Accounting
for Non-financial Managers

Third Edition

John Parkinson
with
Charles Draimin

Captus Press

Accounting for Non-financial Managers, Third Edition

© 2006-2011 by the authors and Captus Press Inc.

Captus Press Inc.
Mail: Units 14 & 15, 1600 Steeles Avenue West
   Concord, Ontario
   L4K 4M2
Tel: (416) 736–5537
Fax: (416) 736–5793
Email: info@captus.com
Internet: www.captus.com

Library and Archives Canada Cataloguing in Publication

Parkinson, John M.
   Accounting for non-financial managers / John Parkinson ; with Charles Draimin. — 3rd ed.

Includes index.
ISBN 978-1-55322-222-4

   1. Accounting — Textbooks.   2. Managerial accounting — Textbooks.
I. Draimin, Charles, 1943–   II. Title.

HF5657.4.P37 2010   658.15'11   C2010-902468-0

Canada   We acknowledge the financial support of the Government of Canada through the Canada Book Fund for our publishing activities.

0 9 8 7 6 5
Printed in Canada

Contents

Contents

Contents

Contents

Section 4   Accounting for the Not-for-Profit Sector 443

Chapter 16 Accounting for Not-for-Profit and Government Organizations 445

Contents

Introduction 1

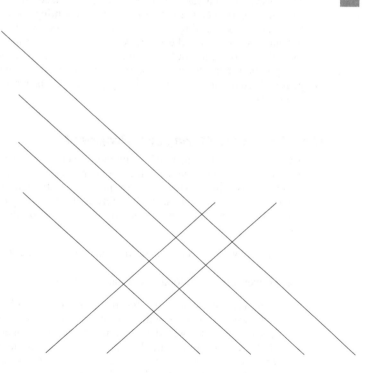

Learning
Objectives

After studying this chapter you should be able to explain the following:
→ Who needs to know about accounting
→ How accounting can be used to keep score
→ How accounting can be used for attention directing
→ How accounting can be used to support decisions

1.1 Accounting: Who Needs It?

The answer is that just about every manager needs it. This book will show why managers need to know about accounting, and will explain the language of accounting and some of the basic techniques. This book is not intended to cover the entire spectrum of accounting, nor is it intended to make accountants out of non-accountants. Its aim, rather, is to bridge the gap between accountants and other managers so that they can intelligently discuss topics of mutual importance. Consider the following three situations.

1.1.1 The Marketing Manager's Proposal

The marketing manager of a medium-sized company is in a meeting with the other managers of the company. He is proposing a marketing campaign to substantially increase product awareness. He is offering his audience the choice of several different ways of implementing the campaign. He is well into his presentation when one of the product managers asks,

"How will this appear in the financial statements?"

His answer may be along the following lines:

"Proposal *A* involves us buying a number of advertising trucks that would drive around the city with illuminated billboards. These purchases would appear in the balance sheet initially, and their amortization would appear in the income statement as expense. Proposal *B* involves renting advertising space on train and bus interiors, which would appear as an expense in the income statement, as incurred. Proposal *A* would initially reduce our liquidity ratios, and this may be a problem for investors, who will perceive us as a riskier investment. Proposal *B* would have minimal effect on liquidity ratios, but would, initially, reduce profits more. Both proposals are expected to increase profitability ratios in the medium term."

Alternatively, he may say,

> "Sorry, but I don't know enough about financial statements to answer you now. I will have to get back to you on that."

The first answer indicates that the marketing manager is familiar with the main financial statements, understands that different types of spending might get treated in different ways, and understands the implications for the users of financial statements. The second answer indicates that he does not fully understand the financial implications of the proposals he is making.

1.1.2 The Human Resources Manager's Situation

The human resources manager is called into her vice-president's office. The human resource department budget is overspent by 12% in the month of March, and the VP wants to know what went wrong. Her reply might be along these lines:

> "When I submitted the budget in October, it was quite clear that there were some uncertainties surrounding the issue of workload — issues over which I had no control. I indicated that the budget I had presented was contingent on the level of hirings and firings being approximately the same as in the previous year. As it happens, there has been a major reorganization in the Quebec region. The number of personnel we let go has increased by 50%, and hirings have also increased substantially. Given this change in workload, it is quite remarkable that we have been able to get by with only two additional staff members and an increase in spending of a mere 12%."

Alternatively, she may have to give some vague answer, such as

> "Well, we needed the extra staff because we were overworked."

or

> "My assistant prepared the budget: I'll have to ask him and get back to you."

The first answer shows that she understands the way a budget is prepared and how it should be used as a control system. The second and third answers show that she knows neither.

1.1.3 The Production Manager's Dilemma

The production manager is proposing the purchase of a new packaging machine. The existing packaging machine is reaching the end of its useful life and needs to be replaced because it is prone to breaking down. Additionally, more modern machines can do more sophisticated packaging, such as integrated full-colour printing and shrink-wrapping. He proposes to spend $100,000 on a state-of-the-art packaging machine that will serve the company's needs for the next 10 to 20 years. The discussion is going well until someone asks if it is possible to lease the machine instead of buying it. His response may be along these lines:

> "Yes, leasing is a possibility. We have a leasing quotation from the supplier. Based on an expected useful life of 10 years, the present value of the lease payments would be $120,000. If we assumed a longer life, the present value of the lease costs would be even higher. So, outright purchase is a better economic alternative. Additionally, the VP of finance informed me that we have adequate cash available for capital investment at this time, and the machine purchase will not strain liquidity."

Alternatively, he may explain that although leasing is a possibility, he has no basis for comparing a capital investment with a series of lease payments, so he cannot decide which is better.

The first answer shows that he is able to deal with the financial implications of his decisions, including consideration of the effect of his proposals on other areas (in this instance, finance and cash flow). The second answer indicates that he is not in command of the appropriate bases for making business decisions, even those within his area of direct control and supposed expertise.

The above three scenarios show that managers need to have a basic understanding of accounting reports and accounting-oriented decision processes. They need this so that they can appear as intelligent, well-informed members of the management team (general background), and so they can plan and control their own operating areas (budgetary control). Furthermore, they can deal with the financial implications of proposals they put forward (decision making).

Given the above hypothetical situations, as a manager, do you want to present yourself as informed and capable of making decisions appropriately? Or, do you want to come across as a narrow specialist who understands his or her own discipline well but has no knowledge of the wider issues of business? Today's business environment suggests that the role of the narrow specialist is decreasing; instead, managers are expected to be able to "talk" accounting as the universal language of business.

This book sets out to deal with situations like the ones faced by the managers above. Section 1 starts out with a description of the main financial statements that are used in external company reporting. It does not go into the detail of recording financial transactions, nor the minutiae of calculating the results. Section 1 does, however, show how the information flows through the system, and deals with the valuation and presentation of the amounts involved. Within each of the chapters in this section, financial ratios are used to explain the relationships between the accounting numbers. These ratios enable the interpretation of accounting data in ways that are meaningful to a wide variety of users.

Section 2 deals with the preparation of budgets and their use as controls. This is partially a number-crunching activity, but we also recognize that budgetary control has serious behavioural implications.

In Section 3, we look at accounting data as the basis for decision making. It covers both short-term operating decisions and longer-term capital budgeting decisions. Section 4 deals with accounting for not-for-profit organizations.

The first three sections conform to one popular classification of accounting that divides accounting into scorekeeping, attention-directing, and decision-making roles.

1.2   Scorekeeping

When a company publishes its income statement and its balance sheet, it is engaged in scorekeeping. That is, the company is reporting to shareholders and other interested parties how well (or how badly) it has performed. These reports are about the past. The income statement covers a period of time that is now completed (the previous fiscal year). The balance sheet is a snapshot of the company at a point in time (usually the last day of the fiscal year).

Scorekeeping is an exercise in stewardship. Investors (and, to a lesser extent, creditors) have allowed the company the use of their resources. The company must, in return, report on what it did with those resources, and how well the investment has performed. With this information, existing investors and creditors can make informed judgments about how advisable it is to continue to be investors or creditors, or whether they should liquidate their holdings in this company and invest or lend elsewhere. In a similar fashion, potential investors and creditors will use the published financial statements to make judgments about whether they should invest or lend, and thus become actual investors or creditors of the company.

By *investor*, we mean the holder of the shares of a company. So, implicitly, we are referring to a limited liability company, the shares of which are listed on a stock exchange. These shares can be bought or sold at market prices by anyone who wants them. North America (particularly the United States and, to a lesser extent, Canada) is a world leader in individual investments in company shares. In other economies, it is more common for people to deposit surplus cash in a bank or buy government securities.

By *creditor* we mean the holder of a company's debt, such as notes or debentures. These are lower risk than shares, and they usually yield a lower return. Like shares, however, they can be bought and sold in a public market, generally a specialized section of the stock market.

The limited liability company with shares listed and traded on a stock exchange is the obvious focus of a book such as this because most large organizations are formed with limited liability. There are also a number of large companies that are "private". Shares of private companies are not listed on any stock exchange. Other forms of business organization include sole proprietor, partnership, not-for-profit, and (in Canada) Crown corporation. While there are no opportunities for buying and selling shares of such organizations, the idea of accounting as the language of business is just as relevant to them as to any publicly listed company. They also have to report their results to someone (owners, members, the government, etc.). Likewise, the attention-directing and decision-making sections following apply to their problems as well.

1.3   Attention Directing

One of the more powerful models of business is that of "management by exception". In this approach a company will go through a series of logically related steps to achieve its objectives:

Step 1:   Define the objectives.
Step 2:   Make plans that would, if achieved, accomplish the objectives.
Step 3:   Carry out the business operations in the plan.
Step 4:   Measure the results of operations.
Step 5:   Compare the results with the plans and the objectives.
Step 6a: If the objectives have been achieved, move on to the next iteration.
Step 6b: If the objectives have not been achieved, instigate corrective action, then move on to the next iteration.

Using this method, corrective action becomes necessary only when things have gone wrong; that is, when there is an exception. Routine activities that are carried out according to plan require no intervention. This cuts down on the amount of purely routine management, and enables management resources to be focused on areas where their use can actually achieve some improvement. Accounting has a major role in the process of defining what will be considered an exception, and in reporting exceptions as they occur.

A major part of organizational planning takes place through budget-setting and budget-approval processes. Only if the budget is capable of achieving the stated objectives and is accepted by all parties should it be approved.

Comparison between the budget and actual results reveals any gaps and should draw management's attention. Depending on the amount and the causes, management can then initiate informed corrective action.

1.4   Decision Making

The third role of accounting is to support decision making or problem solving. Decisions are the essence of business. When made correctly, they will ensure survival of the company and improve profitability. Conversely, when decisions are made incorrectly they will lead, sooner or later, to corporate failure.

As a general rule, decision making should incorporate the following steps:

Step 1:   Specify the problem or decision as precisely as possible.
Step 2:   Choose an appropriate decision technique.
Step 3:   Gather information.
Step 4:   Use the information and the technique to make the decision.
Step 5:   Implement the decision.
Step 6:   Evaluate the outcome.

The basis upon which decisions should be made is not as clear-cut as it may seem. Non-accountants will refer casually to an idea such as "cost" as if it were unambiguous. To the accountant, however, there are as many definitions of *cost* as there are decision situations in which the term would be used. Should the cost be planned or actual? Should it be short-run or long-run? Should it be full cost or variable cost? Do the costs arise in the same time period, or do we need to incorporate the time value of money?

With respect to short-term decision making, we will start by examining the causes of costs, and in particular we shall focus on the modern idea of the "cost driver" — the underlying activities that cause costs to happen. Moreover, we will look at more established models such as the cost-volume-profit model, and at longer-term decision making through the "net present value" model.

1.5 Financial Accounting, Management Accounting, and Auditing

Accounting is so large a subject that a number of specialisms have developed within it. The scorekeeping activities are referred to as financial accounting. Financial accountants are responsible for recording transactions, for measuring, and for disclosing.

Recording transactions is increasingly a routinized, automated activity. When a customer goes through the checkout at a supermarket, when the utility employee zaps a wand at a meter, and in a hundred and one other situations, the transaction data is automatically recorded, and the accounting records on the computer are updated. It may not be long before manual entry of transactions is as outdated as using leather-bound ledgers and quill pens to keep records. However, as of this writing, a number of smaller businesses will still be entering data into the computer records by keying them in at a terminal.

Once the data are recorded, the next step is measurement. Judgment is called for to decide the effect of a transaction. Is the activity to which the transaction refers completed, or is there some residual effect that needs to be recognized as an asset/liability in the balance sheet? To answer these questions, the professional financial accountant has been trained to make appropriate value judgments based on generally accepted accounting principles (GAAP).

Finally, the information has to be communicated. The financial accountants will choose the most appropriate way of disclosing the information, so as to comply with the law and with GAAP, and to meet the needs of external users of financial statements.

Once the financial accountant has prepared the financial statements, an external auditor will review them and the records that support them. The auditor is formally employed on behalf of the shareholders to safeguard their interests. Although the auditor is paid by the company, the shareholders have the right to appoint/reappoint the auditor at the company annual general meeting. If the shareholders are dissatisfied with the auditor's work, they may vote against the appointment. In practice, this shareholders' right is more illusory than real; when the chips are down, management probably has more influence on the decision than the shareholders do.

Management accounting is an internal organizational activity. Its practitioners provide information almost exclusively to managers to assist them in their managerial activities, including the planning and control cycle, and also to support them in decision making.

1.6 Personal Financial Planning

All of the above refers in general to management and managers in organizations. There are also equally important uses for accounting information and accounting techniques in personal lives. There are specialized books that deal with these issues under titles such as *Personal Financial Planning*. Personal financial planning uses accounting information extensively. For example, when making a personal financial plan for the first time, one of the things you have to do is make a complete list of all your assets and liabilities — that is, a personal balance sheet. The difference between your assets and your liabilities is your personal wealth or equity. Also, when making choices about how much to invest in your savings so that you can afford to retire, the decisions are based on personal budgets and net present value techniques.

1.7 Summary

Accounting is the common language of business and is essential for communication in today's market-driven economy. It is necessary that all managers are familiar with the terminology, with the benefits of useful accounting information, and with some of the problem areas where accounting information is less helpful or less clear than it could be.

Accounting has a role in scorekeeping (how well the company has performed); in attention directing (what the managers should be paying attention to); and in decision making (the financial implications of business choices). Accounting is carried out by financial accountants and management accountants within the company, and by external auditors on behalf of shareholders.

Discussion Questions and Problems

Discussion Questions

1. Who needs to know about accounting?
2. Why is accounting called the language of business?
3. What are the main uses of accounting information for managers?
4. Why does an investor need scorekeeping information?
5. What role does accounting have in the planning process?
6. How is control made possible by accounting?
7. What steps should be involved in decision making?
8. Why might the outcome of a decision be different from its expected outcome?
9. What are the main distinctions between financial accounting and management accounting?
10. What is the role of the auditor?

Problems

1. Lafarge Computer Company (LCC) carries out the following actions:
   - (a) LCC pays its monthly rent of $5,000.
   - (b) LCC bills its customers $750,000 for goods and services supplied in November.
   - (c) LCC prepares a detailed list of cash received and cash paid for the month.
   - (d) At a management meeting, the Chief Finance Officer (CFO) complains to the other managers that they are spending more than they are receiving.
   - (e) After consultation with the Chief Executive Officer, the CFO negotiates a bank loan of $500,000.
   - (f) The three product managers present their business plans to the CEO as a first step in preparing next year's budget.
   - (g) LCC sends its annual financial statements to its shareholders.
   - (h) LCC decides to buy the building it has been renting to save on rent expense.

   Required
   For each action, identify whether it is scorekeeping, attention directing, or decision-making oriented.

2. The General Advertising Agency Inc. has been in business for a number of years, providing marketing support for its many clients.

   Required
   For each of the following situations, state whether the parties are investors, creditors, or neither:
   - (a) Marcia Smith owns 5,000 common shares.
   - (b) Bill Smith is Marcia Smith's only son. According to Marcia's will, Bill is going to inherit her shares after her death.
   - (c) Hubert Jones has supplied goods and services to General Advertising Agency Inc. and is owed $25,000.

9

(d) General Advertising Agency Inc. uses the Bank of Tonowanda for all its banking needs. At the end of December, the agency had a checking account with $12,000 in it, plus other deposits that had a total value of $20,000.

(e) General Advertising Agency Inc. owns the building out of which it operates, and there is an outstanding mortgage of $250,000.

(f) Various customers owe General Advertising Agency Inc. a total of $58,000.

(g) General Advertising Agency Inc. has been sued by one of its former employees for $12,500 in an unfair dismissal suit. The matter is scheduled to be heard in court early next year.

(h) There is an unpaid bill of $200 for water supply.

3. The Ideal Computer Co. (ICC) prepared a budget for the year, which planned for a profit of $1,000,000. At the end of the year the profit made was only $750,000. You are given both the budget and the actual data below:

Ideal Computer Co.
Annual Budget

Sales revenue		$7,500,000
Purchase of goods for resale		3,750,000
Gross margin		$3,750,000
Less operating expenses:		
Wages	$1,750,000	
Rent	500,000	
Utilities	200,000	
Other	200,000	
Amortization	100,000	2,750,000
Budgeted profit		$1,000,000

Ideal Computer Co.
Actual Results for the Year

Sales revenue		$8,000,000
Purchase of goods for resale		4,000,000
Gross margin		$4,000,000
Less operating expenses:		
Wages	$2,250,000	
Rent	500,000	
Utilities	200,000	
Other	200,000	
Amortization	100,000	3,250,000
Budgeted profit		$ 750,000

Required

Comment on the year's results. Should management's attention be directed to any specific aspect of the performance?

4. Would the following actions be carried out by financial accounting or management accounting personnel?

(a) Keeping records of goods purchased and goods paid for
(b) Paying wages to staff
(c) Advising on performance-related bonuses for employees
(d) Monthly meetings to discuss budgeted and actual performance
(e) Preparing operating budgets
(f) Preparing annual financial statements
(g) Checking the existence of inventory
(h) Checking whether the inventory is appropriate to the organization's needs

5. (a) Is the auditor's work related to financial accounting or management accounting?
   (b) Who appoints the auditor?
   (c) Who pays the auditor?
   (d) What qualifications does an auditor need?

1

Financial Accounting for Scorekeeping

Financial Accounting:

"The objective of financial statements is to provide information about the financial position, performance and changes in financial position of an entity that is useful to a wide range of users in making economic decisions."

International Accounting Standards Committee Foundation
International Financial Reporting Standards, 2008

The Financial
Statements

2

Learning
Objectives

After studying this chapter you should be able to describe the following:
→ The objectives of financial reporting
→ The accounting equation
→ The four main financial statements
→ The characteristics of accounting information
→ The main accounting concepts

2.1   Introduction

In the first chapter, we established the need for accounting for score-keeping, attention directing, and decision making. We now go on to discuss the information financial accounting provides for scorekeeping. The set of financial reports that are produced for public use by a company consists of the following:

• The balance sheet
• The income statement
• The statement of retained earnings
• The cash flow statement

Each of these statements has a role; together, they provide a rich body of information about the organization. Each will be discussed in detail. First, though, we should establish what it is we are trying to achieve with these reports.

We will concentrate on the reporting process used by incorporated companies. Only incorporated companies are required to report externally. Other entities may choose to make their financial statements public, but they have no legal obligation to do so. The rules that are discussed in this chapter are those that apply to a company registered under the *Canada Business Corporations Act*. The rules that apply to a company incorporated under any of the provincial corporations Acts may differ slightly, but the main points are the same.

Not only is there a difference between publicly traded companies and other types of business entities in the way they publish information, there are also some differences in the reports themselves — mostly in the way owners' equity is treated. Those differences, however, will not be addressed here.

2.2   The Objectives of Financial Reporting

A company is incorporated under either the federal or one of the provincial companies Acts. These acts, together with their associated administrative regulations, require the company to observe certain standards of financial reporting, in particular that

- the company must produce financial statements;
- the financial statements must be distributed annually to the shareholders;
- the financial statements shall consist of an income statement, a balance sheet, a statement of retained earnings, and a statement of cash flows;
- the statements should be prepared in accordance with the standards of the Canadian Institute of Chartered Accountants.

To elicit what the Canadian Institute of Chartered Accountants (CICA) requires, we have to look at the Institute's handbook. The CICA Handbook contains detailed provisions about the treatment of some, though far from all, of the elements of financial statements. For example, the valuation of inventories is discussed at length, but the calculation of sales revenue is not specifically addressed.

It is, therefore, clear that much of the detail of the way in which financial statements are prepared lies elsewhere. Such detail can be found in the professional knowledge that accountants have and use in their work on a day-to-day basis.

In addition to the handbook, the CICA has also published what it believes to be the underlying objectives of financial statements. According to the CICA, financial statements

- are prepared for the use of actual and potential investors and creditors,
- are for the use of those who make investing and lending decisions, and
- should assist users to predict future cash flows.

There are at least two important deficiencies in the way the financial statements deal with the CICA objectives. First, only one of the four statements (see p. 16) actually deals with cash flows: the cash flow statement summarizes past cash inflows and outflows and shows their effect on the cash assets. By contrast, the income statement, the statement of retained earnings, and the balance sheet are all prepared using the accrual concept of resource flows. Where accrual accounting is used, cash flow reporting is replaced by reporting on wealth and changes in wealth. Second, all four statements refer to past events rather than to expectations about the future.

For these two reasons, the linkage between the financial statements and the CICA objectives is somewhat weak. However, whatever their shortcomings, these financial statements are still important, and, in many instances, they are the only information publicly available, so we have to understand them.

The CICA statement of objectives is quite appropriate in the context of the shares of companies that are bought and sold by the general public through stock exchanges. It is also reasonable to state that the legal requirement for providing all shareholders with financial statements has a purpose. This purpose is to be found in the concept of *stewardship*.

The shareholders of the company do not take part in the day-to-day management. They appoint directors (and the directors, in turn, appoint managers) to carry out the actual work of management. This situation is sometimes referred to as the divorce of ownership and control. The financial statements provide some evidence of the extent to which the directors have exercised good (or, sometimes, bad) management. In other words, they enable shareholders to assess whether or not the directors have exercised their stewardship of the company assets effectively.

2.3 The Accounting Equation

Before we discuss any of the financial statements in any detail, it is necessary to introduce the accounting equation. The accounting equation is the logical structure that underlies the recording and reporting of financial results. It is normally expressed in terms of "debits" and "credits". A knowledge of the mechanics of debits and credits is not required for an understanding of accounting. All the same, those who have frequent dealings with accountants and accounting reports may find that some familiarity with debits and credits and the more technical vocabulary of accounting is useful. For those who are interested, an introduction to the basic ideas is presented in Appendix 2.1 of this chapter, and further details are provided in appendices to Chapters 3, 5, and 6.

All four financial statements are drawn from an accounting system based on the accounting equation. This is most evident in the structure of the balance sheet (a financial representation of the company at an instant of time). The balance sheet is essentially a detailed listing of

- what the company owns,
- what the company owes, and
- the owners' financial interest claim on the company.

It is done in a way that satisfies the following equation:

$$\text{ASSETS} = \text{LIABILITIES} + \text{OWNERS' EQUITY}$$

Each capitalized term in the equation represents the total value of all the items of that type that the company has a relationship to. In other words,

- ASSETS is the sum of the value of everything that the company owns;
- LIABILITIES is the sum of all the debt claims on the company (i.e., the sum of all the specific promises the company has made to pay monies to outsiders in the future); and
- OWNERS' EQUITY is the total value of the owners' financial claim on the company.

Thus, one way of looking at the accounting equation is that it is a representation of what the company OWNS on one side — total assets — and a representation of the total CLAIMS on those assets — total liabilities plus total owners' equity — on the other.

To make the nature of this equality clearer in a way that emphasizes the residual nature of the owners' claim, rewrite the accounting equation by subtracting LIABILITIES from each side of the equation, so it reads as follows:

$$\text{ASSETS} - \text{LIABILITIES} = \text{OWNERS' EQUITY}$$

The left-hand side is net assets, the net value obtained after the total claims of the debt holders are subtracted from the total value of the assets. If any transaction that affects the valuation of total assets or total liabilities such that there is a difference between the two changes, then the valuation of owners' equity *must* also be adjusted to maintain the accounting equation.

The income statement, the statement of retained earnings, and the cash flow statement are each summaries of changes in different parts of the accounting equation over a period of time, always respecting the rule that owners' equity is adjusted to reflect changes in net assets. In addition to the accounting equation and the rules for deriving from it the different accounting statements, there are a number of other rules involved in the accounting process, which are collectively called Generally Accepted Accounting Principles (GAAP). These will be discussed throughout Section 1 of this book.

Subject to the limitations of GAAP, financial statements can answer such questions as the following:

• What is the value of the company's assets at the end of the most recent financial year?
• What are the liabilities of the company at the end of the most recent financial year?
• What is the owner's equity (ownership claim) in the company, and how did it evolve in the year?
• How well did the company do this past year in its operations?
• How did the company get cash in the year, and how did it spend it?

Although these are independent questions, and the answers are found on different parts of different statement, they are connected through the accounting equation.

Let us examine some simple transactions to see how they are handled by the accounting equation.

When a company is first organized, it has no assets, no liabilities, and no owners' equity. The accounting equation is satisfied since

$$\$0 \quad = \quad \$0 \quad + \quad \$0$$

As the company engages in transactions, the accounting equation will be used to record the effect of those transactions on the assets, the liabilities, and the owners' equity. In Appendix 2.1, the same transactions will be used to illustrate the mechanics of double-entry accounting.

Transaction #1 The owners invested $25,000 in the company.

• Assets have increased by $25,000.
• Liabilities are unchanged.
• Owners' equity has increased by $25,000.

19

ASSETS   =   LIABILITIES   +   OWNERS' EQUITY
$25,000   = $0   + $25,000

There is only one transaction (the owners invested $25,000 in the company). Note, however, that two separate aspects of the transaction have been recognized in the (revised) accounting equation. First, the company has recorded the fact that it now has $25,000 of assets. Second, the company has recognized that the source of that $25,000 was the owners' investment. The company not only has $25,000, it also has an obligation to the owners to account for the $25,000 they have invested.

It is this recording of the dual effect (on assets and equity, for example) that gives "double entry" bookkeeping its name.

The nature of the obligation to the owners is subtle. It is not a debt that has to be repaid, but the company is responsible for using the resources for the long-term benefit of the owners.

Transaction #2 The company borrowed $10,000 from a bank.

- Assets have increased by $10,000.
- Liabilities have increased by $10,000.
- Owners' equity is unchanged.

ASSETS   =   LIABILITIES   +   OWNERS' EQUITY
$35,000   = $10,000   + $25,000

As with transaction #1, when transaction #2 was recorded, two aspects of the event were captured: (i) the assets were shown as increasing (they started at $25,000; they increased by $10,000; they became $35,000); and (ii) the source of that increase was shown by way of a matching increase in the liabilities. Again, as with transaction #1, the transaction was recorded using the accounting equation, and so the financial records of the company as a whole also continue to conform to the accounting equation.

Transaction #1 increased the owners' equity because the owners parted with some resources, which they let the company have. Transaction #2 did not change the owners' equity: assets increased, but liabilities increased by an equal amount; so the owners' equity (which is always equal to the net assets of the company) stayed the same.

Transaction #3 The corporation bought some inventory (goods for resale) for $8,000, which they paid for in cash.

- Assets (inventory) have increased by $8,000.
- Assets (cash) have decreased by $8,000.
- Liabilities are unchanged.
- Owners' equity is unchanged.

ASSETS   =   LIABILITIES   +   OWNERS' EQUITY
$35,000   = $10,000   + $25,000

We recorded transaction #3 using the accounting equation, as we did with transactions #1 and #2. One asset has increased by $8,000, and another has decreased by $8,000. The total value of the assets has not changed, although the form of the assets has changed. As long as we accept that inventory that cost the company $8,000 is worth $8,000 (at least until we know something different), then the form in which the assets are held is far less important than their dollar total. There was no change in the liabilities; they remain at $10,000. There was no change in the net worth of the company, so owners' equity also remained unchanged.

Transaction #4   The company bought inventory (goods for resale) at a cost of $5,000. The vendor allows 30 days credit on the amount owing.

  The accounting equation treatment of this transaction is as follows: assets (inventory) have increased by $5,000; liabilities have increased by $5,000. Once again, this is an exchange transaction where assets and liabilities of equal value are acquired, and owners' equity remains unchanged.

ASSETS	=	LIABILITIES	+	OWNERS' EQUITY
$40,000	=	$15,000	+	$25,000

Transaction #5   The company sold inventory to a customer for $7,000 in cash; the inventory had cost the company $4,000.

  This is an exchange transaction where the value received ($7,000 in cash) is greater than the value surrendered ($4,000 of inventory). The difference represents an increase in the net assets of the business. This $3,000 is added to the owners' equity. Increases in net assets that arise from regular operations are, by definition, increases in the owners' equity in the business. Also, adding the $3,000 to owners' equity is the only way that the accounting equation can be kept in balance.

ASSETS	=	LIABILITIES	+	OWNERS' EQUITY
$43,000	=	$15,000	+	$28,000

Transaction #6   The company sold inventory to a customer on credit for $9,000; the inventory had cost the company $6,000.

  Transaction #6 is similar to transaction #5, though not identical. In each case inventory has been sold, so in each case the asset inventory has to decrease. In transaction #5 the company clearly has the immediate benefit of the sale, as it now has an additional $7,000 of cash. In transaction #6 the $9,000 sale is represented by money owed to the company by the customer. A decision has to be taken as to what point in time this sale will be recognized. GAAP will recognize this as a completed sale and so will recognize the $3,000 increase in assets (or profit) at the time of the sale. This point will be developed more fully in Chapter 3, "The Income Statement". The $3,000 profit will, as with transaction #5, be added to owners' equity.

ASSETS	=	LIABILITIES	+	OWNERS' EQUITY
$46,000	=	$15,000	+	$31,000

21

Transaction #7 The customer, who had bought the goods for $9,000 on credit in transaction #6, paid for them. What a relief! The worry and uncertainty of having that money owed to the company is now over. The debt has been collected. Is the company any better off, though? We would suggest that it is no better off than before. An asset ($9,000 owed to the company by the customer) has been exchanged for an asset of the same monetary value ($9,000 in cash). There is no increase in the net assets and, therefore, there is no increase in the owners' equity. The company had already recognized the $3,000 increase in owners' equity when the sale was made. Recognizing it again at this point would be double counting. As a general rule, the benefit of a sale is recognized when the sale is made, which is not necessarily when the money is received.

$$\begin{array}{ccccc}
\text{ASSETS} & = & \text{LIABILITIES} & + & \text{OWNERS' EQUITY} \\
\$46,000 & = & \$15,000 & + & \$31,000
\end{array}$$

Transaction #8 The company paid for the inventory it bought on credit ($5,000).

Assets (cash) have decreased by $5,000. Liabilities have decreased by $5,000. There is no change in the owners' equity because there is no change in the net assets.

$$\begin{array}{ccccc}
\text{ASSETS} & = & \text{LIABILITIES} & + & \text{OWNERS' EQUITY} \\
\$41,000 & = & \$10,000 & + & \$31,000
\end{array}$$

Transaction #9 The company paid, in cash, interest of $100 on the bank loan.

Assets (cash) have decreased by $100, resulting in net assets having decreased by $100. Owners' equity has also fallen by $100. This is because the outflow of $100 has not resulted in the acquisition of an asset; rather, it measures an expense. An expense may be thought of as what happens when an asset expires and becomes worthless. There is, of course, a benefit. In this case, the benefit is that the company was allowed the use of a loan for a period of time. Expenses occur in many situations: payment of salaries and wages, rent of premises, fire insurance premiums, etc. In each case, the effect of incurring the expense is to reduce owners' equity.

$$\begin{array}{ccccc}
\text{ASSETS} & = & \text{LIABILITIES} & + & \text{OWNERS' EQUITY} \\
\$40,900 & = & \$10,000 & + & \$30,900
\end{array}$$

Transaction #10 The owners decided to declare themselves a dividend (a cash payment out of profits). They paid themselves $1,000 in cash.

Assets (cash) have decreased by $1,000, resulting in net assets having decreased by $1,000. Owners' equity has fallen by $1,000.

$$\begin{array}{ccccc}
\text{ASSETS} & = & \text{LIABILITIES} & + & \text{OWNERS' EQUITY} \\
\$39,900 & = & \$10,000 & + & \$29,900
\end{array}$$

The 10 transactions above cover the principles behind a lot of the transactions that financial statements have to accommodate. Note the following general points:

- Transactions that involve an exchange of assets and/or liabilities of equal value do not change the net assets of the company, and so do not alter owners' equity.
- Transactions that result in an increase in the net assets of the company result in an equal increase in owners' equity.
- Transactions that result in a decrease in the net assets of the company result in a matching decrease in owners' equity.

Note, too, that all transactions are recorded using the accounting equation. Because each transaction conforms to the accounting equation, the overall records of the company conform to the accounting equation.

2.4 Types of Financial Statements

2.4.1 The Balance Sheet

The balance sheet is a list, at a point in time, of the company's assets, liabilities, and owners' equity. (Yes, that is the same as the accounting equation.) The balance sheet is generally prepared once a year. Chapters 4 and 5 describe the balance sheet in detail. Because the balance sheet is a listing at a point in time, it has been compared to a snapshot or a still photograph of the company.

The balance sheet is used to get an idea of the type and value of the company assets, the amount and repayment dates of the company liabilities, and the net worth of the owners' equity investment.

2.4.2 The Income Statement

During the normal course of trade over a year, the company will probably engage in many transactions that affect the owners' equity. Every time a sale is made or every time an expense is incurred, the owners' equity either rises or falls. The income statement summarizes all these transactions over a one-year reporting period and reports on their overall effect. The net difference between the sales revenue generated and the total of all expenses is the net income or profit of the company for the year.

Because the income statement reports on the events of a period of time, it has been compared to a movie of the company. Although the income statement measures past income, it is used by investors and creditors to make informed judgments about how much income the company is likely to make in future years.

The income statement is described more fully in Chapter 3.

2.4.3 The Statement of Retained Earnings

This is a comparatively short statement that helps link the balance sheet and the income statement. One of the items on the balance sheet of any company is "retained earnings". The retained earnings represent income made on behalf of the owners but that has not been distributed to them by way of dividend. The retained earnings at the beginning of a year are increased by any net income (from the income statement) and decreased by any dividends paid that year. The remaining balance appears on the balance sheet at the end of the year. This information is reported in the statement of retained earnings.

The statement of retained earnings is described more fully in Chapter 3.

2.4.4 The Statement of Cash Flows

The statement of cash flows supplements the balance sheet and the income statement. It reports on the various sources of cash (cash from operations, cash from borrowing, cash from selling assets, cash from raising equity investment) and the various uses of cash (operating losses, repaying debt, buying assets, paying dividends). Because managing the organization's cash resources is so critical to corporate survival, it is as necessary to include this information for the use of investors and creditors.

The statement of cash flows is described more fully in Chapter 6.

2.4.5 Publication of the Financial Statements

Every year, at or before the company's annual shareholders' meeting, the shareholders must receive copies of the four financial statements. The directors are responsible for the preparation of the financial statements. At the shareholders' meeting, the shareholders will vote on whether or not to accept the financial statements. This applies to all companies, whether they are small and privately held (i.e., just a few shareholders) or public corporations that have their shares listed and traded on a stock exchange.

Except for small, privately held companies, the financial statements must also be filed with the director of the *Canada Business Corporations Act*.

Companies that have their shares listed on a stock exchange will also have a responsibility to file their financial statements with the stock exchange and, probably, with a provincial securities commission.

Unless the company is closely held (i.e., no public trading of shares) and the shareholders choose not to have an auditor, the company will also have an obligation to have its financial statements audited; that is, checked by a qualified auditor.

2.4.6 Using Financial Statements to Assess Profitability

The principal objective of most organizations is to make a profit. The dollar amounts of operating income and net profit after interest and taxes will be shown in the income statement. Judging whether or not these are adequate requires that they be compared with the assets. Large companies should produce large profits, while smaller companies need only produce modest amounts.

In reporting the income, it is quite normal to show operating income separately from net income. Operating income is the revenues less the operating expenses incurred in earning the revenues. It specifically excludes interest (which is a financing charge) and taxes (over which management has little control). Operating income is used to judge how well the assets of the business have been used. As such, it is a comment on management efficiency.

Net income is what is left after interest and taxes are deducted from operating profit. Interest paid is an expense that largely depends on the company's capital structure. A company financed entirely from equity capital will have no interest payments, but a company that is financed with a large amount of debt will have a high level of interest expense. Taxes are then deducted, and what is left over is the profit available for the equity shareholders to enjoy. The net income is a measure of how well the company did for its shareholders.

There are two ways of comparing company income to the resources used to generate it.

The ratio of operating income to total assets, or "return on assets" as it is often called, is used to assess the extent to which the assets have been efficiently utilized by management.

The ratio of net income to shareholders' equity is used to assess the effectiveness of the company as an equity investment. It is referred to as the "return on equity". It is also sometimes referred to as the "return on capital employed" or the "return on investment".

Exhibit 2.1 on page 26 shows how the return on assets and the return on equity ratios are calculated.

2.5   Characteristics of Accounting Information

When preparing financial statements, we want the information to be useful. It is not enough to say that the statements should be correct. There are a number of dimensions to the concept of correctness, and each needs to be considered under two important criteria: relevance and reliability.

2.5.1   Relevance

To be relevant, information has to be able to influence a decision or a belief.

Information that causes a bank to decide whether or not to make a loan would be relevant to that lending decision. Suppose a bank looks at the financial statements of a company and discovers that there is already an excessive amount of borrowing and that profits are low. As a result, it estimates that the chances of repayment of the proposed loan are low. The financial statements have provided relevant information. This is sometimes referred to as predictive value. By contrast, suppose that you happen to have a set of financial statements for a major clothing chain, and at the same time you want to buy a coat they stock. You are in possession of information (the financial statements), but it is not relevant to your purchasing decision. The decision to buy is based on factors such as

Exhibit 2.1:   Profitability Ratios

Didier Corporation Ltd. has the following summarized financial statements for 2011:

Didier Corporation Ltd.
Balance Sheet
As at December 31, 2011

Current assets	$200,000	Current liabilities	$110,000
		Long-term liabilities	130,000
Long-term assets	300,000	Total liabilities	$240,000
		Equity	260,000
Total assets	$500,000	Total liabilities and equity	$500,000

Didier Corporation Ltd.
Income Statement
Year Ended December 31, 2011

Sales revenue		$900,000
Operating expenses		800,000
Operating income		100,000
Interest expense	$13,000	
Income taxes	22,000	35,000
Net income		$ 65,000

Return on assets (%):

= (operating income ÷ total assets) × 100%

= ($100,000 ÷ $500,000) × 100%

= 20%

Return on equity (or Return on investment) (%):

= (net income ÷ shareholder's equity) × 100%

= ($65,000 ÷ $260,000) × 100%

= 25%

Because the rate of interest on the borrowed money is less than the return on assets, the return on investment has been leveraged up from 20% to 25%.

the coat's price, availability, style, etc., and not on the financial health of the store.

Suppose an investor has shares in a company. At the year-end the directors send him the financial statements, and the investor is pleased to see that the company has made a reasonable net income, has adequate cash and other resources, and, in general, shows every sign of being well managed. The financial statements were relevant to the investor in supporting his belief that the directors were exercising good stewardship over the assets with which they had been entrusted. This is sometimes referred to as feedback value.

In both of the above situations the information was provided to the user in time for him or her to use it effectively. For example, it would be of no use to the bank to get the financial statements after making the loan. To be relevant, the information must be timely.

2.5.2 *Reliability*

Under the heading "Reliability" we refer to a number of aspects of "correctness". They include verifiability, representational faithfulness, neutrality, comparability, and consistency.

Information should be verifiable. If a number of competent experts look at a set of financial statements' underlying data, they should agree on the accounting conclusions. A transaction might be the purchase of some production machinery. Most accountants would be able to agree that the money was spent and that it was spent on a long-term asset. That indicates verifiability. On the other hand, if those same accountants were to be asked over what period the asset should be amortized, there could be a range of acceptable opinions because this is a judgment call. The amortization expense is, therefore, less verifiable.

Information should have representational faithfulness. The intention of financial statements is to represent various events by means of their monetary values. Suppose a company buys some production machinery for $25,000 cash. If that was the whole of the transaction, then it would be representationally faithful. If, on the other hand, the company had traded in another machine with a realizable value of $10,000, the cash expenditure of $25,000 would not be representationally faithful. It would be better to record this transaction as the sale of the asset traded in (for $10,000), and the cost of the new machine as being $35,000.

Information should be neutral. Information sends strong messages to shareholders and other users. Some of these messages are positive, while others are negative. It is appropriate to have a balanced view: a view without a bias for either good or bad news. Information should not be reported selectively merely because it presents the view that management wants to demonstrate. Suppose a company is being sued by a customer for some fault in a product sold by that company. At the same time the company is suing the supplier of that product, for the same underlying reason. An unbiased report would show both these legal actions and report the company's expectations about the outcome. To show only one legal action, or that the expected outcome is the success of one action and the failure of the other, would be biased. It would lack neutrality.

Information should be comparable. One of the requirements of financial reporting is that the company must report not only on the current year but also on the comparable data for the previous year. If the company has changed one of its accounting practices between the two years (e.g., by changing the number of years over which a machine is amortized), the data is no longer comparable.

Information should be consistent. The reason that the accounting data about amortization is not comparable is that it is inconsistent between the two years. Accounting treatments of events should be consistent. Where they are inconsistent, the nature of the change should be reported so that users may make adjustments in their interpretations and adjustments.

2.6 Accounting Concepts

In order to best pursue the accounting objectives, accountants have agreed on a set of principles that should be applied when accounting transactions are recorded and reported. These principles are more guides to action than they are absolutes. Indeed, some of them are in conflict, so judgment has to be used in their implementation. The concepts most frequently cited are as follows.

2.6.1 Accrual

When reporting resource flows through the income statement, the objective is to capture the revenue generated and the expense incurred in a given period. This may be different from the timing of the related cash flow. Accrual is the name given to reporting revenues and expenditures in the time period when the economic resource is created or used up. In turn, accrual generates the recognition of assets (such as prepayments) and liabilities (such as utilities owed) for which there is no legal documentation, but which cover the ends of accounting periods.

2.6.2 Business Entity

Whatever the legal structure, each business enterprise is considered to be a separate entity for accounting purposes. All the transactions relating to that entity must be recorded and reported, and those transactions extraneous to the entity should be excluded. In practice, this means, for example, that the share capital will be recorded in respect of a company, but other aspects of the shareholders' wealth, such as their personal assets, will not be included.

2.6.3 Historical Cost

Because the price actually paid (historical cost, or entry price) for an asset or an expense is objective and verifiable, it is considered superior to other valuations, and historical cost is the initial valuation of all transactions.

2.6.4 Going Concern

It is assumed that, in the absence of information to the contrary, the business will continue to exist. The implication is that assets will have their value in use as assets of a viable business (restricted to their historical cost), rather than some fire-sale price that they would fetch in a forced sale situation (which would be an exit price).

2.6.5 *Periodicity*

The life of a business entity is effectively unlimited. It does not die as a person would, and it may continue even though its shareholders pass away. It is assumed that partitioning this long life into yearly reports is a meaningful and useful exercise for the shareholders and other interested parties. Without periodicity, companies would present no periodic reports, and no one would know what was going on.

2.6.6 *Disclosure*

There are occasions where presentations in the reports might be misleading. The disclosure principle requires that any such situations be disclosed, generally by way of a "note" accompanying the financial statements. For example, suppose the company is being sued by a customer. The company may believe that the case will go in its favour, and so there are no cost implications and no expenses to report in the financial statements. However, the possibility that the case could be decided against the company should be disclosed in the notes to the financial statements.

2.6.7 *Conservatism/Neutrality*

In calculating income and in valuing assets, the conservatism concept requires that a somewhat biased approach be taken. If there has been a reduction in the value of an asset, that reduction is to be accounted for (shown as a loss). If there has been an increase in the value of an asset, however, its benefit should not be recognized until the benefit has been realized.

Since 2005 there has been a shift of emphasis. Conservatism is no longer so strictly applied. In its place has come a greater emphasis on neutrality. Neutrality means to present information free from bias as much as possible.

2.6.8 *Recognition*

The recognition (or realization) concept governs the point at which a transaction can be said to have happened. It would determine, for example, the rules about exactly when a sale has been made or an asset acquired.

2.6.9 *Matching*

The matching concept is necessitated by the periodicity concept. Periodicity splits the life of the entity into successive 12-month periods. Matching requires that the sales revenue realized in a period be reported in the same period and not in another. Matching also requires that the expenses reported be those that are incurred in the year the sales were recognized.

We will see these concepts being applied on the balance sheet and the income statement in the chapters that follow.

2.6.10 *Materiality*

Financial statement data should only consist of items that are large enough and important enough to be material to their interpretation; trivial amounts may be ignored.

2.6.11 *Constant Dollar*

It is assumed that dollars received or spent at any time are exactly equivalent to dollars received or spent at any other time. Where inflation is significant, this is untrue.

2.7 Published Financial Statements and the Manager

The published financial statements that are covered in this first section of the book are mainly intended for the attention of external users, such as investors and creditors. They have less use for internal managers, such as production, marketing, and human resource managers.

Those internal managers will receive internal reports on the financial dimension of their areas of responsibility. These internal reports will be different from the general-purpose financial statements in two respects: first, they will cover only the items that are under the direct control of those managers; second, they will be in much greater detail.

It would be unusual for internal managers to receive balance sheet or cash flow statements. It is more likely that they would receive a detailed statement of the expenses they had incurred, and, where appropriate, the revenue they had generated. These internal management reports are covered in greater detail in section two of this book.

2.8 International Financial Reporting Standards

Up to 2010 all Canadian companies used Canadian GAAP (generally accepted accounting principles) in preparing their financial statements. With effect from 2011, Canadian companies that are listed on stock exchanges will be expected to replace GAAP with IFRS (International Financial Reporting Standards).

The main differences will appear in the valuation of certain financial instruments, in particular, complex derivatives. For the purposes of the non-financial managers, for whom this book is intended, the changes will be negligible. Canadian companies that are not listed on stock exchanges will be allowed to use either Canadian GAAP or IFRS.

2.9 Summary

The company is required by law to publish financial statements consisting of the balance sheet, the income statement, the statement of retained earnings, and the statement of cash flows.

The objectives of publishing the financial statements are to assist investors and creditors in their investing and lending decisions, and to demonstrate good stewardship of the company assets by the directors.

The accounting equation (assets = liabilities + owners' equity) is the fundamental model used for recording all transactions and for reporting in financial statements.

Accounting information should be relevant. That is, it should have decision usefulness and be timely. Accounting information should be reliable. That is, it should be verifiable, representationally faithful, neutral, comparable, and consistent.

Accounting concepts used in the preparation of accounting reports include accrual, business entity, historical cost, going concern, periodicity, disclosure, conservatism, recognition, matching, materiality, and constant dollars.

Appendix 2.1
The Mechanics of Accounting: The Basics

This appendix and corresponding appendices to Chapters 3, 5, and 6 present the mechanics of double-entry accounting. This is a six-step process carried out over a company's reporting period. The reporting period is typically one year, called the financial year, but it can be as short as one month for a large company. The process is referred to as the *accounting cycle* and the records it generates are the journal and general ledger, informally called the *books* of the company.

The Accounting Cycle

The six steps in the accounting cycle are as follows:

1. Identifying individual transactions and determining how they are to be recorded
2. Recording transactions as entries in the journal
3. Posting journal entries to the general ledger
4. Balancing the general ledger
5. Correcting, adjusting, and closing the books
6. Preparing the financial statements from the ledger balances

1. Identifying Individual Transactions and Determining How They Are to Be Recorded

This step is probably the most important one in the accounting cycle. The rules of accounting, Generally Accepted Accounting Principles (GAAP), determine what is an accounting transaction and what is not, and they also specify how transactions are to be accounted for. Getting these right requires both expertise and experience.

Although a business is engaged in numerous activities every day — both in internal operations and exchanges with those outside the company, such as customers, suppliers, owners, governments, etc. — only some of these events are considered *transactions* by the rules of accounting. A transaction is an event that is recorded in the books of the company. For example a typical sequence of events in a business is taking an order from a customer, shipping the order, invoicing the customer, and finally receiving a cheque from the customer in payment. Although each of these is a distinct and important step in making a sale, GAAP recognizes only the invoicing, shipping, and cheque receipt. As fundamental as getting the customer's order is to the sales process, it is *not* considered a transaction according to GAAP and is thus *not* recorded in the accounting system.

The manner in which a transaction is recorded is also subject to the rules of GAAP. Continuing the same example, if the sale of the goods is on typical commercial terms, the price will be agreed upon when the order is made. An invoice will be prepared and sent when the goods are shipped, specifying when payment is expected — typically within 30 days. The treatment of such a transaction is quite straightforward as we will see below. However, not all sales transactions follow normal commercial terms. Variations include conditions on the selling price that could lead to adjustment of the price depending on market conditions on the date of shipment; payment in advance, delivery later; and allowing the seller a very long time to pay. If special terms of sale apply, the accounting for the transaction may have to be adapted. For example, a software company advertises a radical improvement in one of its popular programs. The upgrade may be just what the market is waiting for and orders flow in from enthusiastic customers with cheques enclosed. As often happens in this business, programming difficulties delay shipments. Despite the difficulties, management will boast of the high rate of new "sales" (they have the orders and the money in hand, have they not?). According to GAAP, however, there is no revenue to record since the goods have not yet been delivered. (In Appendix 3.5, we will see how such transactions are properly recorded.[1])

2. Recording Transactions as Entries in the Journal

In a traditional accounting system, transactions are first recorded as entries in chronological order in the *journal*. The journal entry highlights the individual transaction and allows us to analyze it to ensure that it has been recorded in accordance with GAAP.

3. Posting Journal Entries to the General Ledger

The *account* is the basic building block of the accounting system. The complete set of all accounts for a company is called the *general ledger*. On a regular basis, the journal entries are *posted to* (copied into) these accounts. The general ledger is the core of the accounting system and is the basis for the preparation of the financial statements.

For the purposes of understanding the double-entry method, it is helpful for us to begin with a very simple framework. Accordingly, in this appendix we will start with a *one-write* system — in essence, the system used by computerized accounting systems, one that combines the journal entry and the posting to the general ledger. After we have established the basic framework, we will expand the system to include debits, credits, and journal entries.

4. Balancing the General Ledger

Periodically the general ledger must be balanced. In a computerized system, this is done with each transaction. In a manual system, balancing will be done less frequently but must be done before the books are closed at the end of the accounting period. Balancing the general ledger is a

---

[1] When accounting problems are uncovered in a company's financial statements, they are often related to the inappropriate recording of revenue.

purely mechanical exercise, but as an integral part of double-entry account-ing, it protects against arithmetic bookkeeping errors.

By not permitting unbalanced entries, balancing is automatic in com-puterized systems. For this reason, the topic of balancing is not given much attention today. Still, understanding the nature of out-of-balance error is helpful in understanding how double-entry accounting works.

A balanced ledger is not necessarily correct, but being out of balance is a clear indication of error. The accounting significance of a single error is related to its size. For example, assume a company receives an invoice from its advertising agency for advertising services in the amount of $80,000. A cheque for the correct amount is written, sent, and recorded correctly. The expense, however, is incorrectly recorded as only $8,000. If independent records of cash and expense were maintained — what is known as a single-entry system — the discrepancy might never be discov-ered. The cash account will be correct and it will correspond with the bank statement. On the other hand, the advertising expense itself and total expenses on the income statement will be understated by $72,000. In a small company, this could give a very misleading impression of profit-ability. The strength of the double-entry accounting system is that the recording of the cash payment — the cheque — and the recording of the corresponding expense must be done together *and* must balance. If they do not, the periodic totalling of all the ledger balances will reveal the dis-crepancy. Knowing that an error exists is a necessary condition for correct-ing it. See Exhibit 2A.1, "Finding an Out-of-Balance Error".

If there is a single unbalanced entry in the books, the out-of-balance discrepancy is a measure of the magnitude of the error. However, the con-verse is not necessarily true: an out-of-balance discrepancy does not always mean that there is a single error of that magnitude. The error — actually, errors — could be much larger. If there are two or more out-of-balance errors, large errors can partially offset each other, obscuring their signifi-cance. For example, assume there are two independent errors in an accounting system: the asset account, Buildings, is overstated by $500,000, and the revenue account, Sales, is overstated by $498,300. These two errors act in different directions and they almost cancel each other out, leaving only the small difference between the two of $1,700 as the observed error. Of course, we don't observe the underlying errors, so someone unfamiliar with accounting might conclude that the observed dis-crepancy of $1,700 was the full extent of the error. If the company had total assets close to $10 million, $1,700 would not be considered material and it would be reasonable to disregard the error. That would be a serious mistake: one error of half a million dollars would most certainly be con-sidered material, and two independent errors of that magnitude would mean that the financial statements were seriously misleading.

5. *Correcting, Adjusting, and Closing the Books*

Apart from bringing an out-of-balance ledger into balance, there are other reasons why the ledger might need adjustment. One reason is to correct errors of valuation. Such errors usually arise at the identification or recording stage (step 1 or 2 of the cycle). Errors of valuation do not vio-late the accounting equation, but they are mistakes all the same and can

Exhibit 2A.1:   Finding an Out-of-Balance Error

In a computerized system, the balance in the ledger is effectively tested as the entry is made; if the entry is unbalanced, the transaction will not be accepted. Computers and accounting software are relatively inexpensive and widely used. Still, manual accounting systems are simpler to set up and will be more convenient for any operation that has relatively few transactions. Accounting students, of course, will also have to deal with manual accounting systems. Here are some simple procedures to help you find the cause of a single out-of-balance error when there are two columns of numbers, the totals of which should balance. In fact, beyond accounting, these procedures can be applied to any counting situation where there is a single error and where the magnitude of the discrepancy is known. The procedures are listed in order, the simplest ones first.

Begin by identifying the amount of the discrepancy and the total in each column. Then follow each of these rules in turn:

1. Look for the amount incorrectly posted or posted twice.
2. Scan the source documents for the amount that was not posted to a column.
3. If the error is an even number, look for half the amount in the columns.
4. Apply the rule of nine to the amount.

If none of these rules work, more detailed checking is required. First, check the addition of each column and then look for other arithmetic or posting errors.

These procedures are designed for a situation where there is a single error. Although they will not work if there are two or more errors, any close review of the system is likely to uncover errors. At some point only one will remain and then one of these procedures will work.

Here is an illustration. The two columns below are an example of what you might see if you find a balancing error. The example is consistent with a number of different underlying causes. Depending on which one it is, a different test will lead you to it.

18	13
9	12
5	4
11	8
19	7
62	44

Begin by identifying the amount of the discrepancy and the total in each column. The difference is 18 and the column totals are 62 and 44.

1. **Amount incorrectly entered.** Check first that the "18" in the left-hand column has not been posted there in error. If it shouldn't be there, the two columns will balance to 44. If this is not the problem, try step 2.
2. **Scan source documents for missing amount.** Look for another "18" in the source document that should have been posted to the right-hand column but has not been. If this is the problem, the two columns will balance to 62. If it is not, move to step 3.
3. **Half the error in the wrong column.** Check to see if the "9" in the left-hand column, which is half the error, should have been posted instead in the right-hand column. If that is the case, both columns would then balance with totals of 53. No success? Try step 4.
4. **Rule of nine.** This is a possibility if the discrepancy is divisible by 9, as it is here. If a discrepancy between two totals that should balance is divisible by 9, there is the possibility that there is a transposition error. In this case, for example, if the "13" at the top of the right-hand column should have been its transposition, "31", the difference is 18 and the two columns would in fact balance at 62. A transposition in a sum will always change the total by a number divisible evenly by 9. Thus 74 and 47 have a difference of 27, 649 and 946 have a difference of 297; the difference is always divisible evenly by 9. Satisfy yourself that 0, even if not explicitly written, also follows the rule: 101 is a transposition of 11, 100 of 10, 5000 of 50.

result in material misstatement in the financial statements. For example, if a credit sale is recorded, in error, as $150,000 instead of the correct $50,000, both the entry to revenue and the entry to accounts receivable will be overstated by $100,000. The error would normally be picked up when the customer remits a cheque in the correct amount of $50,000 and the discrepancy is investigated. However, if the transaction takes place late in the financial year and the receivable is not due until early in the next financial year, the current year's financial statements will be wrong: both sales revenue (on the income statement) and accounts receivable (on the balance sheet) will be overstated by $100,000. There are, of course, audit techniques that will find such errors since the balance owing from the customer (the account receivable) can be checked independently of the revenue. (This emphasizes the role and importance of the internal and external *audits* in ensuring the correctness of the accounts and the financial statements that are prepared from them.)

Books of account are permanent records, so when an incorrect entry is discovered, the original entry is not written over, erased, or removed. Rather, a second correcting entry is made as an *adjusting journal entry*. This was the practice when all books were kept in pen and ink and continues with computerized systems. Erasures in handwritten books were considered evidence of tampering. For the same reason, most computerized accounting systems do not permit an entry to be changed after it has been fully entered. The correction must be made as a new entry with a full explanation. The objective is to maintain an audit trail, to ensure that all entries, even incorrect ones, can be traced. If all valuation corrections and other changes are entered as adjusting journal entries, they are open to examination by the auditor.

At the end of each accounting period there is another class of adjusting journal entries to be made. These are not designed to correct errors, but they are non-routine. In most accounting systems, routine entries, including all transactions involving cash, all credit purchases and sales, and, in more sophisticated systems, the cost of goods sold, are made when some transaction takes place with a third party. Certain transactions, however, such as amortization, are a function of time only, and there is no event to trigger recognition; these are recorded periodically — at the end of the month or at the end of the financial year rather than on a day-to-day basis. In addition, in small companies, the cost of goods sold is not recorded for each sale. Instead, at the end of the accounting period, the inventory is counted and valued and only then is cost of goods sold calculated. All of these periodic transactions are entered into the accounts only at the end of each accounting period by means of *adjusting journal entries*. After the adjusting journal entries are made, the general ledger is balanced again, and the accounts are *closed*.

6. Preparing the Financial Statements from the Ledger Balances

At the end of an accounting period, the balances in the general ledger are used to prepare the financial statements: the balance sheet, the income statement, the statement of retained earnings, and the statement of cash flows.

Summary

The accounting cycle is the process of recording transactions in the company's books. A transaction is a single business event that is recorded in the accounting system. On a regular basis, journal entries are posted to the accounts in the general ledger. At the end of each accounting period the general ledger is brought up to date with adjusting journal entries, is balanced, and then closed. GAAP is the name for the set of rules that govern this process.

In the next section, the basics of double-entry accounting will be presented and illustrated using the 10 transactions presented in section 2.3 of this chapter. For the first three transactions, we will use a simplified double-entry system. We will then introduce the standard debit-credit method of double-entry accounting and use it to complete the remaining transactions.

Initially we will focus on steps 1 to 4:

1. Identifying individual transactions and determining how they are to be recorded
2. Recording transactions as entries in the journal
3. Posting journal entries in the general ledger
4. Balancing the general ledger.

After all 10 illustrative transactions are recorded, we will show how end-of-period adjustments are made and how the books are closed (step 5), and, to complete the accounting cycle, how the financial statements are prepared from the ledger balances (step 6). In appendices to subsequent chapters we will use this framework to deal with the more complex transactions presented in those chapters.

A Simplified Double-Entry Accounting System

As we have seen, the accounting equation

$$ASSETS = LIABILITIES + OWNERS' EQUITY$$

forms the structure of the balance sheet. This equation in fact underlies the entire accounting system. For example, the general ledger, just as the balance sheet, has the same form as the accounting equation. When we speak of a "balanced ledger", we mean that the sum of the amounts in the asset accounts equals the sum of the amounts in the liability accounts plus the sum of the amounts in the owners' equity accounts. Moreover, to maintain this balance, each new transaction, which is to say each journal entry, must also be balanced in the terms of the same equation.

In traditional bookkeeping, transactions are first recorded in the journal in chronological order and are then posted (copied) one by one to the accounts in the general ledger. This method has certain advantages for division of labour and for filing, particularly in large, manual systems.

However, for the purposes of demonstrating how the system works, it is more useful initially to combine these two steps and write the transactions directly into the accounts arrayed in the form of the accounting equation.[2] After the basic principle is established using this framework, we will move to the standard format of journal entries followed by postings to accounts in the general ledger.

We will begin by defining the basic accounts. There is an account for every class of *asset*, *liability*, and *owners' equity*. In this appendix, account names will be indicated by the use of an initial capital letter — for example, Cash, Accounts Receivable. We will start with a skeleton set of accounts and expand it as necessary. The first accounts are the main *asset* accounts:

Account	Description
Cash	Primarily money on deposit at a bank; also includes cash on hand
Inventory	Goods purchased for resale
Accounts Receivable	Amounts due from customers for goods they have purchased from the company on credit
Fixed Assets	Assets — e.g., furniture, machines, cars and trucks, building, land — that are purchased for use over several years rather than for resale

Similarly, there are accounts for each different type of *liability*, or debt, such as the following:

Account	Description
Bank Loan	The obligation to repay a loan taken from the bank
Accounts Payable	The obligation to pay money in the future to suppliers from whom the company has purchased goods on credit

A *sole proprietorship* will normally have only one *owners' equity* account on the balance sheet. However, in a *partnership* or an *incorporated company*, owners' equity is divided into different accounts, representing differing legal or accounting aspects of the owners' claim. The example in section 2.3 did not make these distinctions, but now that we are demonstrating actual accounting procedures, they will be necessary. Since most business organizations are incorporated, this will be the form we will use. In an incorporated company, a distinction is made between invested capital and earned capital and thus there are always at least these two owners' equity accounts, usually called, respectively, *Share Capital* and *Retained*

---

[2] This, essentially, is how a computerized accounting system works. Even in a computerized system, however, the information is typically printed in journal entry form or in ledger account form for internal analysis and reporting purposes.

Earnings. Also, since the owners are called shareholders, the entire owners' equity section of the balance sheet is called *shareholders' equity* rather than owners' equity. We will continue to use the term *owners' equity* when referring to the owners' interest in general terms, but the term *shareholders' equity* will always be used when we are referring specifically to the equity section of an incorporated company.

Account	Description
Share Capital	The portion of the shareholders' equity (the claim of shareholders) that arises when new investment is made — i.e., when shares are issued by the company in exchange for assets, usually cash, paid in by the shareholders. Share capital is reduced only in the rare circumstance that shares are cancelled or redeemed. This can happen when a company is reorganized after seeking bankruptcy protection or when it is wound up.
Retained Earnings	That portion of the claim of shareholders that increases as the company operates profitably and is reduced when dividends are paid as losses are incurred.

An important objective of financial accounting is the measurement of the company's operating success, its profitability, in the period. Rather than measure profit directly, transaction by transaction, it is more convenient and informative to measure separately the components of profit, namely, *revenue* and *expense*, for each transaction throughout the accounting period, using accounts with the same names, and then calculate profit (or, as accountants prefer to call it, *net income* or *earnings)* only at the end of the accounting period. Looked at in terms of the basic accounting equation, Revenue and Expense, like Net Income, are measures of *change* in owners' equity. *Revenue* is defined as the gross increase in owners' equity from operations — for example, the period's sales at selling price. *Expense* is the gross decrease in owners' equity necessary to generate revenue — an example would be all the costs incurred necessary to make the period's sales. Netting these two basic gross measures of operations — revenue less expense — gives *net income* (assuming that revenue exceeds expense; if expense exceeds revenue, the net of the two is called *net loss* or, more simply, *loss*).[3]

Account	Description
Revenue	The gross increase in owners' equity from operations
Expense	The gross decrease in owners' equity from operations

---

[3] *Net income* or *net loss* are simply the names for the difference between revenue and expense. One or the other will appear as the bottom line on the income statement, but neither exists as an account in the general ledger. (In some traditional accounting books, a single account called Profit and Loss was used as part of the process of closing the books.)

There are several things to note about Revenue and Expense. First, although Revenue and Expense are treated as individual accounts in this appendix, in practice they each represent *sets* of accounts. A company will normally have one or more particular kinds of revenue, depending on what it actually does to generate it: for example, if the company generates its revenue by selling goods, it is called *Sales Revenue* (or more simply, *Sales*); revenue from selling a service would be either *Service Fees* or *Consulting Fees*, depending on its nature; revenue from real estate is *Rental Revenue*; and revenue from lending money is called *Interest Revenue*.[4] Accounting for revenue, both by line of activity and in total, allows us to keep track of different aspects of the company's business.

All companies will have a number of expense accounts, such as *Salaries*, *Cost of Goods Sold*, and *Amortization*. Keeping separate accounts of expenses, measures of the various costs incurred to earn revenue of the period, is a prerequisite for gauging the efficiency of operations.

Second, although revenue and expense accounts do not appear on the balance sheet, they are nonetheless ledger accounts, sub-accounts of Retained Earnings. Since these accounts are part of the balance in the Retained Earnings account, they have a direct effect on the balance sheet.

The third point is important for understanding how the financial statements are linked. Because revenue and expense are defined in the context of double-entry accounting, there is a corresponding change in an asset or a liability each time revenue or expense is recognized. We will call these changes in assets or liabilities *resource flows*. Resource flows occur in a business for different reasons. Some are simple exchanges — one asset is exchanged for another (buy a building for cash) or an asset is acquired in exchange for debt (take a bank loan). Revenue and expense transactions are different. They are not resource flows themselves; rather, they indicate that the particular resource flow represents a change in the ownership claim — a change in owner's equity — from business operations. We can illustrate this distinction as follows. A merchandising company sells goods for cash. In double-entry terms, this is cash inflow/revenue. Calling this particular cash inflow *revenue* is how the accounting system tags it as an operating resource flow — a resource flow that affects owners' equity. As well, there is another resource flow in a sales transaction — the outflow of the goods that are transferred to the customer. This is the expense part of this transaction. In double-entry terms, this is an inventory outflow/cost of goods sold expense. Calling this asset outflow *expense* is how the accounting system tags the transfer of goods to the customer as an operating resource flow. The goods were transferred for the purpose of earning revenue. Hence the name of the expense — Cost of Goods Sold. Other expenses are not tied to particular revenue transactions, but they are expenses of the period nonetheless. Office supplies and labour, for example, are measures of resources used to earn revenue. In the former, a particular asset is used up (office expense); in the latter, a flow of services is

---

[4] Sometimes you will see such revenue accounts referred to as *Income* — for example, "Rental Income" or "Interest Income". This can be confusing. In business accounting uses, *income* is properly a net concept (revenue less expense), and you should avoid using it as an alternative term for *revenue*.

used up. We can think of the asset labour being created and used instantaneously, but because the company buys it as it is used, we measure the implicit liability to pay the wages as the labour service is used. This is the resource flow tagged as expense. In double-entry terms, this is wages payable/wage expense. (There will be a cash outflow when the wages are actually paid later. This is illustrated in the next paragraph.)

Non-operating resource flows are transactions that involve only assets and liabilities. For example, if a company buys a building for cash, there is an outflow of the asset, cash, in exchange for the inflow of another asset, the building. There is no effect on owners' equity. Another example is the cash inflow that would result if the company were to borrow money: cash is received in exchange for the issuance of debt (the promise to repay the loan with interest in the future); there is again no immediate effect on owner's equity. (Interest expense, the operating cost of borrowing, will be a reduction of owners' equity (i.e., an expense), but only as it accrues in the future.) In the wage example above, the operating transaction is the use of the labour (the expense) and recognition of the wages payable (the operating resource flow). When the workers are paid subsequently, there are non-operating resource flows: cash is transferred to the workers, and the liability (the obligation to pay them) is extinguished.

Dividends is a single account in a class of its own. Dividends (the account name is often written in the plural) is the reduction of Retained Earnings that occurs when assets — normally cash — are distributed to owners *as a result of successful operations* (i.e., after income has been earned). Dividends must not be confused with expenses. Although dividends, like expenses, reduce Retained Earnings, dividends are not a measure of the cost of earning revenue and therefore are *not* an expense.

Account	Description
Dividends	The decrease in Retained Earnings when profits are distributed as cash (or other assets) to shareholders

Like the Revenue and Expense accounts, the Dividends account is a sub-account of Retained Earnings. All the sub-accounts — Revenue, Expense, and Dividends — are temporary accounts, and they are closed at the end of each accounting period to Retained Earnings.

There are other features of accounts that we will need, but we will introduce them as required.

As we proceed, there are three important points to bear in mind:

1. **Money.** All transactions are recorded in money terms; in Canada, that usually means in Canadian dollars. We must be careful to distinguish between the asset money — which we call *cash* to minimize confusion — and money as a measure of value. It is important to remember that, in accounting, the dollar is being used primarily as a unit of *value*. Thus, money valuation is a feature of all accounting transactions, but money as cash is part of a recorded transaction *only* if cash actually changes hands. To avoid the mistakes that many

beginners make, think twice before concluding that because every transaction is measured in money terms, one-half of every double-entry transaction must involve cash. The account Cash is involved in a transaction only if the asset Cash has increased or decreased.

Because the term *money* has so many meanings in business discourse, it is best to avoid the use of the word as much as possible except in a clear valuation sense, as in the phrase "money measurement". Finally, because all figures in the accounts are in dollar terms, by convention the dollar sign is not used in the journal or the general ledger.

2. **Balancing entries involving more than two accounts.** Because of the double-entry nature of accounting, each transaction must affect at least two accounts and the entry must be *balanced*. What this usually means is that an entry of the same dollar value amount will be made in each of two accounts. If three accounts are affected, the sum of the dollar value of the entries in two accounts must equal the dollar value of the entry in the third account (and similarly in the rare case that four or more accounts are affected). Examples given below will make this clear.

3. **Chronology.** In accounting, chronology is important. In these examples we will identify each transaction with a transaction number in the first column to indicate chronological order. If these were actual transactions, each one would be dated instead. All the transactions illustrated in this appendix are assumed to have taken place over the month of December 2011. The identification of the period is necessary for the preparation of the financial statements (see pages 65 and 67).

Entering the Transactions

For the next step, we construct the general ledger in the form of a spreadsheet, reflecting the underlying accounting equation. The accounts are placed under the appropriate section heading of the accounting equation. Asset accounts are on the left-hand side of the spreadsheet, liability and shareholders' equity accounts are on the right-hand side. In Table 2A.1, there are four accounts. (The two that are named Cash and Share Capital are needed for the first transaction; others will be added as we proceed.) Each account is divided into two columns, one representing *increases* to the account, the other representing *decreases*. Note the difference in the labelling of increases and decreases in these two accounts. *If the account is an asset, increases are on the left side of the account and decreases are on the right side.* For accounts on the other side of the accounting equation, the convention is reversed. *If the account is a liability or owners' equity, increases are on the right side and decreases are on the left.* These conventions are maintained in all accounting systems.

Normally the transaction would be written up first in the journal on an entry-by-entry basis. This is the procedure we will in fact follow starting with transaction #4 on page 49, but right now, however, since we are familiar with the basic accounting equation that the general ledger in a spreadsheet form reproduces, it is more convenient to write each transaction directly into the ledger. Although they are not in the standard journal form, each line in the spreadsheet can in fact be read as a journal entry.

Table 2A.1

#	Assets				Liabilities		Shareholders' Equity	
	Cash						Share Capital	
	increase	decrease	increase	decrease	decrease	increase	decrease	increase

Transaction #1 Having set up the ledger in this form, we can now make the first entry into the accounts. To set the stage, recall that initially there are no assets, no liabilities, and no owners' equity; the basic accounting equation is satisfied since both sides are equal to zero. In the first transaction, the owners contribute $25,000, which we will assume to be cash. The increase in the asset Cash is evident, but double-entry accounting means that there must be a corresponding change elsewhere — a change that, together with the increase in cash, maintains the equality of the accounting equation. If we saw only $25,000 cash being received by a company without knowing the reason, we would not know if this was the result of (1) a *decrease* of another asset (an exchange), (2) an *increase* in a liability (borrowing of money), or (3) an *increase* in shareholders' equity (revenue or share issue). In this particular case we know that the cash is being received because the shareholders are making their initial capital contribution, and therefore we can identify the balancing change as an increase in shareholders' equity, specifically, an issue of shares that represents the shareholders' claim.[5]

We can summarize the transaction as follows:

The asset account, Cash, increases by $25,000.
The shareholders' equity account, Share Capital, increases by $25,000.

This being the first entry, it is written on the first line following the account headings, as shown in Table 2A.2. There are, of course, two parts to the entry. Taking the cash part first, we note that Cash is an asset account, so the increase in cash is represented by a sub-entry in the Cash account. For the other part of the entry, we see that Share Capital is a shareholders' equity account, so the increase in share capital, the issuance of shares, is written on the right side of that account.

---

[5] In an incorporated company, *shares* represent the owners' claims. The number of shares issued when the company is first organized is essentially arbitrary. What is important is the *relative* number of shares each owner holds. It will be proportional to his or her investment.

Table 2A.2

#	Assets					Liabilities		Shareholders' Equity	
	Cash							Share Capital	
	increase	decrease		increase	decrease	decrease	increase	decrease	increase
1	25000								25000

After the two parts of the entry are made, there is a positive balance of $25,000 in the asset account, Cash, and a positive balance of $25,000 in the shareholders' equity account, Share Capital. The ledger balances: total assets are $25,000 and total liabilities and shareholders' equity are also $25,000. Although the general ledger is not a balance sheet as such — a balance sheet is a formal document that must show the company name, statement title, and date, and satisfy certain other requirements — it is easy to see how a balance sheet could be drawn up from the information we have in the general ledger at this point. Normally, a balance sheet is drawn up only at the end of an accounting period. Still, if the entries for the period are complete and correct, drawing up the balance sheet and the other financial statements at any time is a relatively straightforward exercise.

Transaction #2   The company has raised its initial capital from its shareholders. This is a shorthand way of saying that it acquired assets in the form of cash by issuing shares. (The cash will be used to buy other assets.) Having done this, it is now in a position to raise the additional funds necessary to begin operations by taking a loan from the bank. Again, the asset acquired is assumed to be in the form of cash, but the corresponding claim is a liability — an obligation to repay the principal amount of the loan as well as interest at agreed-upon rates and times[6] — rather than a permanent ownership claim like share capital. We need to create a new account, Bank Loan, as shown in Table 2A.3.
We can summarize the transaction as follows:

The asset account, Cash, increases by $10,000.
The liability account, Bank Loan, increases by $10,000.

The entry for transaction #2 is written on the line following transaction #1. Again, this being double-entry accounting, there are two parts. As in transaction #1, the increase in cash is represented by a sub-entry of $10,000 in the Cash account. For the other half of the entry, we know that Bank Loan is a liability account, so the increase in the liability, Bank Loan, is written on the right side of that account.

---

[6] These details, as important as they are, are not shown here, but a record of the terms of the loan would, of course, be kept.

Table 2A.3

#	Assets				Liabilities		Shareholders' Equity	
	Cash				Bank Loan		Share Capital	
	increase	decrease	increase	decrease	decrease	increase	decrease	increase
1	25000							25000
2	10000					10000		
account balances	*35000*					*10000*		*25000*

The entry itself is balanced: a $10,000 increase in assets balances a $10,000 increase in liabilities and shareholders' equity (although in this entry only a liability account was affected). Moreover, even though two account balances have changed, the general ledger itself remains balanced. In the third row we confirm this by taking an interim balance of the ledger. (To distinguish balances from entries, balances are written in italics and the row is shaded.) Balancing involves the following steps:

(i)   Finding the balance in each account (if there were decreases in any of the accounts, the decreases would be netted against the increases to come to the account balance)

(ii) Adding up the balances in the asset accounts (there is just one such balance here)

(iii) Adding up the balances in the liability and shareholders' equity accounts

(iv) Comparing the totals in (ii) and (iii) to ensure that they are equal

In this case, the asset side of the ledger totals $35,000 (Cash only), which is equal to the $35,000 in liabilities and shareholders' equity ($10,000 and $25,000, Bank Loan and Share Capital, respectively).

Transaction #3   In transaction #3, the company uses $8,000 of its cash to buy inventory. We need to add another account, Inventory, as shown in Table 2A.4.

The asset account Cash *decreases* by $8,000. This is the first example of a reduction of an account.

The asset account Inventory increases by $8,000.

This entry is written on the line immediately below the interim balance that we took after transaction #2. In this case, since the asset account Cash is being decreased, there is right-side entry in this account. Inventory is increased, so the entry is on the left side.

Because there are entries on both sides of the Cash account, when we strike a balance, we need to do it in two steps. First, each column is sub-totalled ($35,000 and $8,000); then the two columns are netted against each other with the difference ($27,000) being placed as the account balance in the column with the larger subtotal. Since there were more increases to the cash account than decreases, the balance in this case is a net increase. There is an equal and opposite change in the Inventory account so total assets have not changed. There is, of course, no change at

45

all on the other side of the ledger and thus the entry is balanced. (If you compare the balancing that followed transaction #1 with the balancing that followed transaction #2, you will see that there is no particular relationship between the changes in the account balances following a transaction and the overall balance in the ledger [total assets, total liability, and shareholders' equity], which may or may not change. The overall account groups totals have no special significance here; all that matters is that the general ledger remains balanced.)

Table 2A.4

#	Assets				Liabilities		Shareholders' Equity	
	Cash		Inventory		Bank Loan		Share Capital	
	increase	decrease	increase	decrease	decrease	increase	decrease	increase
1	25000							25000
2	10000					10000		
account balances	*35000*					*10000*		*25000*
3		8000	8000					
column subtotals	*35000*	*8000*						
account balances	*27000*		*8000*			*10000*		*25000*

Debits and Credits

At this point we generalize what we have learned so far and then make a change in terminology. This will allow us to formalize the process of balancing the ledger accounts and, more important, to write journal entries.

The division of accounts into a left side and a right side and its connection to balanced entries is an extension of the basic accounting equation. As we have seen, a left-side entry in an asset account *increases* it; but a left-side entry *decreases* a liability or shareholders' equity account. The effect is the opposite for a right-side entry. We also see that a full entry — the representation of a complete transaction that maintains the equality of the basic accounting equation — involves both a left-side entry *and* a right-side entry of equal value. Thus, in transaction #1, an increase in the asset cash, which is a left-side entry, is paired with an increase in shareholders' equity, which is right-side entry. Both have the same value. Transaction #2 is similar, but the right-side entry represents an increase in a liability rather than shareholders' equity. Transaction #3 affects only asset accounts. The left-side entry is the increase in the asset Inventory, and the right-side entry represents the *decrease* in the asset Cash. Again, both have the same value.

We can summarize this graphically. On the left in Figure 2A.1 we list the significance of left-side entries in different accounts, and on the right, the significance of right-side entries. To keep things uncluttered, we show only account groups, assets (A), and liabilities or equities (L/E).

A left-side entry can represent an increase in an asset (+A) or a decrease in a liability or an equity (including an expense and dividends) (–L/E).[7]

A right-side entry can represent an increase in a liability or an equity (including revenue) (+L/E) or a decrease in an asset (–A).

Bars connect all possible combinations of a left-side entry and a right-side entry, such as {+A •▬▬• + L/E} and {+A •▬▬• –A}. These combinations and *only* these combinations of equal value entries satisfy the basic accounting equation. Combinations of entries listed on the same side of the figure, such as {+A and –L/E} in the left-hand column, or {+L/E with –A} in the right-hand column, do *not* satisfy the equation. Similarly, a pair of two identical entries such as {+A and +A} on the left, or {+L/E and +L/E} on the right, do not satisfy the basic accounting equation. Put another way, every possible transaction that satisfies the basic accounting equation involving two accounts can be described by one of the four linked combinations.

Figure 2A.1

Left-side entries   **Right-side entries**

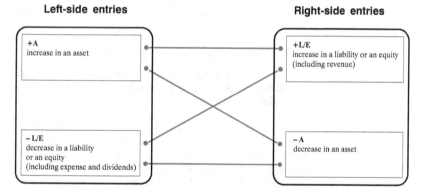

We can illustrate this framework using the three transactions we studied above. Transactions #1 and #2 are both examples of the first combination represented by the top bar: the increase in the asset Cash is combined with an increase in Shareholders' Equity (#1) or with an increase in the liability Bank Loan (#2). Transaction #3 is an example of the second combination represented by the bar sloping down to the right: the increase in the asset Inventory matches a reduction of another asset. We will see examples of the other combinations following.

The rule, then, for recording transactions is as follows:

> **To maintain the basic accounting equation, every accounting transaction must have a left-side entry and a right-side entry of equal value.**

---

[7] We haven't seen an example of the latter yet, but if you guessed that a liability or equity is *reduced* by a left-side entry, you are correct.

There is one more step, and this is purely terminological. Instead of referring to left-side entries and right-side entries, accountants use the terms *debit* entries and *credit* entries, respectively. We can redo the figure using the debit–credit terminology, as shown in Figure 2A.2:

Figure 2A.2

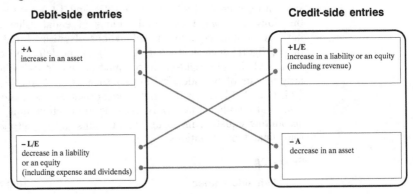

Debit-side entries

+A
increase in an asset

– L/E
decrease in a liability
or an equity
(including expense and dividends)

Credit-side entries

+L/E
increase in a liability or an equity
(including revenue)

– A
decrease in an asset

The rule is now written as follows:

To maintain the basic accounting equation, each accounting transaction must have a *debit entry* and a *credit entry* of equal value.

As shown in Table 2A.5, instead of writing *increase/decrease* for each set of asset account columns, or *decrease/increase* for each set of liability and shareholders' equity account columns, *every* account will be labelled in the same way: *debit* (abbreviated *Dr*) for the left-hand column, and *credit* (abbreviated *Cr*) for the right-hand column. If we redo the general ledger up to transaction #3 using debits and credits, we see that nothing has changed except the headings of the columns, which are now identical for each account: *debit* for the left column, *credit* for the right column.

The process of balancing is unchanged, except that now the account balances are labelled *debit* and *credit* as the case may be, rather than *net increase* and *net decrease*. In a balanced general ledger, total debit balances equal total credit balances, as we can verify in Table 2A.5: total debit balances, all in the asset section, are $35,000; total credit balances, all in the liabilities and shareholders' equity section, are also $35,000. You should note, however, that debit account balances will not always be associated with assets, nor credit balances with liabilities. (We will see examples following.) All that is required for a balanced ledger is that total debit balances equal total credit balances. You can satisfy yourself that even though debit balances do not all correspond only to asset accounts, or credit balances only to liability and shareholders' accounts, if total debit balances equal total credit balances, this is equivalent to saying that total assets equal total liabilities and shareholders' equity from a balancing point of view.

Table 2A.5

#	Assets				Liabilities		Shareholders' Equity	
	Cash		Inventory		Bank Loan		Share Capital	
	Dr	Cr	Dr	Cr	Dr	Cr	Dr	Cr
1	25000							25000
2	10000					10000		
account balances	35000					10000		25000
3		8000	8000					
column subtotals	35000	8000						
account balances	27000		8000			10000		25000

The Language of Debits and Credits

The word *debit* means simply "an entry on the left side of the ledger"; *credit* means, similarly, "an entry on the right side of the ledger". In addition to being the technical terms used in standard accounting systems, the terms *debit* and *credit* offer us a convenient shorthand method of expression. Instead of saying "there is an entry of 25,000 on the left side of the account Cash" that recorded an increase of cash, we say simply "there is debit to cash of 25,000". The words can also be used even more concisely as verbs: "Cash is debited by 25,000", or the bookkeeper might be told to "debit cash 25,000". (The word *dollars* or the dollar sign is always understood.)

By extension, *debit* and *credit* refer to balances as well as entries. As we have seen, an asset account normally has its *balance* on the left side; a liability or shareholders' equity account normally has its balance on the right side. Thus, we call a balance on the left side a *debit balance*, and a balance on the right side a *credit balance*. Bear in mind that if an account has a balance on an unexpected side, it may have to be re-interpreted. Thus, if Cash (the company's record of its bank account) has a credit balance (normally Cash has a debit balance), the company does not have "money in the bank"; rather, it owes the bank money — it has an overdraft.

We will now show how debits and credits allow us to record transactions as standard journal entries. We will also introduce revenue and expense accounts using the language of debits and credits. After we have done this, we will explore why we use debits and credits along with other related questions. We begin by recording transaction #4.

Transaction #4   In transaction #4, the company purchases an additional $5,000 worth of inventory. In this case, however, payment is not made in cash, but instead the company agrees to pay the supplier in 30 days. The deferred payment is called *buying on credit* by the buyer and *selling on credit* by the seller, and the particulars of the arrangement — quite a common one in business transactions — are called *credit terms*. The word *credit* derives from the Latin *credere*, "to believe or to trust" — the Latin word is the source of both the bookkeeping term and the name of the business transaction. In this case, the buyer, the company for which we are keeping the books, will in fact record the liability as a credit in ledger to the account Accounts Payable, but we should resist using this as a mnemonic device; if the company were to "sell on credit", it would record the expected future receipt as a *debit* to the asset account Accounts Receivable (which is exactly what the supplier in this particular example is doing). Thus, two uses of the term *credit* are closely related, but their meanings are quite distinct and they should not be confused.

To summarize:
The asset account, Inventory, increases by $5,000.
The liability account, Accounts Payable, increases by $5,000.

We need to add a new account — Accounts Payable, a liability account, as shown in Table 2A.6.

Now that we know that the asset increase is called a debit and that the liability increase is called a credit, we can write this transaction as a standard journal entry:

		[Dr]	[Cr]
Date			
[Dr]	Inventory {asset}	5,000	
[Cr]	Accounts Payable {liability}		5,000

Transaction #4: Purchase from X Co. Ltd., terms, 30 days.

Leaving aside the date and the narrative (the detailed description of the transaction) at the end, this is read,

"Debit Inventory 5,000; credit Accounts Payable 5,000"

The important pieces of information in the journal entry are the date, the account names and amounts, and the positions of the account names and amounts. The indenting indicates whether an account is being debited or credited. The abbreviations in brackets, [Dr] and [Cr], in the first column under the date and at the top of the debit and credit columns are optional. The account types {asset, liability, etc.} in curly brackets are included in these appendices for teaching purposes only. They do not appear in regular journal entries.

The journal is a chronological record of transactions. As the name implies, journal entries are written up daily as they occur. The information in the journal is subsequently posted to the relevant accounts in the general ledger. These postings are not necessarily made daily, but all the period's journal entries must be posted before financial statements are prepared. Of course, in computerized systems, the initial entry is made in real time and the posting is done simultaneously.

Table 2A.6

#	Assets				Liabilities				Shareholders' Equity	
	Cash		Inventory		Bank Loan		Accounts Payable		Share Capital	
	Dr	Cr	Dr	Cr	Dr	Cr	Dr	Cr	Dr	Cr
1	25000									25000
2	10000					10000				
3		8000	8000							
4			5000					5000		
column subtotals	35000	8000	13000			10000		5000		25000
account balances	27000		13000			10000		5000		25000

Notice again that the general ledger remains in balance: debit account balances total 40,000 (27,000 + 13,000); credit account balances total 40,000 (10,000 + 5,000 + 25,000).

(To keep the ledger uncluttered we have deleted the balances we struck after transaction #2. These were for information only at that time and their removal now changes nothing. This practice will be continued as we proceed.)

Transaction #5 Up to this point, all transactions have involved only accounts that appear on the balance sheet. Transaction #5 is what is called a *revenue transaction*. It involves activities through which the company earns a profit. In this transaction, as shown in Table 2A.7 on page 54, we see an example of *revenue* (i.e., the company sells goods for $7,000) and *expense* (i.e., the goods sold cost the company $4,000).

In the description in section 2.3, transaction #5 was presented as an increase in net assets of $3,000, representing a corresponding increase in owners' equity. In terms of the simplified accounting equation used in section 2.3, this is correct. In terms of debits, credits, and ledger accounts, the story is a little more involved. This net increase in owners' equity represents increases in components of profit: revenue and expense. However, since there will probably be other revenues and expenses of the business before the end of the accounting period, it would be inappropriate to label the $3,000 as a profit just yet. (As it happens, there is both revenue and expense in transaction #6 as well as additional expenses in subsequent transactions.) Profit is the difference between *all* the revenues and *all* the expenses of the period. In fact, the accounting process acknowledges that the measurement of profit is tentative until we have come to the end of the accounting period. Until we close the books, there is no explicit measure of profit in the general ledger. All we see now are some of its components — in this case just sales revenue and cost of goods sold expense (COGS). The process of calculating and recording profit must wait until the accounting period is over and all the other revenues and expenses have been recorded.

A sales transaction is typically recorded in two separate steps: in the first step, the revenue is recorded (5a); in the second, the associated expense is recorded (5b).

Transaction #5a — Sales Revenue
This is a simple cash sale. Revenue, the gross increase in shareholders' equity from operations, is represented by an inflow of cash.

To summarize:
The asset account, Cash, increases by $7,000.
The revenue account, Sales Revenue, increases by $7,000.

An increase in the asset Cash is recorded by a debit of $7,000. The increase in the revenue account Sales Revenue is recorded by a credit of $7,000.

We represent this transaction in journal entry form as follows:

		[Dr]	[Cr]
Date			
[Dr]	Cash {asset}	7,000	
[Cr]	Sales Revenue {SE — revenue}		7,000

Transaction #5a: Sale of goods to Y Co. Ltd., for $7,000 cash.

To emphasize that revenue accounts are sub-accounts of retained earnings and therefore part of shareholders' equity, these entries will be labelled {SE — revenue} in the journal entries. Similarly, expense entries will be labelled {SE — expense}.

Transaction 5b — Cost of Goods Sold
This transaction records the *direct* expense of this particular sale. The cost is the using up (transfer out to the customer) of the goods that have been sold. Whereas the sale is recorded at the selling price, the cost of the goods sold is recorded at the cost price, which will normally be lower. Establishing the actual value of the cost of the goods sold can become a little complicated; we will look at it in more detail below. In this case, we will accept that the cost of this particular sale is $4,000 and leave until later the discussion of the techniques for establishing cost of goods sold.

To summarize:
The asset account, Inventory, decreases by $4,000.
The expense account, Cost of Goods Sold, increases by $4,000.

An expense, even though it is read as a positive number, is a *reduction* of equity. A reduction of equity is represented by a debit. The other side of the transaction is the actual reduction of the asset Inventory. This is the credit.

We represent this transaction in journal entry form as follows:

		[Dr]	[Cr]
Date			
[Dr]	Cost of Goods Sold {SE — expense}	4,000	
[Cr]	Inventory {asset}		4,000

Transaction #5b: Cost of goods sold to Y Co. Ltd. (Transaction #5a)

We can now post both entries to the general ledger and then check the balance. We need to create new accounts in the ledger. These are in fact sub-accounts within Retained Earnings: Revenue — Sales, and Expense — Cost of Goods Sold. (See Table 2A.7 on the next page.)

Having struck a balance in each account, we can balance the general ledger. Debit account balances — now found on both sides of the ledger — total 47,000 (34,000 + 9,000 + 4,000). Credit account balances also total 47,000 (10,000 + 5,000 + 7,000 + 25,000). Notice that we have left the two sub-accounts of Retained Earnings, Revenue — sales and Expense — cost of goods sold, with credit and debit balances, respectively. The process of profit measurement is as yet incomplete. Only when the books are finally closed at the end of the period will all the revenue and expense accounts (there would normally be a number of them) be closed, and net income — i.e., profit — calculated. We will demonstrate this procedure at the end of this appendix.

It is worth pausing at this point to consider the meaning and importance of using debits and credits.

What Do Debit and Credit Mean?

In accounting, the words *debit* and *credit* are just shorthand terms — they have no significance other than "left side of the ledger" and "right side of the ledger". In everyday language, however, these words have other connotations. It is important not to confuse these usages. Although the words *debit* and *credit* are often used in an evaluative way in everyday language, in accounting they have a purely technical meaning. Debits are not bad, nor are credits good. If a building is purchased, the asset account must be increased; this is done by "debiting" the account Building, which will normally have a debit balance. Debits are what increase asset accounts, and an asset account with a positive balance has a debit balance. But with every debit, there is a credit; if the building is purchased for cash, then at the same time that Building is debited, the account Cash is credited, which is simply another way of saying that the account Cash was reduced. None of these transactions imply in any way that the company is worse off. In fact, the transactions simply record trading of assets — cash for building.

Consider a different situation. If the building had been purchased entirely "on credit" — in other words, the money to purchase the building was borrowed — the debit entry would be the same as before, but now, instead of crediting Cash, we would credit Mortgage Loan Payable. *Credit* in this case means the recognition of a liability. It is a different way of financing the purchase and has different implications for future cash management, but in itself, the credit has no moral or judgmental significance.[8] A third method of financing the purchase of the building might be (if the seller would accept it) to pay for the building by issuing new shares. Issuing shares involves a credit entry simply because an increase in shareholders' equity is recorded by a right-side entry. In none of these cases can we say that the company is *ipso facto* better or worse

---

[8] Of course, these other meanings of *debit* and *credit* have some relationship to the accounting terms. Still, strictly speaking, in accounting *debit* and *credit* mean no more than "left side" and "right side".

Table 2A.7

#	Assets				Liabilities				Shareholders' Equity							
	Cash		Inventory		Bank Loan		Accounts Payable		R/E		Revenue—Sales		Expense—COGS		Share Capital	
	Dr	Cr	Dr	Cr	Dr	Cr	Dr	Cr	Dr	Cr	Dr	Cr	Dr	Cr	Dr	Cr
1	25000															25000
2	10000					10000										
3		8000	8000													
4			5000					5000								
5a	7000											7000				
5b				4000									4000			
column subtotals	*42000*	*8000*	*13000*	*4000*		*10000*		*5000*				*7000*	*4000*			*25000*
account balances	*34000*		*9000*			*10000*		*5000*				*7000*	*4000*			*25000*

off because of what the debits or credits record. In fact, in every recorded transaction, total debits equal total credits: that is the nature of double-entry accounting.

Why Should Non-accountants Learn about Debits and Credits?

Why should non-accountants learn double-entry accounting using debits and credits? The short answer is that double-entry accounting underlies all business accounting, and understanding double entry means that you will be less intimidated by financial reports. All standard systems, including all computer systems designed for business use, use standard double entry. While it is true that you don't need to understand double-entry accounting to read a set of financial statements, familiarity with the system has undoubted advantages. Understanding debits and credits is a large part of understanding the language of accounting. Modern financial statements are increasingly complex. A basic accounting course is not going to make us experts; but even if we don't understand a particular transaction or some aspect of statement presentation, a familiarity with basic debits and credits puts us in a better position to follow the explanations of accountants and make intelligent interpretations.

We can now complete the remaining transactions in section 2.3, balance and close the ledger, and show how the financial statements are prepared.

Transaction #6 As noted in section 2.3 of the text, transaction #6 is very similar to transaction #5. The amounts are different, of course; moreover, transaction #5 is a cash sale and this sale has been made on credit. In practical accounting terms, the difference in the terms of sale is reflected solely in the asset account debited: it was Cash in transaction #5, and will be Accounts Receivable in this transaction. As explained in section 2.3, under GAAP, credit sales are normally recognized as completed sales and we will follow that convention here. This question is explored in more detail in Chapter 3.

Again, this sales transaction is recorded in two separate steps, as illustrated in Table 2A.8 on page 57: in the first step, the revenue is recorded (6a); in the second, the associated expense is recorded (6b).

Transaction 6a — Sales Revenue

This sale is a credit sale, a sale "on account". The increase in shareholders' equity is represented by a claim on the customer for a *future* payment of cash. It is not a receipt of cash now, so it is *not* an increase in the account Cash. The account representing a claim for a future payment is Accounts Receivable.

To summarize:
The asset account, Accounts Receivable, increases by $9,000.
The revenue account, Sales Revenue, increases by $9,000.

An increase in the asset, Accounts Receivable, is represented by a debit of $9,000. The increase in the revenue account, Sales Revenue, is represented by a credit of $9,000.

The journal entry is as follows:

		[Dr]	[Cr]
Date			
[Dr]	Accounts Receivable {asset}	9,000	
[Cr]	Sales Revenue {SE — revenue}		9,000

Transaction #6a: Sale of goods to Z Co. Ltd., for $9,000 on account, terms, 30 days

Transaction 6b — Cost of Goods Sold

As in transaction #5b, transaction #6b records the *direct* expense of the revenue earned in transaction #6a. The expense is the expired cost of the asset transferred to the customer — the cost of the goods that have been sold.

To summarize
The asset account, Inventory, decreases by $6,000.
The expense account, Cost of Goods Sold, increases by $6,000.

We represent this transaction in journal entry form as follows:

		[Dr]	[Cr]
Date			
[Dr]	Cost of Goods Sold {SE — expense}	6,000	
[Cr]	Inventory {asset}		6,000

Transaction #6b: Cost of goods sold to Z Co. Ltd. (Transaction #6a)

We can now post entries #6a and 6b to the general ledger. We need to create one new account in the ledger: Accounts Receivable. (Accounts Receivable is an asset account. The account name is written in the plural since we normally have more than one account receivable. At this point, of course, there is just the one.) We have not verified that the general ledger balances, but you should do that yourself as an exercise. (See Table 2A.8 on the following page.)

We will write the journal entries for transactions #7 through #10 before posting them to the general ledger in Table 2A.9 on page 60.

Transaction #7 This is the collection of the receivable created when we made the sale in transaction #6a.

To summarize:
The asset account, Cash, increases by $9,000.
The asset account, Accounts Receivable, decreases by $9,000.

An increase in the asset Cash is represented by a debit of $9,000. The decrease in the asset account Accounts Receivable is represented by a credit of $9,000.
The journal entry is as follows:

		[Dr]	[Cr]
Date			
[Dr]	Cash {asset}	9,000	
[Cr]	Accounts Receivable {asset}		9,000

Transaction #7: Collection of accounts receivable from to Z Co. Ltd. (Transaction #6a)

Table 2A.8

#	Assets						Liabilities				Shareholders' Equity								
	Cash		Accounts Receivable		Inventory		Bank Loan		Accounts Payable		R/E		Revenue —Sales		Expense —COGS		Share Capital	
	Dr	Cr	Dr	Cr	Dr	Cr	Dr	Cr	Dr	Cr	Dr	Cr	Dr	Cr	Dr	Cr	Dr	Cr
1	25000																	25000
2	10000							10000										
3		8000			8000													
4					5000					5000								
5a	7000													7000				
5b						4000									4000			
6a			9000											9000				
6b						6000									6000			

Transaction #8   This is the settlement of the liability (Accounts Payable) incurred in transaction #4: purchase of inventory on account.

To summarize:
The liability account, Accounts Payable, decreases by $5,000.
The asset account, Cash, decreases by $5,000.

An decrease in the liability Accounts Payable is represented by a debit of $5,000. The decrease in the asset account Cash is represented by a credit of $5,000.
The journal entry is as follows:

		[Dr]	[Cr]
Date			
[Dr]	Accounts Payable {liability}	5,000	
[Cr]	Cash {asset}		5,000

Transaction #8: Settlement of account payable to X Co. Ltd.
(Transaction #4)

Transaction #9   This is the payment of bank loan interest. As explained in section 2.3, interest is an expense. The account is called Interest Expense to distinguish it from Interest Revenue, which doesn't appear here but can arise.

To summarize:
The expense account, Interest Expense, increases by $100.
The asset account, Cash, decreases by $100.

An increase in the expense Interest Expense is represented by a debit of $100. (Remember, an expense represents a *decrease* in Retained Earnings.) The decrease in the asset account Cash is represented by a credit of $100.
The journal entry is as follows:

		[Dr]	[Cr]
Date			
[Dr]	Interest Expense {SE — expense}	100	
[Cr]	Cash {asset}		100

Transaction #9: Interest on bank loan for the period.

Transaction #10   The company has had a period of profitable operations, and the directors have decided to pay the owners a cash dividend. There are actually two stages to this transaction: the declaration of the dividend by the board of directors, and later, after the list of shareholders is updated, the payment. In this case, both stages are recorded as one transaction.

To summarize:
The dividend account, Dividends, increases by $1,000.
The asset account, Cash, decreases by $1,000.

An increase in the dividends account Dividends is represented by a debit of $1,000. (Remember, dividends reduce Retained Earnings.) The decrease in the asset account Cash is represented by a credit of $1,000.

The journal entry is as follows:

		[Dr]	[Cr]
Date			
[Dr]	Dividends {SE — dividends}	1,000	
[Cr]	Cash {asset}		1,000

Transaction #10: Declaration and payment of a dividend of $1,000.

Now we can post the four last transactions and balance the ledger. We need to create two new accounts in the ledger: Interest Expense and Dividends. Interest Expense is in fact another sub-account within Retained Earnings and it will be included here in the column headed Expenses. (See Table 2A.9.)

In balancing the ledger, notice that two of the accounts have fallen to zero: the Account Receivable was collected and the Account Payable paid. You can verify that the ledger balances: total debits = total credits = $51,000.

At this point we will make one additional entry, one that was not made in section 2.3, but that is the type of entry that would normally be made at the end of the period.

A standard accounting system is designed to recognize and record, as they take place on a day-to-day basis, all transactions involving cash; most systems will record credit purchases and credit sales as well. In general, any standard business transaction that involves an organization or individual outside the company will trigger an accounting entry. Transactions #1 through #10 are good examples of the sorts of entries that a standard accounting system will capture as they occur.

When we come to the end of the accounting period, however, any event that is deemed to affect the balance sheet or income statement according to GAAP must be recorded. This includes events that have not yet triggered an accounting entry because cash has not been involved and no invoice has been received or sent. For example, imagine that the period covered by transactions #1 to #10 is one month and the books must now be closed. At the beginning of this period, we hired an office assistant on a part-time basis. The agreement was that she was to be paid a monthly salary of $900 for this work, to be paid to her one week after the end of each month. At the end of this accounting period, she has worked for one month but will not be paid until another week has passed. According to GAAP, the cost of the work she did — $900 — is an expense of the past month. No payment has been made (an invoice would not normally be sent by the employee in a salary relationship), so there has been no event to trigger an entry. Standard accounting practice provides for such time-based transactions through the use of *adjusting journal entries* (AJEs). The following are some examples of transactions that would be handled by adjusting journal entries:

- Recognizing an expense for part of a billing period that covers two accounting periods (this is called an *accrued expense*, or simply *an accrual*). The salary example above is in effect an example of such an accrual.

59

Table 2A.9

	Assets						Liabilities				Shareholders' Equity									
	Cash		Accounts Receivable		Inventory		Bank Loan		Accounts Payable		Retained Earnings								Share Capital	
											R/E		Revenue — Sales		Expenses		Dividends			
#	Dr	Cr	Dr	Cr	Dr	Cr	Dr	Cr	Dr	Cr	Dr	Cr	Dr	Cr	Dr	Cr	Dr	Cr	Dr	Cr
1	25000																			25000
2	10000							10000												
3		8000			8000															
4					5000					5000										
5a	7000													7000						
5b						4000									4000					
6a			9000											9000						
6b						6000									6000					
7	9000			9000																
8		5000							5000											
9		100													100					
10		1000															1000			
column subtotals	51000	14100	9000	9000	13000	10000		10000	5000	5000				16000	10100		1000			25000
account balances	36900		0		3000			10000	0					16000	10100		1000			25000

- Recognizing revenue for part of a billing period that covers two accounting periods (another *accrual* — in this case, an *accrued revenue*).

- Recognizing that a payment made for something that is of the nature of an expense and was so accounted for when paid, but that is not an expense *this period*, is *deferred* to the next period. (An example would be a payment for six months' rent paid two months before the end of the accounting period. The whole payment is often charged to expense at the time of payment, a common practice since the payment is of the nature of an expense. However, this treatment is correct only if the part of the payment that will be an expense in the next period is removed from this period's expense by means of an AJE.)

- Recognizing that a payment received for something that we will deliver in the next period is not counted as revenue this period but is *deferred* to the next period. (An example was described on page 33.)

- Cost of goods sold for any business that does not record inventory change for each transaction.

- Amortization.

All of these periodic transactions are identified at the end of each accounting period following a review of operations, contracts, and policies, and then entered into the accounts by means of an adjusting journal entry (AJE).

We will make the AJE for the *salary accrual.*

Adjusting Journal Entry —
Accrual of Salary Expense

The assistant's salary has been earned by her for work done in the past month even though it has yet to paid. The value of her labour has been used up in the month and so, like interest in transaction #10, it is an expense for the period. It is normally called Salary Expense.

To summarize:
The expense account, Salary Expense, increases by $900.
The liability account, Salary Payable, increases by $900.

An increase in the expense Salary Expense is represented by a debit of $900. The corresponding increase in the liability account, Salary Payable, is represented by a credit of $900. Salary Payable is very similar to Accounts Payable; for this reason, the two liabilities will be combined and the account simply renamed Payable.

The adjusting journal entry is as follows:

		[Dr]	[Cr]
Date			
[Dr]	Salary Expense {SE — expense}	900	
[Cr]	Payable {liability}		900

Adjusting journal entry: accrual of unpaid salary expense

See Table 2A.10.

Table 2A.10

	Assets						Liabilities				Shareholders' Equity										
	Cash		Accounts Receivable		Inventory		Bank Loan		Payables		Retained Earnings								Share Capital		
											R/E		Revenue — Sales		Expenses		Dividends				
#	Dr	Cr	Dr	Cr	Dr	Cr	Dr	Cr	Dr	Cr	Dr	Cr	Dr	Cr	Dr	Cr	Dr	Cr	Dr	Cr
1	25000																			25000
2	10000							10000												
3		8000			8000															
4					5000					5000										
5a	7000													7000						
5b						4000									4000					
6a			9000											9000						
6b						6000									6000					
7	9000			9000																
8		5000							5000											
9		100													100					
10		1000															1000			
AJE										900					900					

Closing the Books

We assume now that the one adjusting journal entry was all that was necessary and that the books are thus up-to-date and in accordance with GAAP. We begin the closing process by balancing the accounts. These balances will be used to draw up the financial statements. Before continuing, you should confirm that the general ledger itself is balanced. (See Table 2A.11.)

Closing the books does three interrelated things:

1. It calculates the profit or loss for the period and carries it to retained earnings.
2. It sums the dividends for the period and carries that number to retained earnings.
3. It leaves all the temporary accounts — Revenue(s), Expense(s), and Dividends — with zero balances, ready to begin the next period.

The method we use records two closing journal entries, one for revenues and expenses and one for dividends, which are then posted to the general ledger.

Closing Journal Entry —
Revenue and Expense Accounts

We have opened one revenue account, Sales Revenue, and three expense accounts, Cost of Goods Sold, Interest Expense, and Salary Expense. The entry to close the revenue and expense accounts is purely mechanical: the Sales Revenue account is simply debited with the amount of its final balance of 16,000, and each of the expense accounts are credited with the amounts of their final balances, 11,000 in all. Since revenue exceeds expenses — the company has made a profit for the period — the balancing entry to Retained Earnings is a credit of 5,000. Had there been a loss, expenses would exceed revenue, and the balancing amount would have been a debit.[9]

The closing journal entry is as follows:

		[Dr]	[Cr]
Date			
[Dr]	Sales Revenue {SE — revenue}	16,000	
[Cr]	Cost of Goods Sold {SE — expense}		10,000
[Cr]	Interest Expense {SE — expense}		100
[Cr]	Salary Expense {SE — expense}		900
[Cr]	Retained Earnings {SE — R/E}		5,000

Closing journal entry: revenue and expense

---

[9] In this particular case, this is the first month of operations for the company and the opening balance of Retained Earnings is zero. After closing the books, Retained Earnings would have a debit balance. Negative Retained Earnings is call Deficit. If an incorporated company has a deficit, it is normally illegal to declare a dividend.

Table 2A.11

Assets

#	Cash Dr	Cash Cr	Accounts Receivable Dr	Accounts Receivable Cr	Inventory Dr	Inventory Cr
1	25000					
2	10000					
3		8000			8000	
4					5000	
5a	7000					
5b						4000
6a			9000			
6b						6000
7	9000			9000		
8		5000				
9		100				
10		1000				
AJE						
Balances	51000	14100	9000	9000	13000	10000
	36900		0		3000	

Liabilities

#	Bank Loan Dr	Bank Loan Cr	Payables Dr	Payables Cr
1				
2		10000		
3				
4				5000
5a				
5b				
6a				
6b				
7				
8			5000	
9				
10				
AJE				900
Balances		10000	5000	5900
		10000		900

Shareholders' Equity

#	R/E Dr	R/E Cr	Revenue — Sales Dr	Revenue — Sales Cr	Expenses Dr	Expenses Cr	Dividends Dr	Dividends Cr	Share Capital Dr	Share Capital Cr
1										25000
2										
3										
4										
5a				7000						
5b					4000					
6a				9000						
6b					6000					
7										
8										
9					100					
10							1000			
AJE					900					
Balances				16000	11000		1000			25000
										25000

Closing Journal Entry — Dividends Account

The balance in the Dividends account is closed to Retained Earnings in the same way as the revenue and expense accounts. In this case there was only one dividend declared but in practice there might be up to four declared in the year. The closing entry transfers the final debit balance in the Dividends account to Retained Earnings, which has the effect of reducing its balance.

The closing journal entry is as follows:

		[Dr]	[Cr]
Date			
[Dr]	Retained Earnings {SE — R/E}	1,000	
[Cr]	Dividends {SE — dividends}		1,000

Closing journal entry: dividends

Once the closing entries are posted, the general ledger is balanced for the last time. This *post-closing trial balance*, the closing entries, and other information in the ledger are used to prepare the financial statements. (See Table 2A.12.)

Preparing the Financial Statements

To complete the accounting cycle, we prepare financial statements: Income Statement, Statement of Retained Earnings, Balance Sheet, and Statement of Cash Flows. Further discussion, including the interpretation of these statements, will be the subject of the next four chapters and Chapter 15. What is important to note now is the importance of form. Even though all of the information contained in the financial statements can be found in the ledger and journal, these last, the "books", are the internal records of the company. These four financial statements constitute the only *formal* financial record of a company's operations and its financial position.

Example Co. Ltd.
Income Statement
for Month Ended December 31, 2011

Revenue		
Sales		$16,000
Expense		
Cost of goods sold	$10,000	
Interest	100	
Salary	900	11,000
Net income		$ 5,000

Example Co. Ltd.
Statement of Retained Earnings
for Month Ended December 31, 2011

Net income	$ 5,000
Less: dividends	1,000
Closing balance	$ 4,000

Table 2A.12

#	Cash Dr	Cash Cr	Accounts Receivable Dr	Accounts Receivable Cr	Inventory Dr	Inventory Cr	Bank Loan Dr	Bank Loan Cr	Payables Dr	Payables Cr	R/E Dr	R/E Cr	Revenue—Sales Dr	Revenue—Sales Cr	Expenses Dr	Expenses Cr	Dividends Dr	Dividends Cr	Share Capital Dr	Share Capital Cr
	Assets						Liabilities				Shareholders' Equity									
1	25000																			25000
2	10000							10000												
3		8000			8000															
4					5000					5000										
5a	7000													7000						
5b						4000									4000					
6a			9000											9000						
6b						6000									6000					
7	9000			9000																
8		5000							5000											
9		100													100					
10		1000															1000			
AJE										900					900					
Balances	51000	14100	9000	9000	13000	10000		10000	5000	5900				16000	11000		1000			25000
Trial Bal.	36900		0		3000			10000		900				16000	11000		1000			25000
Close R/E												5000	16000			11000				
Close Div.											1000							1000		
Post-closing Trial Bal.	36900				3000			10000		900		4000	0	0	0		0			25000

Example Co. Ltd.
Balance Sheet
as at December 31, 2011

Assets

Cash	$36,900
Inventory	3,000
	$39,900

Liabilities & Shareholders' Equity

Liabilities		
Salary payable	$ 900	
Bank loan	10,000	
Total liabilities		$10,900
Shareholders' equity		
Share capital	$25,000	
Retained earnings	4,000	
Total shareholders' equity		29,000
		$39,900

Example Co. Ltd.
Statement of Cash Flows
for Month Ended December 31, 2011

Cash from operations	
Net income	$ 5,000
Add: decrease in non-cash working capital	7,900
	$12,900
Cash from financing activities	
Cash from issuing shares	$25,000
Cash used for dividends	(1,000)
	$24,000
Change in cash balance	$36,900

You should satisfy yourself that you understand how the information in the general ledger at the end of the period (Table 2A.12) has been used to prepare the first three financial statements shown above. (The balances in the revenue and expense accounts [before closing] are used to draw up the income statement. The net income figure from the income statement along with the balances in the dividend and retained earnings accounts are used to create the statement of retained earnings. The post-closing trial balance provides the figures for the balance sheet.) The fourth financial statement, the statement of cash flows, is also based on information from the general ledger, but the relationship is not so simply described. In Appendix 6.3 we will learn a technique for taking information from the books — or, more directly, from the first three financial statements — to construct the statement of cash flows for the period.

Self-Study Problems

1. Charley Farley went into business on October 1, 2011, by opening a doughnut shop. He carried on the business in a rented store in downtown Orillia. At the end of December, he realized that he would have to pay income tax on the business profits, but he had no idea how much profit he had made. He has asked you to advise him how much income to report for the three months he has been in business.

    He has presented you with his bank statements and a pile of invoices and receipts. The following is a summarized list of payments and receipts for the three months.

    Receipts paid into bank account:

1.	Owners' equity	$ 50,000
2.	Bank loan	$ 55,000
3.	Cash sales	$146,500

    Payments made out of bank account:

4.	Suppliers	$104,500
5.	Wages	$ 12,000
6.	Rent	$ 20,000
7.	Utilities	$ 5,000
8.	Insurance	$ 4,000
9.	Equipment	$ 99,000
10.	Repayment of bank loan	$ 4,000

    Required
    (a) Enter the summarized transactions into the accounting equation, and show the balance of assets, liabilities, and equities after each transaction. Assume, for now, that transactions 4, 5, 6, 7, and 8 all reduce owners' equity.
    (b) As at December 31, 2011, the assets total $102,000 according to the accounting equation. What are those assets?

2. The financial statements of Ozark Outfitters show an operating income of $100,000 and a net income of $75,000. Total assets are $1 million, liabilities are $500,000, owners' equity is $500,000.

    Required
    (a) What is the return on assets?
    (b) What is the return on equity?

3. Bombardier Inc. reported operating income of $1,700 million and net income of $391 million for the year ended January 31, 2002. The company's total assets were $27,753 million and owners' equity was $4,090 million as at January 31, 2002.

    Required
    (a) How much were the total liabilities as at January 31, 2002?
    (b) What was the return on assets for the year?
    (c) What was the return on equity for the year?

4. Continue with Problem #3: for the year to January 31, 2004, the operating income for Bombardier Inc. was $246 million, and there was a net loss (for the shareholders) of $89 million. Total assets were $25,569 million, and liabilities totalled $22,319 million.

Required
(a) How much was the shareholders' equity as at January 31, 2004?
(b) What was the return on assets for the year?
(c) What was the return on equity for the year?

Solutions

1. (a)

		Assets	=	Liabilities	+	Owners' Equity
	1.	$ 50,000	=		+	$ 50,000
	2.	55,000	=	$55,000	+	nil
		$105,000	=	$55,000	+	$ 50,000
	3.	146,500	=	nil	+	146,500
		$251,500	=	$55,000	+	$196,500
	4.	−104,500	=	nil	+	−104,500
		$147,000	=	$55,000	+	$ 92,000
	5.	− 12,000	=	nil	+	− 12,000
		135,000	=	$55,000	+	$ 80,000
	6.	− 20,000	=	nil	+	− 20,000
		$115,000	=	$55,000	+	$ 60,000
	7.	− 5,000	=	nil	+	− 5,000
		$110,000	=	$55,000	+	$ 55,000
	8.	− 4,000	=	nil	+	− 4,000
		$106,000	=	$55,000	+	$ 51,000
	9.	−99,000 + 99,000	=	nil	+	nil
		$106,000	=	$55,000	+	$ 51,000
	10.	− 4,000	=	− 4,000	+	nil
		$102,000	=	$51,000	+	$ 51,000

(b) The assets consist of:

Cash at bank	$ 3,000
Equipment	99,000
Total	$102,000

2. (a) Return on assets:

= operating income ÷ total assets
= $100,000 ÷ $1,000,000
= 0.1 (or 10%)

(b) Return on equity:

= net income ÷ owners' equity
= $75,000 ÷ $500,000
= 0.15 (or 15%)

3. (a) Accounting equation:

 Assets = Liabilities + Owners' equity
 $27,753 million = Liabilities + $4,090 million
 Total liabilities = ($27,753 – $4,090) million
 Total liabilities were $23,663 million.

 (b) Return on assets:

 = (operating income ÷ total assets) × 100%
 = ($1,700 million ÷ $27,753 million) × 100%
 = 6.1%

 (c) Return on equity:

 = (net income ÷ owners' equity) × 100%
 = ($391 million ÷ $4,090 million) × 100%
 = 9.6%

4. (a) Accounting equation:

 Assets = Liabilities + Owners' equity
 $25,569 million = $22,319 million + Owners' equity
 Owners' equity = ($25,569 – $22,319) million
 Owners' equity was $3,250 million.

 (b) Return on assets:

 = (operating income ÷ total assets) × 100%
 = ($246 million ÷ $25,569 million) × 100%
 = 0.96% (i.e., less than 1% p.a.)

 (c) Return on equity (or Return on investment):

 = (net income ÷ owners' equity) × 100%

 As there was a net loss, this is not a meaningful calculation.

Discussion Questions and Problems

Discussion Questions

1. It is 1997, and you are thinking about investing in Inco Ltd., a Canadian mining and resource company that is (as of 1997) proposing to open one of the richest metal ore mines in the world, in Voisey's Bay, Labrador. List the information available to you as a potential investor, its source, and its degree of usefulness to your investment decision.

2. As a shareholder of Abitibi-Price Consolidated Inc., a Canadian pulp and paper processor, list the information the company will give to you and assess its relevance and reliability.

3. For some time you have been concerned about the environment. In January of the current year your uncle died and left you 500 shares of the Ford Motor Company. What can you do to make yourself more comfortable about the relationship between Ford, you, and the environment?

4. Banks and trust companies regularly provide mortgage loans to home buyers. What financial information do they require before making their lending decisions? What additional steps do they take to make sure their loans are safe?

5. Owners' equity is described as the residual in the accounting equation. Explain what this means in terms of assets and liabilities. If you are the owner of 10 shares in Bell Canada Enterprises Inc., what is your entitlement to the owners' equity on the balance sheet?

6. When an asset is acquired, it is valued at cost because of the historical cost accounting principle. Under what circumstances would this be inaccurate, and what steps should be taken to make the balance sheet show the correct value?

7. The matching concept requires that expenses be reported in the period that received the benefit of the expense, and not in the period when the cash was paid out. Where in the balance sheet would the effect of this be reported?

8. Where in the financial reports would the financial outcome of an ongoing litigation be reported?

9. Does an audit improve the relevance, or the reliability, of financial reports?

10. What does the term *residual interest* mean when it is applied to common shares?

Appendix 2.1

11. What is a transaction? How does a transaction differ from an event?

12. What is a journal entry? What is the relationship between a journal entry and a transaction? Between a journal entry and an event?

13. What is an account?

14. What is the general ledger?

15. What is a debit?

16. What is a credit?

17. Are debits better than credits?

Problems

1. You are a shareholder of Bombardier Inc., a company listed on the Toronto Stock Exchange. The company has recently mailed you its end-of-year financial statements.

   Required
   (a) Why have they done this?
   (b) When would you expect to receive them?
   (c) What information would you get from the income statement?
   (d) What information would you get from the balance sheet?
   (e) What information would you get from the cash flow statement?
   (f) What information would you get from the statement of retained earnings?
   (g) In what way can you use this information to make an informed choice about your future investing activities?

2. You have just received an inheritance of $120,000. Your objective is to use this as a deposit to buy a house. Your best estimate of the lawyers' fees and closing costs is $20,000, and you believe that most financial institutions insist on a 20% deposit. You want a mortgage loan of $400,000, and you could supply the following documents to support your request:

   (a) A list of your RRSP investments
   (b) A list of the shares you hold in companies listed on the Toronto Stock Exchange
   (c) Your university transcript, which shows that you are an A student
   (d) A professional valuation of your car for $50,000
   (e) A letter from your employer showing that your last year's earnings were $100,000
   (f) A list of your clothes and other personal property and your estimate of what they cost you
   (g) Your bank statements and returned cheques for the last six months
   (h) Details of your divorce settlement and child support obligations
   (i) The names and addresses of your grandparents, who intend to leave you something in their wills

   Required
   Describe how your bank manager would view the documents that you could supply to support your request for the mortgage (use the criteria of reliability and relevance in each case).

3. Tom and Jerry decide to go into business together. They will offer lawn maintenance services in spring, summer, and fall, and snowplowing services in winter. They intend to be rich and independent so that they can retire to Florida by the time they are 35. In the first month of their business, they have the following transactions:

(a) Both partners put $20,000 of their personal savings into a partnership bank account to get the business going.

(b) They have leased a truck, a trailer, a garden tractor with a mower attachment, and a snowplow for a rental fee of $5,000 per month.

(c) They have bought various small gardening tools and equipment for $2,000, which they paid by cheque.

(d) They have arranged with their bank to get a credit card, with a credit limit of $10,000, for the business.

(e) During their first month of business, they bought fuel for $1,000 using the credit card.

(f) They used the credit card to pay for repairs to the truck: $500.

(g) During the first month they mowed 250 houses' lawns and charged each customer $50. All the customers paid by cheque, and all the cheques were put into the bank account.

(h) They mowed the lawns of two customers who paid in cash, $50 each. Tom kept $40 and spent the other $60 on office supplies for use in the business.

(i) During the first month, they mowed the lawn of the Felix Company office building twice, after negotiating a price of $250 per mowing. The company has asked them to bill their services monthly.

(j) The Felix Company has also agreed to pay Tom and Jerry $200 per month to snowplow the company's car park in the winter.

(k) At the end of the first month, they paid the outstanding balance on the credit card and they invoiced the Felix Company for the lawn-mowing services.

(l) At the end of the month, they examined the small tools they had bought for $2,000; the tools seem quite well worn, and their value has depreciated by about $500.

(m) At the end of the month, Tom and Jerry each took $4,000 out of the company bank account for their personal use.

Required
Use the accounting equation to show how each of the transactions would be recorded in their business books of account. (Indicate the effect on assets, liabilities, and equity in each case.)

4. Use the information in Problem #3 to prepare an income statement, a balance sheet, and a cash flow statement for Tom and Jerry for their first month of operation.

5. For Tom and Jerry's business, multiply the first month's income by 12 to get an estimate of the annual income, and then calculate their return on assets.

   Is the idea of multiplying their first month's results by 12 to get an annual figure a reasonable thing to do?

6. You are given the following information about the Bayview Variety Store, as at December 31st:

Assets

Cash	$ 500
Inventory, at cost	17,000
Owed by customers	2,000
Rent deposit	2,500
	$22,000
Store fittings & equipment	10,000
	$32,000

Liabilities

Owed to suppliers	$15,000
Owed for utilities	1,000
	$16,000
Owner's Equity	16,000
	$32,000

Required

Show the accounting equation after each of the following transactions occurred in the January that follows:

(a) Collected $1,500 of the money owed by customers
(b) Sold goods for $25,000 in cash; the goods had cost $10,000
(c) Bought goods from suppliers and paid in cash: $5,000
(d) Bought goods from suppliers on credit for $4,000
(e) Paid suppliers $10,000 of the money owed to them
(f) Paid staff wages: $1,000
(g) Discovered that the customer who owed $500 had run away and was unlikely to pay the debt
(h) Paid $2,500 rent for January
(i) Paid $1,000 for utilities. January's estimated utility usage was $500

7. Use the information in Problem #6 to prepare an income statement for Bayview Variety Store for January.

8. For the Bayview Variety Store, multiply January's income by 12 to get an estimate of the annual income and then calculate the store's return on assets.

Is multiplying January's results by 12 to get an annual income estimate a reasonable method?

9. Exact Metal Inc. had total assets of $800,000 at the end of December; liabilities were $500,000 and owners' equity was $300,000. During the most recent year, Exact Metal Inc.'s operating profit was $200,000, on sales of $1,600,000. Interest payments totalled $50,000 and taxes were $100,000, leaving net income of $50,000.

Required

Calculate the following ratios:

(a) The return on assets
(b) The return on owners' equity

10. Plastic Extrusions Inc. had total assets of $1,500,000 at the end of December, and liabilities were $300,000. During the most recent year, Plastic Extrusions Inc.'s sales were $3,200,000, and cost of

goods sold and other expenses totalled $2,000,000. Interest payments were $50,000, and taxes were $550,000.

Required
Calculate the following ratios:

(a) The return on assets
(b) The return on owners' equity

11. The return on assets and the return on owners' equity are all measures of profitability. Explain the differences between them and explain to whom each one would be most useful.

12. The two owners of County Retail have equity of $500,000 ($250,000 each) in their business but do not pay themselves any salary. Their expectation is that they should each get $75,000 out of the business for their work contribution, plus a 10% return on their investment. Ignoring taxes, how much profit are they hoping to earn?

13. For each of the following situations, state the relevant accounting concepts (note that more than one concept may apply):

(a) Tom and Jerry, who run a garden maintenance service, keep a careful record of when they use their truck for business and when they use it for personal trips.
(b) Bayview Variety Store calculates the income earned each year.
(c) Bayview Variety Store counts and values inventory at the end of December. The valuation is based on the expectation that the goods can be sold the following January.
(d) Bayview Variety Store amortizes the fridges and freezers at the rate of 10% of cost each year.
(e) Tom and Jerry normally require their customers to pay in cash. If any money is owed to them at the end of the year, they deduct 10% against the possibility of bad debts.

14. What is the relationship between the accounting equation and the balance sheet?

15. You are given the following information for Hardy's Retail:

Return on assets	20%
Return on equity	25%
Total assets	$500,000
Income tax expense	$40,000

(There was no interest expense.)

Required
Calculate the $ amount of the liabilities.

Appendix 2.1

16. Prepare journal entries for each of the events described below:

(a) In December, Harriet, an architect, designs a building for a client and bills the client $55,000.

75

(b) In December, Harriet pays her helper, Judy, one month's wages of $2,500.

(c) In June, Thomasina, a computer consultant, carries out a system upgrade for a client. She bills the client $15,000 to be paid the following month; she had bought software for $8,000 and employed a helper for the month for $2,000.

(d) In November, Dick, a food retailer, buys goods for resale at a cost of $50,000. He sets his selling price by marking up his cost by 80%.

(e) In December, Dick realizes that $9,000 worth of food (at retail price) was discoloured, and he is able to sell it only by marking it down to half price.

17. Using the information provided in Problem #3, complete the six-step accounting cycle for Tom and Jerry Garden Services for its first month of business. Use debits and credits, and organize your answer in the following three stages:

(a) Identify and record the transactions as journal entries (steps 1 and 2 of the accounting cycle).

(b) Post the journal to the general ledger. Prepare a spreadsheet along the lines of the one used in the appendix, making the appropriate adjustments for the names of the assets and liabilities. Note that there will be Partners' Equity (one account for each partner) instead of Shareholders' Equity. There will be revenue and expense columns but no retained earnings as net income is divided directly between the partners. There are no dividends in partnership but partners make withdrawals, as agreed. Withdrawals are not necessarily equal in any period. Add as many columns as are necessary to accommodate the accounts and as many rows as necessary to complete the post-closing trial balance.

(c) Use the information from the completed spreadsheet to prepare (i) an income statement for the month, and (ii) a balance sheet as at the end of the month, both in good form.

18. Using the information in Problem #6, complete the accounting cycle for Bayview Variety Store for January 20XX in the same manner as you did for Tom and Jerry Garden Services in Problem #17. (Hint: the opening balances in the general ledger on January 1 are the closing balances of December.)

(a) Identify and record the transactions as journal entries.

(b) Post the journal to the general ledger. Lay out the general ledger in spreadsheet form and complete it up to the post-closing trial balance.

(c) Use the information from the spreadsheet to prepare (i) an income statement for the month and (ii) a balance sheet as at the end of the month, both in good form.

The Income Statement

3

Learning
Objectives

After studying this chapter, you should be able to describe and work with the following elements of the income statement:
→ Revenues
→ Cost of goods sold and expenses
→ Operating income and net income
→ Calculation and use of profitability ratios
→ Calculation of retained earnings
→ Calculation of earnings per share (EPS)

3.1 Introduction

In Chapter 2 we introduced the four main financial statements: the balance sheet, the income statement, the statement of retained earnings, and the statement of cash flows. In this chapter we shall look at the income statement and the statement of retained earnings in greater detail.

In the early days of accounting, the emphasis was on the balance sheet, which shows the "wealth" of the owner(s) at a point in time. More recently, to meet the information needs of investors in companies, the emphasis has shifted to the income statement. The income statement reports changes in wealth over a period of time, typically one year.

The changes in wealth that the income statement reports are the net effect of revenues the company has generated and expenses it has incurred. Expenses are deducted from revenues to leave the bottom line, which is a figure of net income or profit. If the expenses exceed the revenues, a loss will be reported.

Both revenues and expenses are calculated according to the matching principle. That is, only the revenues earned in the period (no matter when the money was received) and the expenses that were consumed in the period (no matter when they were paid for) are counted. This idea of matching is effected through accrual: moving revenues and expenses from one period to another to reflect real resource flows. Accrual/matching is the principal difference between the income statement and a list of payments and receipts.

3.2 Revenues

3.2.1 Sale of Goods and Services

Revenues are resources that flow into the company. They increase the value of the company and, hence, increase the owners' equity. Revenues arise mostly as a result of selling goods or services to customers.

The dollar value of any individual sale is seldom in dispute as it will be clearly stated on the invoice. The time period when revenue should be recognized is more subjective. Let us consider a company with a one-year reporting period from January to December.

The most straightforward situation is where the entire transaction is completed within the year. That means the goods are sold, the cash is collected, and all obligations under the contract of sale are completed within the calendar year. In this simple situation, the sale would be recognized in the year. This is typical of a retail store that sells on a cash basis, especially if, like Honest Ed's in downtown Toronto, there is a sign on the door that reads, No Refunds, No Exchanges. Less straightforward situations will occur where some aspect of a transaction falls outside the year: either occurring before the start of the year, or after the end of the year. When that happens, the matching principle requires that an accrual be made to move a part of the transaction forward or backward in time.

The most common accrual is in respect of credit sales. Credit sales are common in many business situations. Typically, credit terms are for 30 days, after which the invoice value is payable in full.

The resource flow that the accrual accounting/matching process is most interested in locating is the period when the goods were sold. That is generally taken to be the point when, legally, ownership of the goods passes from seller to buyer. In a retail store, that point is when the goods are delivered and payment is made. In a business-to-business situation, it is more likely to be when the goods are delivered. There are some special circumstances where it may be at another point, depending on the nature of the contract between the buyer and the seller.

The revenues for the sale of all goods sold in a given year will be recognized as revenues of that year, even if they have not been paid for.

This raises another problem: what happens if the customer fails to pay? The matching principle requires us to recognize this possibility even if, at the time we are preparing the income statement, we do not have all the information to know which customers will prove problematic. We would, therefore, "accrue" an allowance for bad debts, based on past experience. That would create an expense (bad debt expense) that is matched with the time period. (See Exhibit 3.1.)

Some sales are incomplete when initially made. A publisher, for example, sells books to bookstores, but the bookstore has a right to return some or all of the shipment if the books don't sell as well as expected. To take credit for all the sales at the time of delivery would be misleading, so a percentage of expected returns has to be held back in reporting sales. Another example is the sale of a new car, which will have a warranty (say 50,000 km or three years). While the full value of the car as sold may be treated as revenue, the expected costs to be incurred under warranty should be treated as an expected future payment, but a current expense, and matched by making it an expense in the same year the sale was recorded. So, in both of these examples the invoice (and even the cash received) may be an overstatement of the eventual net sales revenue.

Here's another example. Suppose you pay a subscription to a health club and you are entitled to 12 months' access to the facility. At the end

Exhibit 3.1:   Revenue Recognition in the Retail Industry

Peter's Press is a bookstore, and it prepares its income statement for the 12 months ended December 31 each year.

During the current year, a total of $550,000 has been banked from cash sales to customers. Additionally, during November a customer took a large order of books on credit, for $10,000. By December 31, that order has still not been paid for.

Peter's Press will recognize sales revenue of $560,000 ($550,000 + $10,000) for the year.

The matching concept then requires two further actions.

First, the cost of the goods sold for $560,000 must be recognized as an expense.

Second, the possibility that the $10,000 still owed may not be recovered has to be recognized. If the bookstore manager thinks that there is a 50% chance of non-payment, then $5,000 (50% of $10,000) will be reported as a potential bad debt expense.

Exhibit 3.2:   Revenue Recognition in the Service Industry

Fanatical Fitness is a health club. Its income statement is prepared annually to December 31. At the start of 2011, the club showed an amount of $100,000 on its balance sheet as a liability for memberships received in 2010 but continued into 2011. During 2011, Fanatical received $1,500,000 in cash for annual memberships. At the end of 2011, there was a total of $250,000 worth of continuing memberships that would carry on until sometime in 2012.

In 2011, Fanatical Fitness will recognize $1,350,000 as revenue as follows:

Memberships paid for in 2010 and expired in 2011	$ 100,000
Add: Memberships received in 2011	1,500,000
Deduct: Memberships expiring in 2012	(250,000)
Revenue recognized in 2011	$1,350,000

---

of the financial year, your subscription may still have three months to run. The health club should defer one quarter of your subscription to the following year's revenue. (See Exhibit 3.2.)

Suppose a builder has a contract to construct a new office block. It may take more than a year to complete, so work will be carried out that covers more than one accounting period. A very conservative approach would be to wait until the building is complete and handed over to the client, and then recognize the revenue at that point. A more reasonable approach would be to estimate the revenue earned in each period based on the percentage of the contract completed.

The fundamental question, in each case, is, What would the sales revenue be, for the accounting year, if we had full knowledge of all the eventual outcomes? In the absence of full knowledge we make reasonable assumptions. In cases of doubt, we exercise conservatism so that revenues are not over-reported.

3.2.2 Other Revenues

Other, non-sale, situations that give rise to revenues would include

• interest revenues from bank deposits, GICs, etc.,
• rent revenues,
• commission revenues.

These are not, typically, important sources of revenues for the company.

3.3 Expenses

Expenses are the opposite of revenues. They decrease equity. In measuring the net income we try to match the expenses with the revenues of the accounting period. The same problem that we dealt with in respect of revenues exists for expenses: the cash flow may not be a perfect guide to the resource flow we want to recognize. This means that we will have to make the same sort of adjustment, shuffling expenses from one period to another to get a good match.

Expenses are many and varied. They include items incurred directly in relation to the sale of goods, such as the cost of the goods sold in a retail store, or the cost of manufacturing the goods sold in a production plant. In respect of these direct costs, we can see the link between the revenue-generating process and the associated costs incurred, and matching the two is relatively straightforward. Expenses will also include the many operating costs of the company other than cost of goods sold, such as wages, rent, utilities, etc.

3.3.1 Cost of Goods Sold and Inventory

When a company purchases inventory for resale, the transaction is revenue-neutral. One asset (cash or its equivalent) has been exchanged for another asset (inventory) of equal value. As long as they still have the inventory, no change in equity occurs. When the inventory is sold, it creates revenue, and it also reduces the asset inventory. This reduction in inventory value is recorded as an expense, called cost of goods sold.

Depending on the type of record-keeping system in use, it may be possible to capture the cost of goods sold at the time of the sales transaction. This would always happen where the goods were valuable and specifically identifiable (a car or a washing machine, for example). It would also happen in a supermarket, where the bar code on a product passing through the checkout would trigger the recording not only of the sale but, also, the cost of goods sold (it would also feed into inventory records and re-ordering routines).

Exhibit 3.3:   Cost of Goods Sold in the Manufacturing Sector

Peerless Plastics makes plastic bottles using an extrusion moulding process. Its main raw material ingredient is plastic feedstock. The raw material is kept in a large hopper; once delivered, it is impossible to distinguish any one consignment from the rest. The price of the plastic feedstock varies as it is made from oil.

At the beginning of 2011, Peerless had 2,000 kg of feedstock inventory at a price of $5 per kg. During 2011 the company bought 8,000 kg at a price of $7 per kg. At the end of 2011 the company had 1,500 kg left in inventory. Peerless Plastics uses average costs for valuing cost of goods sold and closing inventories.

Opening inventory, January 1, 2011	2,000 kg @ $5.00	$10,000
Purchases during 2011	8,000 kg @ $7.00	56,000
Total available for sale	10,000 kg	$66,000
Average cost per kg: $66,000 ÷ 10,000 kg = $6.60		
Deduct closing inventory	1,500 kg @ $6.60	9,900
Cost of goods sold	8,500 kg @ $6.60	$56,100

The closing inventory value ($9,900) will appear on the balance sheet at December 31, 2011; the cost of goods sold value ($56,100) will appear as an expense in the 2011 income statement.

Where goods are of relatively small individual value, simpler systems that do not capture cost of goods sold as the sale takes place may be used. In these situations, the cost of goods sold is found indirectly. First, goods purchased during the year are added to the opening inventory. Then, the closing inventory is deducted. The balance is the cost of goods sold. (See Exhibit 3.3.)

Control of the cost of goods sold is carried out in a number of ways. One method is through the gross profit (or gross margin) to sales ratio. Because the relationship between the cost of goods sold and the selling price is known, the gross profit to sales ratio should be precise. If the actual gross margin is lower than expected, then something has gone wrong.

Suppose the selling price is established by adding 50% to the cost. Selling price thus becomes 150% of cost. A cost of $4 will result in a selling price of $6, with the gross profit 33⅓% of the cost. Expressed differently, the cost and the gross profit are 66⅔% and 33⅓%, respectively, of the selling price. If the gross profit falls below 33⅓% of the selling price, an unplanned loss has occurred. This might be due to spoilage, theft, temporary selling price reductions, or a range of other causes. If the difference is significant, it should be investigated and corrective action should be initiated. (See Exhibit 3.4.)

The cost convention tells us that inventory is recorded at cost in the first instance. If the inventory becomes impaired in some way, then the conservatism convention tells us that its value should be reduced. Suppose some of the inventory deteriorates and becomes unsaleable. The value of the inventory should be written down to reflect this, and the

Exhibit 3.4: Gross Profit %

Twin Sister's Restaurant marks up ingredients by 50% to get selling prices. That is, if the cost of the ingredients in a sandwich is $4.00, the restaurant would sell it for $6.00 ($4.00 + 50%), leaving a gross profit of $2. That should result in a gross profit % of 33⅓% ($2/$6 × 100% = 33⅓%).

In January, Twin Sisters sold $800 of sandwiches, but the raw materials had cost $600, leaving a gross profit of $200. The gross profit %, 25% ($200/$800 × 100%), is significantly lower than the expected 33⅓%. Some of the controls must have been lax. Possibly sandwiches are being sold at cheaper prices, or someone maybe stealing ingredients or takings.

Exhibit 3.5: Inventory Valuation at the Lower of Cost or Market Value

Peerless Plastics makes plastic bottles using an extrusion moulding process. Its main raw material ingredient is plastic feedstock. The raw material is all kept in a large hopper; once delivered, it is impossible to distinguish any one consignment from the rest. The price of the plastic feedstock varies as it is made from oil.

At the beginning of 2011, Peerless had 2,000 kg of feedstock inventory at a price of $5 per kg. During 2011 the company bought 8,000 kg at a price of $7 per kg. At the end of 2011 the company had 1,500 kg left in inventory. Peerless Plastics uses average costs for valuing cost of goods sold and closing inventories, but it also applies the rule of valuing inventory at the lower of cost or market value. As at December 31, 2011, the market price of plastic feedstock had fallen to $6 due to the lower price of oil.

Opening inventory, January 1, 2011	2,000 kg @ $5.00	$10,000
Purchases during 2011	8,000 kg @ $7.00	56,000
Total available for sale	10,000 kg	$66,000

Average Cost per kg: $66,000 ÷ 10,000 kg = $6.60

Deduct closing inventory valued at lower of cost ($6.60) or market value ($6.00)	1,500 kg @ $6.00	9,000
Cost of goods sold	8,500 kg	$57,000

Cost of good sold per kg = $57,000 ÷ 8,500 kg = $6.71

The closing inventory value ($9,000) will appear on the balance sheet at December 31, 2011; the cost of goods sold value ($57,000) will appear as an expense in the 2011 income statement.

amount of the writedown becomes an expense. The inventory may also lose value for reasons external to the organization. (See Exhibit 3.5.)

Suppose inventory has been bought at a cost of $66,000. Because of a world oversupply, the market price has fallen. The same inventory could now be replaced for a lesser amount. The conservative treatment requires the value of the inventory to be reported in the balance sheet at the lower of its cost and the market (replacement) cost.

In summary: when inventory is bought, it is an asset. Until it is used, it will appear on the balance sheet as an asset, recorded at cost. If market value falls below cost, the inventory value will be reduced to market value. When it has been sold, it will be reported in the income statement as an expense, and it will no longer appear on the balance sheet as an asset.

3.3.2   *Overhead Expenses*

In addition to the cost of goods sold, expenses also include overhead costs, such as

- wage and salary expenses;
- payroll-related expenses (e.g., employers' pension plan and employment insurance contributions);
- establishment expenses (taxes, rent, utilities, repairs, etc.);
- marketing expenses (advertising, sales commissions, etc.);
- research and development expenses; and
- financing expenses (e.g., interest).

Here the matching process is done indirectly. Most of these overhead expenses cannot be directly linked to any particular revenues. Instead, they are more commonly linked to the passage of time. Matching for these expenses is done by matching the time period to when the revenues were earned, rather than to the revenues themselves.

Take utilities, for example. (See Exhibit 3.6.) For the most part, the electricity bills paid in the year will be for electricity consumed in the year; therefore, they are expenses for the current year. At the end of the year, there may be an unpaid invoice for electricity. That invoice should be included as part of the current year's electricity expense. Moreover, the last invoice of the year may only cover consumption up to December 15, as recorded by the meter reading. Electricity consumed between December 16 and 31 should be estimated and accrued so that it, too, becomes an expense of the current year. Assuming the same process was carried out at the end of the previous year, the electricity expense reported this year would not include the amount owed at the start of the year.

This process of examining the payments and judging whether or not they accurately represent the expense incurred in the year should apply to every expense category.

Sometimes the adjustment will go the other way. Rent or insurance contracts, for example, are often paid in advance, and the expense has to be reduced by the amount of the prepayment. This, in turn, will be added to the "prepaid expense", an asset on the balance sheet. (See Exhibit 3.7.)

In general, we use "accruals" to adjust cash payments to reflect the resource flows and to match expenses to time periods. If the company has incurred an expense, but not yet paid for it, add the accrued expense to the payments. If the company has paid for an expense, but not yet used it up, deduct the prepaid amount from the payments.

Exhibit 3.6:   Accrued Expenses

Twin Sister's Restaurant prepares financial statements annually to December 31 each year. On January 1, 2011, the restaurant owed $800 for electricity used in 2010 but not yet paid for. During 2011, Twin Sisters paid 12 monthly electricity bills for a total of $5,200. As at December 31, there was an unpaid electricity bill of $600 for the month to December 15.

Cash paid in 2011	$5,200
Deduct: Owed from 2010	(800)
Add: Unpaid bill to December 15, 2011	600
Add: Accrued usage from December 16 to December 31, 2011	300
Electricity expense for 2011	$5,300

This expense of $5,300 is matched to the consumption of electricity during 2011.

The balance sheet as at December 31, 2011, will show a liability of $900 ($600 billed but not paid and $300 accrued) for electricity used but not yet paid for.

Exhibit 3.7:   Prepaid Expenses (Expenses Paid in Advance)

Twin Sister's Restaurant prepares financial statements annually to December 31 each year. On January 1, 2011, the restaurant's balance sheet showed a payment in advance for rent of $1,250. (This represents the rent for May 2014, the last month of the five-year lease. It was paid on June 1, 2009, at the beginning of the five-year lease.) During 2011, Twin Sisters made 12 annual rent payments of $1,250 each for a total of $15,000.

Cash paid for rent during 2011	$15,000
Add: Rent paid in advance at start of year	1,250
Deduct: Rent paid in advance at end of year	(1,250)
Rent expense for 2011	$15,000

Rent expense of $15,000 will appear in the income statement for 2011, and rent paid in advance of $1,250 will appear as an asset in the balance sheet at the end of 2011.

3.3.3   Amortization (Depreciation)

When a long-term asset, such as a piece of machinery, is bought, the historical cost principle implies that no expense has yet occurred. The asset cash has been exchanged for the asset machinery, both having equal value. Over time, the machine will be used in the operations of the business. Eventually, it will become worn out and worthless. Although the asset is long-term, its life is not infinite. Over the span of its useful life, it is necessary that the cost be written off as expense in some orderly fashion.

This process is called amortization or depreciation. (Some years ago the Canadian Institute of Chartered Accountants decided that the term *amortization* would be the exclusive term for this concept. Despite this, many organizations continue to use the term *depreciation*.) The most straightforward way to calculate amortization is to assume that the net cost is to be written off in equal annual instalments. Any anticipated salvage or sale value will be deducted from the cost, and the balance divided by the number of years the asset is expected to be in operation, to arrive at the annual expense.

Suppose Harry's Haulage Ltd. buys a truck for $100,000. (See Exhibit 3.8.) On day one, the company has exchanged an asset (cash) worth $100,000 for another asset (the truck), also worth $100,000.

This transaction creates neither revenue nor expense. As time goes by, the asset truck will be used up, and the $100,000, eventually, will all become expense. Amortization will allocate the $100,000 to the periods to which it should be matched.

Suppose the company intends to use the truck for four years and then sell it for $24,000. The amount that has to be amortized is $76,000 ($100,000 − $24,000). This will be spread over the four years as a $19,000 ($76,000 ÷ 4) amortization expense each year.

In the balance sheet, the truck will be reported as having a cost of $100,000. From that cost the accumulated amortization to date will be deducted. At the end of year one, the written-down value will be $81,000 ($100,000 − $19,000). At the end of year two, the written-down value will be $62,000 ($81,000 − $19,000). At the end of year three, the written-down value will be $43,000 ($62,000 − $19,000). At the end of year four, the

---

Exhibit 3.8:   Amortization — The Straight-Line Method

The amortization for Harry's Haulage Ltd.'s new truck, using straight-line amortization, is calculated as follows:

Initial cost	$100,000
Expected life	4 years
Expected terminal value	$24,000

The annual amortization is ($100,000 − $24,000) ÷ 4 = $19,000 per year.

Year	Amortization Expense	Accumulated Amortization	Written-Down Value
2010	$19,000	$19,000	$100,000 − $19,000 = $81,000
2011	$19,000	$38,000	$100,000 − $38,000 = $62,000
2012	$19,000	$57,000	$100,000 − $57,000 = $43,000
2013	$19,000	$76,000	$100,000 − $76,000 = $24,000

Over four years, $76,000 of expired cost is written off as amortization expense, with the expectation that the truck will be sold at the end of 2013 for $24,000.

written-down value will be $24,000 ($43,000 – $19,000). At this point the company could do a number of things.

The truck could be sold for $24,000, as per the original plan. If that is the case, the $24,000 realized will be an exact match for the written-down value, and there will be no effect on the income statement.

Quite possibly, the truck could be sold for a higher amount, say, $40,000. This will result in a gain on sale of $16,000. Or, the truck could be sold for less than $24,000, say, $20,000 and result in a loss on the sale of $4,000. Gains and losses have to be brought into the income statement as revenues and expenses, respectively; but, in reality, they are an admission that the original amortization estimate was incorrect.

Other amortization models also exist. Declining balance amortization applies a constant percentage rate to each year's written-down value. The effect is a higher amortization charge in the earlier years of the asset's life, and lower rates in later years. Suppose this truck were to be amortized using a rate of 30% on the declining balance. The amortization expense would be different from the previous example. It would be $30,000 in year one (30% of $100,000), $21,000 in year two (30% of $70,000), $14,700 in year three (30% of $49,000), and $10,300 in year four (30% of $34,300) with numbers rounded to the nearest hundred dollars. By the end of year four, the written-down value has become $24,000, as before.

The truck could also be amortized on the basis of use. If it is assumed that the truck will run 500,000 km over its life, then the rate of $0.152 per km could be charged as amortization ($0.152 is the $76,000 net cost divided by 500,000 km). The effect would be to charge amortization expense according to how heavily the truck was used each year.

3.3.4   Bad Debt Expense

When sales are made on credit, there is some uncertainty as to whether or not the customers will pay. Most customers pay (eventually), but some turn into bad debts. When looking at revenue recognition (section 3.2), we made it clear that the sales should be recognized when the legal title of the goods is passed to the customer. Good matching requires that we recognize an estimated amount of bad debt expense related to those sales in the same year that the sales are recognized.

The bad debt expense will be an estimate relating to future events, of which the precise details are unknown. (See Exhibit 3.9.) Past history is often a good guide to the amount of bad debt expense that would be prudent to recognize. Suppose the bad debts have worked out to be around 2% of all unpaid accounts each year for the past 10 years. Recognition of bad debt expense in the amount of 2% of the current year's accounts receivable would be prudent and reasonable. We do that by creating a bad debt expense of 2% of the accounts receivable and a matching allowance for doubtful debts.

There is a difference between the bad debt expense and most other expenses. The majority of expenses are identified because there is a transaction involved, normally, a payment for the expense. This transaction is then adjusted through the accruals process to represent the actual resource

Exhibit 3.9:   Bad Debts Expense and Bad Debt Provision

It is December 31, 2010, Mike's Motor Repair Shop is preparing its annual financial statements for its first year of operation. Mike has made a list of the money owed to him by customers. There are 125 customers on the list, and the total amount of the outstanding invoices is $27,000. Looking down the list he can identify three prob-lem customers, whose accounts total $2,000. One has gone bankrupt, one has skipped town, the third has complained that the work has not been done properly and has refused to pay. In addition to these, Mike thinks it would be prudent to assign 2% of the remaining receivables as an allowance for doubtful debts.

2010 Income Statement

Bad debt expense:

3 customers whose accounts are specifically identified as bad debts	$ 2,000
2% on the balance of receivables [2% × ($27,000 – $2,000)]	500
Bad debt expense for 2010 (as per income statement)	$ 2,500

2010 Balance Sheet

Receivables:

Accounts receivable (net of the $2,000 of specific bad debts written off)	$25,000
Less: Allowance for doubtful debts	500
Net realizable value	$24,500

At the end of January 2011, Mike's accounts receivable amount to $30,000. Two customers have defaulted upon their obligations and failed to pay for work, amounting to $400, that was done in 2010. This $400 can be taken away from the allowance for doubtful debts without further recourse to the income statement, or the balance sheet.

January 31, 2011:

Accounts receivable, prior to recognizing bad debts	$30,000
Less: Allowance for doubtful debts (no change from December 31, 2010)	500
Net realizable value	$29,500

The $400 of identified bad debts is then removed from both the receivables and the provision.

January 31, 2011:

Accounts receivable, after recognizing bad debts ($30,000 – $400)	$29,600
Less: Allowance for doubtful debts ($500 – $400)	100
Net realizable value	$29,500

As can be seen, the net realizable value is the same ($29,500) in both cases.

flow that should be recognized as expense. In the case of the bad debt expense, there is no transaction. We create the expense without any payment being involved. To recognize an expense in the absence of a payment requires that we create an allowance for doubtful debts on the balance sheet. The allowance for doubtful debts is a *contra-asset account* and is deducted from the accounts receivable to which it refers. By doing this, it reduces the accounts receivable to their net realizable value.

In the next accounting period, when the actual bad debts come to light, they can be written off by deducting them from the bad debt provision. This means that we can adjust the accounts receivable to accommodate the actual bad debts discovered, without making any additional expenses in the income statement of the "current" year. This is good matching.

3.4 Operating Income

Operating expenses are deducted from revenues to reveal the operating income of the organization. Operating income is a measure of how well the organization did in its chosen line of business. The operating manager is held responsible for this figure. Operating income is monitored through the use of ratios.

3.4.1 Gross Profit Ratio (or Gross Profit to Sales Ratio)

The gross profit ratio, or gross margin %, is the gross profit (revenues less cost of goods sold) expressed as a percentage of the revenues. So, if a company (e.g., Shugamai's Styles Inc. in Exhibit 3.10) has revenues of $1 million and gross profit of $500,000, it has a 50% gross profit ratio. In managing retail outlets, this is a critical control number and is carefully checked against expectations and against what the competition is earning.

3.4.2 Return on Sales Ratio (or Operating Profit to Sales Ratio)

The return on sales ratio is the operating profit (revenues less both cost of goods sold and operating expenses) expressed as a percentage of the revenues. So, if Shugamai's Styles Inc. has revenues of $1 million and operating profit of $100,000, its return on sales ratio is 10%. This is a useful measure of overall performance for virtually every company.

3.4.3 Return on Assets Ratio

To get a sense of how much the operating profit is in relation to the assets employed, we calculate the return on assets ratio. This is the operating income divided by the operating assets (frequently taken to be the total assets). So, if Shugamai's Styles Inc. has operating income of $100,000 and total assets of $500,000, it has earned a 20% return on assets.

Exhibit 3.10: Profitability Ratios

Shugamai's Styles Inc.
Income Statement December 31, 2011

Sales revenue	$1,000,000
Cost of goods sold	500,000
Gross profit	$ 500,000
Expenses	400,000
Operating profit	$ 100,000
Interest and tax expenses	65,000
Net income	$ 35,000

Shugamai's Styles Inc.
Balance Sheet as at December 31, 2011

Current assets			**Liabilities**	
Cash		$ 20,000	Trade payables	$100,000
Accounts receivable		75,000	Long-term liabilities	200,000
Inventory		105,000		$300,000
		$200,000		
Long-term assets				
At cost	$650,000			
Accumulated amortization	350,000			
		300,000	**Shareholders' equity**	200,000
		$500,000		$500,000

Gross profit to sales ratio:

= (gross profit ÷ sales) × 100%
= ($500,000 ÷ $1,000,000) × 100%
= 50%

Operating profit to sales ratio (return on sales ratio):

= (operating profit ÷ sales) × 100%
= ($100,000 ÷ $1,000,000) × 100%
= 10%

Return on assets ratio:

= (operating profit ÷ total assets) × 100%
= ($100,000 ÷ $500,000) × 100%
= 20%

Net income to sales ratio:

= (net income ÷ sales) × 100%
= ($35,000 ÷ $1,000,000) × 100%
= 3.5%

Return on shareholders' equity ratio:

= (net income ÷ shareholders' equity) × 100%
= ($35,000 ÷ $200,000) × 100%
= 17.5%

3.5   Net Income

Financing charges, such as interest expense, are deducted from the operating income, as are income taxes. The result is the net income of the company. If Shugamai's has sales of $1 million, operating income of $100,000, interest expense of $25,000, and income taxes of $40,000, its net income is $35,000.

3.5.1   Net Income to Sales Ratio

To understand how much of each sale's dollars remain as income, we can calculate the ratio of net income to sales:

$35,000 ÷ $1,000,000 = 3.5%.

3.5.2   Return on Equity Ratio (or Return on Shareholders' Equity Ratio)

Net income can be compared with the owners' equity to give the return on shareholders' equity ratio. Suppose that the total liabilities and equity equals $500,000, and the liabilities are $300,000. Owners' equity is then $200,000, and the ratio of net income to owners' equity is as follows:

$35,000 ÷ $200,000 = 17.5%.

3.6   Retained Earnings

Retained earnings is a classification that appears on the balance sheet as part of owners' equity. It is a recognition that net income has been made, but that the net income has not been paid out to its ultimate owners: the shareholders. If nothing were ever given to the shareholders, then retained earnings would be the accumulated net income of the company from its inception to date. Conversely, if all the net income is paid to shareholders as dividends each year, then retained earnings will be zero.

The most common situation is that neither of the above happens. The amount paid as dividends is most likely to be some of the net income, but not all of it. The directors like to give shareholders back something on their investment, but prudence dictates that they not give it all. As a result, the category Retained Earnings on the balance sheet tends to get larger each year.

3.6.1   Statement of Retained Earnings

The statement of retained earnings is a required report for companies. It picks up the opening balance of retained earnings in the balance sheet at the start of a year and adds in the net income for the year. It then deducts dividends paid and any other transactions that reduce retained earnings. The remaining balance is the retained earnings at the end of the year.

**Exhibit 3.11: Statement of Retained Earnings
and Dividend Payout Ratio**

On the balance sheet of XYZ Inc. the accumulated retained earnings from earlier years, as at December 31, 2010, was $220,000. During 2011, the net income was $135,000. A cash dividend of $100,000 was paid. At the end of 2011, the retained earnings were $255,000. The statement of retained earnings would report that information as follows:

XYZ Inc.
Statement of Retained Earnings
for the Year Ended December 31, 2011

Retained earnings as at December 31, 2010	$220,000
Add: Net income for the year	135,000
	$355,000
Less: Dividend paid	100,000
Retained earnings as at December 31, 2011	$255,000

Dividend payout ratio:

= (dividend ÷ net income) × 100%

= ($100,000 ÷ $135,000) × 100%

= 74%

One of the features of laying out the statement in this style is that the amount of dividend that is legally possible is highlighted. Companies may only pay dividends out of net income (i.e., current net income), or retained earnings (accumulated undistributed net income). The intermediate total of $355,000 for XYZ in Exhibit 3.11 is the maximum amount legally distributable as dividend. Other considerations, such as cash availability and the need for investment funds, generally mean that the dividend payout is substantially less than the maximum that is legally distributable.

The relationship of the dividend to the net income for the period may be expressed as a dividend payout ratio (i.e., dividend ÷ net income). A company that paid a dividend of $250,000 out of current earnings of $500,000 is said to have a payout ratio of 50%.

There are some other transactions that are reported in the statement of retained earnings, mostly concerned with the ramifications of issuing or retiring shares, but these are rarer and not usually of prime importance.

There are a number of permissible layouts to this statement. In some presentations the statement is separate. Many companies tack it onto the end of the income statement, so that it is presented as a seamless

---

Exhibit 3.12: Income Statement and Statement of Retained Earnings

Canadian Tire
Statement of Earnings and Retained Earnings for 2010
($ million)

Gross operating revenue	$8,981
Less: Operating expenses and interest	8,384
Operating income (after interest, before taxes)	$ 597
Less: Income taxes	143
Net income	$ 454
Add: Retained earnings at start of year	3,014
	$3,468
Less: Dividends paid	74
Retained earnings at end of year	$3,394

---

continuum. Exhibit 3.12, showing the income statement and statement of retained earnings for Canadian Tire, does exactly that. The effect of changing accounting policies could also be shown here.

3.7   Earnings Per Share

At the end of either the income statement or the statement of retained earnings, most companies will also report a calculation of earnings per share (EPS). This is a statistic widely used by analysts when they attempt to value shares. The proposition is that a share's intrinsic value is the earnings the company makes on behalf of that share. The greater the number of shares in existence (for a given amount of net income), the less each one is worth.

A company that reports a net income of $5 million and has 500,000 common shares in issue will report an EPS of $10 ($5,000,000 ÷ 500,000). Even though the earnings may not be paid out as dividend, it is assumed that plowing the profits back into the company will have beneficial long-term growth effects and will, eventually, result in larger dividends being paid to shareholders.

Many new companies reward their employees with the issue of shares, or options to buy shares, instead of cash. Issuing shares dilutes the EPS for all shareholders. The existence of obligations to issue new shares at some future date will also reduce the EPS. To ensure full disclosure, a "fully diluted" EPS is reported, as well as the basic EPS. This is the EPS that would exist if all the extra shares were issued. (See Exhibit 3.13.)

Exhibit 3.13: Earnings Per Share

Jones Co. had earnings of $6 million in 2011. There were 500,000 shares in issue at December 12, 2011. There is a $100,000, 6% debenture that could be converted into 200,000 common shares.

Earnings per share:

= net income ÷ number of shares in issue
= $6,000,000 ÷ 500,000
= $12 per share

Fully diluted earnings per share:

= (net income + interest saved on conversion) ÷ (number of shares potentially in issue)
= ($6,000,000 + $6,000) ÷ (500,000 + 200,000)
= $8.58 per share

3.8 Summary

The income statement summarizes all the operating revenues and expenses to show the operating income. From that, interest and taxes are deducted to calculate the net income. Revenues, expenses, and time periods are matched with one another through the use of accruals.

Appendix 3.1
Example of
an Income Statement

Canadian Tire is a retailer with outlets all over Canada. Their published financial statements (with all the supporting notes and information) is available on the Web at **www.canadiantire.ca**. (Follow the links: company information | investors | financial reports.)

Canadian Tire Corporation, Limited
Consolidated Statement of Earnings
($ millions)

	For the Year Ended	
	January 1, 2011	January 2, 2010
Gross operating revenue	$8,981	$8,686
Operating expenses:		
Cost of merchandise sold and all other operating expenses except for the under-mentioned items	$8,000	$7,788
Interest	103	147
Depreciation & amortization	247	247
Employee profit-sharing plan	33	25
Total operating expenses	8,383	8,207
Earnings before income taxes	$ 598	$ 479
Income taxes		
Current	$ 133	$ 135
Future	11	9
Total income taxes	144	144
Net earnings	$ 454	$ 335

Appendix 3.2
Methods of Amortization

There is more than one pattern of amortization expense. In this appendix, we shall discuss the three commonly used models: the straight-line amortization method, the declining balance method, and the units of production method.

It should be recognized that the management of a company has some choice here. GAAP requires the cost of long-term assets to be amortized over the life of the asset, but GAAP does not specify what amortization model must be used. Therefore, managers can elect to use any rational amortization policy. Of course, once they have made that selection, they are expected to stick with it, so that the financial statements are comparable. They are also expected to disclose the amortization policies and rates, so that users can judge the effects of this policy choice.

The Straight-line Amortization Method

In the straight-line model the cost (net of any expected salvage or disposal value) is divided by the expected life of the asset to give an equal annual amortization instalment:

= (cost – disposal) ÷ number of years
= annual amortization expense

Example: Acto purchased a new filling machine on January 1, 2011, for $100,000. The company expected to use it for five years and then sell it for $8,000.

Straight-line amortization:

= ($100,000 – $8,000) ÷ 5 years
= $18,400 per year

Total amortization expense over five years:

= $18,400 × 5
= $92,000

Declining Amortization Balance Method

Under the declining balance amortization method, the annual amortization amount is a percentage of the asset's written-down value as at the beginning of the year. Because the percentage is being applied to a steadily reducing amount, the amortization expense is less each year. To get to a similar end point as the straight-line method, declining balance amortization has to start with a higher amortization expense, and the annual expense becomes lesser and lesser toward the end of the asset's life.

> **Example:** If Acto used the declining balance amortization method on the new filling machine it purchased for $100,000 on January 1, 2011, and Acto still expected to use it for five years and then sell it for $8,000, the amortization would be calculated as follows:

Declining balance amortization @ 40% per annum:

Cost on January 1, 2011	$100,000
Amortization 2011: 40% × $100,000	40,000
Written-down value as at December 31, 2011	$ 60,000
Amortization 2012: 40% × $60,000	24,000
Written-down value as at December 31, 2012	$ 36,000
Amortization 2013: 40% × $36,000	14,400
Written-down value as at December 31, 2013	$ 21,600
Amortization 2014: 40% × $21,600	8,640
Written-down value as at December 31, 2014	$ 12,960
Amortization 2015: 40% × $12,960	5,184
Written-down value as at December 31, 2015	$ 7,776*

* (which is approximately equal to $8,000)

An advantage of declining balance amortization is that it sometimes represents a better matching of the decline in an asset's value than the straight-line method. Also, it is a better match with Canada Revenue Agency's (CRA) ideas on amortization (for a note on this topic, see Appendix 3.3 to this chapter).

The disadvantages are that it is a little more complex to calculate and you get a different amortization expense each year, so it is untidy.

In general, to achieve a similar total amortization effect over the life of the asset, a declining balance amortization rate has to be about twice the straight-line amortization rate. In the example above, the straight-line rate is 20% (1 ÷ 5 years = 20%), while the declining balance rate is 40%.

Units of Production Amortization Method

The units of production method of amortization is intended for those assets where a measurement of the amount of work produced is possible. This would include motor vehicles (measured by kilometres travelled), production machines (measured by hours run or tonnes processed), mines and gravel pits (measured by tonnes extracted), and woodlots (measured by board feet of lumber won). In the units of production method, an attempt is made to exactly match the expense with the activity.

The total activity over the life of the asset is estimated. This is used to divide the cost to give a rate per unit. Each year, the number of units processed is multiplied by the rate to get the amortization expense.

Example: Assume Acto's newly purchased, $100,000 filling machine is expected to fill 92 million bottles over its five-year life, and will have a resale value of $8,000. The amortization expense, using the units of production method, will be calculated as follows:

Amortization rate:

= ($100,000 – $8,000) ÷ 92,000,000 fills
= $0.001 per fill

Actual usage of the filling machine and related amortization expense is:

2011	25 million fills	$ 25,000
2012	25 million fills	25,000
2013	20 million fills	20,000
2014	15 million fills	15,000
2015	7 million fills	7,000
Total amortization over five years:		$ 92,000

Purchase of Machine on January 1, 2011	$100,000
Amortization 2011: 25 million fills × $0.01	25,000
Written-down value as at December 31, 2011	$ 75,000
Amortization 2012: 25 million fills × $0.01	25,000
Written-down value as at December 31, 2012	$ 50,000
Amortization 2013: 20 million fills × $0.01	20,000
Written-down value as at December 31, 2013	$ 30,000
Amortization 2014: 15 million fills × $0.01	15,000
Written-down value as at December 31, 2014	$ 15,000
Amortization 2015: 7 million fills × $0.01	7,000
Written-down value as at December 31, 2015	$ 8,000

Summary

Each of these three amortization methods results in the same or similar total amortization expense ($92,000) being charged over the five-year life of the asset. The overall effect in the long term is, therefore, immaterial. However, the different methods do report different operating profits year by year. The difference lies in the allocation of expense to different years. In general, the three methods can be characterized as follows:

• The straight-line method is most straightforward.
• The declining balance method writes off the expense sooner, so it is more conservative. (It defers income to the later years of the asset's life.)
• The units of production method is most precise.

Appendix 3.3
Capital Cost Allowances and Deferred Taxes

Companies pay taxes on their income. Under GAAP, the reported tax expense is the tax that would be due if the company paid tax on its reported profit. If the reported net income were precisely the same as the taxable income, there would be a neat matching of the actual tax paid and the tax expense. However, such neatness rarely happens. In general, the amount on which a company is assessed for taxes is different from the amount of its reported net income.

There are two broad classes of difference: permanent differences and timing differences. A permanent difference is the result of some rule that says an amount reported as income or expense in the income statement is not subject to tax (or, in the case of an expense, not allowable against tax). Permanent differences result in a change in the tax expense compared to that based on the current year's income.

A timing difference, on the other hand, is an item that is shown in the income statement in one year, but that will be assessed or allowed for tax in a later year.

One of the principal timing differences is the treatment of amortization. Because amortization rates (what percentage is used) and amortization models (the choice between straight-line and declining balance methods, for example) are both within the choice of management, the CRA rejects such amortization expense reporting by the company and replaces it with its own version, which is referred to as CCAs, or capital cost allowances.

CCAs are a set of allowances at prescribed rates that companies are allowed to charge in lieu of amortization. They are mostly declining balance rates, though a few are based on the straight-line method.

Some sample CCA rates are as follows:

100%: Class 12 — miscellaneous tools or utensils costing less than $200;
 30%: Class 10 — automotive equipment and data-processing equipment;
 25%: Class 9 — electrical generating equipment;
 20%: Class 8 — machinery and equipment not elsewhere described;
  4%: Class 1 — buildings (straight-line).

So, when a company is being assessed to taxes, the amortization expense is eliminated from the income statement and replaced by the CCAs.

The effect of this (and other adjustments to the taxable income) is that the tax paid is no longer the same as the tax expense as calculated according to GAAP. Companies go to considerable pains to ensure that they do not pay any more taxes than they have to, and that they pay those they have to as late as possible. They will actively manage their

99

affairs so as to first reduce the tax payable, and where that is not possible, defer the tax payable to a later date. It is therefore likely that the GAAP-based tax expense will be higher than the tax actually paid in any given year.

The difference between the tax expense and the actual tax paid is referred to as deferred tax. It is tax that is not due at the time of the balance sheet, but that may, eventually, become due at some unspecified later date. We use the words "may become due" because it is by no means certain that the tax will ever be paid. This, in turn, has led to a degree of controversy over how deferred taxes should be reported.

On the one hand, there are those who say that deferred taxes are a liability, of which the timing may be uncertain, and even remote, but from which there is no escape. They would, therefore, have deferred taxes reported on the balance sheet as a liability: probably in the long-term liabilities section. This is the treatment required by the Canadian GAAP.

On the other hand, there are those who say that the historical evidence is that most companies have put off paying these deferred taxes indefinitely, and they are likely to continue to do so. If this is true, the logical way of reporting deferred taxes is to treat them as part of equity. They may have to have some special treatment within equity to show that they are not distributable (and cannot be paid out as dividends to shareholders), but they are not liabilities because they are so unlikely ever to be paid as tax.

Let's say Energen Inc. has reported earnings of $108,000, and its basic tax rate is 35%. Included in the reported income are the following:

- $10,000 of dividends received from Canadian companies that are tax-exempt
- $2,000 of hospitality expense that is not tax-allowable
- $30,000 of amortization expense

In addition, the total CCAs claimable are $50,000.

Reported earnings	$108,000	
Less: Non-taxable income	(10,000)	These are permanent
Add: Non-allowable expense	2,000	differences
Reported income for tax expense	$100,000	
Tax expense (35%)	$ 35,000	
Reported income for tax assessment	$100,000	
Add: Amortization expense	30,000	These are temporary
	$130,000	differences
Less: CCAs	(50,000)	
Taxable income	$ 80,000	
Tax payable (35%)	$ 28,000	

On the balance sheet, this would be reported as follows:

Current liability: tax payable	$ 28,000
Long-term liability: deferred taxes	7,000
Tax expense for the year	$ 35,000

Appendix 3.4
Example of a Statement
of Retained Earnings

The presentation of the statement in this appendix is more complex than the simplified version provided in the main body of Chapter 3 because Canadian GAAP requires a lot of additional information, but the essence is the same. Concentrate on the link between the net earnings for the two years ($454 and $335) and the way that those numbers change the retained earnings that were brought forward from the previous year ($3,013 and $2,752): with the adjustments for dividends and other items this shows how the retained earnings in the final balance sheet are calculated ($3,395 and $3,014).

Canadian Tire is a retailer with outlets all over Canada. Its published financial statements (with all the supporting notes and information) is available on the Web at **www.canadiantire.ca**. (Follow the links: company information | investors | financial reports.)

Canadian Tire Corporation, Limited
Consolidated Statement of Comprehensive Income
($ millions)

	For the Year Ended	
	January1, 2011	January 2, 2010
Net earnings (from income statement)	$ 454	$ 335
Adjustments in respect of gains/losses on derivative securities	8	(141)
Comprehensive income	$ 462	$ 194

Canadian Tire Corporation, Limited
Consolidated Statement of Shareholders' Equity
($ millions)

	For the Year Ended	
	January 1, 2011	January 2, 2010
Share capital		
Balance, beginning of year	$ 720	$ 715
Transactions	(9)	5
Balance, end of year	$ 711	$ 720
Contributed surplus		
Balance, beginning and end of year	$ 0	$ 0
Retained earnings		
Balance, beginning of year	$ 3,014	$ 2,752
Transitional adjustment on adoption of new accounting policies		1
Net earnings for the year	454	335
Dividends	(73)	(69)
Share repurchase		(6)
Balance, end of year	$ 3,395	$ 3,014
Accumulated other comprehensive income (loss)		
Balance, beginning of year	$ (47)	$ 97
Other comprehensive income	8	(143)
Balance, end of year	$ (39)	$ (47)
Retained earnings and other comprehensive income	$ 3,354	$ 2,967

Appendix 3.5
The Mechanics of Accounting:
The Income Statement

In this appendix we present an introduction to accounting for operating transactions: the debits and credits of revenue and expense. In addition to the basic journal entries to record revenue and expense, the appendix also covers such issues as accounting for deferred revenue, inventory, accruals and deferrals, amortization, and bad debt expense. The treatment emphasizes the linkage between adjustments to revenue and expense on the income statement and changes in the balance sheet accounts.

Revenue

Basic Revenue and Expense

The general considerations for recognition of revenue and related transactions are illustrated in Exhibit 3.1. The transactions described involve cash and credit sales, cost of goods sold, and bad debt expense. We deal initially with the entries for the sales and cost of goods sold, deferring the discussion of bad debt expense to later in this appendix.

We saw examples of cash and credit sales transactions in Appendix 2.1, and we will record similar entries here as a review. We will also take this opportunity to formalize the writing of journal entries. The entries will be written in a standard form. Each set of entries will be organized under the following column headings: Date, Accounts/Description, Dr, and Cr. (See Table 3A.1.) Each new transaction will be indicated by a date in the first column. In the second column will be the names of the accounts affected — accounts to be debited will be left-aligned, and accounts to be credited indented. In the third column is the dollar amount of debit entries; in the fourth column, the dollar amount of credit entries.

Usually, there is only one debit line in a journal entry, but if there are more accounts to be debited in the entry these will be written in the same manner immediately following the first debit line. Credit lines follow the debit lines, the account name indented in the second column, followed by the dollar amount in column four. Again, there is usually only one credit line in an journal entry; but if there are more credit lines, these follow right after the first credit line. The last line of the entry is the description, left aligned in column two. We will continue to label the accounts by their nature, such as {asset}, {SE — revenue} though it should be remembered that this is a pedagogical device only; these labels are not used in regular journal entries.

If there is a series of entries written together, a space followed by a date indicates a new entry.

The entries that follow for sales and cost of goods sold are based on the transaction described in Exhibit 3.1 on page 80.

Table 3A.1

Date	Accounts/Description	Dr	Cr
① Jan.–Dec. 31/200X	Cash {asset}	550,000	
	Sales Revenue {SE — revenue}		550,000
	Cash sales for the year 200X		
② Nov. Y/200X	Accounts Receivable {asset}	10,000	
	Sales Revenue {SE — revenue}		10,000
	Credit sales transaction in November 200X		
③ Dec. 31/200X	Cost of Goods Sold {SE — expense}	392,000	
	Inventory {asset}		392,000
	Cost of goods sold in 200X. Peter's Press has determined that cost of goods sold is 70% of revenue.		

We will comment on the three transactions in Table 3A.1 and then post them to the ledger accounts.

1. A revenue transaction always has the same form. The debit indicates the resource flow: this can be an increase in an asset (usually cash or accounts receivable) or (rarely) a decrease in a liability. The credit is always to a revenue account: this indicates that this particular resource flow is an increase to owner's equity from operations.

2. The credit to the revenue account does not distinguish between cash sales and credit sales. A sale "on credit" would only be concluded if the seller has satisfied him or herself that payment will be received as promised. Receipt of cash or the assurance that cash will be received as agreed is one of the tests of *realization*, the basis for calling a transaction "revenue". Once it is decided that the transaction is revenue, no distinction is made in the revenue account; credit and cash sales are treated identically. Of course, the cash or credit nature of the transaction is recorded on the debit side of the journal entry but when the entries to Sales Revenue are totalled, there is just one combined total for all revenue transactions, regardless of their nature, and this is what is reported as sales for the period. No doubt some credit sales will not be collected, but there is a separate procedure to account for expected bad debts. We will examine this at the end of this appendix.

3. There are a number of ways of recording cost of goods sold. Depending on the system used, cost of goods sold is measured either transaction by transaction as each sale is made, or periodically, when the financial statements are drawn up. In either case, the entry is as follows: debit Cost of Goods Sold, credit Inventory. We will look more closely at the different methods used.

Now we can post the first three entries to the accounts. This step is identical to what we did in Appendix 2.1 of Chapter 2 except that now, in the interests of simplicity, we show only the accounts that are affected by the entries being made. For these three journal entries, five different ledger accounts are affected. They are Cash, Accounts Receivable, Inventory, Sales Revenue, and Cost of Goods Sold. Because only a selection of ledger accounts are shown, there is no need to present them in spreadsheet form. Instead, we arrange them separately in a convenient order on the page. Since the accounts are now separate, we can simplify them, drawing only a top line under the account name and a centre line separating debits from credits. Drawn in this way, each one is called a **T-account**. A T-account is a simplified representation of a general ledger account. All T-accounts have the same form:

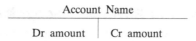

Account Name
| Dr amount | Cr amount |

We can now lay out the five accounts affected by these three transactions from Table 3A.1 and post the entries:

	Cash				Accounts Receivable				Inventory	
200X				200X				200X		
	X	X			X	X			X	X
①	550,000			②	10,000			③		392,000
	X	X			X	X			X	X
to B/S	A			to B/S	B			to B/S	C	

	Sales Revenue			Cost of Goods Sold
200X			200X	
	X			X
①	550,000	③	392,000	
②	10,000			
to I/S	D	to I/S	E	

*X*s have been added to represent other entries that have been or will be made to these accounts. In addition, we have indicated final account balances with bold letters: **A, B, C**, etc. These year-end balances, which incorporate the three entries we have made, will appear in the financial statements. The final balances in the asset accounts — Cash, $A; Accounts Receivable, $B; and Inventory, $C — appear on the balance sheet (B/S). They are not underlined because they are carried forward as the opening balance in the account in the next period. The final account balances in Sales Revenue, $D, and Cost of Goods Sold, $E, show on the income statement (I/S). These balances are double-underlined to indicate that these accounts are closed at the end of the period and reopened with zero balances in the next period.

One point that must be emphasized is that because this is double-entry accounting, any change (or correction) in one number in the books will, in general, affect *both* the balance sheet and the income statement. If, for example, a customer draws to our attention an error in a sales invoice and we agree that he owes us $200 less, not only is Accounts Receivable on the balance sheet lower by that amount, but Sales Revenue in the period must also be $200 less. Similarly, if, after a review of the records, we realize that final inventory was not $C but instead $3,000 less (i.e., $C – $3,000), not only would the inventory figure on the balance sheet at the end of December be $3,000 lower, the Cost of Goods Sold on the income statement would be $3,000 *higher* (and net income would be $3,000 lower). You should follow through the effect of revising the journal entries to satisfy yourself that all these changes would occur. We will see further examples of this phenomenon in the illustrations that follow.

Issues in Revenue Recognition

The journal entry for a revenue transaction is quite straightforward. It is always "debit asset (or liability), credit revenue". The problems that arise in accounting for revenue are not in the form of the transaction, but rather in knowing exactly *when* a resource flow that has some of the characteristics of a revenue transaction actually *becomes* a revenue transaction. We call this the question of *revenue recognition*. Consider, for example, Exhibit 3.2: Revenue Recognition in the Service Industry. There are typical timing issues illustrated here: how to account for the fact that some of this year's membership were paid for last year, and some part of this year's membership payments are for next year's memberships. In both cases, there is a question of revenue timing: how much revenue is recorded in this period and how much in the next. We will begin by examining the *principle of revenue recognition* and then show, in each case, how an examination of the transaction in the light of this principle helps us establish the correct accounting treatment.

The Principle of Revenue Recognition

A sale is made when the following three conditions are met: (i) the seller and a potential buyer agree on the terms of the sale, (ii) the goods are delivered, and (iii) payment is made. To be more precise, the *earnings process* is considered to be complete when the following three criteria are satisfied:

1. There is an arm's length transaction, an agreement on the terms of an exchange.
2. The ordered goods are delivered to the buyer.
3. The seller receives the agreed amount of cash, another asset of equivalent value, or an enforceable claim to cash or equivalent asset.

The first criterion means that we must have an agreement on the terms of the sale made at arm's length. There are two aspects to this — an agreement to complete the transaction and the notion of arm's length. An *agreement on terms* implies that both parties have concluded that they cannot do better under the circumstances and that they intend to carry out the transaction. *Arm's-length agreement* means that the two contracting parties are pursuing independent interests. The seller is trying to get the highest possible price; the buyer, to pay the lowest possible price. Since both parties are trying to get the best terms and are not forced to conclude the transaction, it is deemed to be fair.

The second and third criteria appear self-evident: the buyer must enjoy the benefit of the good or service in the period, and the seller has the benefit of the proceeds of the sale in the period. Generally the situation itself is obvious: either the customer has the goods or he does not; he has paid or he has not. Sometimes, however, conditions on delivery or the nature of payment mean that it is not always clear that these two criteria are both satisfied. Not surprisingly, when questions arise about the validity of a company's revenue recognition policies, we typically find that an unorthodox interpretation of one or more of these criteria has been made.

But even aside from questions of interpretation, the fact that there are three independent criteria for the completion of the earnings process means that what appears to be a revenue transaction may not yet be one because not all the criteria have been satisfied. There are of course many situations we are familiar with in which all three criteria are satisfied simultaneously. For example, a customer comes into a store, selects a product marked with a price, pays cash to the store owner, and leaves with her purchase. The earnings process is complete and the store recognizes the revenue for that particular transaction at that moment. This is true even if the customer pays with a debit card (cash is exchanged electronically rather than physically), or uses a credit card (through agreements both the customer and the merchant have made with the credit card issuer, the merchant has an enforceable claim for payment against the credit card issuer, which in turn has an enforceable claim for payment against the customer).

Although the simultaneous satisfaction of the three criteria defining the completion of the earnings process is common, it can happen that the three criteria are *not* all satisfied at the same time. When they aren't, there is a question as to when and how revenue is realized in the books of the seller. There are a number of possibilities, each with its own recognition solution. We will examine two of them here.

Consider first a customer who tells a merchant that he likes a particular household accessory but that he is not sure that it is the right colour for his room. The store owner tells him to pay for it, take it home, and try it; if it works, he keeps it; if not, he has a week to return the piece for a full refund, no questions asked. There is payment, there is delivery, but there is no sale. The price is not an issue — it has been agreed upon and a payment made; the customer has the goods — there has been delivery. But all this is conditional: only when the customer agrees to keep the goods one week after delivery can revenue be realized by the seller. If the customer returns the product, his payment is returned. There was no sale and no revenue was realized.

The second possibility that we will examine is deferred delivery. A customer comes into the store in late December 2010, near the end of the store's financial year, and describes the product she wants. The store owner says that he can get it on special order. The customer agrees to pay the full price at the time of order to facilitate the transaction. She pays (cash, debit card, or credit card) and leaves with an invoice for goods "to be delivered in four to six weeks". It would be natural to speak of this as a sale. In all likelihood, both the customer and store owner would see it this way as it is only a matter of time until the goods are delivered, the more so if it is agreed that the price is final. Still, from an accounting point of view, timing is an issue. The sale cannot be recognized in 2010 because the goods have not yet been delivered. Even though deliv-

---

**Exhibit 3A5.1: Magazine Revenue Recognition
— Peerless Publishers Inc.**

During 2011, Peerless Publishers received a total of $400,000 from subscriptions to magazines. It is estimated that three-quarters of the magazines for the paid subscriptions had been sent to the subscribers during the year. The other quarter represented issues to be sent during 2012.

December 31, 2011:

Total received for magazine subscriptions	$400,000
Less one-quarter for issues not yet sent	100,000
Net sales recognized in 2011	$300,000

The $200,000 related to the issues not yet sent would be classified as deferred revenue and treated as a liability as at December 31, 2011.

In 2012, when the outstanding issues were all sent out, the deferred revenue, $100,000, would then be recognized as revenue.

---

ery is expected to be made in four to six weeks, the revenue will not be recognized until delivery is made, which will fall outside the store's current financial year and into the next accounting period.

Deferred Delivery

Some goods or services are paid for when they are ordered, but delivery takes place over an extended period. Peerless's magazine subscriptions are a good example. Peerless sells $400,000 worth of subscriptions in 2011 but only three-quarters are delivered in this financial year. The revenue for one-quarter of the issues must thus be postponed or *deferred*. The $300,000 for the magazines delivered in 2011 is credited to Sales Revenue in the year; the $100,000 received in 2011 for magazines to be delivered in 2012 is a liability at the end of 2011 (see the first journal entry below). Note that Deferred Revenue is not a revenue account but a liability account. The liability is the obligation to supply magazines to subscribers in 2012.

In 2012, as the magazines are published and delivered, the liability is reduced as the balance is effectively transferred to Sales Revenue in 2012 (see the second journal entry below).

Date	Accounts/Description	Dr	Cr
① Jan.–Dec./11	Cash, Accounts Receivable {assets}	400,000	
	Sales Revenue {SE — revenue}		300,000
	Deferred Revenue {liability}		100,000
	Subscriptions received 2011		
② Jan.–Dec./12	Deferred Revenue {liability}	100,000	
	Sales Revenue {SE — revenue — 2012}		100,000
	Prepaid subscriptions delivered 2012		

Cash, Acc. Rec.

2011		
	X	X
① I	400,000	
	X	X
to B/S	XX	
2012		
	X	X

Deferred Revenue

2011		
	X	X
I ①		100,000
to B/S		100,000
2012		
② I	100,000	

Sales Revenue

2011	
I ①	300,000
to I/S	**300,000**
2012	
I ②	100,000

Expense

Cost of Goods Sold

In the past, because of the bookkeeping costs involved, keeping track of the day-to-day movements of inventory was only worthwhile if the individual items, such as cars or jewellery, were valuable enough. Now the use of bar coding and information technology make a *perpetual inventory system* advantageous for many merchandising operations. In such cases, the inventory account is adjusted for all movements of goods in and out of stock, and the goods sold expense is recorded for every sale.

A purchase of goods on account costing $5,000 on September 3, 2011, with a $300 delivery charge and 13% HST[1] would be recorded as follows:

Date	Accounts/Description	Dr	Cr
① Sep. 3/11	Inventory {asset}	5,300	
	HST Due {liability}[2]	689	
	Accounts payable {liability}		5,989
	Purchase X Co., invoice #1234		

Notice that the delivery cost is as much a part of the cost of the goods as is the invoice price. In practice, the invoice cost and the delivery charges might be segregated in separate accounts for analysis purposes

---

[1] The harmonized sales tax (HST) is a value-added tax, incorporating both federal and provincial components, in five provinces. The HST rate varies by province: in British Columbia it is 12%; in Ontario, Newfoundland, and New Brunswick, 13%; and in Nova Scotia, 15%. In provinces where there are separate federal and provincial taxes, the federal value-added tax is called the goods and services tax (GST). The same procedures are used to account for the HST and the GST.

[2] Whether HST Due is an asset or a liability depends on the balance. In principle, one might have one account for HST paid {asset} and another for HST due {liability}; but at period end, one will be netted against the other, and typically the amount due will exceed the amount paid since the volume of sales normally exceeds purchases.

(Purchases, Transportation In), but by the end of the accounting period the balances of the delivery account would be transferred to the Inventory account. On the other hand, because of strict rules for accounting for HST and other sales taxes, HST (due or paid) would be segregated from trade payables and accounts receivable.

If half of this shipment were to be sold for $4,500 one week after it was purchased, there would be, in addition to the revenue transaction, an entry in a perpetual inventory system recognizing the cost of goods sold:

Date	Accounts/Description	Dr	Cr
② Sep. 10/11	Accounts Receivable {asset}	5,085	
	Sales Revenue {SE — revenue}		4,500
	HST Due {liability}		585
	Sale to AA Co., sales invoice #5678		
③ Sep. 10/11	Cost of Goods Sold {SE — expense}	2,650	
	Inventory {asset}		2,650
	COGS, sale to AA Co., sales invoice #5678		

The entries in the general ledger accounts affected would look like this:

Accounts Receivable

2011		
② I	5,085	

Inventory

2011		
① I	5,300	
I ③		2,650
	2,650	

HST Due

2011		
① I	689	
I ②		585

Accounts Payable

2011		
I ①		5,989

Sales Revenue

2011		
I ②		4,500

Cost of Goods Sold

2011		
③ I	2,650	

In the traditional *periodic inventory system*, the costs of each purchase is debited to the inventory account in exactly the same way they were recorded in the perpetual system (transaction #1) since in all inventory systems purchases are always accounted for as they are made.

The difference in accounting treatment in the periodic system is at the time the goods are sold. In this case, only the sale is recorded (transaction #2 but not transaction #3). In other words, under the periodic system only the first two transactions are recorded at the time they occur. The cost of good sold is recorded only at the end of the accounting period (as is in fact developed on the following page).

In this illustration of the periodic inventory system, we assume that the year-end is December 31. In this system there must be a physical count of inventory in the company's warehouse at the end of each financial year. (Periodic physical inventory counts are usually taken in perpetual systems as well as a check on the record system, but these can be done at any time, not necessarily at year-end.) This physical count is then costed, item by item, taking account of other purchase costs, such as transportation-in cost, to arrive at the *cost of closing inventory*. (In this connection a flow of costs must be assumed — see Appendix 4.2.)

Let us assume that the cost of closing inventory on December 31, 2011, is $350,000. This same exercise would have been done at the previous year-end. Assume that the inventory cost then was $280,000. Satisfy yourself that this year's opening inventory must be the same as last year's closing inventory. Finally, assume that total inventory purchases in 2011 were $640,000 plus $83,200 HST. We do the following calculation to find Cost of Goods Sold:

Opening inventory	$280,000
Purchases	640,000
Cost of goods available for sale	$920,000
Less: Closing inventory	350,000
Cost of goods sold	$570,000

An adjusting journal entry simultaneously records Cost of Goods Sold and reduces the Inventory account to the correct value.

Date	Accounts/Description	Dr	Cr
Dec. 31/11	Cost of Goods Sold {SE — expense}	570,000	
	Inventory {asset}		570,000
	AJE: Cost of goods sold		

We now post this entry to the general ledger. We have not shown the journal entries for purchases or sales. These would have been recorded on a day-by-day basis as they occurred throughout the year. We show only the summary entries to Cash & Accounts Receivable, Inventory, Accounts Payable, Sales Revenue, HST Due, and Cost of Goods Sold. Cash and Accounts Receivable are combined here for convenience, and HST Due represents the net of HST paid and HST collected as normally done in practice. (Sales Revenue, both cash and on account, is assumed to be $975,000 plus $83,200 HST for 2011.) Recall that the opening balance in the Inventory account is not the result of an entry for that amount; it is simply the previous year-end Inventory Account balance brought forward.

Cash & Accounts Receivable			Inventory		
2011			**2011**		
	1,023,750		Opening inventory	280,000	
			Purchases	640,000	
			AJE COGS		570,000
				350,000	

Accounts Payable			Sales Revenue		
2011			**2011**		
		672,000			975,000

Cost of Goods Sold			HST Due		
2011			**2011**		
	570,000			83,200	
					126,750

111

Inventory Allowances

Inventory records are kept on a cost basis. Normally, these same costs are the basis for the reporting of inventory on the balance sheet and cost of goods sold on the income statement. Occasionally, however, it happens that purchase prices fall by year-end, and the cost of replacing the inventory would be lower than the actual costs incurred. When this occurs, GAAP requires that the value of the inventory on the balance sheet be reduced to the replacement cost. (Note that *replacement cost* refers to the current market price at the year-end. It is not a question of whether the company has paid these lower prices for any of its inventory or even plans to do so. It is most likely, in fact, that most of the company's inventory was purchased at the older, higher costs. If all or most of its inventory had been purchased at the new, lower price, the question of replacement cost being less than the actual price would not arise.)

Exhibit 3.5 on p. 83 illustrates this situation. The journal entry helped explain why the "write-down" of inventory increases expense and reduces net income. If an asset account, Inventory, is overvalued, some of the asset — the *value* of the asset, to be precise — must have expired. And recall that "expired asset" is a definition of expense.

Date	Accounts/Description	Dr	Cr
Dec. 31/11	Cost of Goods Sold {SE — expense}	9,000	
	Inventory {asset}		9,000
	AJE: Reducing inventory to market price		

Often the inventory records are left at average cost — $6.60 a litre in this case — especially if the price decline is considered to be temporary. In such a situation, the adjustment to the Inventory is done by crediting an *allowance account* rather than reducing the Inventory account. This allowance, what is known as a "contra-asset" account, is deducted from the asset Inventory and only the net amount is reported on the balance sheet. The debit to Cost of Goods Sold is the same as in the previous journal entry.

Date	Accounts/Description	Dr	Cr
Dec. 31/11	Cost of Goods Sold {SE — expense}	9,000	
	Allowance for Inventory Reduction {asset}		9,000
	AJE: Lower of cost and market price, allowance method		

The financial statements will be the same in either case, the direct write-down or the allowance method. The difference is in the underlying records and particularly in the Inventory accounts. Allowance accounts are commonly used in accounting for bad debts as well — see the following.

Overhead Expenses

Cost of goods sold is a direct expense. The revenue is earned because goods are delivered to customers; the matching process starts with this physical transfer. As section 3.3.2 explains, in the case of overhead expenses there is no direct relationship between the use of the resources and the revenue: it is, rather, a case of matching the use of resources to the financial year. Typically, the accounting system will record the payments for the resources. Proper matching of expenses, however, requires that we look at the invoices to ensure that expense reflects the resources used in the period rather than the resources paid for in the period. This involves *accruing* expenses that have been incurred but not yet recorded and *deferring* expenses that have been paid but not yet used.

Accruals. The electricity example in Exhibit 3.6 is a typical accrual. We will show the journal entries, but the story is best understood by following the sequence of postings in the T-accounts.

The first entry is the accrual, entered as an adjusting journal entry on December 31, 2010, to correct the electricity expense for 2010. The accountant would find this information either by examining the invoice in January before she closed the books, or by telephoning Hydro to determine unbilled electricity usage to December 31, 2010. The second entry, a composite of entries made throughout 2011, records the payment of electricity invoices received in the year (including the $800 that was accrued at December 31, 2010). The next entry includes the last invoice received, for usage up to December 15, 2011, which was entered as an accrual even though it was still unpaid at year-end. Note that the debit is to 2011 electricity expense. To ensure that the full expense for the year is recorded, we make the year-end accrual the final entry: the estimate of a half-month electricity usage from December 16 to December 31, 2011.

Date	Accounts/Description	Dr	Cr
Dec. 31/10	Electricity Expense [2010] {SE — expense}	800	
	Accounts Payable {liability}		800
	AJE: Electricity expense accrual		
Jan.–Dec./11	Accounts Payable {liability}	800	
	Electricity Expense [2011] {SE — expense}	4,400	
	Cash {asset}		5,200
	Cash payments to Hydro 2011		
Dec./11	Electricity Expense [2011] {SE — expense}	600	
	Accounts Payable {liability}		600
	Electricity invoices to Nov. 16–Dec. 15/11		
Dec. 31/11	Electricity Expense [2011] {SE — expense}	300	
	Accounts Payable {liability}		300
	AJE: Electricity expense accrual Dec. 16–31/11		

	Cash			Accounts Payable	
2010			**2010**	X	X
	X	X	2010 accrual		800
to B/S	XX		**to B/S**		800
2011			**2011**		
	X	X	2011 invoices payment	800	
2011 payments		5,200	2011 accruals		600
					300
to B/S	XX		**to B/S**		900

113

Electricity Expense

2010

2010 accrual	800
to B/S	**800**

2011

2011 payments	4,400
2011 accruals	600
	300
to I/S 10	**5,300**

Deferrals. An accrual records an expense that has not yet been paid or otherwise recorded. A deferral has the opposite effect. It postpones (defers) to the next period a cost that has not been incurred but has been prematurely charged (debited) to expense this period. (As we have seen, revenues can also be accrued and deferred. For example, if a sale is booked because payment has been received but the goods have not yet been delivered, the revenue must be deferred.)

The need for an expense deferral usually arises because a payment, or part of a payment, is made in advance of the use of goods or services purchased. The rent example in Exhibit 3.7 is a typical deferral. In addition to paying each month's rent at the beginning of that month, the lessee was required by the lease agreement to pay the last month's rent on the first day of the lease (in this case, the last month of the five-year lease is May 2014 and the first day of the lease was June 1, 2009). With the exception of the last month's rent, all the rent payments are expense in the period they are paid. In such circumstances, it is common that the company adopts the policy of debiting each rent payment as expense in that month. However, the double rent payment of June 2009 will require correction (i.e., deferral) the first time the books are closed, which will be December 31, 2009. The payment must remain deferred through to May 2014. This is how the asset "Rent Paid in Advance" (alternatively, "Prepaid Rent") described in Exhibit 3.7 arose.

The following entries would have been made in 2009:

Date	Accounts/Description	Dr	Cr
① June 1/09	Rent {expense}	2,500	
	Cash {asset}		2,500
	Rent for first and last month		
	(June 2009 and May 2014)		
② July 1/09	Rent {expense}	1,250	
	Cash {asset}		1,250
	Rent for July 2009		

[There will be an identical entry each subsequent month until April 2014.]

③ Dec. 31/09	Rent Paid in Advance {asset}	1,250	
	Rent {SE — expense}		1,250
	To defer May 2014 rent paid in advance		

Rent Paid in Advance (or Prepaid Rent), which first appeared on the December 31, 2009, balance sheet, will show on successive balance sheets — December 31, 2010, December 31, 2011, etc., until the end of the lease, at which time it will be expensed in that last month. (There will be no rent payment that month.)

	Cash				Rent	
2009				**2009**		
	X	X			X	X
①		2,500		①	2,500	
②		1,250		②	1,250	
					.	
					.	
				③		1,250
					8,750	
					.	
				2010	.	
				2011		
					15,000	
					.	
				2014	.	
					X	
				④	1,250	

	Rent Paid in Advance	
2009		
③	1,250	
.	1,250	
.		
.		
2011		
	1,250	
.		
.		
.		
2014		
	1,250	
④		1,250
	0	

Amortization

Amortization (sometimes called *depreciation*) is the process of expensing a long-term asset over its estimated useful life.

In the example in section 3.3.3 and Exhibit 3.8, Harry's Haulage purchases a new truck early in 2010 for $100,000. The truck has an estimated useful life of four years and an expected salvage value of

$24,000. The amortizable (or depreciable) cost is $76,000, which the company has decided to amortize on a straight-line basis. If the financial statements are prepared annually, an entry will be made at the end of each year to amortize 25% of the amortizable cost, which is $19,000. The first set of entries are written on the assumption that Harry's Haulage keeps the truck until the end of 2013, at which point the company disposes of it at its net book value (the amortized cost of the truck on its books at that point — $24,000).

Date	Accounts/Description	Dr	Cr
Jan. 1/10	Truck {asset}	100,000	
	Cash {asset}		100,000
	Purchase of truck		
Dec. 31/10	Amortization Expense {SE — expense}	19,000	
	Accumulated Amortization {asset}		19,000
	Amortization of truck 2010		

[Identical entries recording amortization are made on December 31, 2011; December 31, 2012; and December 31, 2013.]

Dec. 31/13	Cash {asset}	24,000	
	Accumulated Amortization {asset}	76,000	
	Truck {asset}		100,000
	Disposal of truck at net book value		

Cash

2010 truck purchase	X	X 100,000
	X	X
2013 truck disposal	24,000	

Truck

2010 truck purchase	100,000	
to B/S 2010	100,000	
2011 to B/S 2011	100,000	
2012 to B/S 2012	100,000	
2013 truck disposal		100,000
to B/S 2013	0	

Accumulated Amortization

2010 amortization		19,000
to B/S 2010		19,000
2011 amortization		19,000
to B/S 2011		38,000
2012 amortization		19,000
to B/S 2012		57,000
2013 amortization		19,000
truck disposal	76,000	
to B/S 2013		0

Amortization Expense

2010 amortization	19,000	
to I/S 2010	19,000	
2011 amortization	19,000	
to I/S 2011	19,000	
2012 amortization	19,000	
to I/S 2012	19,000	
2013		
amortization	19,000	
to I/S 2013	19,000	

Amortization expense of $19,000 is recorded each year. In essence, we are recognizing that the cost of the asset, truck, is expiring at that rate. Note, however, that the credit of $19,000 is not to the truck account itself but to the contra-asset account, Accumulated Amortization. The reason for not crediting the asset account itself is that readers of the financial statements want to know the scale of the long-term assets — remember, physically they are not disappearing. Amortization simply allocates their cost to expense over their useful lives. For example, on the balance sheet or in the notes to the financial statements we see both the original cost of the truck as well as its net book value, as the following partial balance sheet at the end of 2010 shows:

Harry's Haulage Ltd.
Partial Balance Sheet
as at December 31, 2010

Long-term assets	
Truck, at cost	$100,000
Less accumulated amortization	19,000
Net book value	$ 81,000

In the example above we happened to sell the truck after four years at exactly its estimated salvage value, $24,000 — the net book value at the end of its expected useful life. Had we been able to sell it for $40,000 because of favourable market conditions, the final entry would read as follows:

Date	Accounts/Description	Dr	Cr
Dec. 31/13	Cash {asset}	40,000	
	Accumulated Amortization {asset}	76,000	
	Truck {asset}		100,000
	Gain on disposal {SE — revenue}		16,000
	Sale of truck for $40,000		

The debit to Accumulated Amortization and the credit to the Truck account are unchanged — both these accounts must be brought to zero since the asset has been sold. Following GAAP, the difference between the proceeds and the net book value of the truck is treated as a gain on disposal in 2013 even though, as pointed out in the chapter, it really represents a correction of the original estimated salvage value. You should satisfy yourself that if the truck were sold for, say, $20,000, there would be a debit to the expense account, Loss on Disposal, of $4,000.

Bad Debt Expense

Companies offer credit terms to their customers because it is convenient for both parties to separate buying and selling from paying and collecting. As well, being able to buy on account is standard practice in many industries.

While no business would knowingly sell to a customer who cannot pay, at the same time experience tells us that some customers do default. Proper matching of expenses to sales requires that the loss be expensed in the period the sale was recognized. We do this using the *"allowance method"*.

The allowance for bad debts, like any other accrual, involves a debit to expense matched by a credit to an asset (or to a liability). Accounts Receivable is the relevant asset in this case, but, as we saw in the accounting for Inventory, there are detailed records of receivables from individual customers that must agree with the balance in the general ledger account. Thus, apart from everyday transactions, such as the receipt of a payment from a customer, we should credit Accounts Receivable only if we "write off a particular account" — that is, declare it non-recoverable and remove it from the detailed list. This is the reason we use the allowance method for recognizing bad debts: it permits us to reduce the asset based on some statistical assessment of probable defaults without actually crediting the asset account itself.

We can illustrate this using the example of Mike's Motor Repair Shop in Exhibit 3.9. In this case, we see examples of both direct write-offs and of the allowance method. In 2010, his first year of operations, Mike identifies three accounts, let us say, Mr. A, Ms. B, and Mr. C, totalling $2,000, that are not worth pursuing for payment. In the first adjusting journal entry below, Mike writes off these three accounts from both Accounts Receivable and from his list of debtors. The debit is to bad debt expense.

However, Mike knows that it is likely that there will be further uncollectible accounts among the $25,000 of receivables remaining. After discussing the matter with his accountant, he estimates that 2%, $500, is a reasonable allowance. This is the second adjusting journal entry. Again, the debit is to bad debt expense, but because no particular accounts have been identified as bad and no accounts are written off, the credit is to a contra-asset account, Allowance for Doubtful Debts (alternatively, Allowance for Doubtful Accounts).

Date	Accounts/Description	Dr	Cr
Dec. 31/10	Bad debt expense {SE — expense]	2,000	
	Accounts Receivable {asset}		2,000
	AJE: To write off as uncollectible the accounts of A, B, and C.		
Dec. 31/10	Bad debt expense {SE — expense]	500	
	Allowance for Doubtful Debts {asset}		500
	AJE: Bad debt expense 2010.		

These entries are posted to T-accounts on page 119. The effect on the income statement and the balance sheet can be seen in Exhibit 3.9 on page 88.

Now that we are using the allowance method to estimate bad debt expense, subsequent write-offs have no effect on the net value of accounts receivable, nor do they affect bad debt expense directly. We can confirm this by considering the treatment of two receivables that are deemed uncollectible in January 2011. Ms. D and Mr. E owed Mike's Repair Shop $400 for work done in 2010. It is clear to Mike that he will not collect this money, and he has decided to write off these two accounts. Since a general provision was made for such an eventuality, the write-off is against the contra-asset account, Allowance for Doubtful Debts. There is no effect on the net value of Accounts Receivable, and the Bad Debt Expense account is not involved.

Date	Accounts/Description	Dr	Cr
Jan. 30/11	Allowance for Doubtful Debts {asset}	400	
	Accounts Receivable {asset}		400
	AJE: To write off as uncollectible the accounts of D and E.		

Since Accounts Receivable and the contra-account, Allowance for Doubtful Debts, are both reduced by the same amount, net accounts receivable does not change. (See Exhibit 3.9.)

Although bad debt expense is not affected by this transaction, there is an indirect effect at year-end when the bad debt estimate is made by taking a percentage of the year-end accounts receivable, as Mike does. Assume that Mike's gross accounts receivable at the end of 2011 are $40,000. Assume also that he continues the practice of having his year-end allowance be 2% of receivables. The allowance must be $800; but since there is already a balance in the Allowance account, the entry — and the year's bad debt expense — is only $700.

Date	Accounts/Description	Dr	Cr
Dec. 31/11	Bad debt expense {SE — expense]	700	
	Allowance for Doubtful Debts {asset}		700
	AJE: Bad debt expense 2011.		

Indirectly, then, the write-off does affect the bad debt expense. Satisfy yourself that had we written off more than $400 in January, the debit to Bad Debt Expense at year-end would have been higher; had we written off less, it would have been lower.

	Accounts Receivable			Allowance for Doubtful Debts	
2010			**2010**		
	X	X			
	27,000				
write off A, B & C		2,000	bad debt expense 2010		500
to B/S 2010	25,000		to B/S 2010		500
2011			**2011**		
write off D & E		400	write off D & E	400	
	X	X	bad debt expense 2011		700
to B/S 2011	40,000		to B/S 2011		800

	Bad Debt Expense	
2010		
write off	2,000	
bad debt expense 2010	500	
to I/S 2010	2,500	
2011		
bad debt expense 2011	700	
to I/S 2011	700	

Self-Study Problems

1. Charley Farley went into business on October 1, 2011, by opening a doughnut shop. He carried on the business in a rented store in downtown Orillia. At the end of December, he realized that he would have to pay income tax on the business profits, but he had no idea how much profit he had made. He has asked you to advise him how much income to report for the three months he has been in business.

    He has presented you with his bank statements and a pile of invoices and receipts. The following is a summarized list of payments and receipts for the three months.

    Receipts paid into bank account:

1.	Owners' equity	$ 50,000
2.	Bank loan	$ 55,000
3.	Cash sales	$146,500

    Payments made out of bank account:

4.	Suppliers	$104,500
5.	Wages	$ 12,000
6.	Rent	$ 20,000
7.	Utilities	$ 5,000
8.	Insurance	$ 4,000
9.	Equipment	$ 99,000
10.	Repayment of bank loan	$ 4,000

    You are given the following additional information:
    (i) The cash received from sales was $161,500. Charley Farley took $5,000 each month from the cash sales for his own living expenses before paying the balance into the bank.
    (ii) Charley has a coffee delivery arrangement with a nearby office. He delivers the coffee daily; they pay him weekly. At the end of December they owed him $500.
    (iii) The $104,500 paid for supplies is not exactly the amount used: Charley owes suppliers another $5,000, and there is inventory on hand that had cost him $1,500.
    (iv) The $20,000 paid for rent consists of $5,000 per month payment for October, November, and December, plus the "last" month of the lease of $5,000.
    (v) In addition to the $5,000 paid for utilities, another $1,000 is owed.
    (vi) The insurance premium of $4,000 gives him cover from October 1, 2011, to September 30, 2012.
    (vii) Amortization expense on the equipment should be taken as $9,000 for the three months to December 31, 2011.

    [Note: This is a continuation of Self-Study Problem #1 in Chapter 2 on page 68. You may need to refer back to that problem for help in doing this one.]

Required
(a) Prepare an income statement for Charley Farley for the three months to December 31, 2011.
(b) What was the ratio of gross profit to sales?
(c) What was the ratio of operating profit to sales?

2. Fanatical Fitness is a health club. At the start of 2011 there was a liability on the company's balance sheet of $200,000, representing the unused balance of members' subscriptions paid in 2010 but extending into 2011. During 2011 the company sold $1,800,000 of new subscriptions. At the end of 2011 the amount of subscriptions that customers had paid in advance was $500,000.

Required
How much membership revenue should Fanatical Fitness recognize for 2011?

3. Fenella's Fashions had inventory on hand that cost $27,500 on January 1, 2011. During the year the owners bought goods for resale at a cost of $450,000. Inventory on hand at December 31, 2011, cost $56,000.

Required
(a) What was the cost of goods sold for 2011, based on the information given above?
(b) The closing inventory had a cost of $56,000. If you were told that it would be sold in the normal course of trade during 2012 for somewhere between $120,000 and $130,000, in what way would you change the cost of goods sold for 2011?
(c) The closing inventory had a cost of $56,000. If you were told that it had a market value of only $43,000 due to changes in styles and colours, what would be the cost of goods sold for the year 2011?
(d) Which accounting principles/concepts are relevant to your answers to (a), (b), and (c) above?

4. Farmer Giles has bought himself a new hay baler. It cost $30,000. He plans to use it for 15 years and then abandon it in the corner of his 40-acre field with all the other worn-out farm implements.

Required
(a) How much amortization expense should he report for the baler each year?
(b) The day after he bought the baler, a new, better model was introduced at a cost of $25,000. How does this affect the amortization calculation?
(c) If it had been his intention and expectation to use the baler for five years and then sell it for $15,000, how much would the annual amortization expense be?

5. Go back to the information provided in Self-Study Problem #1. Prepare a statement of owners' equity for Charley Farley for the three months ended December 31, 2011.

Solutions

1. (a)

Charley Farley's Donut Shop
Income statement for the three months
ended December 31, 2011

				%
Sales revenue				
Cash banked		$146,500		
+ withdrawals		15,000		
+ owed by customer		500	$162,000	100.0%
Less: Cost of goods sold				
Paid to suppliers		$104,500		
+ owed to suppliers		5,000		
– closing inventory		(1,500)	108,000	
Gross profit (or gross margin)			$ 54,000	33.3% (b)
Less: Expenses				
Wages		$ 12,000		
Rent	($20,000 – $5,000 prepaid)	15,000		
Utilities	($5,000 + $1,000 owed)	6,000		
Insurance ($4,000 – $3,000 prepaid)		1,000		
Amortization		9,000	43,000	
Operating profit			$ 11,000	6.8% (c)

2.

Subscriptions paid in advance at January 1, 2011	$ 200,000
Add: Subscriptions sold in 2011	1,800,000
	$2,000,000
Less: Subscriptions paid in advance at December 31, 2011	500,000
Revenue recognized in 2011	$1,500,000

3. (a)

Opening inventory	$ 27,500
+ Goods purchased	450,000
Goods available for sale	$477,500
– Closing inventory	(56,000)
Cost of goods sold (COGS)	$421,500

(b) No adjustment is necessary; cost of goods sold is still $421,500. We never anticipate profit; we wait until it is realized.

(c) The closing inventory must be valued at the lower of cost or market value: $43,000.

Opening inventory	$ 27,500
+ Goods purchased	450,000
Goods available for sale	$477,500
– Closing inventory	43,000
Cost of goods sold	$434,500

As a result, operating profit will be reduced by $13,000.

(d) The matching principle and the cost principle are used in (a), (b), and (c); additionally, the conservatism concept is used in (b) and (c).

4. (a) Straight-line amortization:

$$= (\text{cost} - \text{scrap value}) \div \text{number of years}$$
$$= (\$30,000 - \$0) \div 15$$
$$= \$2,000 \text{ per year}$$

(b) No change: the baler has been bought to use, not to trade, so the cost principle is used to value it (do not use the lower of cost or market value for long-term assets).

(c) Straight-line amortization:

$$= (\text{cost} - \text{scrap value}) \div \text{number of years}$$
$$= (\$30,000 - \$15,000) \div 5$$
$$= \$3,000 \text{ per year}$$

5.

Charley Farley
Statement of Owners' Equity for the three months
ended December 31, 2011

Owners' equity as at October 1	nil
Add: Cash invested	$50,000
Add: Net income for the period	11,000
	$61,000
Less: Withdrawals	15,000
Owners' equity as at December 31, 2011	$46,000

Discussion Questions and Problems

Discussion Questions

1. What is the purpose of the income statement?
2. The income statement provides a link between successive balance sheets: how does it do this?
3. Why is the income statement prepared for a one-year period, unlike the balance sheet, which is prepared at a point in time?
4. Which is more useful to the shareholder, the income statement or the balance sheet? Which is more useful to the creditor?
5. Explain what is meant by revenue matching in the income statement.
6. Give a practical example of matching expenses against a time period.
7. In calculating cost of goods sold, explain how the inventory adjustment makes matching possible.
8. What happens when the historical cost concept is in conflict with the conservatism concept?
9. What is the purpose of the allowance for bad and doubtful debts?
10. What is the accounting principle that underlies the amortization calculation, and how is this achieved by the amortization expense?

Appendix 3.5

11. (a) Provide an example where cash is received in the period *before* the associated revenue is recognized.
    (b) Provide an example where cash is received in the period *after* the revenue is recognized.
12. Why do we need a cost flow assumption when the goods in inventory are physically identical?
13. What is the principle that underlies the practices of accrual and deferral in accounting for expenses?
14. What is the principle underlying amortization?
15. Why do we bother with the complicated procedures involved in estimating a period's bad debts using the allowance method? Would it not be simpler to recognize a bad debt expense when it is finally clear that a particular receivable cannot be collected?

Problems

1. Intrepid Architects Inc. has a busy practice designing manufacturing plants in southern Ontario. In 2011, the following transactions occurred:

   • A total of $1,250,000 was billed to 52 clients for design services completed.
   • During 2011, a total of $1,100,000 was collected from clients. This included $180,000 in respect of work that was carried out in 2010.
   • Of the $330,000 owed by clients at the end of 2011, one customer — John Smith & Co. — who owed $70,000, had gone bankrupt and no cash is expected to be received.
   • Excluding the John Smith account, which is definitely a bad debt, Intrepid Architects has decided to provide a provision for bad and doubtful debts at 5% for the remaining accounts receivable.

• At the end of December 2011, Intrepid Architects was working on five new projects. Two, valued at $50,000 each, were at the proposal stage. The other three, valued at $100,000 each, were approximately 25% completed.

Required
(a) Calculate the gross practice income (sales revenue) for 2011.
(b) Calculate the bad debt expense for 2011.
(c) Describe the accounting principles that apply to Intrepid Architects Inc.'s situation.

2. Jantzen & Co. is a firm of chartered accountants with a busy practice in Welland, Ontario. During 2011, the following transactions were recorded:
   (i) Collected $200,000 cash from clients who owed bills from 2010.
   (ii) Collected $800,000 cash from clients for work done in 2011.
   (iii) Collected $100,000 deposits from clients whose work will be started in 2012.
   (iv) Collected $50,000 from Niagara Auctioneers from the sale of a piece of artwork the firm had owned for 25 years.

Total cash collected: $1,150,000.
   In addition, you are told that clients owed Jantzen & Co. $250,000 for work done in 2011.

Required
Calculate the gross practice income (sales revenue) for 2011.

3. Mary Williams operates a fashion store. About half the sales are for cash or direct debit, so there is no problem identifying the store's sales revenue. The other half of the sales are put on credit cards, and Mary has to wait two to three weeks before she receives the cash. At the end of 2011, a woman had ordered a wedding dress for $1,000 for delivery in January 2012, and her $250 deposit had been banked with the regular takings.
   Cash banked from cash sales and debit card transaction in 2011 was $660,000. The amount owed to Mary from the credit card companies at the start of 2011 was $75,000. Cash received from the credit card companies in 2011 was $585,000, and at the end of 2011 the credit card companies still owe her $40,000.

Required
(a) Calculate Mary's sales revenue for 2011.
(b) How much provision would you suggest Mary makes for bad and doubtful debts? Explain your answer by using the relevant accounting principles.

4. Jessie Baynes has a retail store specializing in greetings cards. On average, the cards cost $1.25 and she sells them for $2.50, though some are more expensive and some are cheaper. The following data apply to the month of January 2011:

• Inventory on hand as at January 1, 2011 (at cost): $1,250
• Cards purchased during January 2011: $7,500

- Inventory on hand as at January 31, 2011 (at cost): $750
- Sales revenue for January 2011: $15,000

Required
(a) Calculate the cost of goods sold for January 2011.
(b) Calculate the gross margin for January 2011.
(c) Calculate the gross margin as % of sales for January 2011.
(d) Is there a problem with the gross margin %?
(e) Is there a problem with the closing inventory?

5. Jessie Baynes runs a retail store specializing in greeting cards. On October 1, 2011, she took out a fire insurance policy on the store and its contents at an annual cost of $2,000. She also used the same insurance company to insure her personal car at a cost of $6,000 per year. She paid for both policies using the store's bank account on November 1, 2011.

Required
(a) How much fire insurance expense will Jessie include in the store's income statement for 2011?
(b) How much car insurance expense will Jessie include in the store's income statement for 2011?
(c) Does it matter *when* the insurance was paid for?

6. Jessie Baynes runs a retail store specializing in greeting cards. Her electricity bills come in quarterly, and the following electricity billings relate to 2011:

- Electricity owed as at January 1, 2011: $80
- Bills received for electricity consumption:
  - from December 1, 2010, to February 28, 2011: $240
  - from March 1 to May 31, 2011: $200
  - from June 1 to August 31, 2011: $180
  - from September 1 to November 30, 2011: $300

Required
Calculate the electricity expense for 2011.

7. Miller Haulage operates a trucking business. Expenses include truck licences. The following licence expenses relate to 2011:

- Licence fees paid in advance as at January 1, 2011: $6,500
- Cash paid for licence fees in 2011: $40,000
- Licence fees paid in advance as at December 31, 2011: $7,200

Required
Calculate the licence fee expense for 2011.

8. Miller Haulage operates a trucking business. On January 1, 2011, the company owed drivers a total of $50,000 for trips in December 2010. During 2011, it paid drivers a total of $795,000. As at December 31, 2011, Miller Haulage owed drivers $75,000.

Required
Calculate the wage expense for 2011.

9. Carron International had accrued wages owed to employees of $120,000 on January 1, 2011. During 2011, the company paid out $3,550,000 for wages. The wage expense recorded in the 2011 income statement was $3,600,000.

Required

Calculate the accrued wages as at December 31, 2011.

10. Carron International had sales of $20,000,000 in 2011. Gross margin was $12,000,000. Operating income was $2,000,000, and net income was $500,000.

Companies in similar businesses normally report a gross margin of 75% and an operating income as % of sales of 12.5%.

Required

(a) Calculate the gross margin as % of sales.
(b) Calculate the operating income as % of sales.
(c) Is Carron International doing well or doing badly?
(d) If shareholders expect a return of 16%, what would be an appropriate amount for the shareholders' investment?

11. Carron International purchased a new milling machine in 2011 at a cost of $50,000. It is the company's intention to use it for 10 years and then dispose of it for no residual value.

Required

Using the straight-line amortization method, calculate the annual depreciation expense for the milling machine.

12. Dwight Inc. purchased a bottle-filling machine for $50,000 in 2011. The company expects to use it for four years and then sell it for $20,000.

Required

Using the straight-line amortization method, calculate the annual depreciation expense for the milling machine.

13. Dwight Inc. purchased a bottle-filling machine for $50,000 in 2011. The company expects to use it for four years and then sell it for $20,000. If the company sells it after three years for $25,000, what amortization expense amounts would be reported for years 2011, 2012, and 2013?

14. Purdon Ltd. had sales of $5,000,000, gross margin of $2,500,000, operating income of $1,000,000, and net income of $500,000. Total assets were $10,000,000, and shareholders' investment (equity) was $4,000,000.

Required

Calculate the following:

(a) Gross margin as % of sales
(b) Operating income as % of sales
(c) Operating income as % of total assets
(d) Return on shareholders' investment (return on equity) %

15. Quartz Ltd. had sales of $9,500,000, gross margin of $2,200,000, operating income of $1,000,000, and net income of $750,000. Total assets were $8,000,000, and shareholders' investment (equity) was $6,500,000.

Required
Calculate the following:

(a) Gross margin as % of sales
(b) Operating income as % of sales
(c) Operating income as % of total assets
(d) Return on shareholders' investment (return on equity) %

16. Brinkswell had retained earnings at the start of 2011 of $2,500,000. During 2011 it made operating income of $500,000 and net income of $400,000. The company paid a 2011 dividend of $150,000. At the end of 2011 there were 5,000 common shares in issue.

Required
Calculate the following:

(a) Retained earnings as at December 31, 2011
(b) Earnings per share for 2011
(c) Dividend payout ratio for 2011
(d) Dividend per share for 2011

17. Corcoran Inc. had earnings per share of $10 in 2011. The dividend payout ratio was 60%. April, who owned 25% of the common shares, received a dividend cheque for $120,000.

Required
Calculate the following for 2011:

(a) Amount of the dividend per common share
(b) The number of shares April owned
(c) The total number of shares in Corcoran Inc.
(d) Net income
(e) Assuming that this was the first year of operations, the balance of retained earnings as at December 31, 2011

18. The assets of Greenham Co. totalled $2,000,000 at the end of 2011. The liabilities and equity were as follows:

Trade accounts payable	$250,000
Short-term bank loan	$150,000
Long-term loan	$500,000
10% convertible debenture	$600,000
Retained earnings	$400,000
10,000 common shares	$100,000

The above balances were after the company had made net income of $500,000 and paid out a dividend of $200,000. At any time the company chose to do so, the 10% debenture holders could convert their debenture into 10,000 common shares.

Required

(a) Show how the statement of retained earnings would appear.
(b) Calculate the following for 2011:
    (i) The dividend payout ratio
    (ii) The amount of interest expense on the 10% debenture
    (iii) Earnings per share for the common shares
    (iv) Fully diluted earnings per share, assuming conversion of the debenture

19. Direct Marketing Ltd. started business on January 1, 2002. In the 10 years to December 31, 2011, it made net income averaging $5,000,000 per year. No dividends were paid. What was the amount of the retained earnings on December 31, 2011?

20. Excalibur Inc. had retained earnings of $250,000 on January 1, 2011. During 2011, the company made net income of $100,000 and paid a dividend of $75,000. What was the amount of the retained earnings on December 31, 2011?

21. Fordham Co. had retained earnings of $250,000 on January 1, 2011. During 2011 the company made net income of $100,000 and paid a dividend of $125,000.

Required

(a) What was the amount of the retained earnings on December 31, 2011?
(b) Was the dividend payment legal?
(c) Was the dividend payment prudent?

Appendix 3.5

22. Write journal entries for the transactions described in Problem 1.

23. Write journal entries for the events described in Problem 6 to the end of December 2011.

24. Doncaster Co. Ltd. is a mattress wholesaler. At the end of 2010, the company purchased a mattress wrapping machine for $80,000. At the time, it was expected that the machine would be used for four years at which time it would be disposed of at an estimated salvage value of $20,000. At the end of the third year of service Doncaster learned that there was now a more advanced machine available that would do a better and faster job at wrapping mattresses. The old machine was still very useful for smaller operations and so the company found no difficulty selling it for $45,000. Using T-accounts, account for the purchase, use and sale of the mattress wrapping machine. Briefly describe how the machine would be reflected on the company's Balance Sheet and Income Statement in the financial statements issued at the end of 2013.

The Balance Sheet (1):
Sheet (1):
Assets

4

Learning
Objectives

After studying this chapter you should be able to list and explain the following components of the balance sheet:

→ Current assets (cash, accounts receivable, inventory)
→ Long-term assets and amortization

You should also be able to assess efficiency through asset turnover ratios (receivables, inventory, total assets).

4.1 Introduction

In Chapter 2 we introduced the four main financial statements: the balance sheet, the income statement, the statement of retained earnings, and the cash flow statement. In this chapter we shall look at the balance sheet in greater detail.

The accounting equation (assets = liabilities + owners' equity) is the fundamental model for recording and reporting transactions. The balance sheet is laid out in the same way as the accounting equation. The assets (the left-hand side of the accounting equation) are listed and totalled. The liabilities and the equities (the right-hand side of the accounting equation) are listed and totalled. The two totals are agreed to show that the accounting equation is in balance. It is, therefore, a list showing a point in time: what a company owns, what it owes, and what owners' equity remains.

The balance sheet is laid out with a format that focuses on the term of both assets and liabilities. The assets that are most readily realizable are listed first, and at the end of the list are the assets that the company will be realizing either not at all or only after a long delay. Likewise, the liabilities are listed, with those that are immediately payable first and those with a long timeline last.

This ordering of the assets and the liabilities helps the user to assess the liquidity of the company, and the probability of the company's being unable to pay its debts. (See Exhibit 4.1.)

The dollar values that appear on the balance sheet are those that are recognized by the accounting equation when transactions occur: i.e., the historical cost. In general, this will give a fair idea of their value, but there are at least two problems with the historical cost approach.

First, the transactions are an incomplete record of the events that are important to the company. There are plenty of events that make the company richer or poorer but that are not captured by transactions, and so go unrecorded. These would include actions by competitors and unusual successes or failures of the company's activities.

The second problem with the historical cost approach is that it sometimes misrepresents the value of assets or liabilities. The true value of an

Exhibit 4.1:   The Balance Sheet

The balance sheet lists items in order of liquidity:

ASSETS	**Everything the company owns**
Current assets:	realizable within one year
Cash	available immediately
Short-term investments	realizable quickly
Accounts receivable	collectible within two months
Inventory	saleable and therefore convertible into receivables within a couple of months
Long-term assets:	those that will be used indefinitely in the course of operating the business

LIABILITIES	**Everything the company owes**
Current liabilities:	payable within one year
Trade payables	payable within a month or at most two months
Short-term debt	payable within one year
Long-term liabilities:	payable beyond one year
OWNERS' EQUITY	**Owners' equity is what is left over**
	the owners cannot insist on their equity being repaid

asset or the true value of a liability may be understated or overstated by its historical cost. The accounting concept of conservatism is a major influence on how we deal with such issues. If the historical cost of an asset is higher than its value in use, conservatism requires that we reduce the historical cost to a more reasonable amount, and if the historical cost of a liability is an understatement, conservatism requires that we increase it to its likely actual future cost. Assets that are undervalued and liabilities that are overvalued by the historical cost approach are not increased, which is an application of conservatism.

We shall see applications of these adjustments next in respect of current assets, such as accounts receivable and inventories, and in respect of the amortization of long-term assets.

4.2   Assets

An asset is anything that is valuable and is owned by the business. In order for the asset to appear in the balance sheet, it must have been acquired at a measurable cost (because of the historical cost basis used in valuation).

When carrying out an audit, the auditors will seek to establish the existence, the ownership, and the basis of valuation of the business assets. The existence of assets is established by physical inspection, counting, etc. For example, the auditors will probably attend when the company staff counts the inventory at the year-end.

The ownership is established by looking at the paper trail. For example, the registration documents for a car show who the owner is, and the auditor would expect to see them.

The basis of valuation is where the accounting expertise comes in: assets are normally valued at their original cost, less any amortization. The auditor would check that the amortization rate is reasonable, considering the nature of the asset.

On the balance sheet, assets are grouped into current assets and long-term assets.

4.2.1 Current Assets

The first grouping of assets on the balance sheet is current assets. An asset is defined as current if its term is one year or less. That means that within a year it is likely to be realized (or is available for realization). Assets with terms longer than one year are classified separately as long-term assets.

Realization means different things in respect of different assets. Cash is always taken to be a current asset because it may be spent immediately. Realization of receivables means collection of the money owed. Realization of inventory means using it in the manufacture of goods, or selling it.

Note that the one-year cut-off is somewhat arbitrary. There is no magical difference between a receivable that is due in 364 days and one due in 366 days. Yet one is treated as a current asset, and the other is treated as a long-term asset. However, some cut-off has to be made, and one year ties in with the idea of an annual reporting cycle (normally, balance sheets are prepared at one-year intervals, and the income statement covers one year).

4.2.1.1 Cash

Cash is the most readily available current asset. It is immediately available for the payment of any company obligation, such as paying a debt that is due, or a recurrent expense, such as payroll. Because of its immediate availability, it comes first in the list of current assets.

The balance sheet does not distinguish the form in which cash is held. Traditionally, cash means notes and coin, but for the balance sheet, money in a chequing account is treated as cash, too. Money in any bank account that is immediately available would be treated as cash.

Money in a term deposit would not be treated as cash, as there is a waiting period before it is available. Because the interest rate on a term deposit is significantly higher than the one (if any) on a chequing account, the company will want to pay particular attention to balancing the objective of making the most out of the available resources against both the objectives of staying liquid and of appearing liquid on the balance sheet.

All the various sites (till balances, floats, chequing accounts, etc.) where cash is held would be added together to give one total figure of cash to appear on the balance sheet.

4.2.1.2 *Short-term Investments*

Short-term investments are relatively liquid and easily realizable assets. If the company has a cyclical pattern of operations, it may have a temporary surplus of funds. Rather than tie up those funds by investing them in plant or using them up by paying the shareholders a dividend, the company can put the money into a term deposit or buy money market certificates, or even shares of other companies. In each case, the asset is one that either has a fixed date of maturity in the near future, or there exists a well-established market where it can be bought or sold at any time.

Note that it is the intention of the company as to the holding period that determines whether or not an asset is a short-term investment. An investment in the shares of a company may be a short-term investment. If the plan is to sell those shares in three months, when the cash is needed for some purpose, it is short-term. An investment in the shares of the same company that was made for strategic reasons and with the intention to hold these shares indefinitely would be a long-term investment. Short-term investments usually earn interest.

4.2.1.3 *Accounts Receivable (or Receivables)*

Sales of goods to customers are frequently made on credit terms. The customer takes the goods (or services) but does not pay for them immediately. The customer is expected to pay according to the "terms of trade". These may vary from one industry to another, but a credit period of 30 days is common.

Thirty days may be the requested credit period, but sometimes customers stretch their payments to longer periods. In extreme cases, customers may lose the privilege of credit sales and be put on a "cash with order" or "cash on delivery" basis. Companies are reluctant to do this, however, as it makes selling more difficult. There is often a difference of opinion between the sales force, who wants to sell as much as possible and who will want to use credit terms as a customer inducement, and the accounting department, who only want to allow credit sales to customers who pay on time.

The worst customers do not pay ever. When the credit sale is first made, a receivable arises. It is not known for certain whether the customer will settle the debt or not. While most customers pay eventually, some credit sales generally turn into "bad debts". When the balance sheet is drawn up, it is unclear which accounts are good and which are bad. The balance sheet accommodates the expected bad debts using an "allowance for bad and doubtful debts".

The bad debt expense was introduced in the previous chapter. Because the bad debt expense has been recognized without any transaction to support it, a matching quasi-liability (or "contra-asset") has to be created, called the "allowance for bad and doubtful debts". This provision is deducted from the historical cost of the receivables, reducing them to their expected eventual collectible cash value.

How well the company is managing receivables may be assessed through the receivables turnover ratio. (See Exhibit 4.2.) In this ratio, the receivables at the end of the year are compared to the sales for the year.

**Exhibit 4.2:   Receivables Turnover Ratio
and Receivables Collection Period**

Continental Containers has a receivables balance of $10,000 as at December 31, 2011. Sales for the year 2011 were $73,000.

Receivables turnover ratio:

= annual sales ÷ end of year receivables
= $73,000 ÷ $10,000
= 7.3 times per year

Receivables collection period (days' sales in receivables):

= end of year receivables ÷ (single day's sales)
= end of year receivables ÷ (annual sales ÷ 365)
= $10,000 ÷ ($73,000 ÷ 365)
= 50 days

   The company is turning over its receivables 7.3 times each year, or, alternatively, the company is collecting its receivables in 50 days, which is less than two months.

Companies with low receivables will have a high turnover ratio. Companies that are slow in collecting their receivables will have a low turnover ratio.

   A similar conclusion can also be attained by dividing the receivables by the amount representing the single days' sales. This shows how many days' sales the receivables represent.

   There are no absolute standards about how high the receivables turnover should be: it will be affected by the terms of trade. The trend of the ratio over time is probably as important as the ratio itself. A company that has increased its receivables turnover ratio (e.g., 6.0 last year to 7.3 this year) is collecting its debts more quickly and, all other things being equal, is becoming more efficient.

4.2.1.4   *Inventory*

Inventory represents assets that are owned by the company and that have been bought for resale or for use in production.

   In a service organization, inventory will probably be trivial. This is because such organizations have neither goods for resale nor raw materials for manufacture. An architect's office, for example, might have only paper and drawing supplies as its inventory.

   In a merchandising company, the inventory will be the goods bought for resale: that is, all the stock on the shelves, plus goods kept in stockrooms and warehouses, ready for sale.

   In a manufacturing company, inventory will consist of three separate classes. There will be inventory of raw material, awaiting use in the production process; there will be inventory of products that are partway through the production system (work-in-process inventory); and there will be inventory of finished goods, awaiting sale.

Inventory has to be both counted and valued. Counting establishes the quantities involved and is normally not controversial: inventory is either there or not. Valuation puts a dollar value on the things that are there and is much more problematic.

Because of the "historical cost" principle, the value of inventory is taken to be what it cost to buy it. In a merchandising company, and in respect of the raw materials in a manufacturing company, this is relatively straightforward. Valuing finished products in a manufacturing company, however, is more complex.

One of the valuation issues is that of making appropriate inventory flow assumptions. If inventory is always bought at the same price, then it really does not matter which units of goods purchased have been used up (e.g., sold) and which units are still in inventory. If the prices at which inventory is bought are different, then we have to make some decisions about the inventory flows and their related cost flows. There are three possible methods: specific identification, average cost, and first-in-first-out. We shall not go into the details of any of these here since they are discussed in Appendix 4.2. Suffice it to say that depending on which assumption is made about how the inventory flows through the system, inventory may have a higher or a lower value placed on it.

This is important from the perspective of both the balance sheet and the income statement. If closing inventory has a relatively high value attributed to it, then the cost of goods sold will be lower. This, in turn, raises operating income and net income. Conversely, if inventory has a lower valuation, cost of goods sold will increase, and operating income and net income will decrease.

Inventory Valuation in Manufacturing Companies: Variable Cost vs. Full Cost

In a manufacturing company, it is necessary to value raw materials. It is also necessary to value both work-in-process and finished goods, and that presents a special problem in respect of the treatment of fixed costs. Tracing the direct materials and direct labour that have been used to produce inventory is normally straightforward, through the use of cost records. The same cost records will also be used to allocate overhead to inventory (overhead allocation is covered in Chapter 11).

The allocated overhead will be a mix of variable cost and fixed cost. Variable overhead includes such costs as electricity and supplies. It fluctuates according to the level of activity. Fixed overhead, on the other hand, is not affected by changes in the volume of production.

Everyone would agree that inventory should carry its fair share of variable overhead because the production of the inventory causes the overhead to be incurred. Including the fixed overhead is, however, more problematic.

Fixed overhead includes such costs as rent, property taxes, amortization, supervisory salaries, etc. However, the argument for including them in inventory valuation is not as strong, even though incurring these costs provides the production capabilities that enable production.

While these fixed overhead costs have clearly expired, goods manufactured during the same period may have been sold or they may remain in inventory. If the goods are still in inventory, there is a choice: to treat the associated fixed overhead as an expense of the current period, or to treat it as inventory value. If the latter is selected, the associated costs will get carried forward on the balance sheet. They will become an expense in a future accounting period when the goods eventually get sold. This is, therefore, an important choice, for it has the effect of moving expense from one period to another, thus changing net income in both periods. (See Exhibit 4.3.)

One perspective on fixed overhead costs is that they were incurred to provide production capacity during a period of time. Once that time period has expired, the costs should be expensed. Even if inventory that was made during the time period exists, these "period" costs confer no benefit on any future time period. It is, therefore, improper to carry such inventory forward. When inventory is valued at variable cost, it is referred to as "variable"

Exhibit 4.3: Inventory Valuation Using Variable Costing vs. Full Costing (Direct vs. Absorption)

Pergammon Peripherals Inc. (PPI) makes computer equipment, including printers. One of the company's popular models is the B2200. Its cost records indicate the following:

Variable costs	Cost per unit
Materials	$ 60.00
Labour & variable overhead	50.00
Total variable cost	$110.00
Fixed manufacturing cost	40.00
Total full cost	$150.00
Markup (33⅓%)	50.00
Selling price	$200.00

At the beginning of January, PPI had no inventory of B2200 printers. During the year, the company manufactured 2,500 B2200 printers and sold 2,000 of them. At the end of December, PPI had 500 B2200 printers in inventory. The total cost incurred was $150 per unit × 2,500 units, which is $375,000.

If PPI had sold all 2,500 units, the whole of the $375,000 would become cost of goods sold; since the company sold only 2,000 units, part of the cost of manufacture must be treated as inventory. There is a choice about valuing the inventory: either it can be valued at variable cost (500 @ $110 = $55,000) or it can be valued at full cost (500 @ $150 = $75,000).

	Variable (direct) costing	Full (absorption) costing
Total manufacturing cost	$375,000	$375,000
Less: Inventory	55,000	75,000
Cost of goods sold	$320,000	$300,000

If variable costing is used to value the inventory, the cost of goods sold will be $20,000 higher and the reported income will be $20,000 lower than if full costing is used.

---

or "direct" costing. All other things being equal, it will result in a lower income in the current period, and increased income in the subsequent periods.

The alternative perspective on fixed overhead costs is that the full cost of goods produced in the current period should include a fair share of manufacturing costs, including fixed manufacturing costs. If they are in inventory at the end of the period, then that full cost is to be carried forward and is expensed only when the goods are sold. This is referred to as "full" or "absorption" costing. All other things being equal, full costing has the effect of increasing current income (by deferring cost) and reducing future income by the same amount.

In either case, the effect is not to change the total amount of net income reported but to change its allocation to accounting periods.

Inventory Valuation: Lower of Cost or Market Price

Once the cost has been determined, a further comparison is done between the cost and the market price. If the market price is less than the cost, then the inventory value for the balance sheet is reduced to that level. Note that if the market price is higher than cost, the inventory value is not increased. This is described as valuing inventory at the "lower of

---

Exhibit 4.4: Inventory — Lower of Cost or Market Price

Burlington Spa Inc. sells hot tubs and related equipment. At the end of December the company did an inventory count and determined that it had the following on hand:

- Ten new hot tubs, which had cost $4,000 each and normally retailed for $6,000 each. Due to inflation, the replacement cost for the same units would now be $4,500 each, and Burlington Inc. intends to increase the selling price to $6,750 in January.

- Various spare parts and accessories that had cost $10,000. In the normal course of events, they would be sold for $20,000. Of those parts, approximately one-quarter (by value) were obsolete or damaged and unsaleable. The remainder is saleable for $14,000.

- Various chemicals, which had cost $5,000 and would normally be sold for $7,500. Due to intense competition and the declining price of commodities, these could currently be replaced for $4,000.

In the balance sheet for December, inventory would be valued as follows:

	Cost	Market price	Lower of cost or market price
10 hot tubs @ $4,000 each (at cost)	$40,000	$45,000	$40,000
Spare parts & accessories			
$10,000 (cost) less 25% obsolete or damaged	7,500		7,500
Chemicals (at replacement market price)	5,000	4,000	4,000
Inventory on balance sheet			$51,500

**Exhibit 4.5:   Inventory Turnover Ratio
and Days' Sales in Inventory**

Continental Containers has an inventory total of $7,300 as at December 31, 2011. Sales for the year 2011 were $73,000.

Inventory turnover ratio:

= sales for the year ÷ inventory at year-end
= $73,000 ÷ $7,300
= 10.0 times per year

Days' sales in inventory:

= inventory at year-end ÷ (sales ÷ 365)
= $7,300 ÷ ($73,000 ÷ 365)
= 36.5 days

    The company is turning over its inventory 10 times each year, or, alternatively, it is selling its inventory every 36.5 days, which is a little more than one month.

---

cost or market price". (See Exhibit 4.4.) Market price can mean the replacement price, or it can mean the price the goods will be sold for.
    The lower of cost or market price rule is an example of conservatism in accounting. Conservatism implies taking the hit immediately if a loss is apparent but not anticipating any profit before it is realized.

Inventory Turnover Ratios

How well the company is managing its inventory may be assessed through the inventory turnover ratio. In this ratio the inventory at the end of the year is compared to the sales for the year. (See Exhibit 4.5.) The company that has low inventory will have a high turnover ratio. The company that is slow in selling its inventory will have a low turnover ratio.
    A similar conclusion can be attained by dividing the inventory by the amount of a single day's sales. This shows how many days' sales the inventory represents.
    Analysts use the inventory management ratios to assess the relative efficiency of companies. According to *The Wall Street Journal* (23/3/2009, page B1), Honda had 125 days of inventory of its small cars in the United States, while Toyota had 175 days; Chrysler, 205 days; and GM, even more. Honda was, therefore, seen as the most efficient of the four companies.

4.2.1.5   *Other Current Assets*

Any assets with a term of one year or less that do not fall under the headings Cash, Short-term Investments, Receivables, or Inventory would be listed as "Other Current Assets". The most common of these is the "prepaid expense".

Exhibit 4.6: Prepaid Expense

Boxer Balloons started business on April 1, 2011. The company paid an annual business insurance premium of $2,000, on April 1. When the company prepared its financial statements as at December 31, 2011, it recognized the following:

- Nine months of the premium (April through December 2011) had been used up, and so $1,500 should be treated as an expense and recorded in the income statement.

- Three months of the premium (January through March 2012) was still unused, so a prepaid expense of $500 should be reported as an asset (a short-term asset) on the balance sheet.

When a company has an expense, the contract sometimes calls for paying the bill before receiving the services. A heating system maintenance service contract, for example, might specify a quarterly payment, in advance, of $200. If, at the end of an accounting period, some of this maintenance time is not yet expired, the company would recognize that as an asset called Prepaid Expense. Another common type of prepaid expense is business insurance. (See Exhibit 4.6.) Deposits are also found under this heading.

4.2.1.6 *Total Current Assets*

The total of the current assets is always shown on the balance sheet.

The cash assets are stated as cash values. The receivables are stated as realizable values (i.e., gross amount owing, less allowance for bad and doubtful debts). The inventories are stated at the lower of cost or market price. This is a consistent approach. Because they are going to be realized, all the current assets are stated at cost or at realizable or exit values: what they are expected to bring in when, as expected, they are disposed of. This contrasts with the long-term assets, where the historical cost is more dominant in the valuation.

Showing the total of current assets facilitates the calculation of the liquidity ratios, which compare the current assets against the current liabilities they have to pay.

4.2.2 **Long-term Assets**

Assets the company intends to hold for periods longer than one year are listed under the heading Long-term Assets (sometimes called Fixed Assets). The general intention is that they will be used in the company business to generate sales. Because the intention is to hold the long-term assets indefinitely, it is not so important to indicate their relative liquidity. Instead, major sub-headings that identify the different classes of long-term assets are generally presented in this order: land, buildings, plant and equipment, intangible assets, and investments in associated companies.

141

4.2.2.1 *Land*

Land owned by the company is an asset that has no effective time horizon. The land may be owned by the company forever (unless the company sells it). The historical cost (what was paid for it) is used as the value. Given the nature of money, inflation, and property markets, it may be that this understates the land's market value. Because of the conservatism principle, any such increases in value are ignored. Conversely, if the land has suffered a drop in value, the conservatism principle requires that the reduction in value be recognized and the balance sheet value reduced accordingly. Consequently, the longer the time between the acquisition of the land and the balance sheet date, the wider any discrepancy between market price and cost is likely to be.

4.2.2.2 *Buildings*

Land, which lasts forever, should be kept separate from the buildings that stand on the land. Unlike land, buildings deteriorate over time, and that has to be recognized in the financial reports. If land is bought separately, and the buildings are then constructed on the land, it is relatively easy to keep the cost of the land separate from the cost of the buildings. If, as is common, land and buildings are purchased together, it becomes necessary to apportion the cost between the two.

Suppose a company were to buy a building for $800,000. (See Exhibit 4.7.) Its expected economic life is 20 years, and it will have no residual

---

Exhibit 4.7: Amortization of Building

Harry's Video Store has just bought a building and the land it stands on for $1 million. The appraised value of the land is $200,000 and of the building is $800,000. The building was built five years ago and had, at that time, a 25-year expected useful life. It therefore has another 20 years of expected life at this time. The cost ($800,000) will be amortized in 20 equal instalments of $40,000 per year over the useful life.

Balance Sheet

Year 1:	Cost	$800,000	
	Less accumulated amortization	40,000	$760,000
Year 2:	Cost	$800,000	
	Less accumulated amortization	80,000	$720,000
Year 3:	Cost	$800,000	
	Less accumulated amortization	120,000	$680,000

And so on for each year, until the written-down value is reduced to zero:

Year 20:	Cost	$800,000	
	Less accumulated amortization	800,000	$ nil

value. The entire $800,000 must be charged as an amortization expense of $40,000 per year for each of the next 20 years.

Note that by the end of year 20 the asset's value has been completely written off by way of 20 amortization charges of $40,000 each ($20 \times $40,000 = $800,000$). Even though written down to zero value on the balance sheet, the asset is still owned by the company and may even continue to have some use. It will continue to appear in the balance sheet (as an asset with nil value) as long as it continues in use. Only when its use is discontinued will it be taken out of the balance sheet.

Effectively, having an asset on the balance sheet with a value of $0 means that the amortization was too aggressive and the asset written off before its useful life was over.

4.2.2.3 Plant and Equipment

One of the largest categories in most balance sheets is plant and equipment. This covers the various items that the business needs to operate, including production machinery, office equipment, computers, motor vehicles, hand tools, furniture, retail store fixtures, computing hardware, software, passenger cars, trucks and so on. For purposes of calculating amortization, they will probably be grouped into a number of different subcategories, with the assets in each category being amortized on a common basis. Like buildings, plant and equipment is recorded at cost initially and will gradually be retired through the amortization process. Because of the nature of the assets, it is probable that plant and equipment would be written off over much shorter time periods than the buildings, but the principle is the same. (See Exhibit 4.8.)

Other patterns of amortization exist. Suppose you buy a new truck. It is probable that the major loss of value occurs in the initial years of the truck's life, while the later years should bear a lesser charge. This can

---

Exhibit 4.8: Amortization of Plant and Equipment

Terri's Tools has just bought a new delivery truck. The cost was $60,000. The company expects to keep the truck for two years. At the end of two years, Terri's Tools will sell it and replace it with a new one. The expected selling price in two years is $40,000.

Cost	$60,000	
Expected selling price	40,000	(residual value)
Total loss in value over two years	$20,000	
Annual amortization charge	$10,000	($20,000 ÷ 2)

The general formula for (straight line) amortization is as follows:

(cost – residual value) ÷ number of years = annual amortization charge

In the balance sheet the net "written-down value" of an asset is as follows:

initial cost of the asset – (sum of all amortization expense for that asset to date)

---

be achieved by calculating amortization as a constant percentage of the written-down value (declining balance amortization). It is also possible to relate amortization to use (units of production amortization). If you assume the truck will last for 200,000 km, you could charge 1/200,000 of the cost to each period when a kilometre was travelled. (These amortization methods are described in detail in Appendix 3.2.)

4.2.2.4 *Intangible Assets*

Some assets have similar characteristics to plant and equipment (in that they are owned and used over a long time period), but they have no physical form. These are called intangible assets, and would include things like patents, trademarks, and goodwill.

Patents and Trademarks

Patents and Trademarks represent a legally enforceable right to a particular process or product.

A patent is normally granted for a new invention, which the developer registers to safeguard his right to exploit. (A patent lasts for 17 years under Canadian law.) When the Xerox Corporation developed its photocopying method, the company patented the design. No one else had the technology to carry out the task, so Xerox had a monopoly of the market. The cost of acquiring and registering that patent was an asset on Xerox's balance sheet. The value on the balance sheet was probably a major understatement of the true value of the company's monopoly position, but its cost was all the historical cost convention would permit recording.

A trademark is the legally enforceable uniqueness of a product. Competitors are allowed to produce similar but not identical products. Thus, Pepsi-Cola competes against Coca-Cola, but Pepsi cannot call its product "Coke". It has been estimated that if Coca-Cola lost the right to the name, the bottle shape, and all the other trappings of its product, it would cost the company about $74 billion (Interbrand, 2010) to replace the brand, the image, and the product recognition in the mind of the public. Again, the accounting model only permits the recognition of the cost of the trademark, not its replacement value. The $74 billion does not appear anywhere on the corporate balance sheet because its value has been built up gradually, over time, and the cost has been written off as expense along the way. If another company were to buy the Coke brand, though, that cost could appear on its balance sheet.

Goodwill

When one company buys the assets of another company, the net assets acquired are valued. There are three possible relationships between the value of the net assets acquired and the purchase price.

If the purchase price is the same as the net value of the assets, the assets will be recorded at their valuations, and no problem exists.

If the valuation of the assets is more than the purchase price, the price is prorated over the assets, and they are all reduced in value proportionately.

If the value of individual assets is less than the purchase price, the buying company is said to have bought "goodwill". Goodwill is recognition that the earning power of the purchased company (because of things such as employees, brands, and reputation) is greater than the sum of the individual values of its assets. Goodwill is an intangible asset and appears on the balance sheet as such.

Goodwill appears only when a company has been bought. Instead of amortization, goodwill is periodically subjected to an "impairment" test, and any deficiency is written off at that time.

4.2.2.5 Total Assets

When all the above assets are added together, the total represents all the assets the company has control over. This total is used by analysts to get an objective measure of the size of the company. The greater the total assets, the larger the company, and so the greater the profit it should make.

There are different amortization methods and rates for the various types of long-term assets. Which method and rate to use depends on the assumptions made by management about asset lives. For example, Sara Lee is a conglomerate that has interests in a range of consumer products. The company's financial statements for 2010 reported its assets as being amortized as follows:

> Property is stated at cost, and depreciation is computed using principally the straight-line method at annual rates of 2% to 20% for buildings and improvements, and 4% to 33% for machinery and equipment.

4.3 Asset Turnover Ratio

The extent to which assets have been used efficiently or inefficiently is measured by the asset turnover ratio. This is calculated by dividing the sales revenue by the total asset figure. (See Exhibit 4.9.) An organization that uses a large amount of assets to create its sales is less efficient; the organization that requires the smallest asset base is the most efficient. Assets are there for the purpose of creating sales revenue: the smaller the asset base for any given level of sales, the better the organization is managing its assets. There are two reasons for this.

First, a larger asset base means that more money has been invested by the owners. For any given level of profit, a larger asset base will lead to a lower return on equity (and profit is driven by sales volume). Second, assets create costs: a larger asset base means more plants, more machinery, more vehicles, etc. All of these have to be operated by people, and that leads to a higher wage expense as well as other operating expenses.

The passenger vehicle industry across the world is plagued by overcapacity. The industry has relatively low asset turnover ratios. It is no surprise that we regularly hear announcements by the big auto manufacturers that they are closing plants. They are trying to improve their asset turnover ratios.

Exhibit 4.9: Asset Turnover Ratio

The efficiency with which the assets have been used to generate sales can be measured using the asset turnover ratio.

Philomena's Fashions had total assets of $500,000 at the end of 2010 and $550,000 at the end of 2011. Sales in 2010 were $5,000,000, and $6,600,000 in 2011. Assets have increased (by 10%), but sales have increased even more (32%).

Asset turnover ratio:

= sales ÷ total assets

2010: $5,000,000 ÷ $500,000 = 10 times
2011: $6,600,000 ÷ $550,000 = 12 times

The company is turning over its assets more quickly in 2011, indicating that it is more efficient, all other things being equal.

4.4 Summary

In this chapter we have dealt with how the balance sheet reports the assets of the business. The assets are broadly divided into two groups: the current assets (cash, receivables, inventory, etc.) and the long-term assets (plant, vehicles, real estate, intangibles, etc.). Current assets are expected to be going through a continuous process of realization and replacement, whereas long-term assets are generally owned over the long term and are bought to be used rather than to be sold.

When deciding the dollar amounts that will go on the balance sheet, the assets must be owned in the first place, and then they must be valued. Current assets are valued conservatively: that is, they are valued at the lower of their cost or their market value. Long-term assets are typically valued at cost, less an allowance (accumulated amortization) for the proportion of their cost that is expired.

Appendix 4.1
Example of a Balance Sheet

Canadian Tire is a retailer with outlets all over Canada. Its published financial statements (with all the supporting notes and information) is available on the Web at **www.canadiantire.ca**. (Follow the links: company information | investors | financial reports.)

Canadian Tire Corporation, Limited
Consolidated Balance Sheet
($ millions)

	As at	
	January 1, 2011	January 2, 2010
Assets		
Current assets		
Cash and cash equivalents	$ 554	$ 870
Short-term investments	196	64
Accounts receivable	662	836
Loans receivable	2,481	2,275
Merchandise inventories	902	933
Income taxes recoverable	99	95
Prepaid expenses and deposits	38	40
Future income taxes	72	83
Total current assets	$ 5,004	$ 5,196
Long-term assets		
Long-term receivables	$ 101	$ 110
Long-term investments	76	49
Goodwill	72	72
Intangible assets	291	265
Property & equipment	3,220	3,180
Total long-term assets	$ 3,760	$ 3,676
Total assets	$ 8,764	$ 8,872

continued....

Canadian Tire Corporation, Limited
Consolidated Balance Sheet (Continued)
($ millions)

	As at	
	January 1, 2011	January 2, 2010
Liabilities		
Current liabilities		
Bank Indebtedness	$ 118	$ 84
Deposits	616	863
Accounts payable	1,356	1,392
Current portion of long-term debt	22	309
Total current liabilities	$ 2,112	$ 2,648
Long-term liabilities		
Long-term debt	$ 1,079	$ 1,101
Future income taxes	55	50
Long-term deposits	1,264	1,197
Other long-term liabilities	187	189
Total long-term liabilities	$ 2,585	$ 2,537
Total liabilities	$ 4,697	$ 5,185
Shareholders' Equity		
Share capital	$ 712	$ 720
Accumulated Other Comprehensive income (loss)	(39)	(46)
Retained earnings	3,394	3,014
Total shareholders' equity	$ 4,067	$ 3,688
Total liabilities & shareholders' equity	$ 8,764	$ 8,873

Appendix 4.2
Inventory Flow and Inventory Valuation Models

As discussed throughout Chapter 4, inventory has to be both counted and valued. Counting establishes the quantities involved and is a matter of fact: either the inventory is there, or it is not. Valuation puts a dollar value on the inventory. Unlike counting, the valuation process is negotiable. Depending on the assumptions we make, we will get different answers to the question, "How much is the inventory worth?" These assumptions focus on the pattern of how inventory flows through the system.

In situations where the price per unit of inventory is the same at all points through the year, it makes no difference what assumptions we make about inventory flow: they all give identical results in terms of operating profit and the inventory value on the balance sheet. In situations where the price per unit of inventory changes, different inventory flow assumptions will result in different inventory valuations and different reported operating profit. Changing prices are more likely than steady prices, so this is an area where we should spend some time understanding the implications of how we record values in the accounting system.

Three possible cost-flow approaches will be dealt with: specific identification, first-in-first-out (FIFO), and weighted average cost. The last two are used when goods are identical or similar, while specification identification is only used when goods are of very high value, such as cars or expensive jewellery.

Specific Identification

If inventory consists of things that have substantial individual value and unique characteristics, allowing items to be separately recorded, then the specific identification method may be suitable. (See Exhibit 4A2.1.) This method would apply to inventory such as household appliances, computers, etc. — each of which has a unique identification serial number. The cost of each item is recorded. If the item is still in inventory, its cost is recorded as inventory value and will appear on the balance sheet. If the item is sold, its cost is transferred out of inventory and into an account called Cost of Goods Sold, which will appear as an expense on the income statement.

Identical or Similar Goods

In many cases, goods purchased for resale are identical with, or very similar to, goods already in inventory, and the purchases and the existing inventory become mixed together. It may be impossible or impractical to

149

Exhibit 4A2.1: Inventory Valuation — Specific Identification

Mike's Motor Sales has five used vehicles in inventory at the start of January:

Make and Model	Cost
Ford Mustang	$10,000
Pontiac Firebird	15,000
GM half-tonne truck	7,000
Mazda 3	12,000
Toyota Tercel	11,000
Total	$55,000 (a balance sheet asset as at January 1)

By the end of January, the Ford, the GM, and the Toyota have all been sold; the Pontiac and the Mazda are still in inventory. No further vehicles have been bought. Specific identification of inventory would report the following:

Cost of goods sold
($10,000 + $7,000 + $11,000) $28,000   (an income statement expense for January)

Inventory
($15,000 + $12,000)   27,000   (a balance sheet asset as at January 31)

Total accounted for $55,000

---

discover which specific goods have been sold and which are still on hand. Two possible patterns of usage can be considered. We could assume that the first goods bought were the first ones used, or we could assume it appropriate to average out the inventory and the purchases because they were mixed randomly.

FIFO Model

In a "first-in-first-out" (FIFO) system, the assumption is that although the goods are not different, because of the way they are delivered, stored, or used, it is reasonable to assume that those bought earliest get used soonest. This implies that the flow-through of cost to the cost of goods sold account consists of goods that were bought less recently than the goods that remain in inventory. While the expense account in the income statement is valued at the earlier price, the inventory account on the balance sheet is valued at the more recent price. (See Exhibit 4A2.2.)

Weighted Average Model

In many situations, new purchases are mixed with existing inventory, and it becomes impossible to separate them. The only reasonable inventory valuation would be averaging the inventory values. (See Exhibit 4A2.3.)

Exhibit 4A2.2: Inventory Valuation — FIFO

Mike's Gas Station has a convenience outlet attached. Among the products it sells are bread and milk. Because both bread and milk deteriorate over time, the cartons they are delivered in always state on the instructions to "sell old stock first". So, when the new stock is put on the shelf, it is put at the back and the old stock is put at the front. When customers pull the milk or bread off the shelf, they are buying the older stock, and the inventory is always the newer goods.

At the beginning of May the inventory of one-litre 2% milk was 20 packets, each having a cost of $1.10. During the month of May there were eight deliveries, each of 100 packets. The first six deliveries were invoiced at $1.10. For the last two deliveries the price went up to $1.20. At the end of the month the inventory was 10 packets.

		Packets	**Price**		
Inventory at May 1		20 × $1.10			$ 22.00
+ Goods purchased in May	6 × 100 =	600 × $1.10			660.00
	2 × 100 =	200 × $1.20			240.00
Goods available for sale		820			$922.00
– Inventory at May 31		– 10			
Total units sold in May		810			
Cost of goods sold (810 units)	20 + 600 =	620 × $1.10	$682.00		
	190 =	190 × $1.20	228.00		910.00
Inventory at May 31	820 – 810 =	10 × $1.20			$ 12.00

Exhibit 4A2.3: Inventory Valuation — Weighted Average

Mike's Gas Station sells gas. The regular gas tank holds 20,000 litres, and there are deliveries whenever stocks fall to a level of 5,000 litres. The price Mike's pays for gas depends on world gas prices, which can change for every delivery. Once in the tank, of course, all the existing gas is mixed with the new delivery. There were 10,000 litres of regular gas in inventory on May 1, at a cost of $0.55 per litre. Deliveries of 15,000 litres (to fill up the tank) were made on the 1st, 15th, and 22nd of the month, at costs of $0.55, $0.60, and $0.54, respectively. There were 6,000 litres in the regular gas tank at the end of May.

Inventory at May 1	(10,000 × $0.55)	$ 5,500.00
Delivery, May 1	(15,000 × $0.55)	8,250.00
Delivery, May 15	(15,000 × $0.60)	9,000.00
Delivery, May 22	(15,000 × $0.54)	8,100.00
Total	55,000	$30,850.00
Weighted average	$30,850 ÷ 55,000 = $0.56091	
Total units sold	55,000 – 6,000 = 49,000 litres	
Cost of goods sold	49,000 × $0.56091	$27,484.59
Inventory as at May 31	6,000 × $0.56091	3,365.46
Total accounted for	55,000 × $0.56091	$30,850.05

The pattern of inventory flows is a matter of fact. The question of whether to use that actual inventory flow as the model for the accounting resource flow is a separate decision. Perhaps surprisingly, GAAP does not absolutely require that the inventory flow assumption used for financial accounting be the same as the inventory flow pattern that happens in reality. The most commonly used inventory flow assumption in Canada is FIFO.

In times of steady prices, the differences between the methods are small or non-existent. In times of rapidly changing prices, the difference in operating profit caused by using different valuation models will be substantial. The choice of valuation model is, therefore, potentially an important decision.

Appendix 4.3
Consolidation of Groups of Companies

When one company owns a few shares of another company, it is an investment (either short- or long-term, depending on the facts) that appears at cost (or market value, if less) on the balance sheet. Where the shareholding is large, rather than treating them as two separate companies, it may be more sensible to treat both companies as a single economic entity. This is done through a process called consolidation.

In consolidation, the cost of acquiring the shares of the subsidiary company is replaced, on the balance sheet of the holding company, by the assets and liabilities of the subsidiary company.

The consolidated income statement will be the sum of the income statements of the holding company and the subsidiary company. Their revenues and expenses are added together. As a result, the income becomes the sum of the incomes of the two companies.

An exception to this is where the holding company and the subsidiary have traded between each other. In order to reflect the idea that the consolidated accounts are the results of the composite economic unit, intercompany sales and purchases are eliminated from both income statements, and any unrealized profits on intercompany sales are eliminated.

Mike's Motor Sales Inc. is a wholly owned subsidiary of Mike's Motors Inc. In preparing the balance sheet of Mike's Motors Inc., there is an asset, Investment in Mike's Motor Sales Inc., of $25,000. Consolidation would replace that $25,000 with the actual assets and liabilities (but not the equity) of Mike's Motor Sales Inc. The new title of the balance sheet would be "Consolidated Balance Sheet of Mike's Motors Inc. and Its Subsidiary" (see next page).

Minority Interest: Goodwill on Consolidation

Where all the shares in the subsidiary company are owned by the holding company, the consolidation process consists of adding all the assets and liabilities of the subsidiary to the assets and liabilities of the holding company and adding the two income statements together.

Even where the holding company owns less than 100% of the subsidiary, it may still be necessary to consolidate them. Canadian accounting practice requires the consolidation of companies where 50% or more of the shares are held, or where as little as 20% of the shares are held if the holding company can effectively control the subsidiary (e.g., by having the power to appoint the directors of the company).

Mike's Motors Inc.
Balance Sheet as at December 31

Assets
Current assets

Cash		$ 2,000	
Receivables		45,000	
Inventory		23,000	$ 70,000

Long-term assets

Equipment at cost	$50,000		
Less: Accumulated amortization	30,000	$20,000	
Investment in Mike's Motor Sales Inc.		25,000	45,000
Total assets			$115,000

Liabilities and Equity
Current liabilities

Trade payables		$ 5,000
Bank loans		25,000
		$ 30,000
Long-term liabilities		20,000
Total liabilities		$ 50,000
Shareholders' equity		65,000
Total liabilities and equities		$115,000

Mike's Motors Sales Inc.
Balance Sheet as at December 31

Assets

Cash	$ 5,000
Receivables	0
Inventory	24,000
Total assets	$ 29,000

Liabilities and Equity

Trade payables	$ 4,000
Shareholders' equity	25,000
Total liabilities and equities	$ 29,000

Mike's Motors Inc. and Its Subsidiary
Consolidated Balance Sheet as at December 31

Assets
Current assets

Cash ($2,000 + $5,000)		$ 7,000	
Receivables		45,000	
Inventory ($23,000 + $24,000)		47,000	$ 99,000

Long-term assets

Equipment at cost	$50,000		
Less: Accumulated amortization	30,000		20,000
Total Assets			$119,000

Liabilities and Equity
Current liabilities

Trade payables ($4,000 + $5,000)		$ 9,000
Bank loans		25,000
		$ 34,000
Long-term liabilities		20,000
Total liabilities		$ 54,000
Shareholders' equity		65,000
Total liabilities and equities		$119,000

In situations where the subsidiary company is less than 100% owned, we have to recognize that there is some part of the net assets that is not owned by the holding company. This is done by showing an item on the balance sheet called Minority Interest.

Another issue is where the amount paid for the shares by the holding company is not precisely equal to the balance sheet value of the net assets of the subsidiary. Where the net assets exceed the cost of the shares, we will show "gain on consolidation" in the equity of the consolidated balance sheet. Where the cost of the shares exceeds the net assets of the subsidiary, we will show an asset Goodwill in the consolidated balance sheet.

In the previous example, suppose the $25,000 that Mike's Motors Inc. paid for shares in Mike's Motor Sales Inc. had bought Mike's Motors Inc. not 100%, but only 60% of the shares. Two items would now have to be recognized: first, the 40% minority interest in the net assets of the subsidiary (40% × $25,000 = $10,000); second, the goodwill of $10,000. Goodwill is calculated as follows:

Net assets of subsidiary ($29,000 – $4,000)	$ 25,000
Less: Minority interest	10,000
Holding company's interest	$ 15,000
Amount paid	$ 25,000
Goodwill ($25,000 – $15,000)	$ 10,000

Mike's Motors Inc. and Its Subsidiary
Consolidated Balance Sheet as at December 31

Assets

Current assets		
Cash	$ 7,000	
Receivables	45,000	
Inventory	47,000	$ 99,000
Long-term assets		
Equipment at cost	$50,000	
Less: Accumulated amortization	30,000	
	$20,000	
Goodwill	10,000	30,000
		$129,000

Liabilities and Equity

Current liabilities		
Trade payables	$ 9,000	
Bank loans	25,000	$ 34,000
Long-term liabilities		20,000
Total liabilities		$ 54,000
Shareholders' equity	$65,000	
Minority interest	10,000	75,000
		$129,000

Instead of amortization, goodwill is periodically subjected to an "impairment" test, and any deficiency is written off at that time.

155

Self-Study Problem

1. Charley Farley went into business on October 1, 2011, by opening a doughnut shop. He carried on the business in a rented store in downtown Orillia. At the end of December, he realized that he would have to pay income tax on the business profits, but he had no idea how much profit he had made or what his assets and liabilities were. He has asked you to prepare a balance sheet.

    He has presented you with his bank statements and a pile of invoices and receipts. The following is a summarized list of payments and receipts for the three months.

Receipts paid into bank account:

1.	Owners' equity	$ 50,000
2.	Bank loan	55,000
3.	Cash sales	146,500
		$251,500

Payments made out of bank account:

4.	Suppliers	$104,500
5.	Wages	12,000
6.	Rent	20,000
7.	Utilities	5,000
8.	Insurance	4,000
9.	Equipment	99,000
10.	Repayment of bank loan	4,000
		$248,500

You are given the following additional information:

(i) The cash received from sales was $161,500. Charley Farley took $5,000 each month from the cash sales for his own living expenses before paying the balance into the bank.

(ii) Charley has a coffee delivery arrangement with a nearby office. He delivers the coffee daily; they pay him weekly. At the end of December they owed him $500.

(iii) The $104,500 paid for supplies is not exactly the amount used: Charley owes suppliers another $5,000, and there is inventory on hand that had cost him $1,500.

(iv) The $20,000 paid for rent consists of the $5,000 monthly rent for October, November, and December, plus the "last" month of the lease of $5,000.

(v) In addition to the $5,000 paid for utilities, another $1,000 is owed.

(vi) The insurance premium of $4,000 gives Charley coverage from October 1, 2011, to September 30, 2012.

(vii) Amortization expense on the equipment should be taken as $9,000 for the three months to December 31, 2011.

(viii) The bank loan is on a five-year term.

[Note: This is a continuation of Self-Study Problem #1 in Chapter 3 on page 120. You may need to refer back to that problem (and even Self-Study Problem #1 in Chapter 2 on page 68) for help in doing this one.]

Required

(a) Prepare a balance sheet for Charley Farley as at December 31, 2011.

(b) Given that the sales for the year were $162,000, what were the receivables turnover ratio and the receivables collection period?

(c) Given that the sales for the year were $162,000, what were the inventory turnover ratio and the days' sales in inventory holding period?

(d) Given that the sales for the year were $162,000, what was the total asset turnover ratio?

Solution

1. (a) Cash account summary:

Cash banked	$251,500	
Owner's withdrawals	15,000	
Total receipts		$266,500
Bank payments	$248,500	
Owner's withdrawals	15,000	
Total payments		263,500
Cash balance		$ 3,000

Charley Farley
Balance Sheet as at December 31, 2011

Assets

Current assets:

Cash	$ 3,000	
Receivables	500	
Inventory	1,500	
Prepaid rent	5,000	
Prepaid insurance	3,000	$ 13,000
Long-term assets:		
At cost	$ 99,000	
Less: Accumulated amortization	(9,000)	90,000
		$103,000

Liabilities and Equity

Current liabilities:

Trade payables	$ 5,000	
Accrued utilities	1,000	$ 6,000
Long-term debt (bank loan)		
($55,000 – $4,000)		51,000
Total liabilities		$ 57,000
Owners' equity:		
Cash introduced	$ 50,000	
Add: Net income	11,000	
Less: Withdrawn	(15,000)	46,000
		$103,000

Before you answer (b), you need to know where the $162,000 sales come from:

$$
\begin{aligned}
\text{Total Sales} \quad &= \quad \text{Cash sales} + \text{Credit sales} \\
&= \quad \$161,500 + \$500 \\
&= \quad \$162,000
\end{aligned}
$$

(b) Receivables turnover ratio:

$$
\begin{aligned}
&= \text{sales} \div \text{receivables} \\
&= \$162,000 \div \$500 \\
&= 324 \text{ times per year}
\end{aligned}
$$

Receivables collection period:

$$
\begin{aligned}
&= \text{receivables} \div (\text{sales} \div 365) \\
&= \$500 \div (\$162,000 \div 365) \\
&= 1.1 \text{ days}
\end{aligned}
$$

(c) Inventory turnover ratio:

$$
\begin{aligned}
&= \text{sales} \div \text{inventory} \\
&= \$162,000 \div \$1,500 \\
&= 108 \text{ times per year}
\end{aligned}
$$

Inventory holding period:

$$
\begin{aligned}
&= \text{inventory} \div (\text{sales} \div 365) \\
&= \$1,500 \div (\$162,000 \div 365) \\
&= 3.4 \text{ days}
\end{aligned}
$$

(d) Total asset turnover ratio:

$$
\begin{aligned}
&= \text{sales} \div \text{total assets} \\
&= \$162,000 \div \$103,000 \\
&= 1.6 \text{ times per year}
\end{aligned}
$$

Discussion Questions and Problems

Discussion Questions

1. Financial statements are prepared annually. Why is one year chosen as the reporting period, as opposed to any other period?
2. Which comes first in the balance sheet, inventory or equipment, and why?
3. How are long-term assets valued for inclusion in the balance sheet?
4. How are short-term assets valued for inclusion in the balance sheet?
5. Give some examples of assets that are important to the company but that are not included in the balance sheet.
6. To whom is the balance sheet more important: investors or creditors?
7. Give one example of the conservatism principle being used in the balance sheet.
8. In what way is the constant value of the dollar in conflict with the historical cost principle in the balance sheet?
9. One of your customers has been buying goods from you regularly for the past six months. He has always paid cash with order, as that is what your company normally does. Today you received a call from your sales department. This customer wants to buy twice as much as he normally does in a month but wants 30 days' credit. Do you say yes or no?
10. Your company manufactures plastic mouldings. A management consultant suggested that you could be more efficient by moving to "just-in-time" ordering of raw materials. One of your plant managers objected, saying that without that inventory, the balance sheet would have fewer assets, and they would all be worse off. Who is right?
11. Why do companies value inventory at the lower of cost and market price?
12. State the advantages and disadvantages of including human resource assets (the value of employees) on the balance sheet.

Problems

1. Superior Software Inc. had the following balances as at December 31, 2011:

   • Petty cash balances in the office: $250
   • Bank chequing accounts: $39,750
   • Bank deposit accounts: $50,000
   • GICs: $110,000

   Required
   What will the company record as Cash at December 31, 2011?

2. As at December 31, 2011, Superior Software Inc. had a total of $1,400,000 recorded as owed by credit sale customers. Of this amount, $190,000 was owed by customers who are never going to pay for one reason or another. In respect of the balance, the company has decided to introduce (for the first time) a provision for doubtful debts of 10% of the amount owed.

Required
(a) What is the bad debt expense for the year 2011?
(b) How would the accounts receivable appear on the balance sheet as at December 31, 2011?
(c) If sales revenue for 2011 was $13,200,000, calculate the receivables turnover ratio.
(d) If sales revenue for 2011 was $13,200,000, calculate the receivables collection period.

3. Crucible Co. had accounts receivable of $290,000 as at December 31, 2011, and the company had a provision for doubtful debts of $20,000. During January 2012 the company discovered that one credit customer owing $5,000 had gone bankrupt, and one credit customer had run away without paying the $2,000 she owed. Both were amounts owed from 2010. During January 2012 a total of $190,000 was collected from the accounts receivable, but no additional credit sales were made.

Required
(a) Show how the accounts receivable would appear on the balance sheet as at December 31, 2011.
(b) Show how the accounts receivable would appear on the balance sheet as at January 31, 2012, after writing off the two bad debts but before recording the collection of cash during January.
(c) Show how the accounts receivable would appear on the balance sheet as at January 31, 2012, after writing off the two bad debts and after recording the collection of cash during January.
(d) What accounting concepts do you apply in the creation of the provision for doubtful debts?

4. Dryall Motors Inc. completed an inventory audit for its stores on December 31, 2011, and identified the following unrecorded items:

(a) 1,000 litres of lubricating oil, which had cost $2.50 per litre (As at December 31, 2011, the replacement price was $3.00 per litre.)
(b) 50,000 litres of regular gas, which had cost $0.75 per litre (As at December 31, 2011, the replacement price was $0.60 per litre.)
(c) Spare parts that had cost $25,000 (Mostly were for vehicles no longer in use; therefore, it was unlikely that they could be sold.)
(d) A replacement engine and transmission for a Ford truck with resale value of $10,000 (Both belong to a customer.)
(e) $20,000 of electronic car parts that were in good working order but had gone beyond their "sell by" dates on the packages

Required
Show how the unrecorded inventory items would appear on the balance sheet as at December 31, 2011, in accordance with the given information.

5. Refer to the information in Problem #4. If Dryall Motors Inc.'s sales for 2011 totalled $780,000 and its inventory is valued at lower of cost or market value, calculate the following ratios:

   (a) The inventor turnover ratio
   (b) The inventory holding period

6. Acme Corporation had sales revenue of $6,000,000 in 2010 and $7,500,000 in 2011. Accounts receivable were $1,200,000 at the end of 2010 and $1,500,000 at the end of 2011.

   Required
   (a) Calculate the accounts receivable turnover ratio for 2010 and 2011.
   (b) Has the management of accounts receivable improved or worsened from 2010 to 2011?
   (c) What are the advantages and disadvantages of selling goods on credit?

7. Acme Corporation had sales revenue of $6,000,000 in 2010 and $7,500,000 in 2011. Accounts receivable were $1,200,000 at the end of 2010 and $1,500,000 at the end of 2011.

   Required
   (a) How much cash did Acme Corporation collect from its customers in 2011?
   (b) If sales in 2012 were expected to be $10,000,000, what would you expect accounts receivable to be at the end of 2012?
   (c) Does a major increase in accounts receivable create any cash management issues?

8. Acme Corporation had sales revenue of $6,000,000 in 2010 and $7,500,000 in 2011. Inventory was $600,000 at the end of 2010 and $800,000 at the end of 2011.

   Required
   (a) Calculate the inventory turnover ratio for 2010 and 2011.
   (b) Has the management of inventory improved or worsened from 2010 to 2011?
   (c) What are the advantages and disadvantages of carrying inventory?

9. Explain how the following purchases would be included in the balance sheet of Superior Software Inc., as at December 31, 2011. In each case, identify the basis of valuation, the dollar value, and the accounting concept(s) that apply.

   (a) At the start of 2011 the company bought a $100,000 automatic software writing program, which is expected to be used for four years and then be replaced. The company uses the straight-line method of amortization.
   (b) The company bought a new delivery van at a cost of $50,000 two years ago. The van was expected to be used for five years

and then be sold for $10,000. The company uses the straight-line method of amortization.

Due to changes in technology, the delivery of software is now done electronically and the delivery van is no longer used. Its resale value as at December 31, 2011, is $25,000.

(c) The company operates out of an office condominium in downtown Hamilton. The suite cost $1,000,000 five years ago. The current resale value is $2,200,000.

(d) The company owns computer hardware that cost $250,000 in 2011. It will probably remain "state of the art" until the end of 2012, by which time it will need replacement or a major upgrade.

(e) The company commissioned an independent contractor to write the software for a new computer game called "Granny Goes Shopping" aimed at the Junior Miss segment of the market. Development costs paid in 2011 totalled $45,000. Unfortunately, market research now shows that the project is unlikely to be successful, and the company is thinking about cancelling it.

(f) The company has just signed a contract with a major politician who will shamelessly promote Superior Software's programs in TV ads and personal appearances. It is expected that his $500,000 salary will be reflected in huge increases in sales and profits: profits in 2012 will increase by $500,000, and in 2013 by a further $250,000.

(g) Superior Software owns proprietary rights to a total of 17 software applications, all of which are protected by copyright law and which are the basis of their revenues and profitability. The cost, as at January 1, 2011, was $1,000,000 and accumulated amortization at that time was $750,000. During 2011 the company added software at a cost of $400,000. It plans to write off 25% of the cost each year.

10. You have just bought $250,000 of building materials from Home Depot. Home Depot is quite willing to give you one month's credit, but, alternatively, it would give you a 5% discount if you paid cash now. You can pay in cash but only by borrowing the money from your bank at 15% interest or by putting it on your credit card at 25% interest.

Required
Work out the best payment plan for this situation.

11. List the order in which the following assets would appear in the balance sheet:

- Plant & equipment
- Accumulated amortization on plant & equipment
- Accounts payable
- Accounts receivable
- Cash
- Inventory
- Prepayments

- Deposits
- Bank chequing account
- Patents & trademarks
- Investment in a subsidiary company

12. Steamboat Brewery started business in Oakville in 1980. The company invested in beer-brewing equipment at a cost of $500,000. This was amortized over its expected useful life of 20 years. As of 2011, it was still in use, and because it has been well maintained, it was still fully functional. The company had no plans to discontinue its use any time soon.

Required

(a) In which section of the balance sheet would this asset appear?
(b) What would be the basis of valuation (i.e., what accounting concepts apply)?
(c) Show how the asset would appear on the balance sheet on the first day it was owned.
(d) Show how the asset would appear on the balance sheet after 10 years of use.
(e) Show how the asset would appear on the balance sheet as at December 31, 2011.
(f) If they disposed of this equipment on January 1, 2012, for $80,000, what would be reported in the income statement and in the balance sheet?

13. Urban Outfitters had the following balances as at December 31, 2011:

Cash balances in the tills at retail outlets	$ 56,000
Accounts receivable	$492,000 (net of doubtful debts)
Petty cash balances in head office	$ 2,000
Chequing account at the Bank of Toyland	$ 58,000
Accounts payable	$566,000
Inventory of goods for resale (at the lower of cost or market value)	$950,000
Term deposits with Investor's Trust	$500,000
Land & building	$500,000 (at cost)
Accumulated amortization on building	$ 50,000
Mortgage owed to Property Trust Inc.	$325,000
Bank loan (repayable on demand)	$245,000
Utility deposit with City Hydro	$ 2,000
Utility expense owed to City Hydro	$ 5,000
Rent paid in advance	$ 5,000
Shares in Union Carbide Inc.	$200,000 (at market value)
Plant & equipment	$750,000 (at cost)
Accumulated amortization on plant	$200,000
Intangible assets	$235,000 (at cost)

Required

(a) Show how these would be reported in the current assets section of the balance sheet for December 31, 2011.
(b) Show how these would be reported in the long-term assets section of the balance sheet for December 31, 2011.

(c) What is the total asset value on the balance sheet as at December 31, 2011?

14. The balance sheet of Steel Traders Inc. as at December 31, 2011, was as follows:

Current assets		Current liabilities	
Cash	$ 25,000	Trade payables	$ 265,000
Receivables	200,000	Bank loan	150,000
Inventory	625,000	Income tax due	35,000
Total	$ 850,000	Total	$ 450,000
Long-term assets	500,000	**Long-term liabilities**	450,000
		Total liabilities	$ 900,000
		Shareholders' equity	
		Share capital	$ 50,000
		Retained earnings	400,000
		Total	$ 450,000
Total	$1,350,000	Total	$1,350,000

You are told that the sales revenue for 2011 was $4,800,000 and that the company made a net income of $500,000 in 2011.

Required

(a) Calculate the following ratios:

(i) Current ratio
(ii) Quick ratio
(iii) Receivables turnover ratio
(iv) Receivables collection period
(v) Inventory turnover ratio
(vi) Inventory holding period

(b) Is the company liquid?

15. Pharmacy Research International had made a number of payments in 2011, which are listed below:

(a) $900,000 for basic research into the elusive cure for the common cold
(b) $350,000 for advertising the company's new on-line prescription drug service
(c) $500,000 for the design of a new company logo
(d) $600,000 for a two-year contract (2012 and 2013) for the rights to manufacture a well-established and successful slimming pill
(e) $500,000 for testing a new depression medication; the trials were successful and the drug will be put on the market in 2012

Required

For each payment, show the dollar value that would be included in the company's balance sheet as at December 31, 2011, and list the accounting principle(s) that apply.

The Balance Sheet (2):
Liabilities and Equity

5

Learning
Objectives

After studying this chapter you should be able to list and explain the following components of the balance sheet:
→ Current liabilities
→ Long-term liabilities
→ Equity share capital

And you should be able to analyze and critically comment on the following through the use of appropriate accounting ratios:
→ Liquidity
→ Risk associated with debt

5.1   Liabilities

According to the accounting equation, the assets are funded by a combination of equity and liabilities:

ASSETS = LIABILITIES + OWNERS' EQUITY

Liabilities are all the amounts the company owes to outsiders and do not include the owners' investment in the business (owners are not outsiders). Liabilities are included whether they are due immediately or at some time in the future. When the liabilities are listed in the balance sheet, the order of liquidity is used to differentiate those that are more current from those that are less current. This is similar to the presentation of the assets in the balance sheet.

5.1.1   Current Liabilities

Current assets are defined as those likely to be realized within one year. Current liabilities are defined as those that are due within one year; many are due even sooner. Current liabilities are one of the biggest threats to a company's existence. Failing to pay the current liabilities when they are due is the easiest way to get into bankruptcy. Therefore, however good the longer-term prospects are, the company has to manage the current liabilities to ensure that there is always enough liquidity to deal with them. Comparing the current liabilities with the current assets gives some idea of whether the company is about to face a liquidity crisis. The main types of current liability are

- trade payables;
- accrued expenses;
- deferred revenue;
- taxes due; and
- short-term loans.

5.1.2 *Trade Payables*

The largest current liability is generally the amount the company owes to its various suppliers for goods and services received. In the same way that the company sells goods on credit (and creates the asset Accounts Receivable), it will also buy on credit. Any unpaid accounts at the end of the year will become a liability (called *Trade Payables* or *Accounts Payable*).

In the case of accounts receivable, it was necessary to make an allowance for bad or doubtful debts. There is no need to make any such reduction in the trade payables; they will be stated on the balance sheet at their full face value, as that is what the company will be paying.

Trade credit is generally offered on a 30-day basis, so it is reasonable to assume that the total amount shown as trade payables is due within a month. Some industries, though, have traditionally operated on shorter or longer periods of trade credit. If there are enough current assets available in the form of cash (and short-term investments) to pay the trade payables, the company probably has enough liquidity. If the company has to collect its receivables before it can pay the trade payables, the company is a little riskier. And if the company has to sell its inventory before it can pay its trade payables, then its risk position may be even greater.

There is no interest payable on trade credit as long as it is paid by the due date. The implication is that it is free money. If that is the case, a business would be foolish to ignore this opportunity for free financing. As the amounts involved can be very large, this is a serious issue.

If the buyer has the cash available, she or he may be able to negotiate a lower price (a cash discount) for paying "cash with order" or "cash on delivery". If that happens, the trade credit is not free. Its cost is just disguised in the invoice price.

Some sellers offer a combination of trade credit and a cash discount for prompt settlement. Terms "2/10, net 30" on an invoice mean that the

---

Credit Management: Automated Payments

The costs of maintaining the trade credit records are substantial. It is necessary to keep a record of every occasion when something is bought on credit. The delivery of the goods or receipt of the services has to be recorded. The goods have to be counted and checked for quality and conformance with specifications. The prices on the invoice have to be checked against the contract. The calculations on the invoice have to be checked. All the invoices for a month have to be added, and the total agreed with the supplier's monthly statement of account. Only when all this paperwork is complete and in order is the buyer in a position to write a cheque for the amount owing.

In the modern management environment, organizations have taken steps to deal with the costs and uncertainties of trade credit. Major Japanese motor manufacturers have arrangements with their suppliers whereby the supply of parts is governed by long-term contracts and just-in-time scheduling of deliveries. The delivery automatically triggers a direct transfer of the cost of the goods from the buyer's bank account to the seller's without the need for invoices, goods received notes, or cheques.

buyer may deduct a 2% discount from the face value of the invoice by making payment within 10 days; failing that, the full (net) amount of the invoice is due at the end of 30 days. All other things being equal, this means that the 2% discount is given for the 20-day difference between payment at day 10 and payment at day 30. The effective annual interest rate on this is 43%! (There are 18.25 20-day periods in a year. The effective annual interest rate is 1.02 to the power of 18.25, minus 1, which is 43%.) This is so high a rate that any company in its right mind would take the opportunity.

In practice, buyers often stretch the payment terms beyond the 30 days they are allowed. If that is the case, the benefit of the 2% prompt payment discount becomes significantly less.

To combat late payers, many sellers are now writing into sales contracts a clause that charges interest on accounts not paid on time.

Look at your latest utilities bill. It will show one amount due for payment by the due date and another, higher amount for payment after the due date. This is effectively charging you interest for late payment.

Look at your latest phone bill. It will state that accounts not paid by their due date are liable to have interest added on.

5.1.3   Accrued Expenses

In addition to trade credit, companies may owe money to suppliers of other goods and services. For some of these transactions, the process is very similar to trade credit: goods or services are supplied, an invoice is issued and, if unpaid, represents a liability. Occasions also arise where the amount owing has to be estimated because the invoice is not yet available.

Suppose it is the end of the fiscal year, December 31. A company may have an unpaid bill for electricity usage for the month up to December 20 (which was the last time the meters were read). The company would record the unpaid bill as a liability. It would also estimate the electricity usage for the 11 days from December 21 to 31 (based on past usage patterns). This would be an accrued expense in the balance sheet. Accrued expenses are typically small in total, by comparison with trade creditors.

Companies must pay income tax on their profits. The taxes are assessed annually and are paid in a lump sum. At the end of the fiscal year, the taxes owing on the profit of that year will be unpaid. Because they will be due soon after the year-end, they will also be a current liability.

5.1.4   Short-term Debt

Trade credit, accrued expenses, and taxes due all arise, almost automatically, out of the normal operation of a business. None of them has an explicit cost. By contrast, both short- and long-term loans are the result of a definite decision to borrow, and interest is payable on the amount borrowed.

If the company has borrowed money on a short-term basis, the amount due will be shown as short-term debt. This would include a short-term loan from a bank, a trust company, or other lending institution.

A short-term loan might be due at a specific date (e.g., a 90-day loan), or it might be potentially payable within a short period of time (e.g., a loan that is "callable" on seven days notice, meaning one on which the bank can insist on repayment after seven days), even though the intention of both parties is for the loan period to be longer.

Companies should use short-term borrowing to meet short-term financing needs. Thus, if the cash budget shows that there is a liquidity crunch in the months of June and July, the company will try to match the time of its borrowing to the period where cash is in need: i.e., by borrowing short-term for June and July. It would be foolish to borrow money for the entire year if the money would be sitting idle in a chequing account for 10 months.

If there is a long-term loan that is payable in instalments, that part that is due for repayment within a year is included in the short-term debt section, not as long-term debt.

5.1.5   Assessing Risk through Liquidity Ratios

Short-term debt is a significant source of risk for the company. Failure to pay liabilities when they fall due is the immediate cause of bankruptcy (though its origins may go back to unprofitable business operations). To assess the likelihood of the company's getting into a liquidity crisis, it is common to calculate liquidity ratios. These set the short-term liabilities against the funds available to pay them.

The current ratio compares all the current assets against the current liabilities. (See Exhibit 5.1.)

Exhibit 5.1:   Liquidity Ratios

Mike's Motors' balance sheet shows current assets of $99,000, current liabilities of $34,000, and inventory of $48,000:

Current ratio:

= current assets ÷ current liabilities
= $99,000 ÷ $34,000
= 2.9 : 1

Quick ratio:

= (current assets – inventory) ÷ current liabilities
= ($99,000 – $48,000) ÷ $34,000
= 1.5 : 1

In general, creditors will look for a current ratio of 2 : 1 or higher, or a quick ratio of 1 : 1 or higher to be sure that there is adequate liquidity. Mike's Motors, with a current ratio of 2.9 : 1, and a quick ratio of 1.5 : 1, comfortably exceeds these levels.

Liquidity Management at *The New York Times*

In times of falling profits and reduced liquidity, companies are sometimes forced to take desperate measures. The New York Times Group is selling off some of its non-core assets, such as the Florence, Alabama-based *TimesDaily* (*The Wall Street Journal*, March 25, 2009, p. B5). This will enable the company to pay back debt that falls due soon.

One of the criticisms of the current ratio is that it assumes all current assets are available to pay current liabilities. In fact, some are more liquid than others. In particular, inventory tends to be a rather slow-moving asset. A more stringent test is the quick ratio (acid-test ratio). This ratio compares current assets, excluding inventory, to current liabilities.

In general, the current ratio is expected to be 2 : 1 or higher, and the quick ratio 1 : 1 or higher.

5.1.6 *Long-term Debt*

Amounts owed for which the term is longer than one year are shown as long-term debt. It is important that these obligations be listed, as they will have to be repaid eventually. It is also desirable to separate them from the short-term debt, on the one hand (which has to be repaid very soon), and the equity, on the other hand (which does not have to be repaid, ever). The company has the use of long-term debt but not forever. The two most frequently encountered types of long-term debt are mortgage loans and debentures and notes.

5.1.6.1 *Mortgage Loans*

When anyone (companies included) buys real estate (land and buildings), the cost is often more than they have available to spend. A mortgage loan is money advanced to assist in the purchase of such an asset, for which the real estate itself is used as security. A legal agreement is signed in which the borrower undertakes to repay the loan with interest. The repayment is either in regular instalments or in a lump sum at the end of a specific period. The interest is at a specified rate (e.g., 5% per annum). If the terms of the agreement are kept up, eventually the purchaser will have repaid the debt and the interest, and will own the real estate unencumbered. If the purchaser fails to make any of the payments due under the agreement, the asset may be sold and the proceeds used to repay the debt and any outstanding interest. The lender thus has very good security for the loan.

Mortgaging any asset means using it as the collateral security for a loan. When that happens, the asset is no longer available to any other creditors. Until the mortgage loan is repaid, the asset's value is legally tied up, and the fact that the asset is mortgaged must clearly be shown in the financial statements.

5.1.6.2 *Debentures and Notes*

Debentures and notes are written acknowledgements of a debt. They are used so that the company can borrow money under stated terms of interest and repayment. The lenders may be members of the general public, banks, or other financial institutions. Sometimes debentures have specific assets pledged as security, in which case they may be called mortgage debentures, but mostly they do not. The lender is relying on the reputation and past history of the company for getting paid.

A debenture is a contract and contains numerous terms. Some of the more important ones cover

- the amount of the loan;
- the date when the loan is issued;
- the date when the loan is repayable (or a schedule of repayment dates if repaid in instalments);
- the interest rate payable;
- the dates on which interest payments will be made;
- any assets specifically pledged as security.

Debt instruments of both companies and governments are traded in a part of the stock market known as the bond market. The market for interest rates on these borrowed funds is very precise. The return on a given debenture will rise or fall as the market rises or falls. It will also change because of factors specific to the issuer. If lenders lose trust in a company's ability to fulfill the terms of a debenture, the lenders will react by selling that company's debentures, and/or by requiring a higher return. This does not affect the company directly, but there are important implications to its cost of borrowing from new sources.

5.1.7 **Total Liabilities**

The total of all liabilities, long-term and short-term, will be shown on the balance sheet. This total is a useful number to know: it shows how much of the company's assets have been financed by borrowed funds, as opposed to the equity funds provided by the owners. This relationship (debt vs. equity) is referred to as the leverage of the company, and is one measure of company risk. The greater the percentage of the assets financed through debt, the riskier the company.

5.1.8 **Assessing Risk through Debt Analysis**

One way to measure a company's level of risk is to look at the amount of debt it has compared to its equity. A company that is financed mostly from equity capital is low risk because the shareholders have no right either to the return of their capital, or to any dividends from the company. Debt, however, implies an obligation to pay interest on a regular basis and an obligation to repay the loan at the end of its term.

If a company has a loss-making year (or even a series of loss-making years), the company financed by equity will have some unhappy shareholders but may be able to struggle through. The company with a higher

---

Exhibit 5.2:   Assessing Risk through Debt Ratios

The balance sheet for Mike's Motors shows a total debt of $54,000, equity of $65,000, and total assets of $119,000.

Debt-to-equity ratio (%):
= ($54,000 ÷ $65,000) × 100%
= 83.1%

Debt-to-assets ratio (%):
= ($54,000 ÷ $119,000) × 100%
= 45.4%

   Both of these ratios are within the usual range for acceptable levels of risk (100% and 50%, respectively).

---

level of debt will find that its obligations give rise to a higher probability of bankruptcy.

   To assess the level of this risk it is common to calculate either debt as a percentage of equity or debt as a percentage of total assets.

   Debt is the sum of all short-term and long-term liabilities. As total assets is defined through the accounting equation as being equal to debt plus equity, the two debt ratios give identical economic information — they just express it in different ways. (See Exhibit 5.2.)

   In Canada and the United States, it is common for the debt-to-equity ratio to be kept below 100%. That is also equivalent to keeping the debt-to-assets ratio below 50%. At levels higher than these, creditors and investors start to worry about excessive risk.

5.2   Equity

Equity is the accounting way of describing the owners' interest in the business. Technically, it is a residual: what is left over after liabilities are deducted from assets. That is more than a trite rearrangement of the accounting equation (remember: assets = liabilities + owners' equity). What it means is that we use valuations to arrive at our totals for assets and liabilities: the dollar value of each element is individually determined when it is included in the balance sheet. We do not do the same thing for equity. We merely recognize it as what is left over when all the other things have been valued.

   There are a number of ways that the value of equity can be changed. Initially, of course, the company has no equity, but one of the first transactions a company is likely to be involved in is when the initial investors put some of their funds into the business to get it going. Putting their money in increases the company's assets. Double-entry recording requires that some balancing entry in the records be made to recognize where that increase in assets came from, and equity is the title given to it. So, equity starts off as zero and then increases because of the owners' investment.

Owners' investment can happen later in the company's life, as well as at the start. If more money is pumped into an ongoing business by investors, that also is recognized as equity. That investment typically happens when a company wants to expand, and it needs more capital to do so.

5.2.1   Shares

Investment in a company is in the form of "shares". We all have an understanding of the word *share* from common English usage: it means that two or more people have equal rights to part of something. The share of the company means exactly the same thing. Each shareholder has an equal right with each other shareholder to enjoy the benefits of owner-ship of the company. It is perhaps a more formalized relationship, and it is evidenced by a piece of paper called a share certificate, but it is funda-mentally a recognition of this equality between a number of individuals in their ownership of the company.

In theory, as owners, the shareholders have the last word in company decisions. In practice, however, it is not as simple as that. It would be impractical for the large modern corporation to have every shareholder actively involved in the running of the day-to-day business. Just imagine the number of shareholders in a company such as General Motors or Bell Canada, and you will get a sense of how difficult that would be. Instead, professional managers (called directors) run the company on behalf of the shareholders. This is referred to as the divorce of ownership and control. It is this separation that makes it so necessary to have financial reports prepared and sent to shareholders to keep them informed of how well the company is being run on their behalf.

The rights of the shareholders may be summarized as follows:

• Attending the annual general meeting
• Voting on issues such as accepting the financial statements, appointing the auditor, and electing the directors at the annual general meeting
• Being kept informed by receiving financial statements annually

Ultimately, if shareholders don't like the way the company is being run, or its performance, they have the right to sell their shares on the open market to anyone who will buy them.

This last right, selling shares, is actually more powerful than it looks. If one small shareholder sells his or her shares, the effect is probably insignificant. If an institutional shareholder with a large holding sells out or a number of smaller shareholders all sell at the same time, then there may be a dramatic effect on the share price. Selling pressure can lower the share price quite sharply.

Conversely, if there are many potential buyers trying to purchase shares of the company, market forces will push the share price up. Company directors constantly monitor the share price and use it as a measure of how well the company is perceived by investors.

The shareholder gets two potential benefits from owning the shares: dividends and capital appreciation.

In the past, the initial investment in common shares would have had a "par" or "nominal" value. For example, a company might have issued one million shares of $1 each to raise $1 million of share capital. Current practice, however, is to issue shares "of no par value": i.e., they do not have a nominal value, they are just recognition of a proportional share in the company, on an equal footing with all other common shares.

If a company has shares with a par value, then complications can arise when subsequent issues of shares are made at prices in excess of par value. The excess over par has to be recorded as a separate category of the owners' equity, called contributed surplus. With no-par shares, this situation does not arise.

5.2.2   *Dividends and Capital Growth*

If the directors choose to do so, they can propose a dividend. This is a periodical payment (typically once a year) made to shareholders as a way of distributing some or all of the profit to them. It is, in effect, a repayment of part of the shareholders' investment in the company. From an accounting perspective, assets are reduced and owners' equity is reduced. Legally, dividends can be paid only to the extent that there are retained earnings. (This is supposed to protect creditors by keeping the share capital intact.) In practical terms, of course, dividends can be paid only out of cash.

If investors recognize a company as a good investment, they will exert buying pressure on the shares, and that will make the price rise. As share prices increase, so, too, will the value of existing shareholders' investments. What forces make investors think a share is a good buy? Essentially, it is a forecast of the company's future prospects. That forecast will be heavily influenced by how well the company has done in the past, along with other factors, such as an assessment of its market possibilities. Dividend payment is part of the information used to judge a company: it sends signals to investors about how well the company has done, and what it expects to do in the future. So, while the initial effect of paying a dividend is to lower the company's assets (and hence, logically, the value of each share), in the medium term dividend payment can encourage investors and have a positive effect on share price.

When the company makes a profit, the directors may choose to pay a dividend. Legally, the dividend must also come out of retained earnings. The directors have to strike a balance between their wish to send positive messages to the shareholders by paying high dividends and their need to plow back earnings into the company to finance expansion. Realistically, if the company is growing, every dollar paid out as dividend has to be replaced with a dollar of new equity raised or a dollar of new borrowing.

5.2.3   *Retained Earnings*

When no dividend is paid, or the dividend is less than the full amount of earnings, a fund of undistributed earnings builds up. To record this on the balance sheet, a category of equity is established called retained earnings. It is increased by net income, and decreased by net loss and/or dividends paid each year. Movements of this fund are reported in the financial statement called the Statement of Retained Earnings.

In well-established companies, the balance of retained earnings may be substantial. It may be far higher than the balance in the common share capital account. The fact that many shares are worth more on the market than their initial issue price is reflected in the large size of these companies' retained earnings. Companies that distribute all their earnings as dividends tend to stay the same size: companies that reinvest earnings tend to grow.

It should be noted that increases in the share price are a direct benefit to the shareholders. They can sell their shares at a price greater than what they paid for them. The company gets no direct benefit from a rise in the share price; however, the company does get an indirect benefit. If the company were to make a new issue of shares, those shares could be sold at the new, higher market price. In this way, the company can get more cash for issuing the same number of shares. That is another reason that directors monitor the share price of their companies on a regular basis.

5.2.4   *Preferred Shares*

In addition to common shares, some (but not all) companies issue preferred shares. Preferred shares are a special class of shares that have some sort of preferential right attached to them. Typically, this is a right to receive a dividend before the common shareholders receive theirs. This can mean that the preferred shareholders get a dividend, while the common shareholders do not. To offset the advantage of the dividend preference, it is usual for the preferred dividend to be restricted in some way.

Other forms of preference exist, but they are less common and far less important. The preference may, for example, extend to preference in repayment of capital if the company is wound up. Some preferred shares have preferential voting privileges, too. An 8% cumulative preferred share, for example, may get nothing if the company has had a really bad year. It may get a dividend of 8%. If it does, the common shareholders may also get a dividend. The term *cumulative* in the name means that the 8% dividend accumulates if it is not paid and must be made good before common shareholders are entitled to anything.

A preferred share has a lower risk than a common share, and we would expect this to be reflected in a lower share price, as risk and return are positively correlated. For some investors, a lower-risk, lower-return investment is more suitable than a higher-risk common share, even in the same company.

There are other elements that may appear in the equity section of the balance sheet, but the ones referred to above (retained earnings, common shares, and preferred shares) are the important ones. The main thing to

---

Exhibit 5.3:   Changes in Owners' Equity

The following reasons exist for changes in owners' equity:

A. Increases
  1. Initial investment in the company:
     → assets increase, owners' equity (common shares) increases.
  2. New share issue in an established company:
     → assets increase, owners' equity (common shares) increases.
  3. Issue of preferred shares:
     → assets increase, owners' equity (preferred shares) increases.
  4. The company makes a profit (net income):
     → assets increase, owners' equity (retained earnings) increases.
  5. The assets are revalued:
     → assets increase; owners' equity (undistributable reserve) increases.

B. Decreases
  1. The company suffers a loss:
     → assets decrease, owners' equity (retained earnings) decreases.
  2. A dividend is paid:
     → assets decrease, owners' equity (retained earnings) decreases.
  3. Shares are repurchased and retired:
     → assets decrease, owners' equity (common shares or preferred shares and retained earnings) decreases.
  4. The company is discontinued:
     → all assets are realized; all liabilities are paid.
     → if there is anything left over, i.e., (assets – liabilities) > 0, it is distributed to the shareholders: first to preferred shareholders; then, the remainder to common shareholders.

---

remember is that owners' equity represents the owners' residual interest in the net assets of the company. (See Exhibit 5.3.)

Legally, this would mean that if the company were to be liquidated, preferred shareholders would get anything left after the creditors had been paid off. In practice, this seldom happens. Instead, shareholders realize their investment by selling their shares through a stock market.

5.2.5   *Limited Liability*

One of the most important features of shares is that they give the owner a limited exposure to risk. In the case of an individual trading on his/her own, or in the case of a partnership, the owners are exposed to a high level of risk. If the business fails, not only can the business assets be used to pay the business debts, but also the personal property of the owners can be seized to pay business debts. If the business is incorporated as a limited liability company, then shareholders cannot be held personally responsible for company debts.

This is only realistic: if a shareholder in a major corporation were to be personally liable for all corporate debts then no one would ever risk investing and the capital market could not function. The concept of limited liability is essential to the functioning of a society where the management of major corporations is separate from their ownership.

This does not imply that shareholders cannot lose money: they most certainly can, but their maximum loss is measurable, so that they can make intelligent investing decisions.

If a shareholder invests money directly into a company by buying its shares, that investment is always "at risk". If I invest $100,000 in a start-up company and that company fails, I will lose my $100,000. If an investor buys shares through the stock market (from an existing shareholder) for $100,000 and the company fails he will lose his $100,000. In both cases, however, the maximum loss will be the $100,000 invested: no one can ask the shareholder for any additional contribution, no matter how badly the company fails and no matter how big its debts were when it failed.

The limited liability concept applies to all classes of shares: common (ordinary) shares, preferred shares, and others.

The limited liability of shareholders is probably the main reason a company would decide to incorporate rather than trade as a partnership or as an individual.

5.3   Summary

According to the accounting equation (assets = liabilities + equity) the assets of the business are funded either from borrowings (liabilities) or by owners' equity. Liabilities are listed on the balance sheet under the general headings of current liabilities (to be paid within a year) and long-term liabilities (to be paid beyond a year). Liabilities are valued at the amounts for which they are going to be settled. The difference between the total value of assets on the balance sheet and the total value of liabilities on the balance sheet is the equity, which is owned by the shareholders. The equity may include sub-classifications for different types of share (e.g., preferred shares, common shares) and will also include the balance of retained earnings or undistributed profits.

Appendix 5.1
Sarbanes-Oxley Act and Bill 198

As a direct response to corporate accounting scandals that had occurred in companies such as Enron, WorldCom, and Xerox, in 2002 a piece of U.S. legislation called the *Sarbanes-Oxley Act* was passed. Canadian companies that have U.S. operations and report to U.S. authorities are directly affected by Sarbanes-Oxley.

Canada followed the Sarbanes-Oxley lead by passing Bill 198 shortly afterward. This affects all Canadian public companies. Although they are not identical, the effect of both pieces of legislation is similar.

A greater responsibility for the financial statements and the control systems that underlie them has been placed on the chief executive officer and the chief financial officer of public companies. They will both have to sign explicit statements that they have satisfied themselves that both the control systems are adequate and the financial statements are accurate. These declarations may be used as evidence if it is subsequently discovered that controls were inadequate and/or the financial statements were inaccurate.

Auditors will be required to be more independent of their clients than they were previously: for example, they will not be allowed to act as both auditor of and management consultant to any client.

In separate Canadian legislation a Canadian Public Accountability Board has been established to provide independent oversight of the audit process.

The objective throughout all these changes is to increase investor confidence in the information that companies publish about their financial activities.

Appendix 5.2
The Mechanics of Accounting:
The Balance Sheet

This appendix continues our introduction to the debits and credits of accounting. It will, however, be briefer than the last one. As we saw in Appendix 3.5 of Chapter 3, every revenue and expense transaction has a direct effect on the balance sheet: for example, every revenue transaction has a debit to Cash or to Accounts Receivable as well as a credit to Revenue; the measurement of Cost of Goods Sold also revalues the Inventory account. In short, we cannot separate income measurement from balance sheet changes — it is the nature of double-entry accounting. The following table lists the balance sheet account transactions we have already seen when we studied the corresponding income statement transactions in Appendix 3.5 of Chapter 3.

Income statement account transaction (Chapter 3, Appendix 3.5)	Balance sheet account affected
Revenue	Cash
	Accounts Receivable
	Other Liabilities
	— Liability for Book Returns
	— Deferred Revenue
Bad Debt Expense	Accounts Receivable (including Allowance for Doubtful Debts)
Cost of Goods Sold	Inventory
	Accounts Payable
	Cash
Overhead Expenses — accruals	Accounts Payable
— deferrals	Prepaid Expense
Amortization	Buildings, Plant, and Equipment (including accumulated amortization)

As we can see, the basic accounting for transactions involving a number of balance sheet accounts, including most of the important asset and current liability accounts, have already been covered in Appendix 3.5 of Chapter 3. In this appendix, we will complete our coverage of the mechanics of accounting for the balance sheet and income statement with the following three topics: intangible assets, borrowing money, and share issue.

Although the presentation in this appendix for each of these topics is complete in itself and can be read on its own, it may be helpful to refer to the general discussion in this and the next chapter:

- Intangible assets — Chapter 4, section 4.2.2.4
- Borrowing money — Chapter 5, sections 5.1.4 and 5.1.6
- Share issue — Chapter 5, section 5.2.1

Intangible Assets

We have studied the accounting for tangible long-term assets, such as property, plant, and equipment. In all cases the cost of these assets is *capitalized* (shown as an asset on the balance sheet), and, with the exception of land, the cost (less any estimated salvage value) is then amortized over its expected useful life on one basis or another. (See Exhibit 5A4.1,) Only land, which has an indefinite useful life, is not amortized. Natural resources is another tangible long-term asset, commonly seen on the balance sheets of industries involved in primary resource exploitation. The accounting is very similar to plant and equipment — the asset is written off over its expected useful life. The difference is that the expense is called *depletion* rather than amortization. The credit is made to a contra-asset account called *accumulated depletion* or directly against the asset account.

Accounting for long-term *intangible assets* is in some respects the same as for tangible long-term assets, but under new provisions of GAAP there is an additional distinction to be made, and then, for one class of these assets, a different accounting treatment.

Just as for tangible long-term assets, only those intangible assets acquired at a cost are accounted for. It is important to emphasize this in discussing intangible assets because many of them have a value far beyond their cost. The example of Coca-Cola's trademark is cited in the text. The value of this trademark is estimated at $74 billion. Although it is difficult to identify the carrying cost of the Coca-Cola trademark itself carried on the company's balance sheet (all the company's trademarks are aggregated on the balance sheet, along with other intangibles), it cannot be much more than $2 billion and is probably less. Although trademark costs have been written off over the years (see below), it is most unlikely that the total costs capitalized over the years have been much above the current carrying cost.

There are two categories of intangible assets: finite-life and indefinite-life intangible assets. *Finite-life* intangible assets are those that can be said to have a limited life. Examples are patents, copyrights, and leasehold improvements. Once this life has been established, these assets are subject to amortization like tangible long-term assets. The differences are that typically there is no residual value and the credit side of the amortization entry is made directly against the asset, rather than to a contra "accumulated amortization" account. There is also one proviso (which is also true for tangible long-term assets): if there is reason to think the carrying value (unamortized cost) of the intangible has been *impaired*, the asset must be written down to its realizable value. This is discussed in the next paragraph.

Indefinite-life intangible assets have an unlimited life. Indefinite-life intangible assets include trademarks and goodwill. These assets are not subject to amortization. On the other hand, they are subject to an annual impairment test. If it is deemed that the carrying value of the intangible

Exhibit 5A4.1

You will often see the terms *expense* and *capitalize* used as verbs. This use arises when something is purchased and a decision must be made as to whether the *cost* is to be debited to an expense account or to an asset account. This decision is independent of how the purchase is financed — payment by cash, on account, or through the issue of long-term debt or shares.

Let's consider an example. You own a small restaurant. Nearby is a delivery pizza outlet whose owner, John Tucci, wants to retire. The pizzeria has a well-recognized name in the neighbourhood with the name serving also as the phone number, PIZZA99. You can easily continue his business and integrate it with your current operations at relatively low additional cost beyond staff and ingredients. It will be a profitable addition. You know the name is valuable and the owner is ready to sell it, but he wants to sell everything related to the business. His premises, including kitchen equipment, are rented but he has a large, relatively new outside sign and a six-month supply of pizza boxes and advertising flyers, all with the name and phone number prominently displayed. After some negotiations, you agree to pay him $50,000 for the trademarked name, the phone number, the sign, and the flyers. It is all of value to you. You would need a sign and it would cost you $10,000. His has a 10-year useful life, with no residual value. The boxes and advertising material, always necessary, would cost $3,000 and $1,000, respectively. The terms are $5,000 cash and the balance in one year at 5% simple interest. How do you account for the transaction? (It is now June 1, the middle of your financial year.) The boxes and advertising material are consumables, so you must *expense* these. The rest is *capitalized*: the sign as equipment and the balance as an indefinite-life intangible, trademark, or goodwill. The entry will look like this:

Date	Accounts/Description	Dr	Cr
June 1/XX	Supplies {SE — expense}	3,000	
	Advertising {SE — expense}	1,000	
	Equipment {asset}	10,000	
	Trademark {asset}	36,000	
	Cash {asset}		5,000
	Note Payable {liability}		45,000

Purchase of assets of pizzeria, for cash and one year note @ 5%

Starting at year-end, the equipment will be amortized (see Chapter 3, Appendix 3.5). We discuss the treatment of the trademark above; loans and other borrowings are dealt with below.

has been *impaired*, i.e., that it will not be realized in the normal course of business, the impairment loss must be recognized; in other words, the asset must be written down to its realizable value. Assume that purchased goodwill was being carried on the balance sheet at $500,000. If, after the annual impairment test, its fair value was deemed to be $200,000, the difference would have to be written off against the year's operations as follows:

Date	Accounts/Description	Dr	Cr
Year-end XX	Impairment Charge {SE — expense}	300,000	
	Goodwill {asset}		300,000

Recognition of the loss of goodwill after impairment test.

Borrowing Money

A liability or a debt is a promise to transfer an asset — usually, but not always, cash — to the creditor in the future. It typically arises out of a transaction undertaken before the balance sheet date, with the settlement, the transfer of the asset, to take place in the future. The asset transfer, when it occurs, extinguishes the liability.

One liability we have studied is deferred revenue, which arises out of an incomplete revenue transaction that will be settled when the goods or services contracted for are delivered to the customer. Actually, deferred revenue is somewhat exceptional as liabilities go since it will be settled with goods or services, not cash. Most liabilities are settled by the company's paying cash. Such liabilities are what we usually think of as debts — an obligation to pay money in the future. A common characteristic of a debt is that it usually accrues an interest charge from when it is contracted until it is repaid. Accounts payable and accrued liabilities, which arise out of the company's purchase of goods and services on credit, comprise one common type of liability. We have seen examples of the accounting treatment of accounts payables and accrued liabilities. Loans are the other important type of liability, and when companies take advantage of such debt financing, the liability on the company's balance sheet can be quite significant. Although interest may or may not be charged by trade creditors on accounts payable, interest will always be charged by lenders on loans, and the resulting expense on the income statement is usually material.

Bank Loans. For most companies, even those that are just marginally profitable, day-to-day operations are largely self-financing. Cash is required to pay employees, suppliers, and other trade creditors; the cash comes from cash sales and collection of receivables. There is typically an annual cycle, however, and even if over the whole year operating cash flow is positive, there is variation from month to month. In some months the cash flow is positive but in others it is negative. Providing cash to bridge these cycles is the role of banks and other short-term lenders (see section 5.1.4.). Once a bank agrees to lend a company money, "demand loan" financing is relatively flexible. Within the terms of the loan, the amount borrowed can be increased when necessary and is reduced whenever possible.

Consider the following situation. A company has an agreement with its bank that it can borrow in units of $5,000 and can repay it on the same basis. Interest is charged at the end of each month on the average daily balance of the loan in the month and deducted from the company's chequing account. The company must provide the bank with annual financial statements through the period of this agreement and monthly statements at any time that there is loan balance outstanding — in this example, covering the first quarter of 2011. Fashion Fabrics Distributing Ltd. borrows $40,000 on January 1, 2011, increases the loan by $20,000 on February 1, reduces the loan by $50,000 on March 15, and pays off the entire balance on March 31, 2011. The current interest rate is 6% per annum. The relevant journal entries and T-accounts, January through March 2011, are shown as well as the relevant sections of the financial statements at the end of the quarter. The only evidence of the loan on the statements is the interest expense on the income statement. Since the loan was completely paid off by the end of March, no liability remains on that date. If a balance sheet had been drawn up while money was owing, Bank Loan would be the first item under current liabilities.

Date	Accounts/Description	Dr	Cr
Jan. 1/11	Cash {asset}	40,000	
	Bank Loan {liability}		40,000
	Demand loan advance		
Jan. 31/11	Interest Expense {SE — expense}	204	
	Cash {asset}		204
	Interest on demand loan, Jan.: {31/365 × 40,000} @ 6%.		
Feb. 1/11	Cash {asset}	20,000	
	Bank Loan {liability}		20,000
	Demand loan advance		
Feb. 28/11	Interest Expense {SE — expense}	276	
	Cash {asset}		276
	Interest on demand loan, Feb.: {28/365 × 60,000} @ 6%		
Mar. 15/11	Bank Loan {liability}	50,000	
	Cash {asset}		50,000
	Demand loan repayment		
Mar. 31/11	Bank Loan {liability}	10,000	
	Interest Expense {SE — expense}	174	
	Cash {asset}		10,174
	Demand loan repayment & interest, Mar.: {(15/365 × 60,000) + (16/365 × 10,000)} @ 6%		

Cash

2011	X	X
Jan. 1 loan advance	40,000	
Jan. 31 interest		204
	X	X
Feb. 1 loan advance	20,000	
Feb. 28 interest		276
	X	X
Mar. 15 loan repayment		50,000
Mar. 31 loan repayment		10,000
Mar. 31 interest		174
	X	X

Bank Loan

2011		
Jan. 1 loan advance		40,000
Jan. 31 balance		40,000
Feb. 1 loan advance		20,000
Feb. 28 balance		60,000
Mar. 15 loan repayment	50,000	
Mar. 31 loan repayment	10,000	
Mar. 31 balance	0	

Interest Expense

2011	
Jan. 31	204
Feb. 28	276
Mar. 31	174
bal., 1st Q.	654

Interest accrues and is payable monthly. At any time the balance in the Bank Loan account shows the amount owing. If financial statements were drawn up at the end of the quarter, we would see interest expense on the income statement:

Fashion Fabrics Distributing Ltd.
Partial Income Statement
for First Quarter, 2011

....

Expenses

....

Interest on bank loan $654

....

Long-term Debt. Long-term debt is usually incurred for reasons other than normal operations, such as the purchase of property plant and equipment, repayment of long-term debt coming due, or the development of a new line of business or general expansion (either of which could include the purchase of another company). As a rule, such loans are large relative to the size of the company; moreover, by definition, the principal repayments are far in the future. To protect the lenders against all the risks this entails, the terms of such loans tend to be quite complex (see section 5.1.6), with the consequences of default clearly spelt out. One standard feature of long-term debt contracts is a fixed schedule of repayment of interest and principal. We will follow through such an example.

No Down Time Ltd. is a successful Web hosting company. Using internally generated funds, the company has financed its growth from an operation with one refurbished server in the owner's basement to a state-of-the-art installation, generating revenues of $500,000. The company has a reputation for uninterrupted service thanks to the hard work of the owner, Joya Dutt, but she is now in the unenviable position of having to turn away business because of the capacity limitations of her equipment. She has accumulated $50,000 in investable funds but the next logical stage of expansion requires an investment in equipment of approximately $250,000.

It is now early January 2011. On the strength of her reputation and prospects, a hardware supplier is prepared to sell her $225,000 worth of equipment (including tax, delivery, and set-up) for $25,000 cash, taking back the balance of $200,000 as a term loan secured on the computer assets. Ms. Dutt has accepted the offer and the transaction is to go through on February 1, 2011. The loan interest rate is 4.63%, payable semi-annually. The principal is to be repaid in $50,000 instalments at the end of years 2, 3, 4, and 5 (i.e., February 1, 2013, 2014, 2015, 2016). The company's year-end is December 31.

The supplier is essentially lending its customer $200,000 for the purpose of purchasing this equipment. In that sense it is as if No Down Time is buying goods on credit with an extended-term account payable. The difference is that interest is now an explicit feature of the debt. As a result, pre-determined payments of both interest and principal as well as year-end accruals must be made on specified dates. The accounting is, accordingly, more involved. The journal entries are as follows.

Date	Accounts/Description	Dr	Cr
Feb. 1/11	Computer Equipment {asset}	225,000	
	Cash {asset}		25,000
	Term Loan {liability}		200,000
	Purchase of computer equipment for cash and term loan		
Aug. 1/11	Interest Expense {SE — expense}	4,630	
	Cash {asset}		4,630
	Term loan interest payment, 6 months to Aug. 1, 2011 $200,000 @ 4.63% × 6/12		
Dec. 31/11	Interest Expense {SE — expense}	3,858	
	Accrued Interest Payable {liability}		3,858
	Accrued term loan interest to Dec. 31, 2011 $200,000 @ 4.63% × 5/12		
Feb. 1/12	Accrued Interest Payable {liability}	3,858	
	Interest Expense {SE — expense}	772	
	Cash {asset}		4,630
	Term loan interest payment, 6 months to Feb. 1, 2012 $200,000 @ 4.63% × 6/12		

[On August 1, 2012, and December 31, 2012, entries identical to the August 1, 2011, interest payment and the December 31, 2011, accrual will be made.]

Date	Accounts/Description	Dr	Cr
Feb. 1/13	Accrued Interest Payable {liability}	3,858	
	Interest Expense {SE — expense}	772	
	Cash {asset}		4,630
	Term loan interest payment, 6 months to Feb. 1, 2013 $200,000 @ 4.63% × 6/12		
Feb. 1/13	Term Loan Payable {liability}	50,000	
	Cash {asset}		50,000
	First instalment of term loan repayment		

[The cycle of entries — interest and repayment — continues until the loan is fully repaid on February 1, 2012. Each year's interest cycle — August 1 payment, December 31 accrual, and following February 1 payment will be smaller as the principal is reduced at the beginning of the cycle. For example, the six-month interest payments on August 1, 2013, and February 1, 2014, will each be $3,473. The related accrual on December 31, 2013, will be correspondingly smaller as well.]

Shares Issue

In Appendix 2.1 to Chapter 2, on pages 43–44, transaction #1, shares were issued for Example Co. Ltd. However, we had not introduced the journal entry form at that point, so we will take this opportunity to review this transaction as a standard journal entry.

We know that the shares were issued for $25,000. These will be common shares because there must always be a residual class of shares outstanding — usually called *common shares* — and thus the first shares issued must be common shares. The number of shares issued was not indicated. In a sense, the number of shares in the first issue is arbitrary. All the same, the number would have to be specified at this point. If there is only one shareholder, there need be only one share, worth 100% of the company. (Crown corporations owned 100% by the government may issue one share, but this is exceptional.) Typically, the number of shares is big enough to allow for the division of ownership envisaged for the company. It is convenient for this to be multiples of 100 shares or more. (Of course, if there are subsequent share issues, the number of shares outstanding will increase.) In this case, let us assume that the initial share issue is 1,000 shares. That means that on the date of issue, a share is worth $25. We will assume that these are not par value shares, which is normally the case for common shares. What this means is that the full amount of the proceeds is credited to share capital.

Date	Accounts/Description	Dr	Cr
Dec. 31/11	Cash {asset}	25,000	
	Common shares {SE}		25,000
	Issue of 1,000 shares @ $25		

Note that the actual account within the share capital (or capital stock) section of shareholders' equity to which the common shares are credited is called *Common Shares* (or, less commonly in Canada, *Common Stock*).

Self-Study Problems

1. As at December 31, 2011, Charley Farley had owner's equity of
    $46,000. He owed $5,000 to his suppliers and there was a long-term
    bank loan of $51,000. Accrued utilities amounted to $1,000.

    [Note: This is a continuation of Self-Study Problem #1 in Chapter 4
    on page 156. You may need to refer back to that problem to help
    in doing this one.]

    Required
    (a) Show how these would appear in the Liabilities and Equity
         part of his balance sheet.
    (b) What was the current ratio?
    (c) What was the quick ratio?
    (d) What were the debt-to-equity and debt-to-assets ratios?

2. As at January 31, 2001, Bombardier Inc. had a balance of retained
    earnings of $2,660 million. During the year ended January 31, 2002,
    the company made net income of $391 million. Dividends (and other
    minor adjustments) were $266 million.
      The share capital as at January 31, 2001, was $1,170 million:
    $300 million of preferred shares and $870 million of common shares.
    New common shares were issued under employee share option plans
    in the amount of $26 million.

    Required
    (a) Prepare a statement of retained earnings for the year ended
         January 31, 2002.
    (b) What was the maximum dividend legally payable as at January
         31, 2002?
    (c) Calculate the balance of preferred shares, common shares, and
         total share capital.

3. Bombardier Inc. had 12 million preferred shares, each of $25, for
    a total of $300 million of preferred shares in issue as at January
    31, 2002. These paid a quarterly dividend on $0.34375 ($1.375
    per share per year). As at February 18, 2003, they were trading
    at $17.25 per share. The preferred shares were cumulative and
    redeemable.

    Required
    (a) How much was the total annual dividend on the preferred
         shares?
    (b) If the dividend on the preferred shares was passed up in 2003,
         what would happen in 2004?
    (c) What return on equity did the dividend represent for someone
         buying a Bombardier preferred share as at February 18, 2003?

Solutions

1. (a) **Liabilities and Equity**
Current liabilities:

Trade payables	$ 5,000
Accrued utilities	1,000
	$ 6,000
Long-term liabilities (bank loan)	51,000
Total liabilities	$ 57,000
Owners' equity:	46,000
Total liabilities & owners' equity	$103,000

(b) Current ratio:

$\quad$ = current assets ÷ current liabilities
$\quad$ = $13,000 ÷ $6,000
$\quad$ = 2.2 : 1

(c) Quick ratio:

$\quad$ = (current assets − inventory) ÷ current liabilities
$\quad$ = ($13,000 − $1,500) ÷ $6,000
$\quad$ = 1.9 : 1

(d) Debt-to-equity ratio:

$\quad$ = total debt ÷ owners' equity
$\quad$ = ($57,000 ÷ $46,000) × 100%
$\quad$ = 124%

Debt-to-assets ratio:

$\quad$ = total debt ÷ total assets
$\quad$ = ($57,000 ÷ $103,000) × 100%
$\quad$ = 55%

2. (a)

Bombardier Inc.
Statement of Retained Earnings
for the Year Ended January 31, 2002 ($ million)

Retained earnings as at January 31, 2001	$2,660
Add: Net income for year ended January 31, 2002	391
Available:	3,051
Less: Dividends paid	266
Retained earnings as at January 31, 2002	$2,785

(b) The maximum dividend legally payable would have been $3,051.

(c)

Bombardier Inc.
Share Capital
as at January 31, 2002 ($ million)

Preferred shares (same as opening balance)		$ 300
Common shares		
Opening balance	$870	
Issued during the year	26	
Balance of common shares		896
Total share capital		$1,196

3. (a) Total annual preferred share dividend:

      = 12 million × $1.375

      = $16.5 million

(b) Because the share is cumulative, if the preferred share dividend is passed up in any year it is carried forward, and it must be made good before the common shares can receive a dividend.

(c) Return on equity (based on dividends):

      = dividend ÷ share price

      = ($1.375 ÷ $17.25) × 100%

      = 7.97%

Discussion Questions and Problems

Discussion Questions

1. What is the definition of a *liability*?
2. What is the definition of *equity*?
3. How are liabilities valued for inclusion in the balance sheet?
4. Which accounting principle(s) apply to valuing liabilities?
5. In what order do liabilities appear in the balance sheet?
6. What are the distinguishing features of a preferred share?
7. Why is retained earnings shown separately from common equity?
8. Is retained earnings cash, or is it some other type of asset? Who owns it?
9. How is common equity valued for inclusion in the balance sheet?
10. Which would you rather have: $10,000 owed to you by a company or $10,000 invested in the company's equity?

Appendix 5.2

11. "... we cannot separate income measurement from balance sheet changes — it is the nature of double entry accounting (p. 179)."
    (a) Give three examples of transactions that combine income measurement with a balance sheet change.
    (b) Give one example of a transaction that measures income (revenue or expense) that does not involve a balance sheet change.
12. A patent is a finite-life intangible asset, whereas a trademark is a finite-life intangible asset. Why are these two assets in different categories and how do the accounting treatments differ?

Problems

1. Crete Co. has $5,000,000 of retained earnings and $2,000,000 of common shares. The company owes $500,000 in income tax, which is due next month. The company has borrowed $1,600,000 from the bank as a demand loan (payable whenever the bank calls it). There is a 5-year mortgage of $7,000,000 on the company's property. Trade payables are $3,250,000, and trade receivables are $4,850,000. Unpaid wages are $250,000. There is a debenture loan of $3,000,000, payable in 10 years. Accrued expenses are $4,000,000. Preference shares are $1,000,000. The dividend paid was $1,000,000, and interest expense for the year was $2,550,000.

    Required
    Show how these amounts would be shown in the liabilities and equity section of the balance sheet.

2. Damart Inc. has the following assets and liabilities:
    - Cash: $75,000
    - Inventory: $900,000
    - Trade receivables: $725,000
    - Long-term assets (net of amortization): $900,000
    - Trade payables: $775,000

- Bank overdraft (short-term): $500,000
- Debenture loan: $300,000

Required
(a) Calculate the current ratio.
(b) Calculate the quick ratio.
(c) Is the company adequately liquid?
(d) What would happen to the liquidity ratios if the company issued $850,000 of new common shares for cash?
(e) What would happen to the liquidity ratios if the company borrowed $850,000 of long-term debt?
(f) What would happen to the liquidity ratios if the company borrowed $850,000 of short-term debt?

3. Elegant Ltd. has the following assets and liabilities:
- Cash: $90,000
- Inventory: $185,000
- Trade receivables: $275,000
- Long-term assets (net of amortization): $550,000
- Trade payables: $275,000
- Debenture loan: $550,000

Required

(a) Calculate the following ratios:
    (i) The debt-to-equity ratio
    (ii) The debt-to-assets ratio
(b) Comment on the leverage of the company.

4. Farhan Inc. has common shares of $1,000,000 and retained earnings of $1,000,000. Show how each of the following independent transactions would affect the common shares and retained earnings:

(a) Paid a dividend of $200,000 in cash.
(b) Issued additional common shares for $500,000 in cash.
(c) Issued additional common shares to acquire a competitor's business. (The acquired business had a fair market value of $600,000.)
(d) The company made a net loss of $200,000 for the year.
(e) Half the common shares were repurchased by the company for $400,000 cash.

5. GB Co. has the following balance sheet:

Current assets			Current liabilities		
Cash	$ 25,000		Trade payables	$ 200,000	
Trade receivables	475,000		Bank loan	100,000	
Inventory	100,000			$ 300,000	
	$ 600,000				
			Long-term liabilities	300,000	
Long-term assets	900,000		Total liabilities	$ 600,000	
			Equity		
			Common shares	$ 350,000	
			Retained earnings	550,000	
				$ 900,000	
	$1,500,000			$1,500,000	

Required
(a) Calculate the current ratio.
(b) Calculate the quick ratio.
(c) Is the company liquid or illiquid?
(d) Calculate the debt-to-assets ratio.
(e) Calculate the debt-to-equity ratio.
(f) Is the company over-leveraged?

6. GB Co. has the following balance sheet:

Current assets		Current liabilities	
Cash	$ 25,000	Trade payables	$ 200,000
Trade receivables	475,000	Bank loan	100,000
Inventory	100,000		$ 300,000
	$ 600,000		
		Long-term liabilities	300,000
Long-term assets	900,000	Total liabilities	$ 600,000
		Equity	
		Common shares	$ 350,000
		Retained earnings	550,000
			$ 900,000
	$1,500,000		$1,500,000

GB Co. has just gone bankrupt. The following amounts were collected from the realization of the assets:

• Cash: $25,000
• Trade receivables: $200,000
• Inventory: $50,000
• Long-term assets: $500,000

Required
(a) Show how much total cash the shareholders would get.
(b) Would it have made any difference to answer (a) if the long-term liabilities were secured against the long-term assets?

7. Haldimand Inc. has the following balance sheet:

Current assets		Current liabilities	
Cash	$ 10,000	Trade payables	$ 250,000
Trade receivables	370,000	Bank loan	200,000
Inventory	520,000		$ 450,000
	$ 900,000		
		Long-term liabilities	300,000
Long-term assets	600,000	Total liabilities	$ 750,000
		Equity	
		Common shares	$ 350,000
		Retained earnings	400,000
			$ 750,000
	$1,500,000		$1,500,000

The directors are considering giving out dividends, and they have two options:

• Making a cash dividend of $100,000
• Making a stock dividend of $100,000 (that is, they will give the shareholders additional shares with a value of $100,000)

Required

(a) If the directors decide to go with cash dividend, is that legal?

(b) Is it possible for the company to make that cash dividend?

(c) What is likely to happen to the value of individual shares after the cash dividend is paid?

(d) If the directors decide to go with stock dividend, is that legal?

(e) Is it possible for the company to issue stock dividend?

(f) What is likely to happen to the value of individual shares after the stock dividend is paid?

8. State what will happen to the owners' equity in a company's balance sheet in each of the following transactions:

(a) The promoters of the company made an initial investment of $500,000, receiving 500 common shares in exchange.

(b) The promoters borrowed $400,000 from the bank.

(c) The promoters listed the company on the Toronto Stock Exchange and sold 2,000 shares to the general public for $2,000,000.

(d) The promoters sold 100,000, 10% cumulative preference shares to the general public for $1,000,000.

(e) The company paid interest on the bank loan of $40,000.

(f) The company made a net loss of $50,000 for its first year of trading.

(g) The long-term assets of the company are re-valued. The assets had cost $250,000, but their assessed worth is now $300,000.

(h) In the second year of trading, the company made a profit of $500,000.

(i) The company paid a dividend on the preference shares, $100,000, in respect of year one, plus $100,000 for year two.

(j) The company paid a $200,000 dividend on the common shares.

9. In November 2008 you bought 500 shares in Nortel for $0.90 each. The Nortel shares were recommended by a friend as a good recovery prospect (the shares had been over $1,000 in 2000 and over $1.00 earlier in 2008). Due to the economic slowdown, Nortel did not do well, and it is reporting a huge loss for 2008. In January 2009 the company filed for Chapter 11 bankruptcy protection. How much will you lose?

10. Klaxon Co. has the following balance sheet:

Current assets			Current liabilities		
Cash	$ 100,000		Trade payables	$ 500,000	
Trade receivables	255,000		Bank loan	300,000	
Inventory	345,000			$ 800,000	
	$ 600,000				
			Long-term liability	300,000	
Long-term assets	600,000		Total liabilities	$1,100,000	
			Equity		
			Common shares	$ 50,000	
			Retained earnings	50,000	
				$ 100,000	
	$1,200,000			$1,200,000	

Additional information:

• The long-term liability is a mortgage loan secured on the long-term assets.
• The bank loan is secured against the trade receivables.
• The trade payables are secured against the inventory.

The company has filed for bankruptcy. The trade receivables were collected and realized at $250,000. The inventory was sold for $200,000, and the long-term assets were sold for $400,000.

Required
Show how the proceeds of sale of the company assets would be allocated to the various creditors and the shareholders.

Appendix 5.2

11. Wilkins Ltd. has an arrangement with the bank to borrow money on a demand loan basis to finance large inventory purchases from late summer through mid-fall. The loan is repaid over the winter. Interest is charged at the end of each month to Wilkins's chequing account on the average daily balance of the loan outstanding that month. In 2010, Wilkins borrowed $75,000 on September 1 and another $50,000 on October 15. It made a $40,000 repayment on December 15 and paid off the balance at the end of February 2011. The interest rate was 5.5% in September 2010; on October 1, it fell to 5.25% and remained there until June 2011. Wilkins's year-end is December 31.

Required
(a) Prepare journal entries for the transactions related to the demand loan in 2010 and post them to T-accounts.
(b) Assuming that these are the only loan transactions, show how they would appear on the balance sheet and income statement in the December 31, 2010, financial statements.

12. On March 1, 2011, Dorricks Ltd. borrowed $500,000, issuing a five-year mortgage bond. No principal payments are due until the end of the five-year loan period, but interest, at a nominal annual rate of 4%, is to be paid every six months beginning September 1, 2011.The company's year-end is December 31.

Required
(a) Using T-accounts, record the 2011 transactions related to the mortgage bond.
(b) Show the relevant sections of the balance sheet and income statement in the December 31, 2011, financial statements.

13. Prepare journal entries for the transactions described in Problem 8.

6

Statement of Cash Flows

Learning
Objectives

After studying this chapter you should be able to describe and explain the following:

→ The components of the statement of cash flows (statement of changes in financial position)

→ The relationship between the statement of cash flows and the other financial statements

---

6.1   Introduction

In the previous chapters we dealt with three of the required financial statements: the income statement, the balance sheet, and the statement of retained earnings. In this chapter we shall deal with the statement of cash flows.

One of the crucial aspects of running a business is to ensure that it does not run out of cash. If there is insufficient cash available to pay the creditors, the company is in danger of being declared bankrupt and closed down. This is a serious external threat, and it happens to large numbers of companies every year. Avoiding bankruptcy may be impossible in some circumstances, but short-term cash management can help in avoiding unnecessary bankruptcy.

Within the company, the chief financial officer (CFO) will engage in cash forecasting and cash budgeting. Based on existing cash, accounts receivable, inventory, sales forecasts, trade credits, other payables, production plans, capital expenditure plans, etc., the CFO will prepare a detailed prediction of cash flows for the immediate future. This cash budget should alert management to any impending problems coming up in the next one to six months. If the company receives adequate notice, it may be able to avoid a potential problem. The company can arrange perhaps to take a short-term loan from the bank, or delay payment on its trade payables, or defer purchase of some plant and equipment. Cash budgets are discussed more fully in Chapter 8.

All well-managed companies carry out cash budgeting. When applying for a bank loan, one of the most important questions the bank lending officer will ask is to see the company's cash budget to ensure the loan is planned and its repayment is a realistic probability. Cash budgets are, however, rather confidential documents, and apart from sharing them with a potential lender, they are not publicly available.

What *is* publicly available is one of the financial reports called the Statement of Cash Flows (or Statement of Changes in Financial Position). This reports on the past (like all the financial statements) rather than predicting the future (as a budget would). It deals exclusively in cash flows, not in the accrual-based revenues and expenses of the income statement.

The cash flow statement is presented in four parts:

1. Cash from operations
2. Cash from (or used in) financing activities
3. Cash from (or used in) investing activities
4. Change in cash

We will discuss each part in detail using the 2010 cash flow statement of Google Inc.

6.2   Cash from Operations

In this section the cash generated from the normal business of the company is reported. The starting point is net income. From operating income, interest and taxes are deducted: these are related to ongoing operations, and they have to be paid in cash. In the simplest of businesses, run entirely on a cash basis, net income is the same as cash inflow. In more complex businesses, the operating income has to be adjusted in several ways to get cash flow.

First, there may be expenses included in the annual income statement that are not represented by cash outflows at this time. Principal among these is the amortization expense. Amortization, you will remember, refers to a situation where a long-term asset has been bought, and its cost is gradually allocated to the income statement over its useful life. The cash outflow in respect of that asset took place when it was bought. The amortization expense is a non-cash-flow expense. All amortization expenses and the like are added back to the operating income. If there were any non-cash revenues (these are much rarer), they would be deducted from operating income.

With the exception of amortization, the rest of the revenues and expenses in the income statement are more closely (though not perfectly) represented by cash receipts and cash payments. There may be differences, and if there are, they are reflected in changes in working capital. An expense that is not identical to its related cash flow results in an increase or decrease in payables and accruals. If the cash payment is less than the expense, the payables will rise; if the cash payment is more than the expense, the payables will fall. Revenue that is more than cash received results in receivables increasing; revenue that is less than cash received results in receivables falling. Inventory that is constant does not affect cash flows; inventory that is increasing causes a cash outflow; inventory that is decreasing results in a cash inflow.

We can address all these changes by looking at the working capital (current assets less current liabilities). In practice, because the fourth part of our cash flow statement will deal in the changes in cash itself, cash would be eliminated from the working capital. Operating income, then, is to be increased by any net fall in non-cash working capital, and decreased by any net increase in non-cash working capital

---

Exhibit 6.1: Cash from Operations — Google Inc.

Cash from operations is calculated as follows:

		Net income
	+	amortization (non-cash expense)
	+	net decrease in non-cash working capital
OR	–	net increase in non-cash working capital
	=	cash from operations

	2010 (US $ millions)
Net income (after tax and interest)	$ 8,505
Add: Amortization and other non-cash expenses	2,675
Less: Decrease in net current assets	(99)
Cash from operations	$11,081

In some circumstances, the result can be a negative figure: if, for example, instead of having an operating income, there is an operating loss; or, if the decrease in non-cash working capital is larger than the net income plus amortization. In those circumstances there would be a net amount of cash *used* in operations.

A positive flow of cash from operations is a sign of corporate health. Without it the company has to borrow to even stay alive. A company that shows cash used in operations is in a precarious situation.

For 2010, Google reported a net income (that is, income after charging all expenses, including tax and interest) of $8,505 million (all figures are in US dollars).

Included in the net income was a total of $2,675 million of expense (such as amortization) that did not result in a cash outflow, so this is added to the net income. Also, during 2010, Google's net current assets decreased by $99 million, so this is deducted from net income. The final tally is that Google's normal business operations caused an inflow of cash of $11,081 million. (See Exhibit 6.1.)

6.3 Cash from Financing Activities

The second section of the cash flow statement is cash from (or used in) financing activities. (See Exhibit 6.2.) Financing activities are those connected with the issuance or redemption of shares and the borrowing or repaying of long-term loans. Items such as interest and dividends that relate to financing may also be reported here.

Exhibit 6.2: **Cash from or Cash Used in Financing Activities — Google Inc.**

	2010 ($ millions)
Cash used in repurchasing shares, net of new issues	$ (413)
Cash from issuing long-term debt, net of repayments	3,463
Exchange rate adjustment	(19)
Cash from financing activities	**$ 3,031**

Google had a few small transactions in respect of the issue of incentive-based share awards, totalling $388 million and repurchased $801 million of stock. The net effect is that share transactions were a use of funds totalling $413 million. Google repaid $1,783 million of long-term debt and issued new short-term debt to bring in $5,246 million. The net cash inflow in respect of debt was $3,463 million. There was a minor adjustment of negative $19 million in respect of exchange rate adjustments. Total cash inflow from financing activities was $3,031 million.

If the company pays a dividend it appears in this financing section, as a use of funds. Google did not pay a dividend in 2010.

6.4 Cash from and Cash Used in Investing Activities

The third category in the report is the cash used to buy long-term assets (or, conceivably, the cash generated by selling long-term assets).

In 2010 Google spent $4,018 million on buying property, plant, and equipment. They also bought and sold marketable securities and other long-term assets at a net cash cost of $6,662 million. In total, $10,680 million was used in investing activities. (See Exhibit 6.3.)

Exhibit 6.3: **Cash from or Cash Used in Investing Activities — Google Inc.**

	2010 ($ millions)
Purchase of property, plant & equipment	$ 4,018
Purchase of other long-term assets, net	6,662
Cash used in investing activities	**$ 10,680**

Exhibit 6.4:   Statement of Cash Flows — Google Inc.

	2010 ($ millions)
Cash from operations	$ 11,081
Cash from financing activities	3,031
Cash used in investing activities	(10,680)
Increase in cash during the year	$ 3,432
Cash at start of 2010	10,198
Cash at end of 2010	$ 13,630

6.5   Change in Cash Balance

The last category in the cash flow statement is the change in cash itself, which can be obtained by comparing the cash level in the current year's balance sheet with the one in the previous year's.

In the case of Google Inc., the cash on hand at the start of 2010 was $10,198 million. The net effect of operations, financing, and investing activities was an increase in cash of $3,432 million. At the end of 2010 the cash balance was $13,630 million.

The whole cash flow statement for Google Inc. is shown in Exhibit 6.4.

6.6   Interpreting the Statement of Cash Flows

From the statement of cash flows in Exhibit 6.4, we observe that Google is a wildly successful company: it had a large positive cash flow from its normal trading operations. It invested in new long-term assets (which is a good sign of a company that is "investing for the future"). Apart from the minor transactions in respect of shares, the only question a rational analyst might ask is why Google issued long-term debt when it has such a substantial amount of cash sitting idle on the balance sheet?

6.7   The Statement of Cash Flows and the Functional Manager

This book is written for the use of functional mangers: by that we mean managers who are in charge of functional areas within the business, and that would include managers of production, marketing, research and development human resources, etc.

In the normal course of their day-to-day activities we would not expect the functional manager to be much involved with the cash flow statement. They have no role in creating it, they will seldom use it. Occasionally they would be involved. An awareness of the sources and uses of cash, and the normal amounts involved each year should inform managers about the likely reaction to their business suggestions.

For example, in the case of Google Inc., there is a ton of money available on the balance sheet and the "normal" business operations are bring in more cash each year. Knowing that, all the managers at Google should be asking themselves questions about what to do with it. Are there any competitors we could usefully buy? Is there a piece of equipment we could usefully purchase?

6.8   Summary

Cash flow analysis is one of the important parts of analyzing a company's past activities and future prospects. A stable, profitable company is internally self-sufficient in cash flow, and this is likely to be seen in a positive flow of cash from operations. The company's financing and investing activities are clearly revealed by referring to the cash flow effects of the actions it has taken. Cash from (or used in) operations, financing activities, and investing activities are reported in the statement of cash flows (also known as the statement of changes in financial positions).

Appendix 6.1
Example of a Cash Flow Statement

The cash flow statement demonstrated in the chapter is intentionally simple. A complete version for a large company such as Canadian Tire is rather more complex.

Canadian Tire is a retailer with outlets all over Canada. Its published financial statements (with all the supporting notes and information) is available on the Web at **www.canadiantire.ca**. (Follow the links: company information | investors | financial reports.)

Canadian Tire Corporation, Limited
Consolidated Statement of Cash Flows ($ millions)

	For the Year Ended	
	January 2, 2010	January 3, 2009
	(52 weeks)	(53 weeks)
Cash generated from (used for) operating activities:		
Net earnings	$ 335	$ 375
Items not affecting cash		
Depreciation & amortization	248	227
Net provision for loans receivable	181	87
Future income taxes	9	(42)
Employee future benefits expense	6	6
Other	4	8
Impairments on property, equipment & investments	3	5
Gain on disposals of property & equipment	(2)	(8)
Changes in fair value of derivative instruments	(11)	56
Gain on sales of loans receivable	(39)	(74)
Securitization loans receivable	(39)	(52)
	$ 695	$ 588
Changes in working capital components	(276)	(407)
Cash generated from operating activities	$ 419	$ 181
Investing Activities:		
Net securitization of loans receivable	$ (532)	$ (32)
Additions to property & equipment	(220)	(360)
Investment in loans receivable, net	(209)	(140)
Additions to intangible assets	(68)	(77)
Other long-term investments	(51)	(20)
Short-term investments	(38)	0
Other	(7)	(4)
Purchase of stores	(6)	(36)
Long-term receivables and other assets	(3)	(27)
Proceeds on disposal of property & equipment	28	240
Proceeds on disposal of mortgage portfolio	162	0
Cash used for investing activities	$ (944)	$ (456)

continued....

Canadian Tire Corporation, Limited
Consolidated Statement of Cash Flows ($ millions)

	For the Year Ended	
	January 2, 2010 (52 weeks)	January 3, 2009 (53 weeks)
Financing Activities:		
Net change in deposits	$ 917	$ 1,024
Issuance of long-term debt	200	0
Class A Non-Voting Share transactions	(1)	7
Repayment of long-term debt	(165)	(156)
Dividends	(69)	(67)
Cash generated from financing activities	$ 882	$ 808
Cash generated (used) in the year	$ 357	$ 535
Cash & cash equivalents at start of year	429	(106)
Cash & cash equivalents at end of year	$ 786	$ 429

Appendix 6.2

International Financial Reporting Standards

Introduction

Canadian Generally Accepted Accounting Principles (Canadian GAAP) have been the rule for all financial reporting in Canada. Effective January 1, 2011, they will co-exist with International Financial Reporting Standards (IFRS) for some Canadian companies.

One perspective on accounting has always been that there is "one best way" and that once that way has been decided upon, all companies everywhere should conform to it. However, the struggle to find that one best way has not been easy. In recent years this discussion has resolved to two main camps: on the one hand, there are the U.S. financial accounting standards; on the other hand, there is a worldwide movement toward IFRS.

The U.S. GAAP, driven by that country's extremely litigious society, is rules-based. All accounting situations are considered and the "correct" treatment is explicitly laid down as a rule. IFRS, by contrast, is more principle-driven. A consideration of the objectives of accounting is laid down, and appropriate accounting treatments are developed that aim to achieve those objectives while allowing for some flexibility of execution.

The completely opposite perspective to the "one best way" approach is that of international accounting: different situations call for different approaches to accounting. Countries will have different social, economic, political, and legal backgrounds; as a result, there are different methods of financial reporting. This gives rise to a diversity of GAAPs, either based on individual countries or on groups of countries that share similar backgrounds.

Unfortunately, however justified international accounting may be, it is a serious barrier to international investment. With the greater globalization of business generally and with particular respect to cross-border capitalization, many companies would wish to use the world's major capital markets to access funds. If a company is using a set of local accounting standards, then it will face problems accessing those markets.

Until recently, the problem was solved through a process known as reconciliation. If a company wanted to have its securities listed on the New York Stock Exchange (NYSE), it could do so supported by its local accounting reports, but it was required to add a statement that showed the effect of using U.S. GAAP on all the information reported.

As of 2011, more than 100 countries have adopted IFRS, and all Canadian Publicly Accountable Entities (PAEs) are required to use IFRS starting 2011. PAEs include all companies listed on a stock exchange. For non-PAEs, the situation remains that they may prepare their accounting reports using Canadian GAAP, but they have the option of using IFRS if they prefer to do so. Thus, IFRS and Canadian GAAP will exist side by side for now.

The differences between Canadian GAAP and IFRS may be grouped under three headings: changes in the conceptual framework; changes in presentation, and changes in measurement.

Changes in the Conceptual Framework

IFRS is more explicit than Canadian GAAP about the conceptual framework that underlies accounting. It retains the idea of presenting a "true and fair view" of the company and its financial position and notes that there may be a wide range of users to whom this information is directed. It also notes that the financial statements may not contain all the economic information that a user needs.

Four over-riding qualitative characteristics that all accounting reports should have are understandability, relevance, reliability, and comparability. In general, these (and their component parts) are the same as the parts that make up Canadian GAAP, with the possible exception that the more neutral "prudence" has replaced "conservatism" and that the idea of trading off one principle against another to enhance the true and fair view is mentioned.

Changes in Presentation

There are some changes suggested (though not required) to the titles of accounting reports:

- The balance sheet will be referred to as the statement of financial position.
- The income statement will be referred to as the statement of comprehensive income.
- The statement of retained earnings will be referred to as the statement of changes in equity.
- The cash flow statement will be referred to as the statement of cash flows.

Under IFRS the separation of extraordinary (i.e., unusual and non-recurring) items from the rest will disappear.

On the statement of financial position, the order of current and non-current liabilities will be reversed and the equity will appear before the liabilities, not after them.

Changes in Measurement

Treatment of current assets, such as cash, accounts receivable, and inventories, as well as liabilities, will not change in any material respect. With respect to inventory, the last-in-first-out inventory flow method will not be acceptable, which is in line with Canadian GAAP.

Long-term assets may be stated at cost (as before) but may also be revalued to a higher level, where it can be established that the increase can be reliably measured. This increase would be reported as income but would not be added to retained earnings: instead, it would be added to a "revaluation surplus" account.

Perhaps the biggest changes will occur in respect of financial instruments. Where these are held with the intent that they be sold in the near future, they will now have to be valued at fair value. Fair value is measured according to market prices, where there is a ready market, and on the basis of expected net present value, where the market is less reliably observable. This is a major departure from the cost model that dominates Canadian GAAP. The result is the likelihood (especially in turbulent economic times) of major write-downs when markets are low and major write-ups when markets are buoyant. This will make reported income much more volatile than it would otherwise have been.

Summary

This text is aimed at managers and those training to be managers and, for the most part, managers who will be unaffected by these changes. Managers are much more concerned with internal accounting issues, such as preparing budgets and dealing with management control reports and accounting-based decisions. However, the changes are sufficiently substantial that this appendix has been added to summarize the new situation.

Appendix 6.3
The Mechanics of Accounting: Cash Flows

The *statement of cash flows*, **SCF** (also called the cash flow statement), *explains the change in cash over the accounting period in terms of the changes of the other balance sheet accounts*. This is illustrated schematically in Exhibit 6A3.1. If cash has changed by some amount from the end of year 0 to the end of year 1 (illustrated here as a decrease), the double-entry nature of accounting means that there must be an equal change in all the other balance sheet accounts taken together.

This can be stated more clearly in algebraic terms. From the accounting equation:

$$A = L + S/E$$

Break each side down into its components, using the acronyms in Exhibit 6A3.1:

$$C + NCA + LTA = NCL + LTL + CS + RE$$

Date the components using subscripts, C_0, NCA_0, etc., for the account balances at the end of year 0, and C_1, NCA_1, etc., for the balances at the end of year 1.

We then have one accounting equation representing the end of year 0 (the beginning of year 1) and another representing the end of year 1.

$$C_0 + NCA_0 + LTA_0 = NCL_0 + LTL_0 + CS_0 + RE_0 \tag{1}$$

$$C_1 + NCA_1 + LTA_1 = NCL_1 + LTL_1 + CS_1 + RE_1 \tag{2}$$

Subtract equation (1) from equation (2) to get the change in each component over the year, $C_1 - C_0$, $NCA_1 - NCA_0$, etc. Writing these as ΔC, ΔNCA, etc. we have

$$\Delta C + \Delta NCA + \Delta LTA = \Delta NCL + \Delta LTL + \Delta CS + \Delta RE \tag{3}$$

The change in cash plus the change in the other assets equals the change in the liabilities plus the change in the equity accounts.

The signs on each term, ΔC, ΔNCA, etc., can be positive or negative. If a particular account, say CS, has increased over the year, then ΔCS will be positive; if it has decreased, it will be negative.

Rearrange to isolate the change in cash on the left-hand side:

$$\Delta C = -\Delta NCA - \Delta LTA + \Delta NCL + \Delta LTL + \Delta CS + \Delta RE \tag{4}$$

The change in cash is equal to the change in all the other balance sheet accounts taken together. For example, *all other accounts unchanged*, an

Exhibit 6A3.1: Statement of Cash Flows

Assets | **L & S/E**

$Cash_0$	Non-cash current liabilities	NCL_0
C_0	Long-term liabilities	LTL_0
Non-cash current assets	Shareholders equity	CS_0
NCA_0		
Long-term assets		
LTA_0		RE_0

B/S$_0$

The statement of cash flows explains the change in cash over the reporting period *in terms of changes in the other balance sheet accounts.*

Assets | **L & S/E**

$Cash_1$	Non-cash current liabilities	NCL_1
C_1	Long-term liabilities	LTL_1
Non-cash current assets	Shareholders equity	CS_1
NCA_1		
Long-term assets		
LTA_1		RE_1

B/S$_1$

increase in cash could be associated with a *decrease* in another asset account, such as non-cash current assets or long-term assets. Or, it could be associated with an *increase* in a liability or a shareholder equity account, such as non-cash current liabilities, long-term liabilities, or capital stock.

As with the other financial statements, form is important for conveying information. The statement of cash flows arranges these balance sheet changes in a particular way, grouping them into three categories: changes that are the result of *operating activities*, changes that are the result of *investing activities*, and changes that are the result of *financing activities*.

Operating activities are the regular business activities of the company. In accrual accounting, these activities are summarized on the income statement where the objective is to measure the growth of shareholders' equity. For the purposes of the statement of cash flows, we are interested in the cash consequences of operations — net cash flow from operations: in other words, operating cash receipts less operating cash disbursements. In practice, however, we often measure operating cash flows indirectly by starting with net income and adjusting this figure for non-cash transactions. As this method is still commonly used, it will be followed in this appendix. You should be aware, however, that the *direct method* — showing cash receipts from operations less cash disbursements — will be seen increasingly in published financial statements.

Investing activities are purchases and disposal of long-term assets (ΔLTA). Long-term assets include property, plant and equipment, intangibles, as well as securities (shares and bonds) held as long-term investments. *Financing activities* are reflected in the changes in the long-term liabilities (ΔLTL), capital stock (ΔCS), and dividend payments (the part of ΔRE that is attributable to dividends). In all cases, we are concerned with both increases and decreases. Rearranging equation (4), we have the statement of cash flows in algebraic form:

change in cash	=	operating activities
ΔC		ΔRE (NI) + ΔNCA + ΔNCL
	+	investing activities
		ΔLTA
	+	financing activities
		ΔLTL + ΔCS + ΔRE (DIV) (5)

There will be some variation from case to case, but the general principle always holds: *The statement of cash flows explains the change in cash in terms of the changes in the other balance sheet accounts organized by type of activity — operating, investing, and financing.*

Unlike the balance sheet, income statement, and statement of retained earnings that we are familiar with, we cannot "read" the SCF directly from the ledger balances. The books are not organized this way. We could go through the cash account and use the other side of each entry to build up the statement, but, apart from companies with a few simple transactions in a period, this would be quite onerous without full access to the books. (There were only 10 transactions in Example Co. Ltd., which was used to illustrate debits and credits in Appendix 2.1, so analyzing these cash transactions is feasible. As an exercise, you might try to see how the information in the journal entries that affect the cash account — use the last version of the spreadsheet — are regrouped to form the statement of cash flows at the end of that section.) Of course, an SCF is a part of every set of financial statements; so, just as for the other statements, it is not necessary for the user to prepare one. Still, an understanding of how an SCF is prepared facilitates its interpretation.

The cash flow statement does not contain new information. It is a reorganization and presentation of information that already exists implicitly in the opening and closing balance sheets, supplemented by information on the income statement and the statement of retained earnings for the period. This is essentially what was done in sections 6.2 to 6.5 in this chapter. The T-account method presented in this appendix formalizes this method of comparing balance sheets. The method developed here makes use of our knowledge of debits, credits, and T-accounts to provide a systematic way of constructing an SCF.

There are four steps to constructing an SCF using the T-account method:

1. Calculate the change in each balance sheet account over the period.
2. Transfer these changes to a set of T-accounts.
3. Reconstruct, in summary form, the transactions that affected cash in the period.
4. Use the summary information to prepare the SCF.

The method will be illustrated using the financial information from Essential Food and Drink Ltd., an organic food supply company, for the 2011 reporting period. The financial statements of Essential Food and Drink Ltd. can be found in Exhibit 6A3.2A and 6A3.2B. There is one additional piece of information that does not appear in the financial statements but may be relevant: equipment purchases in the year totalled $795.

Step 1: Calculate the change in each balance sheet account.

The changes in each balance sheet account are shown in Exhibit 6A3.3. In each account, we compared the balance in the opening balance sheet account to the corresponding balance in the closing balance sheet. If a debit balance increased, the change was classified as a net debit (for example, Inventories); if it decreased, the change was a net credit (for example, Prepaid Expense). There is a corresponding rule for credit balance accounts. If a credit balance increased, the change was a net credit (for example, Long-term Debt); if it decreased, it was a net debit (for example, Accounts Payable). As with any set of self-balancing accounts, the two columns must balance.

Share capital and Contributed surplus are not shown as there was no year-to-year change in either account. Ignoring an account for which the opening and closing balances are the same implicitly assumes that there were no transactions in the account. This may in fact not be true: there may have been offsetting transactions in the period. If information to this effect emerges, these transactions will have to be identified and accounted for.

Exhibit 6A3.2A

Essential Food and Drink Ltd.
Balance Sheets
As at December 31 ($ '000s)

	2011	2010
ASSETS		
Current		
Cash	$ 4,970	$ 467
Accounts receivable	3,617	2,596
Inventories	3,730	3,694
Prepaid expenses	305	394
	$ 12,622	$ 7,151
Property, plant and equipment, net	27,985	29,216
Total assets	$ 40,607	$ 36,367
LIABILITIES AND SHAREHOLDERS' EQUITY		
Current liabilities		
Accounts payable and accrued liabilities	$ 4,124	$ 4,602
Dividends payable	601	541
	$ 4,725	$ 5,143
Long-term debt	$ 7,799	$ 3,557
Future income tax liability	2,382	2,671
	$ 10,181	$ 6,228
	$ 14,906	$ 11,371
Shareholders' equity		
Share capital	$ 18,431	$ 18,431
Contributed surplus	741	741
Retained earnings	6,529	5,824
	$ 25,701	$ 24,996
Total liabilities and shareholders' equity	$ 40,607	$ 36,367

Exhibit 6A3.2B

Essential Food and Drink Ltd.
Statement of Income, Comprehensive Income and Retained Earnings
for the year ended December 31, 2011 ($ '000s)

Net revenue		$ 46,232
Cost of sales		18,617
Gross profit		$ 27,615
Expenses		
Selling	$ (14,631)	
General and administrative	(4,037)	
Interest	(142)	
Amortization	(1,969)	
		(20,779)
		$ 6,836
Other income		304
Income before income taxes		$ 7,140
Future income tax recovery		289
Net income and comprehensive income for the period		$ 7,429
Retained earnings, beginning of the year		5,824
Dividends		(6,724)
Retained earnings, end of the year		$ 6,529

Exhibit 6A3.3

Essential Food and Drink Ltd.
Balance Sheet Changes
for the year 2011 ($ '000s)

	Dr.	Cr.
Cash	4,503	
Accounts receivable	1,021	
Inventories	36	
Prepaid expenses		89
Property, plant, and equipment		1,231
Accounts payable and accrued liabilities	478	
Dividends payable		60
Long-term debt		4,242
Future income tax liability	289	
Retained earnings		705
	6,327	6,327

Step 2: *Transfer these changes to a set of T-accounts.*

Set up T-accounts, one for each of the accounts in the list of balance sheet changes. The cash account should be longer as there will be more transactions to be entered and provision must be made to divide it into three sections: operating, investing, and financing. This account is where the information for the statement of cash flows will be organized. At the top of each T-account, enter one of the balance sheet changes, debit or credit as appropriate, and double-underline it. This is the figure in each account that is to be explained. See Exhibit 6A3.4.

Exhibit 6A3.4

	Cash	Accounts Receivable	Inventories	Prepaid Expenses
Operating	4,503	1,021	36	89

		Property, Plant & Equipment	Accounts Payable	Dividends Payable
Investing		1,231	478	60

		Long-term Debt	Future Taxes Payable	Retained Earnings
Financing		4,242	289	705

Step 3: *Reconstruct, in summary form, the transactions that affected cash in the period.*

Using information from the balance sheet changes that is recorded in the T-accounts, along with information from the income statement and the statement of retained earnings, reconstruct, in summary form, all the transactions that affected cash in the period. We will reconstruct these transactions systematically, beginning with those classified as operating activities. Each summary transaction will be described and recorded as a journal entry. The completed T-accounts are shown in Exhibit 6A3.5 at the end of this section.

(a) **Net income.** Cash from operating activities is measured most directly as cash receipts less cash disbursements. Cash receipts and cash disbursements, however, do not appear anywhere in the books or financial statements and, so, are not particularly recognizable by financial statements readers. For this reason, accountants have traditionally started with net income and adjusted it to arrive at cash from operating activities. We can think of net income as the first approximation to cash from operating activities. Of course, net income is not net cash flow but, rather, net operating flows — net change in shareholders' equity from operations — and we have to find a way to convert them to cash flows. This is what we will do in entries (b) and (c).

First the summary entry for net income:

Entry	Accounts/Description	Dr	Cr
a	Cash (NI)	7,429	
	Retained Earnings		7,429
	First approximation to cash from operating activities		

What does this entry mean? The credit to Retained Earnings of $7,429 is the net income for the year, i.e., all the credits to revenue accounts net of all the debits to expense accounts. With this entry we are treating all the revenue and expense transactions *as if they were all cash transactions* — hence the net debit to cash. Of course these are not all cash transactions — some are close but very few are exactly — and this is what we meant above when we wrote that net income is a first approximation to cash from operating activities. However, once we take account of the non-cash revenue and expense transactions and the changes in the non-cash working capital accounts, we will have calculated the cash provided by (or used in) operating activities.

(b) **Amortization.** The one common operating transaction that clearly does not involve cash is amortization. The transaction looks like this:

Amortization Expense	1,969	
Accumulated Amortization (PP&E)		1,969

Amortization was an expense in the calculation of net income, but it did not entail the use of cash. Therefore, entry (a) above,

213

which records $7,429 as the first approximation to cash from operating activities, understates the cash inflow by $1,969 insofar as it includes amortization. Put another way, the amortization expense of $1,969 has been assumed to have involved a use of cash of $1,969 when it in fact has not. This is corrected by the following entry. Do not be misled by the debit to cash; this does not mean that amortization is a source of cash. It is simply correcting the erroneous entry (a) above, which has implicitly recorded amortization as a use of cash.

Entry	Accounts/Description	Dr	Cr
b	Cash (Amortization)	1,969	
	Accumulated Amortization (PP&E)		1,969
	Correcting net income for amortization		

Since the account Accumulated Amortization is netted against Property, Plant & Equipment (PP&E) in these T-accounts, the credit is made to the latter account.

(c) **Income taxation.** A long-term liability for income taxes can exist for several reasons, most commonly because of a difference between the tax and accounting base of long-term assets (see Appendix 3.3, Capital Cost Allowances and Deferred Taxes). Whatever the reason for the balance, the future income tax liability has declined from $2,671 in 2010 to $2,382 in 2011, reflecting a recovery of future income taxes of $289. This was not a cash recovery, but, as with amortization above, it was treated as an inflow of cash in entry (a). The following entry corrects this error. (By the same reasoning as in entry (b) above, the credit to cash does not represent an outflow of cash; the entry simply corrects the implicit recording of it as an inflow of cash in entry (a).)

Entry	Accounts/Description	Dr	Cr
c	Future Income Tax Payable	289	
	Cash (Future income tax recovery)		289
	Correcting net income for future income tax liability recovery		

This entry accounts for the changes to future income tax liability. When we are satisfied that we have used all the information in an account change, we indicate with a tick that it is cleared. This ensures that we work systematically through all the balance sheet changes. When all the account changes have been ticked, we will be able to see clearly that we have as complete an explanation of the cash flows as our information provides.

(d) **Changes in non-cash working capital accounts.** We have corrected the first approximation to cash from operating activities with respect to two specific non-cash transactions that were treated as cash transactions along with all other revenue and expense items. Now, we deal with the other revenue and expense transactions. Most other revenue and expense transactions that we call "cash" are not in fact cash; they typically are debits or credits to some other current asset or current liability. For example, most sales are a credit to revenue and a debit to accounts receivable. However, within a short period of time, the receivables are collected as cash, and in this extent, treating credit sales as an approximation to cash sales is not a major error. There is an error only to the extent that accounts receivable has changed over the period. We can adjust for this by accounting for the change. In this case, accounts receivable increased by $1,021 over the year, which means that sales exceed cash from sales by the same amount. Using this information, we could adjust cash from sales in entry (a) with the following entry:

Accounts Receivable	1,021	
Cash		1,021

Similar adjustments can be done for the changes in the other non-cash working capital accounts. Rather than dealing with them individually, we make one composite entry:

Entry	Accounts/Description	Dr	Cr
d	Accounts Receivable	1,021	
	Inventories	36	
	Accounts Payable	478	
	Prepaid Expenses		89
	Cash (Changes in non-cash working capital)		1,446
	Adjusting net income for changes in non-cash working capital accounts		

Assuming that there are no other transactions in the non-cash working capital accounts, this entry explains the change in these accounts. The next stage is to account for cash used in or provided by investing activities.

(e) There were net credits of $1,231 to the account Property, Plant & Equipment in 2011. We know also that the credit to accumulated amortization for the year was $1,969. If we had no further information about transactions involving this account, it would be reasonable to conclude that acquisition of PP&E amounted to $738 in 2011. But we do have more information — $795 was spent for the acquisition of PP&E in the year — and so the entry to record this is as follows:

Entry	Accounts/Description	Dr	Cr
e	Property, Plant & Equipment	795	
	Cash (Acquisition of PP&E)		795
	Purchase of property, plant, and equipment		

(f) Evidently there is something missing — we have not accounted for all the changes in PP&E.

So far we have two entries to PP&E:

	Amortization	1,969 Cr entry (b)
	Acquisition	795 Dr entry (e)
	Net	1,174 Cr

But the net change in the account in 2011 was in fact: 1,231 Cr

Leaving a difference of 57 Cr

The credit of $57 could be accounted for in several ways; but if we have no concrete information to support any of them, the simplest assumption is best. The simplest assumption in this case is that the $57 credit represents one type of activity, namely, the proceeds on the sale or PP&E. (It is assumed also that the sale (or sales) must be at book value; otherwise, there would be gains or losses on the income statement for which an adjustment would be made.)

Entry	Accounts/Description	Dr	Cr
f	Cash (Disposal of PP&E)	57	
	Property, Plant & Equipment		57
	Disposal of property, plant, and equipment		

These two entries, (e) and (f), account for all investing activities.

(g) Dividends are considered a financing activity. Dividends declared can be found on the statement of net income, comprehensive income, and retained earnings. However, on a cash basis, we need dividends paid, not dividends payable. Dividends paid are dividends declared plus the increase in dividends payable.

Entry	Accounts/Description	Dr	Cr
g	Retained Earnings (Dividends declared)	6,724	
	Dividends payable		60
	Cash (Dividends)		6,664
	Payment of dividends		

(h) The last entry accounts for the change in the Long-term Debt account. The account has increased by $4,242 over the year, representing an increase in cash for this financing activity:

Entry	Accounts/Description	Dr	Cr
h	Cash (LTD)	4,242	
	Long-term Debt		4,242
	Issue of long-term debt		

This source of cash is classified as financing and is entered in that section of the cash T-account. Since we have no other information about long-term liabilities, we can assume that the net decrease in cash we have accounted for (dividends net of new debt issued) described our financing activities. Long-term liabilities can be considered cleared and explained.

At this point we have explained all the changes in all the accounts, so we can now complete the worksheet. To complete this worksheet, go back to the cash T-account and add the cash provided or used in each section. Operating activities provided $7,663; Investing, $738; and Financing, $2,422. There is a net increase in cash of $4,503, exactly what we identified at the beginning of the exercise through the comparison of balance sheets. We now have all the ingredients for the preparation of the Statement of Cash Flows.

Exhibit 6A3.5

	Cash		Accounts Receivable		Inventory		Prepaid Expenses
	4,503		1,021		36		89
Operating			(d) 1,021		(d) 36		89 (d)
a Net income	7,429		✓		✓		✓
b Amortization	1,969						
c Future income tax recovery		289					
	9,109						
d Δ non-cash working capital		1,446					
Cash from operating	7,663						

			Property, Plant & Equipment		Accounts Payable		Dividends Payable
			1,231		478		60
Investing			(e) 795 1,969 (d)				
e Acquisition of PP&E		795		57 (f) (d)	478		60 (g)
f Disposal of PP&E	57			1,231	✓		✓
Cash used in investing		738		✓			

			Long-term Debt		Future Taxes Payable		Retained Earnings
			4,242		289		705
Financing			4,242 (h) (c)	289		(g) 6,724	7,429 (a)
g Dividends		6,664		✓	✓		705
h Issue of L-T debt	4,242						✓
Cash used in financing		2,422					

Net cash flow	4,503	
	✓	

Step 4. Use the summary information to prepare the SCF.

The information needed for the statement is in the Cash T-account. The finished statement can be seen in Exhibit 6A3.6. Notice that the organization of the statement reflects its objective: it explains the change in cash over the accounting period in terms of the changes of the other balance sheet accounts. The balance sheet changes are grouped by the nature of the activity that generated them — operating, investing, and finance. Finally, at the foot of the statement, the change in cash is reconciled to the opening and closing balance of the cash account.

217

Exhibit 6A3.6

Essential Food and Drink Ltd.
Statement of Cash Flows
for the Year Ended December 31, 2011
($ '000s)

Operating Activities	
Net income for the year	$ 7,429
Add (deduct) items not involving cash	
Amortization	1,969
Future income tax recovery	(289)
	$ 9,109
Net change in non-cash working capital related to operations	(1,446)
Cash provided by operating activities	$ 7,663
Investing Activities	
Purchase of property, plant, and equipment	$ (795)
Proceeds from sale of equipment	57
Cash used in investing activities	$ (738)
Financing Activities	
Dividends paid	$ (6,664)
Long-term debt issued	4,242
Cash used in financing activities	$ 2,422
Net increase in cash	$ 4,503
Cash, beginning of the year	467
Cash, end of the year	$ 4,970

Self-Study Problem

1. You are given the balance sheet as at December 31 for Charley Farley, who went into business on October 1, 2011.

Charley Farley
Balance Sheet as at December 31, 2011

Assets

Current assets:

Cash		$ 3,000
Receivables		500
Inventory		1,500
Prepaid rent		5,000
Prepaid insurance		3,000
		$ 13,000

Long-term assets:

At cost	$99,000	
Less: Accumulated amortization	(9,000)	90,000
		$103,000

Liabilities and Equity

Current liabilities:

Trade payables		$ 5,000
Accrued utilities		1,000
		$ 6,000
Long-term debt		51,000
Total debt		$ 57,000

Owners' equity:

Cash invested	$50,000	
Add: Net income	11,000	
Less: Withdrawals	(15,000)	46,000
		$103,000

[Note: This is a continuation of Self-Study Problem #1 in Chapter 4 on page 156. You may need to refer back to that problem for help in doing this one.]

Required

Prepare a statement of cash flows for the three months to December 31, 2011.

Solution

1.

Charley Farley
Statement of Cash Flows
for the Three Months to December 31, 2011

Cash from operations		
Net income	$ 11,000	
Add: Amortization (non-cash expense)	9,000	
	$ 20,000	
Less: Increase in net non-cash working capital		
($13,000 – $3,000 – $6,000)	4,000	$16,000
Cash from financing activities		
Cash introduced by owner	$ 50,000	
Add: Bank loan	55,000	
Less: Bank loan repaid	(4,000)	
Less: Owners' withdrawals	(15,000)	86,000
Cash used in investing activities		
Purchase of long-term assets		(99,000)
Increase in cash balance		$ 3,000

Discussion Questions and Problems

Discussion Questions

1. What is the purpose of the statement of cash flows?
2. According to economist Milton Friedman, when a company makes a profit it has a duty to pay the whole profit to shareholders as a cash dividend. Discuss the effect of this on the company and on the shareholders.
3. What is the effect of amortization expense on cash flow?
4. What is the effect on cash flow of increasing inventory?
5. Your business allows customers to pay in 30 days: what is the effect on cash flow of allowing customers to pay in 60 days?
6. Why is reporting on cash flows so very important?
7. What are the four main headings in a cash flow statement?
8. Should the cash from operations be positive or negative?
9. If a firm has positive cash from investing activities, what would you infer?
10. If a company is expanding, would you expect cash from financing activities to be positive or negative?

Appendix 6.3

11. Is it always true that changes in a company's non-cash balance sheet accounts over the year taken together will be identical to the change in cash over the same period? Briefly explain your answer.

12. Define each of the following terms in the context of the statement of cash flows:

    (a) Operating activities
    (b) Investing activities
    (c) Financing activities

Problems

1. Alberta Co. had the following cash flow statement for 2011:

Cash from operations	$750,000
Cash used in financing activities	(500,000)
Cash used in investing activities	(100,000)
Increase in cash	$150,000

   Required
   Discuss the implications of this statement for the company.

2. Lumber Ltd. made a net loss of $600,000 in 2011. Amortization expense was $250,000. During the year, accounts receivable increased from $500,000 to $550,000 and inventory increased by $100,000. Trade payables increased by $200,000.

   Required
   Calculate the cash from (or used in) operating activities.

3. In 2011 Newcombe Ltd. had a net profit of $100,000 after charging amortization expense of $50,000. Inventories had increased by $100,000 and accounts receivable had increased by $50,000 over the year. Accounts payable had remained constant at $250,000.

   Required
   Calculate the cash from operations.

4. In 2011 Newcombe Ltd. raised $500,000 from a new issue of common shares. The company paid off a long-term loan of $200,000 and repaid $600,000 of redeemable preference shares. The company also issued a 5% debenture loan that brought in $750,000 and took out a mortgage of $400,000 related to the purchase of a retail store.

   Required
   Calculate the cash from (or used in) financing activities.

5. In 2011 Newcombe Ltd. bought new milling equipment at a cost of $750,000 and bought two new trucks for $75,000 each, trading in two old trucks for a total of $50,000. The company also bought a new retail store for $500,000, taking out a $400,000 mortgage to finance it.

   Required
   Calculate the cash used in (or cash from) investing activities.

6. At the start of 2011, Newcombe Ltd. had $500,000 cash and short-term demand deposits. From the information in Problems #4, #5, and #6, prepare the cash flow statement for 2011.

7. Konrad Co. had the following cash flow statement for 2011:

   Konrad Co.
   Statement of Cash Flows
   Year Ended December 31, 2011

Operations:		
Net income	$500,000	
Add: Amortization	80,000	
Add: Decrease in non-cash working capital	20,000	
Total cash from operations		$600,000
Financing activities:		
Cash from borrowing	$500,000	
Less: Loan repaid	200,000	300,000
Investing activities:		
Purchase of plant assets		(750,000)
Total change (increase) in cash		$ 150,000

   Required
   Comment on the sustainability of the company's activities as revealed by the cash flow statement.

8. Consider each of the following independent events that occurred in Calgary Inc. in September 2011. In each case, state whether the

event would increase cash flow, decrease cash flow, or leave cash flow unchanged.

(a) The company paid accounts payable of $200,000.
(b) The company paid wages of $500,000.
(c) The company bought inventory for $480,000, paying in cash.
(d) The company bought inventory for $340,000 on 30 days credit.
(e) The company sold goods for cash for $900,000.
(f) The company sold goods on credit for $600,000.
(g) The company allowed its payables to increase by $100,000.
(h) The company paid $270,000 off its accounts payable.
(i) The company took out a bank loan of $500,000.
(j) The company repaid amounts owed to credit card companies by $200,000.
(k) The company bought new machinery for $250,000 in cash.
(l) The company bought a new truck for $360,000 in cash, trading in an old truck for $80,000.
(m) The company leased a new bottling machine for $60,000 per month.
(n) The company paid interest for the month on a 5% convertible debenture of $100,000.
(o) A 5% convertible debenture of $100,000 was converted into $100,000 of common shares.
(p) The company issued 200 new common shares, and the new shareholders paid $2,000 per share into the company.
(q) Senior managers were issued $200,000 new common shares as part of their remuneration.

9. Deal Co. had operating income of $250,000 for 2011. Included in the expenses was a total of $50,000 of depreciation and amortization. Net non-cash working capital had decreased by $25,000. Interest expense was $25,000, and income taxes were $100,000.

Required
Calculate the cash from operations for 2011.

10. Deal Co. had 100,000 common shares in issue at the start of 2011. During the year, the company issued an additional 25,000 shares, which were given to managers as bonuses, and bought and retired 5,000 shares from existing shareholders for $25,000. The company paid a total of $50,000 in dividends in 2011 and also borrowed $100,000 as a long-term loan from a bank.

Required
Calculate the cash from financing activities for 2011.

11. Deal Co. had long-term plant assets of $200,000 at the start of 2011. During the year, the company charged $50,000 amortization on these assets. The company bought new assets for $125,000 and sold existing assets for $30,000.

Required
Calculate the cash used in investing activities for 2011.

12. Deal Co. had cash balances totalling $5,000 at the start of 2011. By the end of 2011, the cash balances had increased to $135,000.

    Required
    Calculate the increase in cash for 2011.

13. (a) Based on Problems #9 through #12, prepare the cash flow statement for Deal Co. for 2011.
    (b) Based on the cash flow statement, write a brief report indicating whether Deal Co. has any cash flow issues.

14. You are given the combined income statement and statement of retained earnings for Riley Inc. for the year ended December 31, 2011, and the balance sheets as at December 31, 2010, and 2011:

Riley Inc.
Income Statement for the Year Ended December 31, 2011

Sales revenue		$19,000,000
Operating expenses (includes $1,500,000 amortization)		7,200,000
Operating income		$11,800,000
Interest expense	$ 600,000	
Income taxes	4,800,000	5,400,000
Net income		$ 6,400,000
Add: Retained earnings as at 1/1/2011	.	10,600,000
		$17,000,000
Dividends paid		4,200,000
Retained earnings as at 31/12/2011		$12,800,000

Riley Inc.
Balance Sheet

	As at December 31	
	2010	**2011**
ASSETS		
Cash	$ 1,000,000	$ 1,200,000
Accounts receivable	26,400,000	23,600,000
Inventories	45,000,000	44,200,000
Total current assets	$72,400,000	$69,000,000
Long-term assets (net)	20,000,000	22,500,000
Total assets	$92,400,000	$91,500,000
LIABILITIES & EQUITY		
Current liabilities	$31,800,000	$41,700,000
Long-term liabilities	40,000,000	22,000,000
Total liabilities	$71,800,000	$63,700,000
Common shares	$10,000,000	$15,000,000
Retained earnings	10,600,000	12,800,000
Total equity	$20,600,000	$27,800,000
Total liabilities & equity	$92,400,000	$91,500,000

Required
(a) Calculate the increase or decrease in working capital (current assets – current liabilities).

(b) Calculate the increase or decrease in non-cash working capital [(current assets – cash) – current liabilities].
(c) Calculate the cash from or cash used in operations.
(d) Calculate the cash from or cash used in financing activities.
(e) Calculate the cash from or cash used in investing activities.
(f) Calculate the increase or decrease in cash.
(g) Prepare the Statement of Cash Flows for 2011.
(h) Comment on the Statement of Cash Flows you have prepared.

Appendix 6.3

15. Refer to the financial statements for Example Co. Ltd. on pages 65 and 67 in Chapter 2. Using the T-account method, prepare a Statement of Cash Flows for 2011. (Hint: how do we get the balance sheet changes when there is only one balance sheet shown?) You can check your answer against the SCF on page 67, and you can also reconcile the T-account method to the method that was actually used to prepare the SCF, namely, a review of all the transactions in the year.

16. Here are the working capital accounts for Algonquin Manufacturing Ltd. as at December 31 in thousands of dollars:

	2010	2011
Current Assets		
Cash	$ 0	$ 440
Accounts receivable	880	700
Inventories	970	1,100
Total current assets	$ 1,850	$ 2,240
Current Liabilities		
Bank overdraft	$ 230	$ 0
Accounts payables	680	460
Total current liabilities	$ 910	$ 460
Net working capital	$ 940	$ 1,780

The income statement for 2011 shows net income of $1,380 including amortization of $725.

Required
(a) Calculate the net cash flow for the year.
(b) Using the T-account method, prepare the operating activities section of Algonquin's Statement of Cash Flows.
(c) If you subsequently learned that you had not noticed a line on Algonquin's 2011 Income Statement, "Gain on Disposal of Equipment, $250", would this lead you to change your answer to (a) above? To (b)? Explain.

17. Use the T-account method to prepare a Statement of Cash Flows for 2011 for Riley Inc. using the data provided in Problem #14.

2

Budgeting for Planning & Control

Management Accounting:

"...the process of identification, measurement accumulation, analysis, preparation, interpretation and communication of information that assists managers in making decisions."

C.T. Horngren, G.L. Sundem, W.O. Stratton, H.D. Teall & P. Beaulieu
Management Accounting, 6th Canadian Edition
Toronto, Pearson Education, 2012

Budgeting 7

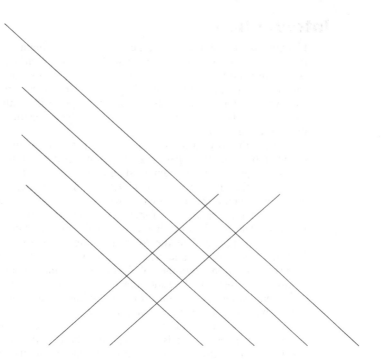

Learning
Objectives

After studying this chapter you should be able to do the following:
→ Identify planning and control as the main objectives of budgeting
→ Identify a number of different approaches to budget preparation:
  → Prepare an operating budget for a service department of an organization
  → Prepare an operating budget for a production department of an organization
  → Prepare an operating budget for a simple organization
→ Understand the role of participation in budget setting

7.1   Introduction

Planning is one of the five "functions of management" identified by Fayol (the others are organizing, commanding, co-ordinating, and controlling). Any competently run organization will make plans about its future. The source of planning information is generally the managers and other senior staff who run the organization: each manager will contribute information from his or her own area of expertise, which together will become the organizational plan.

When the organizational plan is expressed in financial terms, it is called a budget. The operating budget is the budget for all the activities that get reported in the income statement, and it is presented in the same format as the income statement. The main difference is that the income statement summarizes past events, while the budget forecasts future events. The cash budget is a list of forecast receipts and payments and their effect on cash balances. In this chapter we shall consider how operating budgets can be prepared, and in the following chapter we shall consider how cash budgets are prepared and used. In Chapter 9 we show how budgets may be used for control (another of Fayol's five management functions). In the control exercise, actual results are compared to budgeted results to see if the organization is on track or not. Without the budget that judgment would be more difficult or even impossible to make.

While planning and control are the most common uses to which budgeting will be put, it is also true that both perform valuable service in communicating information to managers (e.g., by implication, they map out the organizational structure, and they also communicate profit expectations) and that they may be used as motivational devices to encourage managers to strive for organizational goals.

Because the budget has so many purposes, it is a very important part of the management process. Also, because budgets can be prepared with several different uses in mind, it is sometimes unclear as to how they should best be executed.

If the primary purpose of the budget is to support the planning process, then its most important characteristics should be, first, that it is integrated with the organizational objectives and strategy, and, second, that it should be accurate. Use of the budget for planning is probably of greatest interest to top management, such as the board of directors, or the chief executive officer and his immediate area managers.

If the primary purpose of the budget is to enable control, then its most important characteristics should be, first, that it is linked to the responsibility areas over which functional managers have control, and, second, that it represent a fair basis for the control process. Fairness can be achieved by both the parties (the manager exercising control and the manager being controlled) agreeing to the budget before it is put into use. Control of activities is normally exercised by (and on) functional managers, such as plant managers, marketing managers, and human resource managers.

Although communication and co-ordination are unlikely to be primary purposes of any budget, they should be borne in mind when considering the accuracy of the picture they give of the organization. The structure of the budget should not mislead the observer as to the reality of the organizational structure.

In sales and marketing situations (and occasionally in production and service units) the budget may have a major motivational objective. In that case, the budget should represent some challenging, but achievable, level of performance.

As a further gloss on this situation, the degree to which budgets are regarded as important varies among organizations. In some, the budget is regarded with almost religious fervour, and achieving or not achieving the budget is strongly linked to rewards and punishments. Those who exceed budget expectations are likely to receive bonus payments and promotions, while those who fail to meet their budgets will be denied such rewards. In other organizations the budget is treated more lightheartedly: it is a source of valuable information, but rewards and punishments are unlikely to follow as a result of achieving or not achieving the budget.

7.2 Preparing the Budget for a Service Department

Sarah Smith has recently been promoted from salaries and benefits manager to being in charge of the whole human resource department at Tizer Foods Inc. The previous manager was given a $20,000 severance package in September, and told to go away. Sarah has the most recent departmental cost report on her desk (see Exhibit 7.1), which is for the month of September. It is now mid-October, and she has received a request from the management accounting department for her departmental budget for next year. How should she proceed?

Where is Sarah going to start in setting her proposed budget for next year? Her choices could include the following:

Exhibit 7.1:   Departmental Monthly Cost Report

Tizer Foods Inc.
Human Resource Department
Monthly Cost Report

Details	September Actual	September Budget	Year to date Actual	Year to date Budget
Manager's salary	$ 28,000	$ 8,000	$ 92,000	$ 72,000
Other salaries	75,000	72,000	675,000	658,000
	$103,000	$ 80,000	$ 767,000	$ 730,000
Employee benefits (5%)	5,150	4,000	38,350	36,500
Total staff costs	$108,150	$ 84,000	$ 805,350	$ 766,500
Travelling expense	5,300	15,000	104,500	135,000
Advertising expense	10,700	17,500	173,200	157,500
Amortization expense	2,000	2,000	18,000	18,000
Occupancy expense (500 metres^2 @$200)	10,000	10,000	90,000	90,000
Total	$136,150	$128,500	$1,191,050	$1,167,000

1. Previous Year's Budget

Take the current year's budget ($128,500 per month) and say that it can be used again next year.

There are a number of issues with approach #1. First, the world does not stand still, and prices tend to rise through time, so with inflation in Canada running at around 2% (2010) per year, last year's budget will not be enough for next year. Sarah would be unwise to commit herself and her co-workers to meeting an unrealistic budget, based on out-of-date data.

2. Previous Year's Budget + Inflation Adjustment

Take the current year's budget ($128,500 per month) and add 2% for general inflation, to make it $131,070 per month.

Although that is a little more realistic, there are still some issues with approach #2. The 2% inflation rate will not necessarily be relevant to all expense items. Some (salaries is a good example) may rise at rates higher than inflation. Others (amortization, for example) may not rise at all.

We can also see that the actual expenses (both for the month of September and for the year to date) are greater than the budgeted expenses. Why was this? Was the budget inadequate, or was control lax? At this point Sarah does not know. It would be reckless to commit to a budget without full information.

3. Previous Year Actual + Inflation Adjustment

Take the current month's actual expenses ($136,150) and add 2% for inflation, to make the budget $138,873 per month.

In approach #3 we institutionalize whatever was going on in September and immortalize it in our budget. Any inefficiencies that happened now become part of next year's budget request. In addition to any uncontrolled overspending in the month, closer examination of the cost report shows that the $20,000 severance payment for the previous HR manager is included, for example, and that the travelling expenses were underspent by $10,000. It would be incorrect for Sarah to base next year's budget on the expenses that were incurred in September as September was not typical. Probably any given month is atypical in some respect.

4. Zero-Based Budget

If Sarah were to go back to basics, she would go through each line of the budget and try to justify the dollar amount. So, her salary as manager would be line 1, and the budget would be based on her expected actual salary for next year — likewise for the remaining employees, the employees' benefits, travelling, advertising, etc. Her monthly budget might appear as follows:

Details	Monthly Budget
Manager's salary	$ 7,500
Other salaries	72,000
	$ 79,500
Employee benefits (5%)	3,975
Total staff costs	$ 83,475
Travelling expense	12,000
Advertising expense	17,500
Amortization expense	2,000
Occupancy expense (500 metres^2 @ $200)	10,000
Total	$124,975

Approach #4 is often referred to as "zero-based budgeting" as it assumes a starting point of zero, and every expense item has to be justified before being included. President Jimmy Carter introduced zero-based budgeting to the U.S. government because he was appalled by the waste in government offices. Sadly, its two big problems soon became apparent: first, it takes an unreasonable amount of time to prepare budgets this way; and second, managers who are preparing budgets soon become adept at sneaking unjustified expenses into the list to pad the budget, thus frustrating its main objective. Although it may be unmanageable to do zero-based budgeting every year, as an occasional exercise in cost control it has much to recommend it.

5. The Padded Budget

While talking to other department managers, Sarah might have heard that whatever budgets were put forward, the management accounting department routinely cut them back by 10% to get rid of the fat. That being the case, whatever budget she wants to finish up with (say, for example, the budget of $124,975 per month in #4), she would add 10% to each of the line items so that the total budget she puts in for will be $137,472.50.

What started off as a rational process has now become a political foot-ball. The only reason the management accounting department should have to cut back a budget by an arbitrary amount is if it expects managers to pad the budget in the first place, so the remedy is giving rise to the dis-ease here.

6. The Compromise Budget

A compromise solution, which many organizations are comfortable with, is to base the budget of one year on that of the previous year but to make appropriate adjustments in respect of routine changes, such as inflation, and also challenge some of the major assumptions that underlie the budget. In this department, for example, salaries are the largest line item: there would be a periodic review of what the employees do and how that contributed to the goals and strategy of the organization.

7. Activity-Based Costing

Taken to its logical conclusion, both zero-based budgeting and challenging major assumptions lead to the identification of the activities the unit is carrying out and why it is doing so, and the related cost that should be incurred to carry out the activities. This is currently referred to as the idea of "activity-based" costing and management (ABC/ABM). The underlying theme of ABC/ABM is that there is a chain of activities that add value to the product or service the organization is selling. All activities that the organization executes should be part of the value chain, otherwise they should be eliminated. ABC/ABM is discussed more fully in Chapter 11.

8. Benchmarking

Some organizations are lucky enough to be able to compare the cost of their activities with those of competitors. Car makers, for example, rou-tinely share cost and efficiency information at various car plants world-wide. If that information is available, then budgets may "benchmarked" against the best standards in the industry. Sarah probably does not have this information to help her.

9. Kaizen System

The Japanese "Kaizen" approach to budgeting regards standing still as unacceptable. Each period's costs must be lower than those of the previous period, so a continuous series of efficiency-based improvements is required. By itself, any single improvement may be trivial, but cumulatively they may add up and keep efficiency on a steady upward path. The Kaizen system is widely used in manufacturing situations, but in theory, at least, it could be applied to any activity.

Whatever budget amounts Sarah submits, we must recognize the bud-get it will then become part of a negotiation process. Whoever is co-ordinating the budget for the whole organization has the right to ask Sarah to reconsider her submission. If the overall operating budget is not able to meet the organization's profit expectations, then everyone will have to rethink how their contribution affects that overall picture. Only when all parties agree that the budget is possible and that it will achieve organizational objectives should it be approved and implemented.

7.3 Preparing the Budget for a Production Department

In the previous example, Sarah Smith was preparing the budget for a department that provided a service to the rest of the organization (human resources management). The managers of any service department, including HR, accounting, marketing, research and development, and maintenance, would face a similar task. In the case of service departments, the budgeting issue is somewhat (but not totally) separated from the issue of how much work they are expected to do.

Production departments face a different situation. In the case of a department that makes a product or that renders a service for sale to customers, there are some costs that behave like service department costs (essentially fixed costs) and others that would be expected to rise or fall with the number of products made or the number of services sold: these are called variable costs, as they vary in direct proportion to activity.

Barbara Byng is the production manager of the Coated Nut Division of Tizer Foods Inc. Her monthly operating budget for the current year is shown in Exhibit 7.2.

When Barbara Byng prepares her operating budget for the following year, not only will she have to think about all the issues that Sarah Smith had to consider (such as changing prices), but she will also have to think about how many kg of coated nuts are planned for production.

If the output of coated nuts is going to rise by 10% (from 600,000 kg to 660,000 kg), then even if the rate per kg stays the same (variable cost is currently $1.50 per kg), the budgeted cost would rise by 10% (from $900,000 to $990,000). Likewise, if the budgeted output of coated nuts were to be 20% lower (480,000 kg) then the budgeted total variable cost would fall by 20% (from $900,000 to $720,000).

The fixed costs have a current budget of $450,000. Price changes and increased efficiency may make the following year's budget for fixed costs different, but the level of activity should not change the budget for fixed costs. It would not matter if the output was the same (600,000 kg), was lower (e.g., 480,000 kg), or was higher (660,000 kg), these would still be expected to be $450,000 (plus or minus any price or efficiency changes).

Suppose Barbara Byng is preparing her budget for the next year. She has been given the following information to help her:

1. The sales department plans on selling an average of 750,000 kg of coated nuts per month (an increase of 25%).
2. The purchasing department expects the following price changes:
   • The cost of nuts will increase to $0.60 per kg.
   • The cost of coatings will increase to $3.00 per kg.

Exhibit 7.2: Departmental Operating Budget for Current Year

Tizer Foods Inc.
Coated Nut Division
Operating Budget for Current Year

Activity: Budgeted monthly output of coated nuts		**600,000 kg**
Variable operating costs:		
Raw materials and packaging		
Nuts	500,000 kg @ $0.500	$ 250,000
Coating	100,000 kg @ $2.750	275,000
Packing materials	600,000 kg @ $0.050	30,000
Labels and inserts	600,000 kg @ $0.075	45,000
Total		$ 600,000
Labour	8,000 hours @ $25	200,000
Other variable operating costs	8,000 hours @ $12.50	100,000
Total variable costs ($1.50 per kg of output)		$ 900,000
Fixed operating costs:		
Supervisory salaries (5 @ $5,000 each)		$ 25,000
Rent & taxes		100,000
Utilities		50,000
Maintenance		75,000
Amortization of plant & equipment		200,000
Total fixed operating costs ($0.75 per kg of output)		$ 450,000
Total operating costs ($2.25 per kg of output)		$1,350,000

- The cost of packing materials will decrease to $0.04 per kg.
- The cost of labels and inserts is not expected to change.
3. The human resources department will agree to a new collective bargaining agreement that will increase wage rates by $5 per hour.
4. Automation of the nut-roasting process will reduce the required labour hours to 0.01 labour hours per kg of output.
5. The other variable operating cost rate will increase to $15 per labour hour.
6. One supervisor will be let go, at a cost saving of $5,000 per month.
7. The remaining four supervisors will be paid $6,000 each per month.
8. Amortization will increase by $50,000 per month.

In Exhibit 7.3 we show how Barbara Byng would prepare the monthly operating budget for next year for her division.

Note that 750,000 kg is a 25% increase in activity over the current year, so the quantities of all the variable cost inputs will have to increase by 25% before considering any price changes.

The budget in Exhibit 7.3 shows the following:

- Variable costs have risen from $1.50 per kg to $1.565 per kg: mostly this is due to rising raw material costs.

Exhibit 7.3:   Departmental Operating Budget for Next Year

Tizer Foods Inc.
Coated Nut Division
Operating Budget for Next Year

Activity: Budgeted monthly output of coated nuts		**750,000 kg**
Variable operating costs:		
Raw materials and packaging		
Nuts	(500,000 kg + 25%) @ $0.600	$ 375,000
Coating	(100,000 kg + 25%) @ $3.000	375,000
Packing materials	(600,000 kg + 25%) @ $0.040	30,000
Labels and inserts	(600,000 kg + 25%) @ $0.075	56,250
Total		$ 836,250
Labour	(750,000 × 0.01) hours @ $30	225,000
Other variable operating costs	(750,000 × 0.01) hours @ $15	112,500
Total variable costs ($1.565 per kg of output)		$1,173,750
Fixed operating costs:		
Supervisory salaries (4 @ $6,000 each)		$ 24,000
Rent & taxes: no change		100,000
Utilities: no change		50,000
Maintenance: no change		75,000
Amortization of plant & equipment ($200,000 + $50,000)		250,000
Total fixed operating costs ($0.6653 per kg of output)		$ 499,000
Total operating costs ($2.2303 per kg of output)		$1,672,750

- Fixed costs have risen in total (from $450,000 to $499,000) but have actually decreased on a dollar per kg output basis (from $0.75 per kg to $0.6653 per kg) because of the increased production activity: the fixed cost is spread over a greater quantity of production.
- Total cost has decreased from $2.25 per kg to $2.2303 per kg: considering the substantial raw materials cost increases, this is a remarkable achievement.

7.4   The Master Budget

In addition to the various production and service departments creating budgets for their individual responsibility areas, there will be an operating budget for the whole organization. It will look like an income statement, listing the budgeted sales revenues and the budgeted costs and expenses incurred. It will also show the budgeted operating income and the budgeted net income.

In addition to the operating budget, most organizations will prepare budgets for a range of other items, such as a capital budget (for major investment expenditures), a cash budget (for movements in the cash balances), and a budgeted balance sheet. We shall discuss the cash budget in the next chapter because it is so important for organizational survival that all managers need to be aware of the effect their actions have on cash flow, but the rest of the master budget can safely be left to accounting experts and will not be discussed here.

In Exhibit 7.4 we show the relationship between the various elements of the master budget.

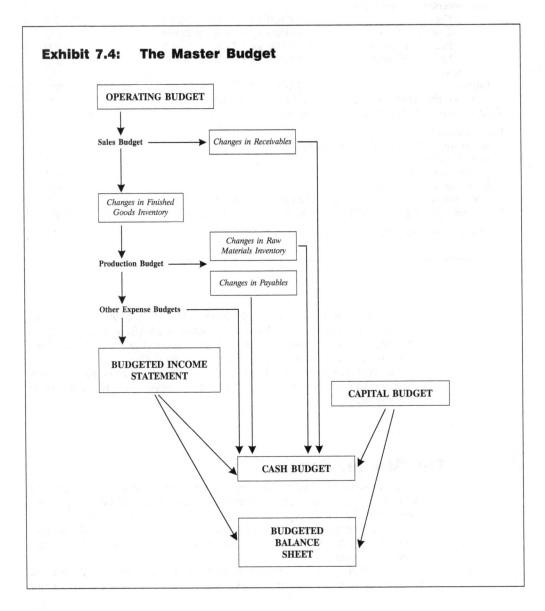

Exhibit 7.4:   The Master Budget

7.5 The Operating Budget

The process starts with a forecast of sales. All organizations are subject to some limiting factor that determines the highest level of activity at which they could operate. Because we live in a vibrant modern market economy, sales level is almost always the limiting factor. If potential sales exist, most organizations can somehow find the resources to deal with the additional customers.

Sales forecasts can come from various sources: extrapolations of past trends, the considered opinion of sales and marketing personnel, analysis of market and competitor activity, or any combination of these sources. They will consist of a schedule of products, prices, and volumes that are expected to occur.

In these days of "just-in-time inventory management" it is highly probable that the sales forecast will be virtually identical to the planned production. If, however, the company's plan is to build up inventory over the budget period, then planned production will exceed planned sales. Conversely, if it is planned to run inventories down, then production will be less than sales. Planned production levels, then, will be sales levels adjusted up or down for changes in finished goods inventories.

Production levels drive manufacturing costs. The raw material purchases necessary for the production plan will have to be bought and paid for. As with sales, if there is little or no inventory, raw materials and bought-in parts will be driven precisely by the production plan. Only if there is a build-up or run-down of raw materials inventory will purchase requirements differ from production. Production levels also drive wage costs and manufacturing overhead.

As a separate exercise, expense budgets will also be prepared for service departments, such as sales and distribution, human resources, accounting and administration, research and development, and any other areas of the organization that are separately managed.

Morgan Cars

Morgan Car Co. has been making cars since 1909. By the look of the cars, it seems as though the design may not have changed much in the past 100 years. The traditional appearance, however, masks a thoroughly modern car in many respects. What has not changed is the "craft" mentality used in their construction. Morgan has studiously avoided moving up to large-scale production so that the company can maintain its reputation for quality manufacturing. As a result, demand has consistently outstripped supply in recent years. If you want a Morgan, you can order one, any time, but in the late 1990s the waiting list was an incredible eight years.

As of 2010, the waiting list is still one to two years. Clearly, Morgan cannot use "sales demand" as the starting point for preparing its budget, but it can use "production capacity" as a starting point as that is its binding constraint. All cars are hand-assembled and they make fewer than 1,000 every year.

Fortunately, as an area manager, it will never be your role to put together the master operating budget. That consolidation is done by the accounting staff. The accountants, however, rely on managers for their inputs. As a functional area manager, it is important to realize that your input into the budgeting process is not an empty exercise in number shuffling, but is one of the ingredients that make the whole thing reasonable and accurate. It is, therefore, essential that the process be taken seriously.

As a manager, you will be expected to budget for your area of responsibility. You can expect some base data to be given to you by the budgeting department. The data would consist of expected rates of inflation, wage settlement prospects, activity levels, etc. Translating that into a reasonable budget is your job.

7.5.1 Sales Forecasting

If sales activity is the driving force for other parts of the budget, we should start by considering the sales forecasting process. (Rogers' 2001 launch of its @Home Internet service is an excellent example of poor sales forecasting and its negative impact on a company.)

The past is not a perfect predictor of the future, but it is a very good starting point. Suppose that sales revenue has been growing steadily over the past few years. The most likely projection would be that it would continue to grow as long as the underlying factors have not changed. We might even expect the rate of growth to remain the same.

Shelburne Heating reports that its gross sales revenues have increased every year from 2007 to 2011:

	$ million
2007	5.7
2008	6.1
2009	6.5
2010	7.2
2011	7.9

Rogers@Home

With considerable fanfare, Rogers announced its @Home Internet service. Because it was piped into your house through the TV cable, it was much faster than the phone line connections, which had been the main source of home Internet access up to that point. Rogers was successful: too successful, in fact. The number of customers increased beyond all expectations, including Rogers' own. The sales level was so high that Rogers' systems could no longer handle it effectively. Although the hookup was wickedly fast, it became increasingly unreliable. Customers defected to other services or retreated to old, slow modems. Eventually, a class action suit was brought against Rogers for failing to live up to its promises.

You could say that Rogers had two failures from a budgeting perspective: it had been inaccurate in its sales forecast, and it had taken on additional customers without having the service capacity to provide effective services.

Exhibit 7.5:   A Sales Revenue Graph

Shelburne Heating (2007 to 2011)

Plotting the sales on a graph (see Exhibit 7.5) shows that the increase is roughly the same each year. Alternatively, year-on-year growth rates could be calculated: sales in 2008 were 7.0% higher than in 2007, for example.

Year	Sales ($ million)	Growth ($ million)	% Growth
2007	5.7		
2008	6.1	0.4	7.0 (0.4 ÷ 5.7)
2009	6.5	0.4	6.6 (0.4 ÷ 6.1)
2010	7.2	0.7	10.8 (0.7 ÷ 6.5)
2011	7.9	0.7	9.7 (0.7 ÷ 7.2)
Average growth rate			8.5

On average, sales have grown by 8.5% per annum over the four years since 2007. A reasonable forecast for 2012, on that basis, would be for sales of $7.9 million plus 8.5%, which would be $8.6 million.

A more sophisticated analysis of this data might draw a trend line through the data points, either by eye on the graph or by a calculation, such as a regression analysis. We do not need to go into the mechanics of regression analysis, but the best estimate of sales for 2012 would also be $8.6 million.

Analyzing the trend is quite legitimate if the underlying circumstances are unchanged. If there have been any disturbances in the pattern, however, that might make the trend less reliable. Suppose that you are the manager of Shelburne Heating in Shelburne, Ontario. Superior Propane has just opened a store 500 metres away. It is inevitable that this will affect your sales as Superior Propane is such an effective competitor, and the store is so close to yours. A change such as that would have to be built into the sales forecast.

7.5.2 *Production Forecasting*

Once the sales level has been estimated, we have to consider the implications for the rest of the business.

Ontario Brewery has forecast sales of 12 million hectolitres of beer in 2012. Clearly, the brewery will need manufacturing capacity for 12 million hectolitres. If the brewing process takes a month, the plant capacity will have to be rated at 1 million hectolitres, assuming that a steady production of 1 million hectolitres a month is sufficient to meet the annual demand. This would certainly be true if demand were constant, but demand for beer is very seasonal. It goes up in the summer and at holiday times, and is generally lower in colder weather. Suppose the demand was forecast with a seasonal pattern, as shown in Exhibit 7.6.

If sales demand can only be met with current production, then a plant rated at maximum demand (1.7 million hectolitres a month) will be necessary. Apart from the three months of maximum demand, there will be unused capacity for the rest of the year, when demand is less than 1.7 million hectolitres.

With this pattern of demand, it will be possible to meet demand with a plant rated at 1 million hectolitres per month if the product can be carried in inventory. Storing inventory enables production and demand

---

Exhibit 7.6:   A Demand Forecast

Ontario Brewery
Demand Forecast for 2012

Forecast demand	Millions of hectolitres
January	0.5
February	0.5
March	0.7
April	0.7
May	0.9
June	1.0
July	1.7
August	1.7
September	1.0
October	0.8
November	0.8
December	1.7
Total	12.0

Exhibit 7.7:   A Production Plan

Ontario Brewery
Production Plan for 2012
Hectolitres (in million)

	Opening inventory	Production	Available	Demand	Closing inventory
January	0.0	1	1.0	0.5	0.5
February	0.5	1	1.5	0.5	1.0
March	1.0	1	2.0	0.7	1.3
April	1.3	1	2.3	0.7	1.6
May	1.6	1	2.6	0.9	1.7
June	1.7	1	2.7	1.0	1.7
July	1.7	1	2.7	1.7	1.0
August	1.0	1	2.0	1.7	0.3
September	0.3	1	1.3	1.0	0.3
October	0.3	1	1.3	0.8	0.5
November	0.5	1	1.5	0.8	0.7
December	0.7	1	1.7	1.7	0.0
Total		12		12.0	

to be "uncoupled" and their capacities do not have to be precisely matched. Demand can be effectively met by the production plan shown in Exhibit 7.7.

The brewery is able to build inventory levels up gradually over the light months so that it can effectively meet demand in the heaviest months. Of course, there is a price to pay: the inventory has to be stored. This production plan calls for storage with a peak level of 1.7 million hectolitres. If the company has a plant that could meet the maximum monthly demand every month, then this storage would be unnecessary.

The decision to add 700,000 hectolitres of production capacity, or 1.7 million hectolitres of storage capacity, is one that would have to be made on its own merits.

Although the main focus of the production forecasting exercise was to budget the production activity, there was a spinoff effect: changing inventory levels were planned. In other words, the financial budget is being constructed in parallel with the operating budget.

7.5.3   *Labour Planning*

Once production activity levels have been budgeted, it is possible to schedule the labour force necessary to carry out the production plan. Suppose Ontario Brewery now has a production plan that calls for 1 million hectolitres of beer to be produced each month. A constant level of labour would be appropriate to operate the production plant. Sales, however, are very seasonal, from a low of 500,000 hectolitres to a seasonal peak of 1.7 million hectolitres per month. Planning for the labour requirements in bottling and distribution will have to match that seasonal trend. Either casual workers will have to be added at the busy times, or overtime will have to be scheduled — or some combination of the two.

When budgeting labour costs, do not forget that there are several labour-related costs incurred by the company in addition to the wages paid to staff, including unemployment insurance and workers compensation premiums, the employer's contribution to pension schemes, holiday pay, and so on. Typically, for budgeting, a constant percentage is added to raw labour costs for these fringe benefits.

We have the sales forecast and production plan for Ontario Brewery (see Exhibits 7.6 and 7.7). The production activity requires a workforce of 10 all year round. Production workers are paid $25 per hour and work a 40-hour week. Bottling and distribution workers are needed at the rate of 10 people for every million hectolitres sold. Bottling and distribution workers are paid on average $15 per hour and they, too, work a 40-hour week. There are two supervisors (one for production and one for bottling and distribution), each earning $40,000 per year. Fringe benefits are expected to cost an additional 10% of wage costs. The labour budget would be as shown in Exhibit 7.8.

Exhibit 7.8: Labour Cost Budget

Ontario Brewery
Labour Cost Budget for 2012

Month	Millions of hectolitres produced	Production 10 × $25 × 40 hrs × 4 weeks	Millions of hectolitres sold	Bottling and distribution Sales × 10 × $15 × 40 hrs × 4 weeks
January	1.0	$ 40,000	0.5	$ 12,000
February	1.0	40,000	0.5	12,000
March	1.0	40,000	0.7	16,800
April	1.0	40,000	0.7	16,800
May	1.0	40,000	0.9	21,600
June	1.0	40,000	1.0	24,000
July	1.0	40,000	1.7	40,800
August	1.0	40,000	1.7	40,800
September	1.0	40,000	1.0	24,000
October	1.0	40,000	0.8	19,200
November	1.0	40,000	0.8	19,200
December	1.0	40,000	1.7	40,800
		$480,000		$288,000
Supervisors		40,000		40,000
		$520,000		$328,000
10% fringe benefits, etc.		52,000		32,800
Total		$572,000		$360,800

7.5.4   *Preparing the Operating Budget*

The operating budget for Ontario Brewery for 2012 is shown in Exhibit 7.9.

The brewery plans on selling a total of 12 million hectolitres of beer in 2012, with the demand showing a seasonal peak in the summer with another smaller peak in December, and lower demand in the rest of the year. Beer is retailed in the beer stores for $5 per litre. The beer stores take a 20% margin ($1), leaving $4 per litre as gross revenue for the brewer. The government takes $1.00 for duties and taxes, leaving $3.00 per litre net of tax revenue for the brewer. Total budgeted sales of 12 million hectolitres will result in budgeted revenue of $3,600 million.

Raw material costs and packaging costs are $1.50 per litre. For 12 million hectolitres, this will be a budgeted cost of $1,800 million. Variable distribution and marketing costs are $0.20 per litre. For 12 million hectolitres this will be a budgeted cost of $240 million. Fixed distribution and marketing costs are budgeted to cost $180 million for the year, while fixed general and administrative costs are budgeted to cost $300 million for the year. Interest expense is budgeted at $80 million for the year, and income taxes expense is budgeted to be 40% of the pre-tax profit.

Exhibit 7.9:   **Operating Budget**

Ontario Brewery
Operating Budget for 2012

Sales	12 millions of hectolitres	
	$ millions	
Sales revenue: Gross	$4,800	
Brewing excise & sales taxes	1,200	
Net sales revenue		$3,600
Variable costs:		
Raw material & packaging	$1,800	
Variable distribution & marketing	240	
Total variable costs		2,040
Contribution margin		$1,560
Fixed costs:		
Fixed distribution & marketing	$ 180	
Fixed general & administrative	300	
Total fixed costs		480
Operating income		$1,080
Interest expense		80
Taxable income		$1,000
Taxes: 40%		400
Net income		$ 600

If this business were to be evenly spread over the year, then the monthly budget would be calculated by dividing the annual total by 12. However, we know that it is a very seasonal business, so the budget for each month would have to be separately calculated to include its own level of production and the associated costs.

7.6 Participation in Budgeting

In some organizations the budget is handed down from above as something the unit is expected to achieve, without giving the unit any say in the budget's contents. This is called an imposed budget. In general we can expect the manager of the unit to be suspicious and resentful of an imposed budget, and to have a low level of commitment to it. The organization may find that it has to set up a system of strong sanctions against managers who do not reach their budgets in order that they become realized.

By contrast some other organizations will treat the budget-setting process as a dialogue, with managers sharing information and expectations to agree on a budget. The budget does not become formally adopted until both the manager and her superiors have signed off (a) that they regard it as a reasonable task to undertake and (b) that it meets organizational expectations. This is referred to as a participatory budget. In general we can expect that the manager of a unit who has participated in the budget-setting process will be more highly personally committed to achieving the budgeted results. She will need fewer "sticks and carrots" to persuade her to work enthusiastically toward organizational success. Behaviourally, participatory budgets are superior to imposed ones.

7.7 Budget Preparation and the Functional Manager

In a very centralized organization, the budget will be set by "top management", generally by setting parameters and instructing the management accounting team to prepare the budget in keeping with those parameters.

In a very decentralized organization, functional managers will be responsible for preparing the budget themselves for tasks that lie under their operational control. This means that marketing/sales would be responsible for setting the revenue budgets, production managers would be responsible for setting the production cost budget, and managers of service cost centres (for example, human resource managers and accounting department managers) would be responsible for setting the budgets for the costs to be incurred in their own areas.

Clearly, functional managers cannot be left to set their budgets without any consideration of inter-relationships between units. It would be plain dumb for marketing to set a budget for sales that is inconsistent with the production budget. General Motors made that mistake and went bankrupt as a result.

Likewise, setting the budget for a service cost centre without any regard for the work to be done or its affordability, and without some managerial checks, would be an abdication of management responsibility. Managers in such a situation have a tendency toward empire building, which fosters the consumption of ever greater amounts of the organization's resources.

So what tends to happen is that the responsible managers propose the budgets, which are then vetted by a higher level of management to ensure that the whole plan is co-ordinated and that it achieves whatever organizational objectives have been chosen. As a result, complete decentralization hardly ever exists; and although the process may start with the functional managers, an iterative process is used to ensure the acceptability of their budgets.

7.8 Summary

The management activity of planning is realized through the preparation of budgets, which give the financial dimension of organizational plans. Budgeting consists of estimating operating revenues and expenses and, hence, operating income, as well as planning cash receipts and payments. Budget preparation (covered in this chapter) paves the way for budgetary control, which is covered in Chapter 9.

Appendix 7.1
Budgeting Is Dead:
Long Live Budgeting!

A claim made in recent years is that budgeting is a wasteful and divisive activity that consumes more resources than the value it creates; that it should be got rid of; and that it has been successfully discontinued in a number of major organizations.

Here is the description from the Beyond Budgeting Round Table Web site:

Beyond Budgeting is the first great management idea of the twenty-first century[1]

A radical proposition?

Budgeting, as most corporations practice it, should be abolished. That may sound like a radical proposition, but it is merely the final (and decisive) action in a long running battle to change organizations from centralized hierarchies to devolved networks. Most of the other building blocks are in place. Firms have invested huge sums in quality programs, IT networks, process reengineering, and a range of management tools including EVA, balanced scorecards, and activity accounting. But they are unable to establish the new order because the budget, and the command and control culture it supports, remains predominant.

Gap between rhetoric and reality

The [gap] between the rhetoric and the reality of devolved decision-making is huge. But to succeed in the global market, it must be bridged. Much is at stake. Responding effectively to change, finding and keeping talented people, producing imaginative strategies, reducing fixed costs, building closer relationships with customers, and improving ethical behaviour and reporting — all these key success factors depend, to some degree or another, on winning the battle for the devolved organization together with its culture of personal responsibility. The central planning and budgeting process perpetuates a culture of dependency. It supports the belief that decisions improve the higher in the organization they are taken. This is a ridiculous idea to most employees.

Budgeting has few admirers

Gaming the numbers is pervasive. One large survey of U.S. companies concluded that managers either did not accept the budgetary targets and opted to beat the system, or they felt pressured to achieve the targets at any cost. This pressure is squeezing the life and spirit out of many organizations and their people. It's the mentality that says, "Do what I say or your future is at risk." It is driven by greed

---

[1] Reproduced with permission from the Beyond Budgeting Round Table (BBRT) Web site (**www.bbrt.org/**). Copyright by BBRT. All rights reserved. For further discussion, see J. Hope and R. Fraser, *Beyond Budgeting: How managers can break free from the annual performance trap* (Boston: Harvard Business School Press, 2003).

and a need for instant gratification and immediate results. This was evident at both Enron and WorldCom. The WorldCom culture, say those who worked there, was all about living up to [CEO] Bernard Ebbers's demands. "You would have a budget, and he would mandate that you had to be 2 percent under budget. Nothing else was acceptable."

Beyond Budgeting, a more adaptive and devolved alternative
Replacing the budgeting model with a more adaptive and devolved alternative is the solution that [organizations] need to achieve their goals of becoming devolved networks. Criticizing budgets is not new. But defining a set of principles that guides leaders toward a new lean, adaptive and ethical management model is a new idea — perhaps the first great new idea of the twenty-first century.

If you read more deeply about the companies that have adopted this approach (Volvo, for example), you will find that the major thing that has changed is the use to which budgets are put. No longer is the budget seen as a fixed target, with severe sanctions for not being met. The companies still prepare forecasts (i.e., budgets) but they are used as guidelines, not straitjackets. Budgets, however, in the sense of plans for the future, are still prepared and widely used.

Self-Study Problems

1. Sales revenues for the Bombardier Inc. group of companies were as follows:

Year to January 31	$ billion
1998	8.3
1999	11.3
2000	13.4
2001	15.9
2002	21.6

Required
(a) Calculate the year-on-year increase in sales revenue in both $ and %.
(b) What is your best estimate of the sales revenue for the year to January 31, 2003?

2. One of the products made by Bombardier is the Ski-Doo snowmobile. Assume that in 2011 Bombardier plans to sell 80,000 snowmobiles at a price of $7,500 each. At the start of the year, the company will have 5,000 snowmobiles in inventory. The company would like to have an inventory of 3,000 snowmobiles at the end of the year.

Required
(a) What is the budgeted sales revenue for snowmobiles for the year?
(b) How many snowmobiles should Bombardier plan on manufacturing in the year?
(c) What monthly manufacturing capacity should Bombardier plan to have for the Ski-Doo snowmobile plant?

3. Carlton Co. makes luxury travel bags. They are sold to retailers for $250 each. Material costs are $40 per bag; labour costs are $60 per bag; overhead is a fixed amount of $100,000 per month. The company expects to sell 1,000 bags per month.

Required
Prepare budgets for production and sale of 800, 1,000, and 1,200 bags.

Solutions

1. (a) **$ billion**

Sales revenue	Sales revenue	Increase	Increase %
1998: $ 8.3	1999: $11.3	$3.0	($3.0 ÷ $ 8.3) × 100% = 36.1%
1999: $11.3	2000: $13.4	$2.1	($2.1 ÷ $11.3) × 100% = 18.6%
2000: $13.4	2001: $15.9	$2.5	($2.5 ÷ $13.4) × 100% = 18.7%
2001: $15.9	2002: $21.6	$5.7	($5.7 ÷ $15.9) × 100% = 35.8%

(b) Average sales growth rate over past four years:

$$= (36.1\% + 18.6\% + 18.7\% + 35.8\%) \div 4$$
$$= 27.3\%$$

Estimated sales revenue in 2003:

$$= \$21.6 \text{ billion} + 27.3\%$$
$$= \$27.5 \text{ billion}$$

2. (a) Budgeted sales revenue:

$$= 80,000 \times \$7,500$$
$$= \$600,000,000$$

(b)

Budgeted sales units	80,000
Less: Opening inventory	5,000
	75,000
Add: Budgeted closing inventory	3,000
Budgeted production	78,000

(c) If Ski-Doo snowmobile production is carried out continuously during the year, then the required manufacturing capacity is

$$78,000 \div 12 = 6,500 \text{ per month}$$

If production is seasonal, then a larger capacity would be required. Suppose the plant makes Ski-Doo snowmobiles for only four months, and then changes to making Sea-Doo watercraft. The required capacity is

$$78,000 \div 4 = 19,500 \text{ per month}$$

3.

Number of bags (= n)	800	1,000	1,200	
Sales revenue	$200,000	$250,000	$300,000	(n × $250)
Materials	$ 32,000	$ 40,000	$ 48,000	(n × $40)
Labour	48,000	60,000	72,000	(n × $60)
Overhead	100,000	100,000	100,000	
Total expense	$180,000	$200,000	$220,000	
Operating profit	$ 20,000	$ 50,000	$ 80,000	

Discussion Questions and Problems

Discussion Questions

1. What are the objectives of budgeting?
2. Compare and contrast a budget based on the previous period with a zero-based budget: which is more appropriate?
3. Why does budget preparation start with a forecast of sales?
4. How are sales and production linked in the planning process?
5. Why is it important to distinguish between variable costs and fixed costs in preparing a budget for a production division?
6. Describe the difference between a participative budget and an imposed budget.
7. What is the difference between a budget for a production department and a budget for a service department?
8. Who in the organization is responsible for forecasting sales quantities and selling prices?
9. Who in the organization is responsible for preparing the master budget?
10. What are the advantages and disadvantages of selling goods on credit?

Problems

1. The research & development department at Consumer's Cosmetics Co. is responsible for design and development of new face care products. The following data relate to year 2011:

   (i) The department employed 15 scientists, each paid $80,000 per year, and 30 assistants, each paid $50,000 per year.
   (ii) Employee-related costs added 15% to the basic salary bill.
   (iii) The laboratories and test units cost $500,000 in total operating costs.
   (iv) Travel costs were $120,000.

   In year 2012, the following changes will occur:

   (i) The number of scientists will be decreased to 10 and the number of assistants will be decreased to 20; all the salaries will be increased by $10,000 per person.
   (ii) The employee-related costs will rise to 20% of salaries.
   (iii) The laboratory and test unit costs will rise by 10%.
   (iv) Travel costs will be cut by half.

   Required
   (a) Prepare a budget for year 2012.
   (b) If the R&D department manager is asked to cut this budget by another $100,000, what are his choices?
   (c) If the R&D department manager expected that, whatever budget he proposed, a higher authority would cut it by 10%, what total amount of expense should he put forward to make sure that he had enough left over to meet his expected real needs?

2. The manager of sunscreen products at Consumer's Cosmetics Co. is responsible for all activities related to sunscreen products, including new product development, production, distribution, and marketing. The budgeted and actual departmental results for year 2011 are given below:

Consumer Co.
Sunscreen Products Division
Year 2011
($ millions)

	Budget		Actual	
Sales revenue		$150		$175
Cost of goods sold				
Variable production costs	$30		$40	
Fixed production costs	20	50	22	62
Gross margin		$100		$113
R&D, marketing, and administrative expenses				
Variable	$25		$30	
Fixed	20	45	20	50
Operating profit		$ 55		$ 63

It is expected that sales revenue in year 2012 will be $180 million. Inflation may be assumed to be zero for year 2012, so prices need not be adjusted.

Required
(a) List the assumptions you need to make before compiling the 2012 budget.
(b) Prepare a budget for year 2012.

3. The Toothpaste Division of Consumer's Cosmetics Co. has the following sales revenues in recent years:

2008	$200,000,000
2009	$210,000,000
2010	$220,500,000
2011	$231,525,000

Required
(a) Calculate the year-on-year percentage increase in sales revenue.
(b) Estimate the sales revenue for 2012.

4. The sales revenue (in $ millions) for Hudson's Bay Co. in recent years has been as follows:

2000	$7,194
2001	$7,400
2002	$7,446
2003	$7,384
2004	$7,400

Required
What is your best estimate of HBC's sales revenue for year 2005?

253

5. The Government of Canada's federal revenue was $231,481 million in 2007 and $253,222 million in 2008.

   Required
   (a) Based solely on the data for 2007 and 2008, what is your estimate of the government's revenue for 2009?
   (b) Was there a difference between your estimate and the actual revenue? If so, what would account for it?

6. The Baby Products Division of Consumer's Cosmetics Co. has consistently achieved a 20% market share in the baby products market. In 2010, the total world baby products market was $1,000,000,000. In 2011, due to the introduction of new products, Consumer's Cosmetics Co. expects to get 22% of the market, and due to increased population, the company expects the market total to increase by 5%.

   Required
   (a) Calculate Baby Products Division's sales revenue for 2010.
   (b) Calculate Baby Products Division's expected sales revenue for 2011.
   (c) If the actual total baby products market in 2011 is $1,100,000,000, what is likely to be the effect?
   (d) If the total baby products market in 2011 is $1,100,000,000 and the Baby Products Division's actual sales are $220,000,000, has the division done well or badly?

7. The Fragrances Division of Consumer's Cosmetics Co. is expected to have an inventory of finished product of 50,000 litres of various perfumes, at a total inventory cost of $150,000 at the beginning of 2011. The sales forecast for year 2011 is to sell a total of 120,000 litres of product. Because the company is moving toward a "just-in-time" inventory system, it plans to reduce its inventory of finished product to 10,000 litres by December 31, 2011. Costs are not expected to change between 2010 and 2011. All products are sold to other divisions of Consumer's Cosmetics Co. and the average selling price is $5 per litre. All production costs are variable costs and amount to $3 per litre. In addition to production costs, there is a total of $50,000 of fixed administrative expense.

   Required
   (a) How much should the Fragrances Division budget for production in year 2011?
   (b) What is the division's budgeted sales revenue for 2011?
   (c) Prepare a budget for the Fragrances Division for year 2011.

8. The Fragrances Division of Consumer's Cosmetics Co. is expected to have inventory of finished product of 50,000 litres of various perfumes at the beginning of 2011 at a total inventory cost of $150,000. The sales forecast for the first six months of year 2011 is to sell a total of 60,000 litres of product. Sales in January are expected to be 15,000 litres; February, 20,000 litres; March, 10,000 litres; and April, May, and June, 5,000 litres each. Because the company is moving

toward a "just-in-time" inventory system, it plans to reduce its inventory of finished product to 20,000 litres by June 30, 2011. The production facility can make 10,000 litres per month, but that is the maximum capacity.

Required

(a) Draw up a chart for the first six months of 2011, and enter all the above information in it. The chart should show the following headings: opening inventory; production; available; sales; closing inventory (like the one in Exhibit 7.7 on p. 243 of the text).

(b) Is the production plan feasible?

9. The Human Resource Department at Bill & Ben Inc. had the following actual activities and actual results for the current year:

Number of company employees	1,000
Number of HR employees	25
HR Department	
Salaries	$1,250,000
Office expenses	$125,000
Travel and interview costs	$250,000
Advertising	$75,000

Next year, it is expected that the company payroll will expand from 1,000 to 1,200 employees and that all costs will rise by 5% because of inflation.

Required

Prepare a budget for Bill & Ben's HR Department for next year.

10. The Marketing Department at Freda's Fashions spent $850,000 last year. The department has two employees. One prepares advertising copy, and her salary, inclusive of employer's contributions, cost $50,000. The other employee organizes shows and events, and her salary, inclusive of employer's contributions, cost $70,000. In total, $500,000 was spent on advertising, and $230,000 was spent on shows and events.

Next year, Freda's Fashions plans to double the number of shows and events, so the company will need one extra person in that area. Advertising will stay roughly the same as this year. All costs will rise by 10%.

Required

Prepare a budget for the Marketing Department for next year.

11. Superior Software operates at the cutting edge of designing new software applications, including games, retail support, and product design groups. Typical project time, from concept to first commercial application, is about six months, and typical product life cycle is two years of retail sales. As the competition changes so quickly, it is not possible to know exactly which products will dominate the sales or for how long each product is likely to survive in its market.

After 10 years of operating more like a family than a business, the owner, Bill Doors, wants to make the management more professional, and he has every intention of introducing formal annual budgeting for both sales revenues and costs so that he knows how much profit he will have to play with in the next few years.

It has been suggested that he should use statistical methods such as "time series analysis" to predict sales, "regression analysis" to predict costs, and "just-in-time" inventory management to control production activities.

Required
Is Bill on the right track?

12. Consumer's Cosmetics Co. manufactures face care products. These are sold to retail outlets of all descriptions: from the big-box stores down to convenience stores. There are a number of divisions, each specializing in a particular product line.

Material purchases are handled centrally to enable the negotiation of low prices and to control quality. All labour negotiations are subject to a company-wide collective agreement. Each year, in November, division heads are told by head office what their next year's sales forecast should be and what their budgeted operating expenses are. Divisions are controlled through a strict monthly budget reporting exercise, during which actual results are compared with the budget and any discrepancies are expected to be explained.

Required
(a) Is this a participative budgeting situation?
(b) Is this budgeting system appropriate to this organization?

13. The chief executive officer of Consumer's Cosmetics Co. has been reading about the "Beyond Budgeting Round Table" (see Appendix 7.1). He is quite taken with the idea of eliminating budgeting at Consumer's Cosmetics Co.

Required
List the advantages and disadvantages of eliminating budgeting.

Cash Budgeting

8

Learning
Objectives

After studying this chapter you should be able to do the following:
→ Identify the importance of planning and controlling cash flows
→ Prepare a cash budget for a simple organization
→ Understand the role of short-term and long-term credit on liquidity management
→ Understand the relationship between the internally produced cash budget and the externally published cash flow statement

---

8.1   Introduction

In order for an organization to succeed, it has to get a lot of things right. It has to market a product or service for which there is a demand. It has to offer that product at a price that is acceptable to the target market. It has to produce the product or service at a cost that facilitates the market price and that includes a sufficient markup to satisfy financial obligations (such as interest) and provide an acceptable return to equity investors.

In order for an organization to fail, it only has to get one thing wrong. Whatever the underlying causes, if an organization does not have enough cash to pay its debts when those debts are due, creditors will force it into bankruptcy. Managing the inflows and outflows of cash are therefore critical to an organization's survival. That is called liquidity management, or cash flow management.

8.2   Preparing the Cash Budget for a Simple Organization

8.2.1   The Accruals Method and Cash Flows

Most of the information that goes into a cash budget arises directly from the organization's day-to-day operations: the ones that are reported in the income statement, and the ones that appear in the operating budget for a future period. These will include the following:

• Sales of goods or services will result in cash inflows.
• Direct costs of goods bought for resale will cause cash outflows.
• Operating expenses incurred will cause cash outflows.
• Financial charges, such as interest paid and taxes, will cause cash outflows.

Exhibit 8.1:   Operating Budget

Tizer Foods Inc.
Operating Budget for Quarter 1 ($ thousands)

	January	February	March
Sales revenue	$ 6,800	$ 7,600	$ 8,200
Raw materials (50% of sales)	$ 3,400	$ 3,800	$ 4,100
Wages (10% of sales)	680	760	820
Fixed production costs	2,000	2,000	2,000
Selling & administrative expenses	3,000	3,000	3,000
Total expense	$9,080	$ 9,560	$ 9,920
Operating income (loss)	$(2,280)	$(1,960)	$(1,720)
Interest expense	100	100	100
Net income (loss)	$(2,380)	$(2,060)	$(1,820)
Cumulative income (loss)	$(2,380)	$(4,440)	$(6,220)

Because we use the "accrual" method to prepare the income statement we report the sales, purchases, expenses, etc. in a way that reflects their effect on the wealth of the organization. A sale is "recognized" (that is, included in the income statement) when it is "realized" (that is, when the property in the goods passes from the seller to the buyer). That is not necessarily the same as when the related cash flow occurs. We "recognize" expenses when their value has been used up, and, again, that is not necessarily when the related cash flow occurs. The process of preparing the operating budget (operating budgets were dealt with in the previous chapter) will give us a good estimate of the accrual-based sales, direct costs of sales, operating expenses, and financial charges. It is one of the tasks of cash budgeting to transform those into expected cash flows.

Tizer Foods Inc. has prepared an operating budget for the first quarter of next year, and this is shown in Exhibit 8.1. As can be seen from the budget, Tizer Foods expects to show a loss in each month and to report a total loss of $6.22 million for the quarter.

8.2.2   Cash Receipts

Sales revenues are the main source of cash receipts. In a pure cash business (many retail outlets deal only in cash) the sales revenue will be received immediately, and receipts and revenue will be identical. A business that sells on credit, however, will have to wait to receive its cash until the customer pays. So, in the same way that inventory uncouples production and demand, allowing them each to happen at different rates, making credit sales uncouples the act of making a sale and the collection of the related cash.

Tizer Foods Inc. makes credit sales to some of its customers. The budgeted sales for the first quarter of the year are as follows:

January: $6.8 million
February: $7.6 million
March: $8.2 million

The company's expectation is that

- 25% of all sales will be cash sales, received immediately;
- 75% of all sales will be on 30 days credit terms;
- 50% of all sales (that is, two-thirds of the credit sales) will be collected by the end of the month following the sale;
- 25% of all sales (that is, the remaining one-third of credit sales) will be collected during the second month after the sale.

During the month of March the company would budget to collect the following:

25% of the March sales, received in cash:	
$8,200,000 × 25%	$2,050,000
50% of the February sales, collected in March:	
$7,600,000 × 50%	$3,800,000
25% of the January sales, collected in March	
$6,800,000 × 25%	$1,700,000
Total cash collections in March from sales	$7,550,000

There may be other receipts of cash: from the sale of assets, issuing shares, or from borrowing. Each of these would be carefully estimated as to its expected amount and its timing.

Together with whatever beginning balance of cash existed at the start of the period, these provide a pool of available cash out of which cash payments can be made.

8.2.3 *Cash Payments*

The biggest dollar item of outgoings on the income statement of most organizations will be the direct cost of sales. That is, goods bought for resale in a retail shop; raw materials and direct production costs of a manufacturer; and direct costs of service inputs in a service company. They translate into the biggest cash outflows, too.

In the same way that credit sales "uncouple" the sale and its related cash flows, buying goods on credit uncouples the resources flow that appears in the income statement from the related cash flow. In addition, any change in inventory has to be recognized as influencing cash flows. If inventory is increased, it implies a related cash outflow to buy the additional inventory. By contrast, when inventory is reduced, sales can be made without replacing inventory, and the cash outflow will be less than it otherwise would have been.

Tizer Foods Inc. has budgeted to make the following sales:

November:	$10.4 million
December:	$12.5 million
January:	$ 6.8 million
February:	$ 7.6 million
March:	$ 8.2 million

The direct cost of sales includes raw materials. Raw materials are budgeted to be 50% of the sales amount. The company's plan is to have enough inventory at the start of every month to satisfy the sales for that month. Raw material purchases have to be paid for by the end of the second month following delivery.

Thus, at the beginning of January, the raw materials inventory should be half of $6.8 million, which is $3.4 million, and Tizer Foods has to pay for it by the end of February. The inventory bought in November for December sales was $6.25 million, and it has to be paid for by the end of January.

The direct cost of sales also includes production wages. These are budgeted to be 10% of the sales amount. Production wages are paid in the same month that they are incurred, so the resource flow shown in the income statement is the same as the cash flow.

Fixed production costs amount to $2 million per month. Half of these ($1 million per month) are represented by cash payments that are made in the same month as the expense is incurred. The other $1 million of these expenses is amortization of fixed plant assets. In a current income statement, amortization is the recognition of the gradual expiry over time of an investment in assets made some years earlier. Amortization does not affect current cash flows, so it must be deducted from the expense amount of $2 million to get the net amount of $1 actually paid in the month. Selling and administrative expense is $3 million per month, all paid during the month when it was incurred.

Interest payments amount to $100,000 each month, and these are paid monthly, so the resource flow and the cash flow are the same.

Tizer Foods Inc. plans to pay investors a dividend of $4 million in March, and it also plans to pay $5 million in February to purchase some new equipment. The equipment vendor will expect a cash payment of $1 million and will advance a loan of $4 million.

At the beginning of January, Tizer Foods Inc. expects to have a cash balance of $200,000 on hand. The effect of the above cash flows can be seen in Exhibit 8.2.

In January, sales revenues amounted to $6.8 million. Cash collections were actually much higher than this, as part of the sales of November and December are collected in January. January cash collections total $10.55 million. Cash payments in January are budgeted to be $11.03 million.

Cash inflow of $10.55 million less cash payments of $11.03 million means that cash resources are planned to be reduced by $480,000 in the month. As the opening cash balance is only $200,000, we can see that Tizer Foods Inc. has a problem!

Exhibit 8.2: Cash Budget

Tizer Foods Inc.
Cash Budget for First Quarter ($ thousands)

	November	December	January	February	March
Sales revenue	$10,400	$12,500	$ 6,800	$ 7,600	$ 8,200
Receipts:					
Cash sales: 25%	$2,600	$3,125	$ 1,700	$ 1,900	$ 2,050
Previous month: 50%	?	5,200	6,250	3,400	3,800
2 months back: 25%	?	?	2,600	3,125	1,700
Total cash from sales			$10,550	$ 8,425	$ 7,550
Other receipts: loan			nil	4,000	nil
Total receipts			$10,550	$12,425	$ 7,550
Payments:					
Raw materials (50% × previous month's sales)			$ 6,250	$ 3,400	$ 3,800
Wages (10% × current month's sales)			680	760	820
Fixed production costs			2,000	2,000	2,000
Selling & administrative expenses			3,000	3,000	3,000
Less: amortization expenses (not paid in cash)			(1,000)	(1,000)	(1,000)
Total operating payments			$10,930	$ 8,160	$ 8,620
Other payments:					
Interest			$ 100	$ 100	$ 100
Dividend			nil	nil	4,000
Equipment purchase			nil	5,000	nil
Total			$ 100	$ 5,100	$ 4,100
Total payments			$11,030	$13,260	$12,720
Net cash increase / (decrease) in month			$ (480)	$ (835)	$(5,170)
Beginning cash balance			200	(280)	(1,115)
Ending cash balance			$ (280)	$(1,115)	$(6,285)

In February, the problem gets worse. Cash inflows total $12.425 million and cash outflows total $13.26 million. The net cash outflow for the month is $835,000. According to this budget, a cash shortage of $280,000 is brought forward from January, so a cash shortage of $1.115 million is carried forward to March.

In March, expected cash inflows total $7.55 million and expected cash outflows total $12.72 million. The net cash outflow for the month is $5.17 million. A cash shortage of $1.115 million is brought forward from February, so a cash shortage of $6.285 million is expected at the end of March.

A negative cash balance is clearly unacceptable. The implication is that some payments that were due to be made would not get made, and the outcome would probably be that the creditors who were owed money would seek redress in the legal system and have Tizer Inc. declared bankrupt. As we shall see in the next section, though, this initial cash budget has put Tizer Foods Inc. in a good position to manage its way out of the problem.

8.3   Liquidity Management

According to the cash budget in Exhibit 8.2, Tizer Foods Inc. has a net cash outflow for each month and an expected net cash deficit at the end of each month for the first three months of the year. The question that Tizer Foods Inc. should now address is how the company is going to deal with this situation. Can it make the problem go away? If it can, then it may survive to more profitable times (which should, eventually, solve its liquidity crisis). If the company cannot resolve the current liquidity problem, it must accept that bankruptcy is the likely outcome; and however profitable the company might expect to be in the future, it is not going to survive to enjoy that.

Probably the first issue is to think twice about paying the dividend to the shareholders. A company that is currently expecting to lose nearly $8 million over the next three months is in no position to pay $4 million out as dividend. Dividends are always under the control of the company directors, so they have discretion to cancel it.

The second issue is to consider the proposed payment of $5 million ($1 million net of the vendor's loan) for new equipment in February. Possibly this could be deferred until the company is in better shape to pay for it. Possibly the company could lease the equipment instead of buying it outright.

Even if Tizer Foods can eliminate the payment of the dividend and the payment for the equipment, the company is still not out of the hole it was in. Even in January, the cash outflow exceeds the total of cash inflows and available cash balances. At this point, the company would have to consider financing options.

If Tizer Foods Inc. believes that this is a short-term problem, then it needs a short-term solution. The company may expect that the rest of the year will be very profitable and that the profitability translates into high cash inflows so that its liquidity problem will be automatically solved. If that is the case, the company should approach its bank, show the bank the full year's cash budget, and negotiate a short-term loan to tide it over.

If Tizer Foods Inc. believes that this is a long-term problem, then it needs a long-term solution. The company may expect that this liquidity crisis is going to happen every year due to, for example, seasonal variations in the trade. If that is the case, the company should approach its bank and convince the bank to grant it a long-term loan, or it should approach its shareholders and ask them to inject more permanent capital into the business by buying additional shares.

The point of the exercise is this: if Tizer Foods Inc. fails to prepare a cash budget, then the liquidity crisis will hit the company unexpectedly, and it will not have the luxury of time to seek an appropriate solution. By preparing the cash budget, the company puts itself in a position to seek an appropriate solution and the time to put the solution into effect. It is part of good planning and good management.

8.4 Cash Budgeting and the Cash Flow Statement

The cash flow statement (dealt with in Chapter 6 of this book) is provided to outside parties (such as investors and creditors). It summarizes the inflows and outflows of cash for a past period under three headings:

1. Cash from (or occasionally cash used in) operations (that is more or less the cash flow effect of all the items that go through the income statement).
2. Cash used in (or occasionally cash from) the acquisition or disposal of long-term assets.
3. Cash from or used in investing activities (that is, the net financing from issuing or repaying debt and the net financing from issuing or repaying equity).

The net total of the above three headings is the increase or decrease of the cash for the period, and it is added to or subtracted from the opening balance of cash in order to come up with the closing balance of cash. It is one way of understanding how an organization has managed its cash for that period.

The cash budget that is demonstrated in this chapter tells a similar story, but

1. it deals with a future period rather than a past period;
2. its format is generally closer to the format of the income statement, rather than the headings used in the cash flow statement;
3. it is prepared for use within the organization by managers who are responsible for monitoring and planning liquidity and corporate finance.

Both the cash flow statement and the cash budget, if prepared for the same time period, would tell the same story:

1. How much cash inflow was generated, and where did it come from?
2. How much cash outflow was there, and where did it go to?
3. What was the effect on the cash balance?

8.5 Cash Budgeting and the Functional Manager

External analysts will try to get a handle on how liquid a company is by calculating liquidity ratios, such as the current ratio and the quick ratio, and by examining the contents of the cash flow statement. These, however, are all going to be based on data from published financial statements that refer to the past. While these may be a guide to what will happen after the balance sheet date, they are an imperfect way of forecasting future cash flows and future liquidity.

Internally, the managers of the organization will have access to information that is both more current and more relevant than the information available to external analysts. They will be able to use this information to prepare detailed cash budgets. These will show the sources, amounts, and timing of cash inflows and cash outflows, and their effects on cash balances and cash availability.

Managers of functional areas (production, marketing, human resources, etc.) will not normally be expected to be managing organizational liquidity as such, but they should be thinking about the effects of their decisions and actions when they plan and execute their normal work activities. For example, the marketing manager may have identified an opportunity for a major new customer that would increase sales by 25% next year. Clearly this is going to make the company more profitable, but the additional production will have to be financed and if the sales are on credit, the increased receivables will have to be financed. She should discuss the effect on the company's liquidity with the treasurer or controller before committing to the new business.

Treasurers or controllers will normally prepare the cash budget on the basis of information given to them by other managers. Then, when they are informed by the cash budget they are in a good position to manage cash availability through access to short- or long-term financing, or by planning to put available surplus funds into appropriate investments.

8.6   Summary

Cash flows are critical to an understanding of liquidity. Managing liquidity is a critical task in ensuring that the organization can survive in the short term. Cash flows are budgeted by forecasting how much cash will be generated from sales revenue and when those cash inflows will arrive and by forecasting when cash outflows will occur. Cash inflows and outflows, when combined with expected beginning cash balances, enable the forecast of ending cash balances. Once the organization knows what to expect in respect of ending cash balances, it is in good position to manage the situation, for example, by negotiating short-term loans or additional long-term financing.

Self-Study Problem

1. You are the manager of Excellent Trading Inc. On November 1, 2011, you will have the following balances of current assets:

Cash on hand	$ 10,000
Accounts receivable	120,000 (25% of October's sales)
Inventory	175,000

You will owe $240,000 to trade creditors (50% of October's sales). Actual sales revenues were as follows:

September 2011	$360,000
October 2011	480,000

Budgeted sales revenues were as follows:

November 2011	$600,000
December 2011	720,000
January 2012	240,000

Experience has shown that 75% of the sales will be collected within the month of purchase, and the other 25% will be collected within the month following the purchase.

Goods for resale are marked up by 100% on cost to get selling price: i.e., a product that had cost $5 would be sold for $10. The goods purchased are paid for the month after they are sold (goods sold in October will be paid for in November).

Selling and marketing expenses are 10% of the sales revenue each month and are paid during that same month. General and administrative expenses are $100,000 per month, including $20,000 per month of amortization expense.

Required

(a) Prepare a cash budget for the months of November and December 2011.

(b) Is there a cash flow problem for November and December (and if so, what should you do about it)?

Solution

1.   (a)

Cash on hand November 1, 2011		$ 10,000
Budgeted receipts: November		
Collection of 25% of October's sales	$120,000	
Collection of 75% of November's sales		
($600,000 × 75%)	450,000	570,000
Cash available		$580,000
Budgeted payments: November		
Suppliers: (beginning accounts payable)	$240,000	
Sales and marketing expense (10% × $600,000)	60,000	
General and administrative expense		
($100,000 – $20,000 amortization)	80,000	380,000
Cash balance as at November 30, 2011		$200,000
Budgeted receipts: December		
Collection of 25% of November's sales		
(= accounts receivable at December 1)	$150,000	
Collection of 75% of December's sales*		
($720,000 × 75%)	540,000	690,000
Cash available		$890,000
Budgeted payments: December		
Suppliers ($600,000 × 50%)	$300,000	
Sales and marketing expense (10% × $720,000)	72,000	
General and administrative expense		
($100,000 – $20,000 amortization)	80,000	452,000
Cash balance as at December 31, 2011		$438,000

    * $720,000 × 25% receivable in January 2012

  (b)   Yes, there is a problem: the company has too much cash. The company should investigate useful ways to deploy the surplus funds, such as the following:
- Loan repayments
- Purchase of new equipment
- Dividends to shareholders
- Temporary investments

Discussion Questions and Problems

Discussion Questions

1. What is the objective of cash budgeting?
2. Which managers are responsible for preparing cash budgets?
3. When should cash budgets be prepared?
4. Why does a cash budget start with a forecast of the collection of cash from sales?
5. In a company that makes all its sales as cash sales, is the dollar amount of cash that is forecast to be collected a certain or an uncertain amount?
6. In a company that makes some or all of its sales as credit sales, is the dollar amount of cash that is forecast to be collected a certain or an uncertain amount?
7. What would a company do if the cash budget revealed a cash deficiency?
8. What would a company do if the cash budget revealed a cash surplus?
9. If the cash budget revealed a temporary cash deficiency, what type of financing would be suitable to use as a remedy?
10. If the cash budget revealed a long-term cash deficiency, what type of financing would be suitable to use as a remedy?

Problems

1. As the manager of a new retail outlet in the Jane-Finch Mall, you have been asked to prepare a cash budget for the first three months of year 2012.

   Sales revenue is budgeted to be $100,000 in January, $120,000 in February, $150,000 in March and April. All sales are for cash (or Interac direct debit, which is almost the same as cash).

   Selling price is calculated by adding a mark-up of 100% to the cost of goods sold. The plan is to buy enough inventory in December for the January sales, enough in January for the February sales, and so on. This means that the inventory of goods for resale at the start of any month is sufficient for the sales of that month.

   Goods are paid for in the month when bought (i.e., one month before being sold). Wages are paid during the month when earned and amount to $2,000 plus commission of 10% of sales revenue. Rent of $10,000 per month is paid in advance, with "first and last" month's rent payable on January 1.

   Required
   (a) Prepare a cash budget for the first three months of 2012.
   (b) Identify the point in time when the cash requirement is at a maximum and the amount of cash required at that time.

2. As the marketing manager of Consumer's Cosmetics Co., you are expecting total sales revenues to be as follows:

Date	Sales Revenues ($ millions)
October 2011	600
November 2011	660
December 2011	690
January 2012	600
February 2012	620
March 2012	650
April 2012	700
May 2012	740
June 2012	800

The pattern of sales can generally be grouped as follows:

- 30% of all sales are cash sales.
- 30% of all sales are credit sales collected one month after the sale.
- 25% of all sales are credit sales collected two months after the sale.
- 15% of all sales are credit sales collected three months after the sale.

Required

(a) Prepare a schedule of cash receipts from sales for January, February, and March 2012.

(b) Which month has the greatest amount of cash collections from sales? Explain why.

3. The cash budget for the Western Co. shows the following for the first three months of 2012:

Western Co.
Cash Budget
($ millions)

	January	February	March
Receipts			
Collections from sales	$50	$40	$45
Issue of new shares			10
Total receipts	$50	$40	$55
Payments			
Trade suppliers	$25	$30	$15
Wages and benefits	10	11	12
New equipment		5	
Loan repayment		10	
Dividend to shareholders	10		
Total payments	$45	$56	$27

The cash balance at January 1, 2012, was expected to be $5 million.

Required

(a) Is there a problem?

(b) If there is a problem, are there ways to deal with it?

4. Fitron Inc. is expected to have a cash balance of $100,000 on January 1. Relevant budget information is as follows:

	January	February
Cash collections from customers	$750,000	$950,000
Payments to suppliers	$250,000	$200,000
Direct labour expense	$200,000	$150,000
Production overhead expenses	$250,000	$250,000
Selling and administrative expense	$150,000	$150,000

Required
(a) Prepare a cash budget for January and February.
(b) Is there a problem?
(c) If there is a problem, suggest ways of dealing with it.

5. The Falstaff Co. manufactures toy soldiers, which the company sells in matched sets to toy stores in all major Canadian cities. In struggling to prepare next year's budget the company has collected the following information:

Projected sales, per month	200 sets
Selling price, per set	$100
Expected inventory on January 1	100 sets
Target inventory at the end of February	50 sets
Expected accounts receivable on January 1	$20,000
Direct labour hours, per set	5
Direct labour rate, per hour	$25
Direct materials, per set	$100
Variable manufacturing overhead, per set	$5
Fixed manufacturing overhead, per month	$2,000
Fixed selling & administrative overhead, per month	$5,000

Falstaff pays all costs in the month when they are incurred; the fixed costs include $1,000 per month for amortization. Customers take 30 days credit on all sales. There will be $2,000 cash on hand on January 1.

Required
(a) Prepare an operating budget for January.
(b) Prepare a cash budget for January.

6. Wilson Inc. manufactures sports equipment. In June last year the company borrowed $100,000 from the Wimbledon Bank at an interest rate of 8%. Repayment is to be in 10 annual instalments of $10,000 each on June 30 each year. When each repayment is made, the accumulated interest for that 12-month period is also paid.

Required
(a) How much interest expense will be reported last year, this year, and next year?
(b) Calculate the cash outflow for this loan, last year, this year, and next year.

7. Prince's Sales in December were $750,000. Prince's sales for January are expected to be $600,000, and for February are expected to be $800,000. Collections are normally as follows:

- 60% of customers pay cash and get a 2% discount.
- 30% of customers pay within 30 days.
- 10% of customers pay within 60 days.

Required
Calculate the cash collections from customers for February.

8. Pegler Co. has budgeted its credit sales as follows:

January	$300,000
February	$400,000
March	$600,000
April	$700,000
May	$800,000

Collections are normally as follows:

Collected within 30 days	50%
Collected in 30–60 days	30%
Collected in 60–90 days	15%
Uncollectible	5%

Cash payments are budgeted to be $400,000 per month for January to May. The cash balance on April 1 is expected to be $100,000.

Required
Calculate the cash balance at the end of each of April and May.

9. Maxima Inc. wants a projection of cash receipts and payments for the month of November. On November 28, a note payable will become due, to the bank that issued it, for $98,500 (including interest). The cash balance on November 1 will be $29,600. Accounts payable on November 1 were $280,000. Accounts receivable on November 1 were $132,000.

Sales of Maxima's only product are always $11 each: 70% of sales are collected in the month of sale and the other 30% are collected the following month. Each month the company plans to buy enough inventory to exactly meet demand for the following month. The company takes 30 days credit on all purchases.

Purchase cost of Maxima's product is $7 per unit. All expenses are fixed and amount to $150,000 per month, of which $25,000 is amortization. In November, Maxima expects to pay a dividend of $10,000 and to sell a building for $500,000. The budgeted sales are 40,000 units every month.

Required
Prepare a cash budget for the month of November.

10. Lennox Inc. manufactures heating and air-conditioning units for sales to builders and hardware stores. The area sales rep for Thunder Bay

has recently announced that a major new account has agreed to purchase Lennox's goods. Expected trade is 12,000 units per year, and each unit sells for $500. The new client has asked for two months' credit, as times in the construction trade are hard.

Required

As CFO, discuss the advantages and disadvantages of taking on this new client.

Budgetary Control

9

Learning
Objectives

After studying this chapter you should:
- → Be aware of the way budgets are used in controlling companies
- → Be able to explain the difference between an imposed budget and a participatory budget
- → Be able to explain how responsibility can only be exercised where there is a high level of control
- → Be able to execute budgetary control in revenue centres, cost centres, and profit centres
- → Be able to interpret a simple balanced scorecard
- → Be aware of the behavioural aspects of budgeting

9.1 Control

As was described in the previous chapter, a primary objective of a budget is planning: the budget represents the financial dimension of the organizational plan.

Another objective of a budget is that it enables budgetary control. The budget is used as an objective or standard. It represents an acceptable level of performance. From the perspective of the senior management, achieving the budget is evidence of having achieved the organization's objectives, and failing to achieve the budget indicates that the objectives have not been met.

If the budget in question is a budget for the whole organization, the bottom line will be a budgeted profit, and achieving the budget means bringing in an actual profit at least as big as the budgeted profit. If the budget is for a smaller part of the organization (e.g., a human resources management department), achieving the budget may be a question of keeping actual costs below budgeted costs.

Budgetary control of this type is extremely important, but there are also many other aspects to the control process that are non-financial in nature. Maintaining good customer relations and preserving the organization's reputation for quality products or services, for example, are both control issues, but largely fall outside the strict limits of budgetary control. As we shall see later in this chapter, the balanced scorecard can bring these non-financial controls into a routine control report.

The essence of budgetary control can be found in the idea of "management by exception". This idea proposes that once organizational objectives have been set and communicated to organizational members, then a routine process of comparison of actual outcomes with the objectives will reveal one of two states. Either the objectives will have been achieved, in which case no action is required, or the objectives will not have been achieved (this is regarded as an "exception"), and management will have

Exhibit 9.1:   Management by Exception — Budgetary Control

Establish organizational objectives.
Create an operating budget.

Carry out business activities.

Measure actual outcomes.
Calculate an actual
operating statement for the unit.

Provide explanations.
Implement necessary corrective
actions.

**Compare actual outcomes
with objectives.**
Compare actual profit (or cost)
with budgeted profit (or cost).

**If outcomes do not meet
objectives, investigate and
act as necessary.**
Is actual profit less than
budgeted profit,
or is actual cost greater than
budgeted cost?

**If outcomes meet objectives,
continue to next control period.**
Is actual profit equal to or greater
than budgeted profit,
or is actual cost less than
budgeted cost?

an obligation to investigate the situation so that an explanation of the exception can be found, and appropriate corrective action can be implemented. This can also be described as a feedback loop, and it is illustrated in Exhibit 9.1.

So, a company may have budgeted for a profit of $500,000 for the month of August. If the actual profit were to be $520,000, the company would probably consider it (a) close enough and (b) erring on the plus side rather than the negative. The idea of management by exception would imply that the organizational objectives had been achieved, and they could carry on with business as usual.

275

If, on the other hand, the actual profit were to be $370,000, management by exception would call for an investigation because the variance (minus $130,000) is both large and unfavourable. If the investigation then revealed that there had been production problems and that these had resulted in customers' orders not being fulfilled, then the production manager would be expected to show what changes had been made to prevent it from happening again. Because there was an exception (missing the profit target by $130,000), management action was required (reports and corrections).

A human resources department may have had an operating budget that authorized it to spend $200,000 in August. If the actual expense were to be $190,000, it would probably be treated as "in control". If the actual expense were to be $250,000, then the department manager would have to explain what happened (perhaps she had to deal with an unusually high level of production employee turnover) and show what she had done to prevent the overspending from recurring.

9.2   Imposed and Participative Budgets

In order for the budget to be an effective control it has to have validity: that is, all the people involved have to accept it. There are two broad approaches to achieving acceptability: imposed budgets and participative budgets.

An imposed budget is one that is dictated by the higher levels of management, without the people responsible for carrying it out having any say in what it comprises. The roots of imposed budgets are in a hierarchical approach to management, such as would be found in a military unit. The superiors are recognized as having authority to impose the budget by virtue of their position in the organization. The inferiors are required to accept the budget because they have been ordered to do so, and the order comes from a source with legitimate authority.

There are a number of situations where this is an appropriate way to plan and to exercise control, considering the context in which the organization operates. For example, if there are factors that are known to senior management, but not known to lower levels, then an imposed budget may be the only way that information can be recognized in the organizational plan. More commonly, though, an imposed budget reflects an organizational style of tight control that is caused by the personalities of the senior managers.

One danger of imposed budgets is that they may be set at an unreasonable level of performance. If people know that the budget is impossible to meet, they may become careless and cease trying because they know they are going to fail anyway.

A participative budget, by contrast, is one where the people who have to actually carry out the work engage in an interchange of information with their managers, such that both sides can eventually agree on a budget that is mutually acceptable. This budget represents performance that is acceptable to the senior managers because it meets the organization's objectives, and to the operating staff because they regard it as a reasonable task that is within their capabilities.

As with imposed budgets, a participative budget can be the result of situational factors (such as the operatives having detailed knowledge of things senior managers do not know) and can also be caused by the psychology of the senior managers of the organization, who are more open to discussion and compromise.

There is a high level of agreement that a participative budget is likely to have a higher degree of "buy-in" than an imposed one. The people controlled by a participative budget will be more motivated to achieve it, and they are likely to have a more positive attitude toward their work situation. The downside is that the budget-setting process sometimes allows people to set unreasonably low standards: budgets that have a lot of budgetary slack or padding built in, and that are relatively easy to meet.

Pseudo-participation can be observed where an organization wants to be seen to have adopted a participatory approach, so it introduces superficial participation and seeks the formality of approval by lower level employees, without giving them the reality of being able to say no. Pseudo-participation is most unlikely to result in an appropriate budget or in superior motivation.

Few organizations are likely to run things at either the totally imposed or the totally participative extreme, and most exhibit some budget behaviours of each type. Smart organizations will choose the budget style that matches the underlying factors of each budget situation, rather than insisting on a universal approach throughout.

9.3   Responsibility and Control

Underlying the control process is another management theory: that of responsibility and control. It is a reasonable assumption that you can hold someone responsible for the things they can control, but you should not hold them responsible for things over which they have no control. What is meant by this is that each manager has a responsibility area within which his or her decisions affect the outcomes. They can be held accountable for those outcomes through the control process.

A production manager, for example, has control over the production process, and his or her decisions will affect the quantity and quality of production output. If production is at acceptable levels of quantity and quality, everything is OK. If there is a shortfall of quantity or an unacceptable deterioration of quality that is going to have serious negative consequences for the organization, the control system should be identifying the production area as the problem and, probably, the production manager as being the person responsible.

Further investigation may lead to the conclusion that the problem had been caused by the purchasing department buying below-standard raw materials. If the production manager was not in control of the purchasing decision, he cannot be held responsible for the effects of a purchasing decision. The responsibility then shifts to the purchasing manager.

Like many management theories, this is obviously correct at the extremes but tends to become highly problematic in real cases due to blurred lines of responsibility.

Missing the sales budget, for example, might be caused by the following:

• Marketing decisions, leading to an inappropriate product specification
• Design decisions, leading to a poor design
• Production decisions, leading to poor quality
• Sales decisions, leading to a low level of sales effort
• Marketing decisions, leading to advertising in the wrong media
• Logistics decisions, leading to late deliveries
• After-sales decisions, leading to poor warranty work

An unacceptably high production cost could be impossible to control if several products are made in common facilities, and the company loses track of what costs are caused by which product-related decisions.

Often the costs of common facilities are allocated to departments or products through an overhead recovery system. Although this makes sense in establishing the full cost of operating the department or making the product, it is not a situation where the manager has any control over the cost, so it becomes problematical to hold him or her responsible for these allocated central costs.

9.4 Control in Organizational Sub-Units

We can consider responsibility and control by relating it to the organizational sub-units that have been chosen. Sub-units can be classified as either revenue centres, cost centres, or profit centres. Cost centres can be further divided into those responsible for delivering a service and production cost centres. Profit centres can be further divided into those that have no control over investment in assets and those with investment control. The budgetary control reports should match the realities of what is controlled.

9.4.1 Control in Revenue Centres

A sales department is an example of a revenue centre. It is responsible for making sales. Its success or failure may be judged by the difference between budgeted and actual sales. This can be measured in units, or in sales revenue dollars, or even in terms of the contribution margin the sales have earned. (Contribution margin is the sales revenue, less the variable cost of sales.)

> **Example:** Northgate Supplies has budgeted to sell 2,000 widgets in the month of September, creating $50,000 of sales revenue (before taxes). Actual sales were 2,100 widgets, and actual sales revenue was $54,600. Northgate has exceeded its budget in both units (widgets sold) and revenues, so the company has more than met its budget.

Further investigation shows that the budgeted price was $25 per widget ($50,000 ÷ 2,000 widgets = $25), whereas the actual price per widget was higher ($54,600 ÷ 2,100 widgets = $26 each). This is another cause for satisfaction.

9.4.2   *Control in a Cost Centre 1: Service Department*

A department of human resources management is an example of a cost centre that delivers a service. Its role and objective would be to provide HR services and expertise to the rest of the organization. It has (i.e., its manager has) control over how much HR to provide. How much service the department can provide will be strongly influenced by the resources the HR manager is allowed to consume by virtue of his or her budget. When the budget is established, it would be the HR manager's role to argue the case for an adequate budget to carry out the task at hand (hence the importance of a participative budget). During the execution phase, the manager will allocate resources appropriately to carry out the work. Two linked but separate control questions can then be addressed. First, did the required HR services and expertise get delivered? Second, did the HR department operate within the budget? Clearly, budgetary control as such can only address the second question.

Example: The Southgate Co. has a human resources department with an operating budget of $500,000 in 2011. This is comprised of salaries for the employees, travel and entertainment expenses, supplies, and the costs of operating a computer system for the payroll. The actual expense for 2011 has come out to $565,000, as follows:

Southgate Co.
Budgetary Control Report for Year 2011

	Budget	Actual	Variance
Salaries	$250,000	$300,000	$50,000 U
Travel & entertainment	50,000	70,000	20,000 U
Supplies	10,000	10,000	nil
Computer system costs	190,000	185,000	5,000 F
Total	$500,000	$565,000	$65,000 U

The salaries and travel and entertainment lines are both overspent, while the supplies are exactly on target and the computer system costs are underspent. If asked, the HR manager may have a rational and logical explanation. For example, if the organization had been required to deal with some unexpected hirings and firings or to adapt to new HR legislation, then the overspending could be treated as a legitimate response to a situation that has changed since the budget was set. Conversely, if no such changes from the original business plan could be identified, the HR manager should be in serious trouble for the overspending and should provide a detailed description of the actions that have been taken to avoid overspending in future.

Note that, by convention, any difference between a budget and an actual is called a variance, and variances that decrease profits are called unfavourable (U), while variances that increase profits are called favourable (F). This is easier to deal with than calling them plus or minus.

9.4.3   *Control in a Cost Centre 2: Production Department*

A production department is responsible for producing a good or a service for sale. Because there is some measurable production or service activity, the work done can be expressed not only as a total, but also on a "per unit" basis. This enhances the control process as the effect of changes in the volume of activity can be separated from the effect of price changes or efficiency changes.

> **Example:** Eastgate Co. manufactures ethical pharmaceuticals (i.e., prescription medicines). The budget for the production of Patent Pain Pills for October and the actual results are as follows:

Eastgate Co.
Production Budget for Patent Pain Pills — October

	Budget	Actual	Variance
Volume	**500,000**	**600,000**	**100,000**
Raw material	$ 5,000	$ 6,300	$1,300 U
Direct labour	2,000	2,400	400 U
Allocated overhead			
Variable	4,000	4,800	800 U
Fixed	6,000	7,200	1,200 U
Total	$17,000	$20,700	$3,700 U

The original budget (called a static budget) is for total expense of $17,000 — that is, the materials, the direct labour costs, and the overhead required for producing 500,000 Patent Pain Pills. The overhead is an allocation based on 200% of the budgeted labour cost in respect of variable overhead and 300% of the budgeted labour cost in respect of fixed overhead. Both overhead amounts represent the use of facilities shared by all products made by the company.

The actual cost is made up of the actual raw materials and direct labour, plus allocated variable overhead (200% of the actual labour cost) and allocated fixed overhead (300% of the actual labour cost).

The first thing we would probably notice is that the budget has been overspent — a budget of $17,000 has become an actual reported cost of $20,700 — and that the unfavourable variances total $3,700. However, it is important to note that the budget was for the production of 500,000 units, while the actual was the cost of producing 600,000. Clearly this comparison of totals is unfair because the amount of work done has increased by 20%.

This work increase can be seen, however, if the cost is expressed on a per unit basis. The budget was for 500,000 pills to cost $17,000, which is $34 per thousand units. The actual cost of $20,700 made 600,000 pills, at a cost of $34.5 per thousand units. Although there has still been overspending, it is not as extreme as the crude totals would indicate.

In order to separate the effect of volume changes from the effect of price and efficiency changes, a calculation can be done with the budget that would have been set if the actual volume had been known in advance: this is called a flexible budget (to contrast it with the static or original budget).

Eastgate Co.
Production Budget for Patent Pain Pills — October

Volume	Rate $ per unit	Static Budget 500,000	Flexible Budget 600,000	Actual 600,000
Raw material	$0.010	$ 5,000	$ 6,000	$ 6,300
Direct labour	0.004	2,000	2,400	2,400
Allocated overhead				
Variable	0.008	4,000	4,800	4,800
Fixed	0.012	6,000	6,000*	7,200
Total	$0.034	$17,000	$19,200	$20,700

* Fixed costs are not normally "flexed" in a flexible budget.

The effect of the volume change (increase of production from 500,000 to 600,000) is that we would expect the expense to increase from $17,000 to $19,200. The $2,200 change does not represent an "out-of-control" situation; it represents a reasonable additional expense of making the additional 100,000 units.

The difference between the flexible budget ($19,200) and the actual expense ($20,700) is an amount of $1,500 overspent. In this case it is overspending on materials of $300 plus overspending on fixed overhead of $1,200. As a percentage of the raw materials budget, this is only 5% and may be regarded as relatively unimportant ($300 ÷ $6,000 × 100% = 5%).

We can be clear that materials are overspent by $300. It is not clear at this stage whether that was due to a price increase, or due to a reduction in efficiency, or a combination of the two. The overspending on fixed overhead of $1,200 on a budget of $6,000 is far more serious.

Despite the apparent overspending, this production department is reasonably in control.

This concept of flexing the budget for changes in activity should be applied in all circumstances where there is a relevant measure of the volume of activity. Generally, that means it should be applied for control of all production cost centres.

9.4.4 Control in a Profit Centre

A profit centre is an organizational sub-unit that has control over both revenues and costs and, therefore, over the operating profit. The same techniques that are available for controlling revenue centres and cost centres are available for controlling profit centres. Additionally, control in a profit centre is exercised by comparing the actual profit to the budgeted profit. In the same way that a production department has a physical measure of its activity (the number of units produced), a profit centre also has a physical measure of activity (the number of units sold). This also enables "flexing" of the budget to enable changes in the level of activity to be separated from other spending changes.

> **Example:** The appliance division of Westgate Inc. had budgeted to make an operating profit of $10,000 in September, but its actual operating profit was $15,400.

Westgate Inc.
Appliance Division — Budget Report for September

	Budget per Unit	Static Budget	Actual	Variance	
Units		1,000	1,200	200	F
Sales revenue	$50	$50,000	$62,400	$12,400	F
Less: Cost of goods sold	30	30,000	35,000	5,000	U
Contribution margin	$20	$20,000	$27,400	$ 7,400	F
Less: Fixed costs	10	10,000	12,000	2,000	U
Operating profit	$10	$10,000	$15,400	$ 5,400	F

The operating profit has increased from $10,000 to $15,400. The first thing that can be said is that the profit objectives have been comfortably exceeded. Clearly the increase in sales from 1,000 in the budget to 1,200 actual is a part of the change in profit. Further analysis calls for creating a flexible budget: the expected profit for selling 1,200 units.

Westgate Inc.
Appliance Division — Budget Report for September

	Budget per Unit	Static Budget	Flexible Budget	Actual
Units		1,000	1,200	1,200
Sales revenue	$50	$50,000	$60,000	$62,400
Less: Cost of goods sold	30	30,000	36,000	35,000
Contribution margin	$20	$20,000	$24,000	$27,400
Less: Fixed costs	10	10,000	10,000	12,000
Operating profit	$10	$10,000	$14,000	$15,400

With the flexible budget column added, the volume effect can be separated from any other effects. The original budget called for sales of 1,000 units of product and an operating profit of $10,000. The flexible budget shows that sales of 1,200 units should have resulted in an operating profit of $14,000. The $4,000 increase is due to the additional sales of 200 units, each one of which makes a contribution margin of $20.

The difference between the flexible budget operating profit ($14,000) and the actual operating profit ($15,400) is $1,400. We can explain this line by line from the statement.

Sales revenue was $62,400, compared to the flexible budget's $60,000. We got a $2,400 favourable variance by selling products at prices higher than the budgeted prices.

The cost of goods sold was actually $35,000, compared to the flexible budget of $36,000. Either because we paid less for inputs, such as raw materials and labour (a price effect), or because we used fewer raw materials and less labour (an efficiency effect), we spent less overall than was expected, and created a $1,000 favourable variance.

The budgeted spending on fixed overhead was $10,000. Note that this item does not get flexed in the flexible budget. Whereas revenues and the cost of goods sold are expected to rise or fall when the volume of activity rises or falls, fixed costs are not expected to be affected by volume changes. The actual expense was $12,000, so an overspending or unfavourable variance of $2,000 has occurred.

Summarizing these variances we get the following:

Sales price variance	$2,400 F
Cost of goods sold variance	1,000 F
Fixed cost variance	2,000 U
Net flexible budget variance	$1,400 F

and

Sales volume variance	4,000 F
Total change	$5,400 F

This profit centre has done very well overall. It has generated an additional $4,000 of profit from increasing sales volume and has generated an increased profit of $2,400 by increasing selling prices, and a further $1,000 by reducing the direct cost of goods sold. The profit centre reduced its profit by $2,000 by overspending on fixed costs.

Whoever was responsible for the increased sales and the reduced cost of goods sold is likely to be praised and maybe rewarded. Whoever was responsible for the overspending on fixed costs will have to explain exactly what happened, why it happened, and what corrective actions have been implemented.

9.4.5 Control in an Investment Centre

An investment centre is a profit centre with one addition: in addition to having control over its profit-making activities, it also has control over the investment in assets. An investment centre can be controlled using all the methods available for controlling revenue centres, cost centres, and profit centres. Additionally, an investment centre can be controlled through the ratio of profit to assets employed.

Example: Compass Inc. is a multi-divisional organization for which the budgeted and actual results for 2011 were as follows:

Compass Inc.
Budgetary Control Report for 2011
($ millions)

	Budget	Actual
Sales revenues	$200	$240
Cost of goods sold	150	180
Gross margin	$ 50	$ 60
Operating expense	20	24
Operating income	$ 30	$ 36
÷ Total assets	$300	$450
Return on assets	10%	8%

Exhibit 9.2: A Budgetary Control Report

Compass Inc.
Budgetary Control Report for 2011 ($ millions)

	Aircraft		Motor Vehicles		Consulting		Total	
	Budget	Actual	Budget	Actual	Budget	Actual	Budget	Actual
Sales revenues	$ 50	$ 40	$100	$135	$ 50	$ 65	$200	$240
COGS	25	24	89	109	36	47	150	180
Gross margin	$ 25	$ 16	$ 11	$ 26	$ 14	$ 18	$ 50	$ 60
Operating expense	10	10	5	9	5	5	20	24
Operating income	$ 15	$ 6	$ 6	$ 17	$ 9	$ 13	$ 30	$ 36
÷ Total assets	$150	$150	$120	$170	$30	$130	$300	$450
ROA%	10%	4%	5%	10%	30%	10%	10%	8%

Although sales and profits have increased, so have assets. The budgeted return on assets was 10%, but the actual return is only 8%. Compass Inc. is not performing as well as was expected.

All organizations can be controlled in total as investment centres, as they are all capable of exercising control over both profits and investment. Most large organizations will extend the idea down through the company. They do this by splitting the company up into sub-units that have control over both profits and investment in assets. This creates a decentralized organizational structure and it makes each autonomous sub-unit controllable through the return on assets ratio.

Suppose Compass Inc. had structured itself into three autonomous sub-units: aircraft, motor vehicles, and consulting services. Its budgetary control report might look like Exhibit 9.2. (All amounts that follow are in millions.)

Compass Inc. started off with the expectation of earning $30 of operating income, which is a 10% return on $300 of invested assets. The actual results come out as a higher profit ($36), but also a higher asset total ($450). This is a return of only 8%, so the company has not met its profitability objective of a 10% return on assets. Fundamentally, the $6 of additional earnings do not justify the $150 of additional investment. Because the company controls its three sub-units as investment centres, the location of the discrepancy can be located quite precisely.

The aircraft division expected to make $15 of income on $150 of assets, which is a 10% return. The actual result is a smaller profit ($6) on the same level of assets, for a 4% return. The division contributed to the problem by making insufficient operating profit, while the assets are the same as were budgeted.

The motor vehicles division budgeted to make a profit of $6 on $120 of assets, which is a 5% return on assets. The actual result shows a higher operating profit ($17) on a greater amount of assets ($170), and an actual return that has gone up to 10%. Clearly this division is not the problem!

The consulting division planned to make a $9 profit on $30 of assets, which is a 30% return. Actually the division made a larger profit ($13), but had a massive increase in assets, which rose from $30 to $130, and the return on assets fell to 10%. The division made more profit, but it was not enough to justify the additional investment.

The aircraft division and the consulting division were the culprits in the drop in return on assets from 10% to 8%.

Further ratio analysis can also be carried out on these data. For example, the ratio of gross margin to sales could be looked at, and its budgeted rate could be compared to its actual rate. In the aircraft division, for example, the gross margin was budgeted to be 50% (gross margin: $25 divided by sales revenue of $50 = 50%). The actual gross margin was 40% (= $16 ÷ $40). This goes a long way to explaining why the division did so badly.

Note that as with most budgetary control analyses, the accountant can accurately calculate the effect of a deviation from the budget and measure how much it damages the organization, but the accountant has no idea what the underlying causes are. That part of the management process has to come from the managers who are in control of the sub-units or departments.

9.5 The Balanced Scorecard

One of the criticisms of the budgetary control approach is that it dwells only on financial measures and deals only with what has already happened. Business has wider objectives than can be described purely financially, and management should be about the future, not the past. The balanced scorecard has been developed to change this emphasis. It is a report that considers the past, the present, and the future, and it considers both financial and non-financial information. In this way, the control process can be explicitly linked to the organizational strategy.

Step one is to make an explicit list of the company strategy and the plans that have been put in place to achieve that strategy. For each of the identifiable initiatives a measure of its success or failure should be identified, and a target set. Actual results are then reported against that target to see whether or not it was achieved.

A typical balanced scorecard contains four sections (see Exhibit 9.3):

1. *Financial perspective:* Financial measures such as profitability rates are reported here. Financial measures are not ignored in the balanced scorecard, but their dominance is mitigated by the presence of other measures.

2. *Customer perspective:* The customer's perspective is considered through primary measurement, such as getting customers to fill in questionnaires about service levels and satisfaction, and through indirect measures, such as the number of complaints and the number of

Exhibit 9.3:   The Balanced Scorecard

Carberry Hotels
Balanced Scorecard for September 2011

Objective	Measure	Target	Actual
Financial perspective:			
Shareholder value	Return on equity	15.0%	15.6%
	Share price growth	5.0%	6.0%
Customer perspective:			
Quantity	Occupancy rates	90.0%	93.2%
Quality	Room rack-rate growth	4.0%	5.0%
	Customer satisfaction	9/10	9.3/10
	Written complaints	0	0
Internal business perspective:			
Cleanliness	Random checks	10/10	10/10
Restaurant	Menu changes	5	6
Accessibility	Wheelchair access	98.0%	98.0%
Learning and growth perspective:			
Staff training	Training hours	100	75
Market segments	New segments targeted	2	1
Product development	New facilities	1	0

Assessment: Carberry Hotels has done very well in three areas, meeting or exceeding its targets on each criterion for financial, customer, and internal business perspective. However, it has failed to meet its targets for learning and growth. It is probable that learning and growth, which are about developing the future, have been compromised in the company's efforts to achieve current success.

sales returns. The customer perspective, unlike the financial perspective, is about the present, not the past.

3. *Internal business perspective:* The ways in which the business has changed its internal operations to better achieve its objectives are considered through such measures as process restructuring, technology, and logistics improvements.

4. *Learning and growth:* The organization will have a successful future only if it learns and grows over time. This section is future oriented. It lists the activities that have been engaged in that create that rosy future. Here it would report training initiatives, employee motivation, new product development, and basic research.

A good balanced scorecard has the following characteristics:

• It articulates between strategy and operations.
• It helps to communicate strategy to employees.
• It creates a balanced perspective between financial and non-financial measures for employees.

- It creates a balanced perspective between the past, the present, and the future in the management process.
- It restricts itself to a few key measures.
- It identifies the effect of trade-offs between competing objectives.
- It is integrated with the motivation and reward system.

9.6 The Behavioural Aspect of Budgeting

Budget preparation and budgetary control may seem like mechanical processes: they may be described by a series of rules about how the budgets are prepared, how actual results are compared with budgets, and how management actions arise from the comparison. In reality a substantial degree of influence over how the process is carried out is exerted by the people involved. This is referred to as the behavioural aspect of budgeting.

A unit manager who is responsible for preparing a budget may be motivated to reduce her forecast of sales or increase her forecast of expense, for example. Either of these actions results in a budget that is easier to achieve. A senior manager who approves unit managers' budgets, on the other hand, would only accept their budgets if the budgets have an optimistic estimate of profit, which is an incentive for the units to strive for superior performance. In general, this conflicting situation arises because both the organization and its employees have goals and objectives that are not the same, and the organization's goals can only be met through the actions of the employees.

The ideal situation is where the organization's goals can be met by the employees pursuing their own goals. This is called "goal congruence". One example of how to create goal congruence is through the use of incentive rewards.

Basing part of remuneration on whether or not goals have been achieved is called an incentive-based reward system. It makes the link between doing what the organization wants and the presumed economic objectives of employees immediate and tangible. The typical incentive scheme gives a monetary reward (a bonus) for achieving some small, but clearly defined step that is part of the organization's plan. The rewards are frequently monetary but can also be non-monetary (such as being recognized as "employee of the month"). Threat of punishment for not achieving goals can also be used but tends to set up a negative and confrontational work atmosphere.

Examples of incentives include the following:

- A salesperson might be given a $1,000 bonus for every 1% increase in sales volume.
- A shift of production workers might be given a $250 bonus for every week when no product defects were identified.
- An employee might have his or her picture displayed in the lobby for helping customers beyond the call of duty.
- A manager might be dismissed for failing to meet profit objectives.

Creating a climate of goal congruence should be a carefully thought out process rather than a lucky accident. Ideally, goal congruence fits in with other ideas mentioned earlier in this chapter, such as the creation of realistic budgets, the linkage between responsibility and control, the participative budget-setting process, and feedback loops (which should be frequent and which should clearly and frequently indicate what is going well and what is going badly).

Failure to create a system of goal congruence may lead to dysfunctional behaviours, such as the creating of budgetary slack (such as padding the budget with unnecessary expense), and employees making decisions that benefit them but that frustrate the achievement of the organizational goals.

9.7 Budgetary Control and the Functional Manager

Functional managers have responsibility for the areas where they make resource decisions. Through the control process they can be held accountable for the decisions they make:

- Sales/marketing managers can be held responsible for meeting the sales revenue budgets.
- Production managers can be held responsible for the cost of products.
- Service cost centre managers (such as human resource managers) can be held responsible for the costs of their areas (for example, the cost of a new training program).

Functional managers should not, however, be asked to take responsibility for outcomes over which they have no control.

9.8 Summary

The management activities of planning and control are realized through the preparation and use of budgets. Budgeting consists of estimating operating income, expense, and cash flow, and budgetary control consists of using the budget to keep the organization on track to meet its objectives. Recently, budgeting as a financial activity has been supplemented with the balanced scorecard, which brings non-financial data into the equation and tries to deal with the present and the future as well as the past.

Self-Study Problems

1. Carlton Co. makes luxury travel bags that are to be sold to retailers for $250 each. Material costs are $40 per bag; labour costs are $60 per bag; overhead is a fixed amount of $100,000 per month. The company expects to sell 1,000 bags per month.

   Required
   (a) Should Carlton Co. be controlled as a cost centre, a profit centre, or an investment centre?
   (b) What is the budgeted monthly profit?
   (c) The actual results for August were as follows:

Sales revenue	900 bags @ $260	$234,000
Materials	$ 35,000	
Labour	50,000	
Overhead	102,000	187,000
Operating profit		$ 47,000

   Was the company in control or out of control?

2. The maintenance and cleaning department at Concordia Hospital had the following budget for July:

Wages	$ 500,000
Supplies	300,000
Vehicle expenses	250,000
Office expenses	100,000
Total	$1,150,000

   The actual expense totalled $1,250,000, as follows:

Wages	$ 475,000
Supplies	430,000
Vehicle expenses	250,000
Office expenses	95,000
Total	$1,250,000

   Required
   (a) Should this unit be controlled as a revenue, cost, profit, or investment centre?
   (b) Was the department in control or out of control?

3. As part of an exercise in preparing a balanced scorecard, identify three customer satisfaction measures and say how you would assess them for (a) Tim Hortons (a fast food franchise) and (b) Air Canada (an airline).

Solutions

1. (a) Like most autonomous organizations, Carlton Co. has control over its revenues and its costs and, hence, over its profit, and would also have control over its investment in assets. Therefore, in theory, it should be controlled as an investment centre. In this example, the information presented includes revenues and expenses but does not include investment, so we would have to treat it as a profit centre for control purposes.

   (b) The budgeted monthly profit is as follows:

Sales revenue	(1,000 bags @ $250)		$250,000
Materials	(1,000 bags @ $40)	$ 40,000	
Labour	(1,000 bags @ $60)	60,000	
Overhead		100,000	200,000
Operating profit			$ 50,000

   (c) The original (or static) budget was that Carlton Co. would make an operating profit of $50,000. The actual operating profit was only $47,000, so the company missed its target. The $3,000 gap can be further analyzed as follows. The actual results and the static budget results are the bookends in the following chart. In the middle is the flexible budget. The flexible budget shows that at a sales level of 900 units, we would expect Carlton Co. to make a profit of $35,000.

	Actual 900 bags	Flexible Budget 900 bags	Static Budget 1,000 bags
Sales revenue	$234,000	$225,000	$250,000
Materials	$ 35,000	$ 36,000	$ 40,000
Labour	50,000	54,000	60,000
Overhead	102,000	100,000	100,000
Total expense	$187,000	$190,000	$200,000
Operating profit	$ 47,000	$ 35,000	$ 50,000

   Sales volume effect: The company planned to sell 1,000 bags, but actually sold only 900 bags. Each bag not sold could be expected to earn a "contribution margin" of $150. (The contribution margin is the difference between the selling price [$250] and the variable cost [$40 + $60] and is $150 for this product: see next chapter for a fuller discussion of contribution margin.)

   Variance = 100 bags @ $150 = $15,000 (unfavourable).

   This $15,000 U variance explains the difference between the static budget profit of $50,000 and the flexible budget profit of $35,000.

   Selling price effect: The company planned to sell its bags for $250: the actual price was $260. Each of the 900 bags brought in an additional $10 of sales revenue, due to the price increase.

Variance = 900 @ $10 = 9,000 (favourable).

Materials cost effect: The company planned to spend $40 per bag on materials; for 900 bags, that would be $36,000. The actual cost was $35,000, so the company saved $1,000.

Variance = $1,000 (favourable).

Labour cost effect: The company planned to spend $60 per bag on labour; for 900 bags, that would be $54,000. The actual cost was $50,000, so the company saved $4,000.

Variance = $4,000 (favourable).

Overhead cost effect: The company planned to spend $100,000 (total) on overhead; the actual cost was $102,000, so the company overspent by $2,000.

Variance = $2,000 (unfavourable).

Summary:

Original budgeted profit (static budget)	$50,000
Actual profit	47,000
Difference	$ 3,000 (unfavourable)

Which is explained by the variances:

Sales volume variance	$15,000 U
Sales price variance	9,000 F
Material cost variance	1,000 F
Labour cost variance	4,000 F
Overhead cost variance	2,000 U
Total	$ 3,000 U

Was the company out of control? It is a judgment call as to whether the gap of $3,000 is a serious issue or a relatively trivial one. That $3,000 net unfavourable variance conceals an unfavourable sales volume variance of $15,000, which is almost certainly a cause for concern.

2. (a) This unit should be controlled as a cost centre, specifically a "service" cost centre. The department has a responsibility to clean and maintain and the right to spend $1,150,000 per month to do so, but the department does not produce a saleable product, and it has no revenue.

(b) There is an overspending of $100,000 in the month, which represents a little under 10% of the budget of $1,150,000. This would probably be regarded as a significant amount. The department would have to (at the very least) explain why the overspending happened. Yes, on the face of it, the department is out of control.

On a "line-by-line" examination of the budget we can see that the department actually underspent on each expense area except supplies, so spending on supplies (overspent by $130,000) is the only problem. There may be a good explanation (for example, an unexpected major repair to a piece of equipment or a building), but it is up to the unit manager to justify the overspending.

3. (a) Tim Hortons' customer satisfaction measures:
   - Percentage of customers responding "very satisfied" to a customer satisfaction survey
   - Number of written or e-mail complaints in the complaints log
   - Speed of customer service, as measured by observation

   (b) Air Canada's customer satisfaction measures:
   - Percentage of customers responding "very satisfied" to a customer satisfaction survey
   - Number of written or e-mail complaints in the complaints log
   - Number of flights arriving on time as measured by observation

Discussion Questions and Problems

Discussion Questions

1. What is the purpose of feedback in budgetary control?
2. Who should set a budget: the upper management of the organization or the employees who have to carry out the actual work?
3. How should a service department (such as a human resource department) be controlled?
4. How should a production department (such as a bottle-filling station in a food factory) be controlled?
5. How should a revenue centre (such as a sales team) be controlled?
6. How should a retail store that is a branch of a national chain be controlled?
7. What is the link between responsibility and control?
8. If a product is sold at a higher price than the budgeted price, is it "out of control"?
9. Is spending less than the budget always a good idea?
10. How can the organization create "goal congruence"?
11. What are the four sections usually found on a balanced scorecard?
12. How does a balanced scorecard improve the budgetary control process?

Problems

1. You are given the year's budget and actual financial report for the marketing department at Eros Furniture:

Details	Budget	Actual
Staff salaries	$ 900,000	$ 875,000
Salary-related expense	90,000	87,500
Travel and lodging	300,000	250,000
Equipment-related expense	50,000	50,000
Training	25,000	nil
Total	$1,365,000	$1,262,500

The salaries were below budget because of a vacancy in the last quarter of the year. A new employee will be starting work on January 1. The nine marketing staff earned an average salary of $100,000 each in the current year. Next year, the salaries will average $110,000 (that includes the new employee). Salary-related expenses (health, pension, etc.) are budgeted at 10% of salary expense.

Travel and lodging expenses were down because site visits to stores were fewer than planned (25, instead of the planned 30 visits). Next year, 25 visits are planned. In addition to the change in the number of store site visits, travel and lodging expenses are expected to increase by 5% next year. Training was not carried out as expected this year, but next year a $75,000 training expense is expected.

Required

Was the marketing department "in control" or "out of control"?

2. Below is a list of responsibility areas identified in the Dayglo Cosmetics firm:

   (i) Marketing department (responsible for toothpaste products)
   (ii) Marketing department (responsible for new product development)
   (iii) Toothpaste manufacturing unit
   (iv) Toothpaste logistics and delivery management department
   (v) Manager in charge of toothpaste product line (responsible for all sales and costs)
   (vi) Production manager (responsible for all production costs and production-related investment)
   (vii) Vice-president in charge of personal care products (responsible for all sales, costs, and investments)

   Required
   For each responsibility area, determine if control should be exercised

   (a) through a participative process or through an imposed budget; and
   (b) as a revenue, cost, profit, or investment centre.

3. You are given the following data (in $'000s) for the toothpaste product line of Dayglo Cosmetics:

	Budget		**Actual**	
Total toothpaste market		$10,000		$12,000
Dayglo's market share		10%		9%
Dayglo toothpaste sales		$ 1,000		$ 1,080
Variable costs				
Materials	$200		$240	
Labour	200		200	
Overhead	100		96	
Marketing	200		220	
	$700		$756	
Fixed costs				
Production	$100		$100	
Marketing and administration	50		60	
	$150		$160	
Total costs		850		916
Operating income		$ 150		$ 164

   Required
   (a) Was the toothpaste product line "in control" or "out of control"?
   (b) Which manager(s) would you hold responsible for any deviations from the budget?

4. Truly Inc. is a luggage manufacturer. The company estimated that the Ontario market for suitcases would be 2,500,000 units this year, and it expected to get a 5% share of this market. On average, each case would be sold to stores for $50. Variable costs were budgeted to be $20 per case and fixed costs were budgeted at $1,000,000. As it happened, due to the recession, both holiday and business travel

was much lower than expected, and total suitcase sales were only 1,500,000 for the year.

At the end of the year, the company presented the following results:

Sales revenue (100,000 cases @ $45)	$4,500,000
Actual variable costs	2,500,000
Gross margin	$2,000,000
Actual fixed costs	1,200,000
Operating profit	$ 800,000

Required
Was Truly Inc. "in control" or "out of control"?

5. Truly Inc. is a luggage manufacturer. The company estimated that the Ontario market for suitcases would be 2,500,000 units this year, and it expected to get a 5% share of this market. On average, each case would be sold to stores for $50. Variable costs were budgeted to be $20 per case and fixed costs were budgeted at $100,000,000. As it happened, due to the recession, both holiday and business travel was much lower than expected, and total suitcase sales were only 1,500,000 for the year.

At the end of the year, the company presented the following results:

Sales revenue (100,000 cases @ $45)	$4,500,000
Actual variable costs	2,500,000
Gross margin	$2,000,000
Actual fixed costs	1,200,000
Operating profit	$ 800,000

The total assets of the company last year were $20 million. Because of the downturn in sales and manufacturing activity, Truly Inc. sold off one of its plants and got rid of its fleet of delivery vehicles to pay off a loan, reducing its total assets to $10 million by the end of the year.

Required
Was Truly Inc. "in control" or "out of control"?

6. Truly Inc. is a luggage manufacturer. The budget for the current year was to manufacture and sell 125,000 suitcases, but because of the recession the company only sold 100,000. At the beginning of the year, the company was in process of negotiating an agreement to supply suitcases to Dwellmart, one of the big-box stores. The terms were that Truly Inc. would supply 10,000 suitcases per month to the 500 stores in the Dwellmart chain, and this could turn Truly Inc. into a very profitable business.

The suitcases supplied to Dwellmart would be of the same quality as its existing products, so variable costs, at $20 per case, would not change. To provide the extra production capability, Truly Inc. would have to rent additional manufacturing accommodation at a cost of $120,000 per year.

295

The agreement was that Dwellmart would not pay for the suitcases until they are sold to a customer, and then it would settle the account within 30 days.

Required

(a) Would the Dwellmart contract be a profitable one for Truly Inc. had it been accepted?

(b) What issues would Truly Inc. face if it accepted the contract?

7. Savoy Co. is a retailer of fine foods. The company has two stores: Oshawa and Burlington. The company expects to earn a return of 25% on sales and 20% on investment. You are given the current year's budget and actual results (in $ '000s):

	Oshawa		Burlington	
	Budget	**Actual**	**Budget**	**Actual**
Sales revenue	$1,000	$1,200	$3,000	$3,000
Cost of goods sold	400	500	1,200	1,200
Gross margin	$ 600	$ 700	$1,800	$1,800
Expenses	350	425	1,050	1,060
Operating profit	$ 250	$ 275	$ 750	$ 740
Investment	$1,250	$1,500	$3,750	$3,500

Required

Did the two stores produce the expected return on sales and return on investment?

8. The balanced scorecard has been introduced into a number of organizations in recent years. Comment on its suitability for control in the following forms of organizations:

(a) A retail outlet, such as a Baskin-Robbins High Street ice cream store

(b) A manufacturing unit, such as General Motors's Oshawa truck plant

(c) A sales unit, such as Air Canada's ticketing department

(d) A not-for-profit organization, such as York University

(e) A service unit, such as the accounting department at Loblaws

9. The following is taken from the 2006 Annual Report of the Loblaws Companies:

Facing an increasingly competitive marketplace, Loblaw continues to maximize the return on its assets under the themes "Simplify, Innovate, Grow." By concentrating on its strengths — great brands, great stores and great people — Loblaw's goal is to enhance value for consumers and shareholders. The Company is simplifying its organization by redesigning processes and structures to ensure that the business becomes more efficient and agile. Innovation has been a cornerstone of Loblaw's success: the Company strives to be the best at making healthy living affordable for all Canadians and to offer general merchandise and other services that enhance the customer experience. The Company's "Formula for Growth" defines priorities while the 100 Day Review provides the roadmap for achieving them. With these initiatives in place, Loblaw looks forward to a challenging and rewarding future.

Required

Based on the excerpt above, suggest suitable headings to be included in a balanced scorecard for Loblaws.

10. The Wellness Club runs fitness centres throughout Ontario. Its latest balanced scorecard is as follows:

	Measure	Target	Actual
Financial perspective			
Add shareholder value:	share price	$20	$21
Add franchisees' income:	franchisees' income	+10%	+12%
Customer perspective			
Add market share:	% customer retention	75%	80%
Customer satisfaction:	complaints	0	5
Internal business perspective			
Cleanliness:	survey	9/10	9.5/10
Efficiency:	administration costs	–5%	–6%
Learning and growth perspective			
Training:	training hours/unit	5	3
Customer awareness:	advertising $/unit	$10,000	$7,500

Required

(a) Does this balanced scorecard capture the main issues for this business?

(b) According to the balanced scorecard, how well is the Wellness Club doing?

(c) Does the balanced scorecard suggest any ways that the Wellness Club could improve?

Cost Behaviour and Break-Even Analysis

10

Learning
Objectives

After studying this chapter you should be able to describe and explain the following:
→ Why an understanding of cost behaviour is important
→ How variable costs behave
→ How fixed costs behave
→ How total costs behave
→ How to analyze mixed costs into their fixed and variable cost elements
→ How fixed and variable costs occur in different cost centres
→ How revenues behave
→ How fixed and variable costs and revenues are combined in the break-even model
→ How the contribution margin ratio can be calculated and used

10.1 Introduction

Organizations are bound by some constraints: for example, the prices of their products are constrained by customers' willingness to pay, and the quantity they sell is limited by customer demand and by the actions of competitors. Costs are constrained by the prices and availability of raw materials and labour. Within those constraints, organizations are engaged in making plans to be as profitable as circumstances permit. A good understanding of the reasons that underlie cost behaviours is necessary to do this properly.

Understanding cost behaviour is the basis for making accurate plans and budgets for operational activities. It also facilitates effective budgetary control.

To introduce this topic we shall start with a simple model of cost behaviour. In that approach, all costs will be treated as being either fixed costs or variable costs; or if they are more complex mixed costs, we will assume that they can be simplified into their fixed cost and variable cost elements.

When combined with expectations about sales revenue, this simple model of cost behaviour enables managers to use cost-volume-profit (CVP) analysis to plan operations so that the organization is as profitable as it can be. Cost-volume-profit analysis also enables managers to understand the effect of changing various aspects of their business plans.

The simplified assumption that costs are all capable of being described as either fixed or variable is quite adequate when dealing with simple organizations. A retail store that sells a single type of product is a good example. Its activities can be accurately modelled using CVP. As organizations become more complex, the model fits less and less well. A manufacturing company that makes several different products, or a service operation with many different types of customer, will find that cost behaviour (and possibly revenue behaviour, too) is not described accurately enough by the fixed or variable behaviour pattern. For these situations, it is necessary to treat costs as being caused not just by sales volume but by a more complex mix of activities, in addition to sales volume. This is called activity-based costing (ABC). Activity-based costing enables a more sophisticated approach to planning, decision-making, and control of the organization.

10.2 Cost Behaviour

Cost behaviour describes the relationship between cost and different levels of sales activity. The two main types of cost behaviour that we are concerned with are fixed costs and variable costs. Mixed costs contain an element of fixed cost and an element of variable cost. The two parts of a mixed cost can be separated so that they can be slotted into either the fixed or the variable cost pattern.

10.2.1 Variable Costs

Variable costs are incurred in direct proportion to sales levels. The more you sell, the greater the variable cost. If sales quantities double, then variable costs will double. In statistical terms, a variable cost is positively and perfectly correlated with sales activity.

Variable costs will include the following:

• The cost of goods sold in a retail outlet
• Raw material used in a manufacturing company
• Production labour
• Some overheads: for example, power supplies used to run production machinery
• Sales commissions

For planning and control purposes, it is necessary to understand this variable cost relationship. The higher the level of sales activity that is planned, the higher the budgeted variable cost will be. The higher the level of actual sales activity, the higher the expected variable cost will be.

Leon's Furniture Ltd. has a dining room set in inventory (actually it has lots, but let's stick to one). It is priced at $200, and its cost was $120. If Leon's sells that dining room set, in order to bring its inventory back up to the previous level it will have to replace the one it sold. Replacing the dining room set sold will cost it $120 (as long as input prices have not risen). The $120 cost of the dining room set sold is a variable cost. The variable cost is incurred every time a sale is made. Even if Leon's chose not to replace the dining room set it sold, the accrual accounting model will still treat its $120 cost as an expense.

According to the published financial statements of Leon's Furniture Ltd., its gross profit margin in 2010 was approximately 40%. That is, of every dollar of sales, 60 cents was its direct cost, and 40 cents was

Exhibit 10.1: Variable Costs at Various Sales Levels

Leon's Furniture Ltd.

Sales ($ millions)	Direct costs ($ millions)
$ 0	$ 0
$200	$120
$400	$240
$600	$360
$800	$480

available to pay expenses and provide a return to the shareholders. If we assume that the direct cost of sales is Leon's main variable cost, we can use this to illustrate the variable cost at a range of different sales levels. (See Exhibit 10.1.)

All other things being equal, organizations will try to make the variable cost per dollar of sales as low as it can be by actively managing the sources of products and the rates of other variable costs they incur.

10.2.2 *Fixed Costs*

The behaviour of fixed costs is the opposite of the behaviour of variable costs. Changing the level of sales activity does not alter the fixed costs: they are constant at all activity levels.

Leon's Furniture Ltd. incurs approximately $14 million each year in rent and property tax expense. This expense would be incurred each year no matter what level of sales Leon's managed to make. Actual sales are approximately $650 million per year, but if the sales fell to $500 million or rose to $800 million, the rent and property taxes would still be $14 million. To contrast the fixed costs with the variable costs, the cost behaviour

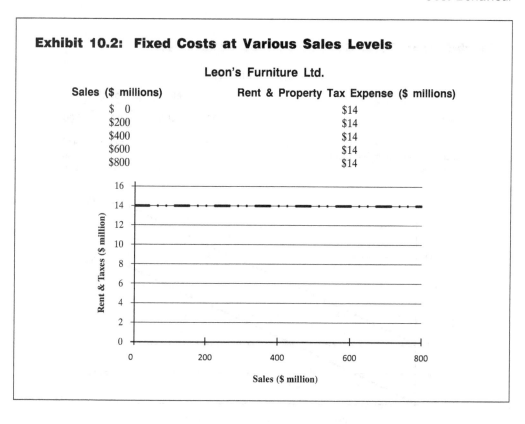

Exhibit 10.2: Fixed Costs at Various Sales Levels

Leon's Furniture Ltd.

Sales ($ millions)	Rent & Property Tax Expense ($ millions)
$ 0	$14
$200	$14
$400	$14
$600	$14
$800	$14

of rent & property tax at various sales is shown in a table and a graph in Exhibit 10.2.

Examples of fixed costs will include the following:

• Staff salaries (but not staff commissions on sales)
• Advertising
• Rent
• Property taxes
• Amortization
• Interest expense

Fixed costs may be treated as capacity costs: they give the organization the potential to carry out their business activities. All other things being equal, organizations will try to manage their fixed costs to as low a level as possible. However, they will not want to reduce their fixed costs below a level where they provide enough facilities to enable the planned business activities.

In the case of Leon's rent and taxes, for example, the company could reduce these by eliminating a store, but this would decrease revenue, so it might not be a good idea. Leon's might try to persuade the landlord to accept a lower rent: that would increase the company's profitability.

Exhibit 10.3: Total Cost at Various Sales Levels

Leon's Furniture Ltd.

Cost	Sales ($ millions)			
	200	400	600	800
Variable cost (60% of sales revenue)	120	240	360	480
Fixed cost ($200 million per year)	200	200	200	200
Total cost	320	440	560	680

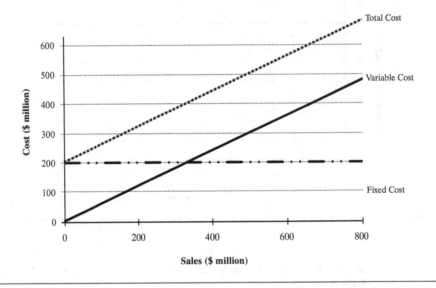

10.2.3 *Total Costs*

Using this simple model of cost behaviour, total cost will be the sum of fixed cost and variable cost. Exhibit 10.3 shows a table and a graph of the total cost if we assume that the fixed cost is $200 million per year and that variable cost is 60% of sales revenue.

10.2.4 *Mixed Costs*

Some costs do not fall neatly into either the variable cost or the fixed cost category, because they contain elements of both types of behaviour. They are made up of a fixed element and a variable element. Power costs, for example, are often made up of a combination of a fixed cost of supply (at a rate of so many dollars per month) plus a variable cost of so many dollars per kwh used. The cost of operating a delivery truck is a combina-

304

tion of fixed costs (including insurance, registration, and amortization) and a variable cost (including fuel and repairs).

If the fixed costs and the variable costs are itemized on the invoice, it may be possible to identify them precisely by analyzing the bills paid. However, the financial accounting records often capture mixed costs in a single category (vehicle operating expenses, for example). Then the management accountants will have to analyze that mixed cost into the fixed and variable cost components.

Suppose a retailer used trucks to deliver goods to customers. The retailer expects that some part of the truck operating expense would be fixed, and some part would be directly related to the sales. In January total sales were $15 million and truck expense was $1,250,000. In February sales rose to $17 million and truck expense rose to $1,350,000.

Both the January and the February truck expense would be made up of a combination of fixed cost and variable cost. We would expect the fixed cost to be similar, if not identical, in both months. If we deduct the January total truck expense from the February total truck expense, then fixed costs (which are included in both) cancel each other out. We also find that the variable cost of operating the trucks in January (when sales were $15 million) would be included in the variable cost of operating the trucks in February (when sales were $17 million), so the variable costs incurred in January cancel each other out.

What we are left with is the variable cost of operating trucks for the difference between January sales and February sales. The variable cost of $100,000 was caused by the additional sales of $2 million. This enables us to calculate the rate of variable cost: $100,000/$2,000,000 = $0.05 per $1 of sales. This is demonstrated in Exhibit 10.4.

Exhibit 10.4: Analyzing a Mixed Cost into Its Fixed and Variable Cost Components

	Sales	Total Truck Expense
January	$15,000,000	$1,250,000
February	17,000,000	1,350,000
Difference	$ 2,000,000	$ 100,000

Variable Cost Rate per $1 Sale = $100,000 ÷ $2,000,000 = $0.05

Substitute $0.05 per $1 of sales in the January total cost equation:

January total cost		=	fixed cost + variable cost
$1,250,000		=	fixed cost + ($15 million × $0.05)
$1,250,000		=	fixed cost + ($750,000)
$1,250,000 – $750,000	= $500,000 =		fixed cost per month

Total Monthly Cost = $500,000 + ($0.05 × $ of Sales)

By substituting the variable cost rate (of $0.05 per $1 of sales) into the January total cost, we can calculate the fixed cost as $500,000 per month. The total cost equation for each month is equal to the total fixed cost each month (i.e., $500,000) plus ($0.05 × # of sales in the month).

10.3 Fixed and Variable Costs in Different Cost Centres

Different types of cost centre are likely to incur greater or smaller proportions of variable and fixed costs.

In a retail sales situation, for example, the main cost will be the cost of goods sold and this is likely to be all variable costs. Sales commissions will also be a variable cost. Fixed costs may include rent and property taxes, sales salaries, and most administration costs.

In a production department of a manufacturing company, an important cost is likely to be the raw materials used in production; manufacturing wages are also likely to be a large proportion of the department's total cost. Both raw materials used and production wages are usually variable costs (though some exceptions to that exist). Some of the manufacturing overhead is also likely to be variable, for example the cost of power used to run the production machinery. Fixed manufacturing costs will include rent, property taxes, amortization, and administrative expense.

Many of the managers for whom this book was written will be operating service departments, such as a marketing department or a human resources department. In service departments, it is common to find that most of the costs are fixed costs. Their costs do not increase automatically just because sales levels increase. Fixed service department costs will include staff salaries and the related costs, such as employers' contributions to pension plans; rent of office space and related property taxes; amortization (if they have any long-term assets); advertising; sales-related travelling expenses, and so on. It is possible that, in the long run, increased sales levels will make all the service departments busier, and it may prove necessary to increase the service departments' budgets, but that increase may not be directly proportional to sales and the increase in their budget may well be separated in time from the event that ultimately caused it.

10.4 How Revenues Behave

It is always assumed that revenues are a purely variable item. That is, the selling price is constant per unit of product sold, no matter when or where the sale occurs and no matter who the customer is.

This is, of course, a considerable simplification of the actual situation, where the product may be sold at a higher or lower price to reflect the additional costs of servicing distant markets, where prices are raised or lowered to match those of local competitors and where some customers may get substantial discounts for buying in bulk.

In economics, for example, the normal expectation is that sales revenue per unit will start off relatively high, and then gradually reduce as the product is sold to customers who are only prepared to pay a lesser price (the downward sloping demand curve). For the purposes of this chapter those complex patterns of the relationship between selling price and quantity will be ignored and we will assume that sales revenue is linear and directly proportional to sales quantities.

So, in the same way that doubling sales causes variable cost to double, when we double our sales units we expect sales revenue dollars to double.

10.5 The Break-Even or Cost-Volume-Profit Model

We can combine the features of the variable nature of sales and variable costs, and the fixed nature of fixed costs into a model that is called the Break-Even model (BE) or the Cost-Volume-Profit (CVP) model. This is a simple way of looking at the relationship between costs and revenues to determine the answers to question, such as the following:

- What level of sales is necessary to cover the fixed costs and avoid making a loss?
- What level of profit will be achieved by a given volume of sales?
- What would be the marginal effect of changing factors, such as the selling price, sales volume, the variable cost, or the fixed cost?

10.5.1 Contribution Margin

When goods are sold revenue is generated. The sales caused variable costs to be incurred. The difference between the selling price per unit and the variable cost per unit is called the contribution margin per unit. The contribution margin (CM) per unit measures how much better off the company is as a result of selling one additional unit. Conversely, the CM per unit measures how much worse off the company is if sales are reduced by one unit. The CM measures the marginal effect of a sale.

Tony's Drinks sells coffee, tea, and soft drinks. Each drink is priced at $0.80 and has a variable cost of $0.50. The contribution margin is $0.30 per drink. In other words, for every drink sold, Tony's Drinks will have an additional $0.30. If 1,000 drinks are sold in a day, the total contribution margin will be $300. If 1,001 drinks are sold, the total contribution margin will be $300.30.

10.5.2 Break-Even Point

Once variable costs are subtracted from sales revenue, the amount left behind is the contribution margin. The contribution is used to pay for the business's fixed costs. When that has been achieved, the business has reached its break-even point. It is useful to know how much business activity is necessary to reach break-even. If this level of activity is unlikely to be reached, there is no reason for the business to exist. If the break-even level is likely to be exceeded, the company will be profitable. Knowing the break-even point enables a sensible decision to be taken as to whether or not to go ahead with a business venture.

To calculate the break-even point, the fixed cost for a given period of time is divided by the contribution margin per unit. The answer indicates how many units need to be sold in that period to reach the break-even point.

Tony's Drinks has fixed costs of $180 per day. Selling price is $0.80 per drink and variable cost is $0.50 per drink. Contribution margin is $0.30 per unit. Break-even is 600 drinks per day ($180 ÷ $0.30). If Tony's can sell 600 drinks in a day the company will break even. (See Exhibit 10.5.) If Tony's sells fewer than 600 drinks, there will be fixed costs not covered by contribution and a loss will occur.

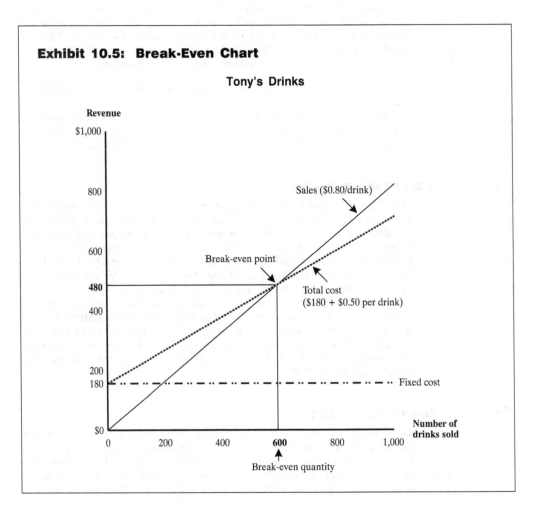

Exhibit 10.5: Break-Even Chart

Tony's Drinks

10.5.3 *Activity Above the Break-Even Point*

At activity levels above the break-even point, the company will be making a profit. For every unit sold above the break-even point, the contribution margin is pure profit. The greater the number sold, the higher the profit becomes.

Earlier, we calculated that Tony's Drinks will break even if it sells 600 drinks per day ($180 ÷ $0.30). Tony, the manager, estimated that his average sales will be 850 drinks per day. His estimated average profit, therefore, will be $75. This may be calculated by totalling the $0.30 contribution margin on every drink sold in excess of the break-even point: $0.30 × (850 − 600) = $75.

Tony's Drinks
Budgeted Daily Income Statement

Sales (850 × $0.80)	$680
Variable cost (850 × $0.50)	425
Contribution margin (850 × $0.30)	$255
Fixed costs	180
Operating profit	$ 75

In addition to paying the fixed costs, an organization may have an expectation or hope about the profit level. This can only come out of the contribution margin earned from sales. Expected profit may be treated in the same way as fixed cost for calculation of the sales level required. The total of the fixed costs and the required profit is divided by the contribution margin to determine the required sales level.

Tony has decided that unless he can make a profit of $120 per day, it's just not worth getting out of bed. To make $120 profit, he has to make enough of the $0.30 contribution margins to pay the fixed costs ($180) plus $120: that is, a total of $300. To make this level of profit he will need to sell 1,000 drinks ($300 ÷ $0.30).

Based on Tony's profit expectation, if he cannot sell 1,000 drinks a day, it is not worth his while being in business. If he estimates that he can sell more than 1,000 drinks a day, then he has a potentially viable business. If his prediction is that he can sell exactly 1,000 drinks a day he has reached a point of indifference: he does not mind whether he is in business or not.

If, as above, his prediction is that he can sell 850 units per day, then his profit objectives will not be met. He will fall short by $45 ($120 − $75).

10.5.4 *Using the Break-Even Model to Analyze Changes*

The break-even model lends itself to simple (but sometimes very effective) "what if" analysis. In a "what if" analysis, the numbers, assumptions, and so on are changed to study the effect of the change. You might want to consider the effect of increasing the selling price, for example. This would increase the contribution margin but (unless the product is perfectly inelastic) would also reduce the sales volume. Or you might want to decrease the selling price, which would increase the volume but decrease the contribution margin. It is almost always the case that changing one variable will also result in change in one of the other variables. Sometimes the effects are extremely complex, with several variables changing at once.

Tony's break-even calculation informs him that he will need to sell 1,000 drinks to pay his fixed costs and get the $120 profit he is hoping for. His best estimate is that he can sell 850 drinks per day at a price of $0.80, which is not enough volume to give him his required profit. Tony is considering two alternatives: he could raise the price of drinks from $0.80 to $1.00, in which case his volume will decrease to 600 units; alternatively, he could decrease the price of drinks from $0.80 to $0.70, in which case volume will increase to 1,600 units.

Selling price	Variable cost	Contribution margin/unit	Volume	Total contribution	Objective
$1.00	$0.50	$0.50	600	$300	Met
$0.70	$0.50	$0.20	1,600	$320	Exceeded

Both actions result in achieving his stated profit objective. Raising the price meets his requirements exactly. Reducing the price gives him his required profit, and another $20 per day. Tony would now have a good basis for making a decision. Which route he chooses would be a matter of personal preference, but both are feasible.

Another calculation to reach the same conclusion would be as follows:

Existing situation
850 units, $0.30 contribution margin per unit; $300 required; shortfall $45.

> *Option 1: Increase Price*
> Effect of decreasing volume: $(600 - 850) \times \$0.30$ =   ($ 75)
> Effect of increasing price: $600 \times (\$1.00 - \$0.80)$ =   120
> Net increase in contribution margin $ 45

Forty-five dollars is exactly enough to meet the $45 shortfall, so the objective has been met.

> *Option 2: Decrease Price*
> Effect of increasing volume: $(1,600 - 850) \times \$0.30$ = $225
> Effect of decreasing price: $1,600 \times (\$0.80 - \$0.70)$ =   (160)
> Net increase in contribution margin $ 65

A net increase of $45 would have been enough to meet the shortfall, so the objective has been met and superseded by $20.

The break-even model can be used to evaluate a wide range of decisions, such as using better raw materials to increase quality, using advertising to boost sales, expanding the product range, and so on.

Tony is considering the effect of advertising on his outlet. At a cost of a mere $60 per day, he can have posters put on all the transit stop benches within one kilometre of his place of business. If he does that he estimates that sales will increase by 250 units per day. His current fixed cost is $180 per day, and his contribution margin is $0.30 per drink sold.

> Additional contribution margin: $250 \times \$0.30$ $75
> Additional fixed cost   60
> Additional net income $15

Advertising increases his net income, so it is a sound business idea. We should also recognize that it makes his business a little riskier. His fixed cost has now increased from $180 per day to $240 per day. His break-even point has increased from 600 units a day ($180 ÷ $0.30) to 800 units a day ($240 ÷ $0.30). Although he is likely to do better, his exposure to risk is higher, as measured by the increased break-even level.

Note that in this calculation, the existing situation is irrelevant, and none of the data about the existing situation enters into the decision. The only relevant facts are those that are marginal to the decision — i.e., those that change as a result of the decision. The increased advertising spending is a marginal cost. The increased contribution from additional sales is a marginal benefit. The net effect is the marginal benefit of the decision to advertise.

10.5.5 *The Contribution Margin Ratio*

The explanation above works really well where the company is selling a single product. Tony was selling only soft drinks and all the products had the same cost per unit and selling price per unit, so the CVP model fits his business. In reality, most companies sell a range of products, and they may all have different selling prices and contribution margins. For these situations we can use a variation of the simple CVP model. Instead of using the CM per unit, we can use the contribution margin ratio.

Joe's Kitchen Store sells kitchen appliances (stoves, fridges, freezers, etc.) and small ware (knives, gadgets, dishes, etc.). When Joe buys goods, he adds a markup on cost of, on average, 25% to get his target selling price. So a stove that he buys for $400 would be sold for $500, giving him a contribution margin of $100. A six-inch knife that he would buy for $10 would have a $12.50 sticker price, and it would include a $2.50 contribution margin.

Although the contribution margins of the two products are different in $ amounts, they are a constant percentage of the selling price. In each case the contribution margin is 20% of the selling price. This is illustrated in Exhibit 10.6.

Exhibit 10.6: Contribution Margin Ratio

Joe's Kitchen Store

	Stove	Six-inch knife
Cost	$400.00	$10.00
Add 25% markup	100.00	2.50
Selling price	$500.00	$12.50

Contribution margin as % of selling price $100 ÷ $500 = 20% $2.50 ÷ $12.50 = 20%

Exhibit 10.7: Using the Contribution Margin Ratio to Set Sales Target

Joe's Kitchen Store

Markup % on cost	25%	
Contribution margin ratio (CM as % of sales)	20%	
Fixed cost per month	$100,000	
Break-even sales	$100,000 ÷ 0.20	= $500,000
Expected profit	$10,000	
Required sales to achieve expected profit	($100,000 + $10,000) ÷ 0.20	= $550,000

In the same way that the break-even point in units is calculated as fixed cost ÷ contribution margin per unit, now the break-even point in sales dollars is calculated as fixed cost ÷ contribution margin ratio.

If Joe's fixed costs are $100,000 per month, then he will have to achieve sales of $500,000 each month to break even. If he wants to make a profit of $10,000 per month, he will have to sell $550,000 of goods to get there. This is shown in Exhibit 10.7.

The CM ratio can be used to analyze changes in the same way that the CM per unit can be used. The difference is that using the CM per unit results in an answer expressed in units, while using the CM ratio results in an answer expressed in sales dollars. Examples are shown in Exhibit 10.8.

10.6 Cost Behaviour and the Functional Manager

Functional managers need to be aware of the dynamics of cost behaviour, as cost behaviour underlies many of the decisions they make and it affects the way their areas are controlled.

A production manager, for example, needs to understand that introducing an automated system to replace a labour-based manufacturing model might have the effect of reducing cost as well as making the organization more risky, as a variable cost (labour) would be replaced by a fixed cost (automated plant). As long as levels of production activity are relatively high, the benefit would be attainable. However, if production activity falls significantly, fixed costs do not go away (unlike labour costs, which can be scaled down). This is a lesson that General Motors learned in the recent recession. The company was disproportionately affected by a slump in sales demand combined with a high level of automation in its plants. When advising management on implementing changes such as this, the human resources manager should bring these considerations to the attention of management. It is not that the decision to automate is inherently

Exhibit 10.8: Using the Contribution Margin Ratio to Analyze Changes

Joe's Kitchen Store current position is as follows:

Sales per month	$520,000
Contribution margin ratio	20%
Fixed cost per month	$100,000

Although business has been good, Joe the owner is looking at ways to increase the store's profit. Below are three that were proposed by his staff:

1. Consider an advertising campaign that would cost $15,000 per month and increase sales by $100,000 per month.

Increased fixed cost	$ 15,000
Increased contribution	20,000 ($100,000 × 20%)
Net increase in operating profit	$ 5,000

This idea increases operating profit, so it is acceptable.

2. Joe's current sales are $520,000 per month. Consider the effect of introducing a new sales commission program that would reduce the contribution margin from 20% to 19% on all sales and increase sales by $250,000 per month.

Fixed cost	no change
Loss of contribution margin on existing sales	$ 52,000 ($520,000 × 1%)
Increased contribution margin on new sales	47,500 ($250,000 × 19%)
Net decrease in operating profit	$ 4,500

This idea reduces operating profit, so it is unacceptable.

3. Consider the effect of raising prices so that the contribution margin ratio increases to 22%. This will cause a 10% drop in sales dollars.

Fixed cost	no change
Contribution margin lost on decreased sales	$ 10,400 ($520,000 × 10% × 20%)
Increased contribution margin on remaining sales	9,360 (($520,000 – $52,000) × 2%)
Net decrease in operating profit	$ 1,040

This idea reduces operating profit, so it is unacceptable.

wrong but more that the decision carries both benefits and risks, and both need to be considered in the decision.

In a service cost centre, such as a human resources department, the effect of cost behaviour may lead to misleading interpretations of the department's efficiency. Almost all the costs in a human resources department are fixed costs. If sales revenue and production activity is rising, then the cost of the human resources department per dollar of sales revenue will fall. This could be interpreted as greater efficiency, even though the actual cost of the department had not changed. Conversely, if sales revenue falls, the costs of the HR department will become a greater percentage of the sales revenue. This could be interpreted as being less efficient, even though nothing in HR had changed and the department's costs remain the same.

10.7 Summary

In this chapter we have discussed the behaviour of variable costs, fixed costs, and revenues. We have brought those ideas together in calculating the break-even model (also known as the cost-volume-profit model). The assumption that costs can be effectively described in this simple way will apply to some companies and to some simple decisions within companies, but a richer model of cost behaviour, known as activity-based costing, will be discussed in the next chapter.

Self-Study Problem

1. Daniel's Dress Shop sells fashions in the Mississauga Mall. The shop buys from manufacturers in Toronto and Singapore. A typical dress costs $12 and is sold for $40. Sales staff get no wages, but receive 20% commission on all goods sold. Insurance, storage, and handling cost $5 per garment. The store pays a rental of $1,000 per month, plus 12.5% of turnover. The manager receives a salary of $5,000 per month. There are incidental operating costs of $2,500 per month.

Required
(a) What is the variable cost per dress sold?
(b) What is the fixed cost per month?
(c) What is the contribution margin per dress?
(d) What is the gross profit to sales ratio?
(e) How many dresses must the shop sell each month to break even?
(f) In a month when the shop sells 1,000 dresses, how much operating profit will it make?
(g) The manager is thinking about advertising Daniel's Dress Shop by mailing a flyer to all the households within five kilometres of the mall. This would cost $2,000. How many additional dresses must be sold to make it worthwhile?

Solution

1. (a) Variable cost per dress:

Cost of dress	$12
Sales commission	8 ($40 × 20%)
Insurance, handling, etc.	5
Part of rent	5 ($40 × 12.5%)
Total variable cost per dress	$30

(b) Fixed cost per month:

Rent	$1,000
Manager's salary	5,000
Incidental expenses	2,500
Total fixed cost per month	$8,500

(c) Contribution margin per dress:

$$= \text{selling price} - \text{variable cost}$$
$$= \$40 - \$30$$
$$= \$10$$

(d) Gross profit to sales %

$$= [(\text{selling price} - \text{cost of goods sold}) \div \text{selling price}] \times 100\%$$
$$= [(\$40 - \$12) \div \$40] \times 100\%$$
$$= 70\%$$

(e) Break-even point (unit):

$$= \text{fixed cost} \div \text{contribution margin}$$
$$= \$8,500 \div \$10$$
$$= 850$$

The shop must sell 850 dresses per month to break even.

(f) In a month when the shop sells 1,000 dresses, it will make an operating profit of $1,500:

Income Statement

Sales revenue	1,000 × $40		$40,000
Cost of goods sold	1,000 × $12		12,000
Gross margin			$28,000
Less expenses:			
Sales commission	$40,000 × 20%	$8,000	
Insurance, handling, etc.	1,000 × $5	5,000	
Rent	$1,000 + ($40,000 × 12.5%)	6,000	
Manager's salary		5,000	
Incidental expenses		2,500	26,500
Operating profit			$ 1,500

OR

Actual sales	1,000 dresses
– Break-even point	850
Sales in excess of break-even point	150
× Contribution margin/unit	$10
= operating profit	$1,500

(g) Additional cost of flyer $2,000
Contribution margin/unit $10

The shop must sell $2,000 ÷ $10 = 200 additional dresses to make the flyer pay for itself.

Discussion Questions and Problems

Discussion Questions

1. Describe the behaviour of a variable cost.
2. Describe the behaviour of a fixed cost.
3. Describe the behaviour of sales revenue.
4. Define and describe the contribution margin.
5. Define and describe the contribution margin ratio.
6. How can the contribution margin be used in decision making?
7. How can the contribution margin ratio be used in decision making?
8. Are the cost behaviour assumptions of the CVP model reasonable or are they unreasonable?
9. Describe how you would deal with a mixed cost.
10. Can you change one variable in a CVP situation without changing something else?

Problems

1. The following is a list of expenses incurred by the Davis Co.:

   (a) Steel used as raw material
   (b) Consumable stores, such as welding rods
   (c) Lubricating and cleaning materials for the production machinery
   (d) Stationary supplies for the accounting department
   (e) Production workers' wages
   (f) Insurance (fire and theft of property)
   (g) Insurance (product and public liability)
   (h) Rent of factory building
   (i) Rent of administrative building
   (j) Property taxes
   (k) Amortization of production equipment
   (l) Amortization of marketing department's computer system
   (m) Amortization of delivery vehicles
   (n) Amortization of salesmen's vehicles
   (o) Amortization of computer system used in human resource department
   (p) Research and development costs
   (q) Quality control department costs
   (r) Heating expense

   Required
   Label each expense as variable, fixed, or mixed.

2. The utilities bill for Davis Co. was $28,000 in January when the plant was closed for its annual winter break. In the months of February through April the utility bills were $52,000 per month on average, and production was 960 units per month.

   Required
   (a) Describe situations where the utility bill for a company is likely to be a fixed cost, a variable cost, or a mixed cost.

317

(b) Assuming the utility bill for Davis Co. to be a mixed cost, estimate the fixed element and the variable cost per unit produced.

3. You are told that the cost for public liability insurance at Davis Co. is a base amount of $100,000 per month, plus 1% of sales revenues. In a year where sales revenues were $5,000,000, estimate the public liability insurance expense.

4. Davis Co. makes office desks. Each desk uses 50 kg of steel, which costs $2 per kg, plus fittings, which cost $40. Direct labour is paid at $25 per hour, and it takes two hours to make each desk. The building in which the desks are made is rented at a cost of $33,000 per month. Amortization of the plant is $10,000 per month. Other production and administrative overhead, which is all fixed, totals $53,000 per month. Packing and shipping is $20 per desk. Each month, 960 desks are made and sold. Desks sell for $460 each.

Required
(a) What is the variable cost per desk?
(b) What is the contribution margin per desk?
(c) What is the total fixed cost per month?
(d) What is the fixed cost per desk?
(e) What is the break-even point per month, in units?
(f) What is the break-even point per month, in sales revenue?
(g) How many desks must be sold per month to make a profit of $150,000?
(h) If Davis Co. plans to make an operating profit of $12,000, how much total sales revenue must be earned?
(i) If Davis Co. sells an average of 960 desks per month, what is the monthly operating profit?
(j) If Davis Co. spent an additional $45,000 on advertising, how many additional desks would the company need to sell to make it worthwhile?
(k) If Davis Co. increased its price for desks from $460 to $500 and there was a 10% decrease in sales quantities, from 960 desks per month to 864 desks per month, by how much would its monthly operating profit change?

5. Fergus Education Inc. runs courses in quality control for production staff in manufacturing industries. The company runs training courses once a month. Each course can accommodate up to 10 trainees. The costs for a recent course with 10 participants were as follows:

Instructor's fees	$1,000	
Refreshments	$100	
Photocopying materials	$200	
Room rental	$270	
Computer hire	$500	($25 per workstation, plus $250 one time only set-up fee)
Software licence	$250	($100 per course, plus $15 per trainee).

The trainees' employers pay $250 each to go on the course.

Required
(a) With respect to trainees, classify each cost as variable, fixed, or mixed.
(b) Separate mixed costs into their variable and fixed components.
(c) Calculate the total variable cost per trainee, and the total fixed cost per course.
(d) Calculate the contribution margin per trainee.
(e) Calculate the break-even point in number of trainees per course.
(f) Calculate the profit for a course with eight trainees.
(g) Course #03.2005Z is full (10 trainees). As a favour, Fergus Inc. is going to allow registration by one additional trainee but charge the employer only the minimum amount such that Fergus Inc. will not lose money. How much will this trainee be charged?
(h) Is the break-even model a good description of the Fergus Inc.'s training course activities?

6. The following is data about the product made by the Zillion Co.:

Selling price per unit	$75
Variable cost per unit	$50
Fixed cost per year	$200,000

Required
Calculate the following:

(a) Contribution margin per unit
(b) The break-even point in units per year
(c) The annual unit sales that must be made to get an operating profit of $500,000 per year

7. Calculate the missing amounts for each of the three situations below:

	Product 1	Product 2	Product 3
Total sales	?	$360,000	$900,000
Total variable cost	$120,000	?	?
Total contribution margin	?	?	?
Contribution margin per unit	$30	?	$30
Total fixed cost	?	$90,000	$225,000
Operating income	$25,000	$60,000	$75,000
Units sold	4,000	7,500	?

8. Leon's Furniture Ltd. had the following results for 2009 (all the numbers have been brutally rounded so that the question is less messy: if you want to see the original data, look up Leon's Furniture on the Web, where their results are posted).

	$ Millions
Sales revenue	$700
Direct cost of sales	420
Gross margin	$280
Fixed costs and expenses	200
Operating profit	$ 80

319

Required
(a) What is the contribution margin ratio?
(b) What is the break-even point (in sales $ per year)?
(c) Based on the 2009 data, how much revenue would the company need to earn an operating profit of $100 million?
(d) If you assume that the fixed cost in 2010 will increase to $220 million and no other changes occur, what would happen to operating income?
(e) If you assume that the contribution margin ratio will increase by 1 percentage point in 2010 and no other changes occur, what would happen to operating income?
(f) If you assume that the sales revenue will increase by 1 percentage point in 2010 and no other changes occur, what would happen to operating income?

9. You are thinking about changing your phone plan. One carrier is offering a plan at $30 per month, including free calling within Canada and the United States. Another carrier is offering a plan with a monthly fee of only $20: calls within Canada would be free, but calls to the United States would be billed at $0.05 per minute. Which plan should you choose?

10. The cost of running a car in Ontario is quite steep. The CAA data for 2010 include the following:

Approximate Annual Driving Costs
— Based on the Chevrolet Cobalt LT

Km driven per year	Annual operating costs (variable)	Annual ownership costs (fixed)	Total cost	Cost per km
12,000 km	$1,512	$6,256	$7,768	64.7 cents
16,000 km	$2,016	$6,256	$8,272	51.7 cents
18,000 km	$2,268	$6,256	$8,524	47.4 cents
24,000 km	$3,024	$6,430	$9,454	39.4 cents
32,000 km	$4,032	$6,662	$10,694	33.4 cents

As an alternative, Zip Cars offers an occasional drivers plan with two car rental options: Option 1 involves an annual fee of $55 plus an hourly rate (on the weekend) of $11.25, and Option 2 asks for a daily fee, which starts from $88 (depending on what car you choose). Under Option 1 there is an unlimited mileage allowed. Under Option 2 there are 200 free km per day and a charge of $0.30 per km in excess of 200 km.

Required
Which should you choose, owning your own car or the Zip Cars alternative?

11

Allocating Overhead: Activity-Based Costing and Product Costing

Learning
Objectives

After studying this chapter, you should be able to describe and explain the following:

→ Why costs are allocated to products
→ How overhead is allocated to products using a single overhead recovery rate
→ How overhead is allocated to products using multiple departmental overhead recovery rates
→ How activity-based costing is used to allocate overhead to products
→ How over- or under-allocations of overhead arise
→ How costs are used to price products and services

11.1 Introduction

A simple organization, dealing in a single product, does not have a cost allocation problem: all the costs are incurred for that single product. Most organizations are much more complex: they sell or make a wide range of products. They need to trace costs to individual products or to groups of similar products so that they can establish prices and assess the costs and profitability of each one.

Where the organization is making a series of unique products (such as a civil engineering company designing and building bridges), the estimated cost of each individual job will be the basis for setting the price of the organization's bid for that job. These organizations are "price setters"; without detailed cost information, they would not know how much to set as a bid price. After the job is completed, the cost information will be used to see if the job was profitable or not.

Where the organization is making products that compete with those of other manufacturers, the problem is a little simpler: a price that is acceptable to the consumer and competitive in the market can be established by looking at what goes on elsewhere. These companies are "price takers". They need detailed cost information to ensure that their estimated costs are low enough that their products are profitable. After each period, the cost information will be used to see if the product was profitable or not.

Some costs are easy to trace: goods bought for resale, for example. For manufacturers, they keep detailed records of raw materials bought and of which products used them. Detailed records of wages are also kept so that manufacturing wages can be tracked to the products for which they were incurred. So, for raw materials and labour, we have detailed records of actual usage, which are used to track costs to products.

Raw material and manufacturing labour are called "direct costs" because they can be directly traceable to the products that caused them to be incurred. This contrasts with overheads, which are called indirect costs because they cannot be traced in the same way.

11.2 How Overhead Is Allocated to Products

Overhead costs are more difficult to relate to products. Overheads will, in any event, probably be a mix of variable costs and fixed costs. Typically, variable overhead is a small proportion of total overhead, while the greater part is fixed overhead. Because overheads are often a large (and increasing) percentage of total product cost, it is highly desirable that they be "attached" to products so that price setting and cost control can be effectively exercised, even though there is no direct measure of their use. Variable overhead may rise or fall in a general sense in sympathy with increased or decreased sales, but a precise variable cost relationship with individual products is often difficult to establish. Fixed overheads can seldom be treated as uniquely identifiable with individual products, and by definition, they do not change as a result of changes in sales levels.

Overheads are "attached" to products by using overhead allocation rates. The following steps show how the rates are calculated and how overheads are used:

1. A cost pool is established and the estimated overhead is charged to it.
2. An allocation base is chosen.
3. An allocation rate is calculated: total estimated overhead in the cost pool divided by the total estimate of the allocation base.
4. Overhead is allocated to products: the product's actual use of the allocation base is multiplied by the allocation rate and that is added to the product cost.

Exhibit 11.1 shows an example of this process using Madoc Inc., a manufacturer of hole punches and staplers. Exhibit 11.2 shows the full allocation of all overhead costs to the two products.

A **cost pool** is a collection of costs, all of which are eventually going to be allocated to the products or services that the organization sells.

Allocation is the process of making sensible decisions about how the cost pool is allocated to products and services. Allocation of costs can be contrasted with tracing direct costs. Tracing direct costs is using specific information to decide which costs belong to which products or services: allocation is an attempt to achieve the same result in respect of overheads that cannot be directly traced to individual products or services.

An allocation base is an indirect measure of activity. You cannot *trace* overhead costs to products (as you would for direct costs, such as raw materials and labour), but what you can do is choose something like direct labour hours or machine hours, which would be expected to increase in step with variable manufacturing overhead. This is called an allocation base.

Exhibit 11.1: Overhead Allocation

The overhead allocation for hole punches at Madoc Inc. is calculated as follows:

1. Estimated total overhead for the year $640,000
2. Machine hours have been chosen as the allocation base because they are highly correlated with overhead being incurred.
   Estimated total machine hours for the year 16,000 hours
3. Overhead allocation rate ($640,000 ÷ 16,000 hours) $40 per machine hour
4. Budgeted number of machine hours used by hole punches 10,000 hours
5. Overhead allocated to hole punches (10,000 hours × $40/hour) $400,000
6. Remaining overhead $240,000

Because Madoc Inc. produces only two products, the remaining overhead would be allocated to the other product (staplers), which used the other 6,000 hours of machine time.

Exhibit 11.2: Overhead Allocation Using Single Cost-Recovery Rate

Madoc Inc.
Budgeted Income Statement

	Hole Punches	Staplers	Total
Sales units	500,000	200,000	700,000
Selling price per unit	$1.64	$2.50	
Sales revenue	$820,000	$500,000	$1,320,000
Direct costs:			
Raw material	$180,000	$80,000	$ 260,000
Manufacturing labour	90,000	40,000	130,000
Overhead:			
Hole punches (10,000 × $40)	400,000		
Staplers (6,000 × $40)		240,000	
Total overhead allocated			640,000
Total cost	$670,000	$360,000	$1,030,000
Operating profit	$150,000	$140,000	$ 290,000
Operating profit as % of sales	18.3%	28.0%	22.0%

As long as the allocation base is well chosen and all the organization's products are similar in their demands on the production system, this allocation system will make a fair allocation of overhead, and this process will give an acceptably fair method of establishing the total cost of each product. While Exhibits 11.1 and 11.2 show overhead allocation for only two products, this approach can be scaled up to deal with any number of different products.

In the example of Madoc Inc., although the company as a whole is profitable (22% return on sales) and the individual products are profitable, management has been putting pressure on the manager in charge of hole punches as his product line's rate of profitability (at 18.3%) is substantially lower than the 28.0% made by the staplers line. The manager of the hole punch line is puzzled by this as he knows he runs an efficient operation.

11.3 Using Multiple (or Departmental) Overhead Rates

Further analysis of the data at the Madoc company reveals that the budgeted overhead of $640,000 is not a homogenous pool of similar costs; instead, it is the sum of the costs of two different operations done in two different departments: machining and assembly. Budgeted overhead in the machining department is $480,000. It is a reasonable assumption that the department should continue to use machine hours as an overhead allocation base for machining department costs. Budgeted overhead in the assembly department is $160,000. The assembly process uses more labour than machinery; therefore, it is more appropriate for the department to use labour hours as the allocation base. The development of the two overhead recovery rates is shown in Exhibit 11.3. While this only illustrates the calculation of two recovery rates, the process could be used equally well to calculate recovery rates for three, four, or many more different departments. In Exhibit 11.4, we show how the budget is revised to include this new cost allocation information.

Exhibit 11.3: Calculating Multiple Overhead-Recovery Rates

Macdoc Inc.
Departmental Overhead Rates

	Machining	Assembly	Total
1. Estimated total overhead for the year	$480,000	$160,000	$640,000
2. Recovery bases:			
Machine hours	10,000	6,000	16,000
Labour hours	2,000	8,000	10,000
3. Overhead allocation rates:			
Machining ($480,000 ÷ 16,000 hours)	$30 per machine hour		
Assembly ($160,000 ÷ 10,000 labour hours)	$16 per labour hour		

Exhibit 11.4: Overhead Allocation Using Multiple Cost-Recovery Rates

Madoc Inc.
Budgeted Income Statement

	Hole Punches	Staplers	Total
Sales units	500,000	200,000	700,000
Selling price per unit	$1.64	$2.50	
Sales revenue	$820,000	$500,000	$1,320,000
Direct costs:			
Raw material	$180,000	$ 80,000	$ 260,000
Manufacturing labour	90,000	40,000	130,000
Overhead:			
Machining department			
Hole punches (10,000 × $30)	300,000		
Staplers (6,000 × $30)		180,000	
Assembly			
Hole punches (2,000 × $16)	32,000		
Staplers (8,000 × $16)		128,000	
Total overhead allocated			640,000
Total cost	$602,000	$428,000	$1,030,000
Operating profit	$218,000	$ 72,000	$ 290,000
Operating profit as % of sales	25.6%	14.4%	22.0%

The following should be observed in comparing Exhibits 11.2 and 11.4:

• The total overhead has not changed: it is still budgeted to be $640,000.
• The total operating profit has not changed: it is still budgeted to be $290,000.
• The operating profit for hole punches has increased from $150,000 to $218,000, and its profitability (return on sales) has increased from 18.3% to 25.6%.
• The operating profit for staplers has decreased from $140,000 to $72,000, and its profitability (return on sales) has decreased from 28.0% to 14.4%.

Our perceptions of the relative profitability of hole punches and staples have now been completely reversed.

11.4 How Activity-Based Costing Is Used to Allocate Overhead to Products

The break-even model is a simplification of the complexities of the real world. There are situations where the model is sufficiently close to reality that it is useful. Tony's Drinks in Chapter 10, for example, is a simple enough situation for the model to be a perfect description of the company activities and decisions.

11.4.1 Fixed Costs and Variable Costs

Many retailers, like Tony's, find that their costs can be adequately described as either variable or fixed. The more we move away from retailing and get into manufacturing, where companies manufacture a huge range of products, the more the simple split between variable cost and fixed cost becomes an inadequate description of cost behaviour. That world of large, complex organizations, with a wide product and customer range, is much more realistic than its simpler counterparts.

To be sure, large and complex organizations still have some variable costs. They still buy goods for resale and use raw materials in production. These will be directly proportional to volume. In activity-based costing, these are referred to as *unit-variable costs* as they change with the number of units sold or produced (activity level).

Likewise, the organizations will have some purely fixed costs. The cost of head office operations, the expenses of the board of directors, the cost of the annual audit, and similar costs are all virtually independent of sales and/or production activities. In activity-based costing these are referred to as *business-sustaining costs*.

11.4.2 Complex Overhead Costs

It is a feature of large modern corporations to have a large amount of what would be described as overhead expenses. Some of it is production overhead, some administrative overhead, and some marketing overhead. Activity-based costing shows how overhead is caused by activities, which are the result of decisions, conscious or unconscious, made by management.

An example of an activity is moving finished goods from the place they were made to the finished goods warehouse. The cost rate for that activity depends on how far the goods have to be moved, which is, in turn, caused by the plant layout and the convenience of the warehouse. The number of times the cost is incurred depends on how often goods are moved, and that depends on factors such as the number of production runs. The number of production runs is a decision made by management. At the extremes, production can be carried out in a single large production run (when only one movement will take place), or in a series of many small production runs (when many movements will take place). So the decision as to how much cost to incur depends on how many production runs are scheduled. In traditional cost accounting systems, costs such as this are lost in a general account called production overhead. In activity-based costing, such costs are analyzed according to their cause.

11.4.3 Activity-Based Costs

If all products (and all customers) were roughly equal in the activities they used, then there would not be too serious a problem. However, where products and customers demand different levels of activities, they should bear the differential cost of those activities. Simple systems of cost behaviour and cost allocation fail to capture these differences. As a result, products may be allocated too much cost (more cost than they generate through their activities), or too little cost (less than the cost they generate through their activities). If we have an incorrect perception of the cost a product is causing, we are likely to make incorrect decisions. This would happen in decisions such as product addition or deletion, product pricing, advertising, product design, and production-run size.

In activity-based costing, in addition to unit-variable costs and business-sustaining costs, at least two further classifications are introduced: batch-level costs and product-sustaining costs.

Batch level costs are a function of the number of times that a batch is run. A batch may be a production run; it may also be the ordering of raw materials or the dispatch of finished goods. The features of batch-related costs are that they are fixed in relation to each batch, no matter how large or how small, and they are variable in respect of the number of batches; so the greater the number of batches, the greater the total batch costs.

In a production run, the batch costs would include scheduling the batch into the production plan, ordering and delivery of raw materials, setting up the machines to produce the product, inspection of the batch for quality control, and dispatching output. These costs will be incurred every time a new batch happens. The size of the batch may be a single product, or it may be a large batch. There are obvious implications for product cost. The larger the batch, the smaller the per unit cost for batch-related costs.

Once the dynamics of the cost of a batch are understood, there is a tendency to make each batch as large as possible. By averaging the (fixed) batch cost over the largest number of units, the cost per unit is minimized. One spinoff effect of this is that substantial inventories of partly produced and finished goods occur. This creates interesting tensions between cost minimization in the production area and cost minimization elsewhere. The plant may be operating on a just-in-time inventory management basis, which tries to avoid inventory. Juggling these competing needs becomes a difficult decision.

Activity-based costing also identifies "product-sustaining costs". These are the costs associated with having the product in existence. Product-sustaining costs would include engineering design and redesign, cataloguing, advertising, and sales education.

11.4.4 *Activity-Based Costing for Products*

There is a tendency toward product proliferation in most businesses. Frequently, the costs of adding a new product or a new variant are poorly understood and not fully factored into the new product decision. Similarly, the decision to delete a product is seldom rigorously addressed.

In the previous chapter we explained how the cost-volume-profit (CVP) model was used to understand cost behaviour in simple organizations, or in simple situations within more complex organizations. That same simplicity is the basis for using a single overhead recovery rate to apply all overhead to products, as shown in the earlier part of this chapter. In the immediately previous section of this chapter, we showed how to use multiple departmental overhead recovery rates to allocate overhead. The basis for that was that overheads behaved in a similar way within each department, but differently between departments. While this will work well for some organizations, it is, again, a simplification that does not match cost behaviour in some other organizations. For the most complex situations, we need to develop a system that reflects all the causes of overhead, and that system is called activity-based costing (ABC). We shall consider the use of activity-based costing information in making good cost allocations. This, in turn, should lead to making good management decisions.

The simple expectation that all costs are either fixed (in relation to sales levels) or variable (rising or falling in the same proportions as sales rise or fall) is true of simple situations (a good example is a retailer that sells a single product). Most modern enterprises, however, are not simple; they are complex. For complex organizations, a more complex approach is required.

Some costs (e.g., raw materials and production labour) may continue to be recognized as purely variable. Other costs (e.g., the organization's central administrative function) may continue to be recognized as purely fixed. Much of the overhead, however, would be better described as the result of "activities".

An example is the overhead cost related to running an adaptable production machine, such as a lathe or a milling machine. This machine has to be set up to start a production run. That is, skilled personnel will re-arrange the machine's settings and tolerances to manufacture a particular product. If only one unit of the product is made, then the set-up cost is a pure variable cost. If the machine, once set up, is run forever, then the set-up cost is a pure fixed cost. But, typically, neither of those extremes happens. The machine is set up, completes a production run, and is then set up to make a different product. Every time the product changes, the set-up cost is incurred; thus, set-up cost is neither purely variable nor purely fixed. The total set-up cost is driven by the number of times the machine is reconfigured to make a different product. Total set-up cost is therefore positively related to the number of production runs and negatively related to the length of each production run.

When companies had a smaller range of products, overhead allocation was a small problem. If product ranges are much greater, the problem is bigger. When overhead was a small percentage of total cost, overhead allocation was a small problem. If overhead is a greater percentage of total cost, the problem is bigger.

Activity-based costing is necessary where a company makes a wide range of products and different products cause different amounts of overheads. Activity-based costing is equally necessary where a company has a range of different customers, each of whom causes different amounts of sales and marketing overheads.

11.4.5 *Applying Activity-Based Costing*

When applying activity-based costing to a company, the following steps should be carried out:

1. Identify the purely variable costs (i.e., costs that should be directly traceable to products).
2. Identify the purely fixed costs (i.e., costs that you might not want to allocate to any specific products).

Once these two costs have been identified, the costs that remain are overhead costs, which must be driven by activities. There could be a number of different overhead costs, caused by different activities. Their cost behaviour is described as activity-driven or activity-based.

3. Identify the activities that drive the activity-driven costs.
4. Set up cost pools, one for each activity.
5. Allocate the costs driven by a particular cost pool to that pool.
6. Select a cost driver for each cost pool.
7. Calculate a rate of $ per unit of cost driver for each cost pool.
8. Use the cost driver to allocate costs to products or other cost objects.

At Madoc Inc., the making of hole punches and staplers is more complicated than was at first supposed. While both products use the production machinery, their production processes do not lead to use that is proportional to machine hours.

Further analysis of the costs reveals that the allocation of overhead on the basis of machine hours is problematic. Machine hours only capture the activity once a production run has started. Hole punches are made in four production runs a year, each of 12,500 units. Staplers, by contrast, are made in a lot of short runs of about 2,000 units each. This means that staplers should be allocated a greater amount of batch-related costs. Additionally, product level support for hole punches is inexpensive as the design has not changed in years, while the stapler line is regularly re-engineered to meet changing tastes in the office. Some overhead is unit-related and can be traced to the two production lines. Some overhead is purely fixed (business sustaining).

A revised product cost report has now been prepared, reflecting this activity-based costing information, in Exhibit 11.5.

As we can see, if activity-based costing is used to allocate costs, those allocated to the stapler line are substantially higher. This reflects the fact that the staplers are the users of activities that result in more costs. The hole punches are a cheaper product to produce. The perception that hole punches were not pulling their weight was altogether incorrect. In fact, their return on sales is far higher than that of the staplers.

Hole punches and staplers may seem trivial, but they are being used to illustrate a more complex reality. A company that manufactures 1,000 products will almost always have some that are more expensive to produce and maintain than others. In particular, the effect of mass production versus small-batch production generally means that the small-scale products are more expensive to produce. This is always disguised by simple overhead allocation bases (such as the machine hour allocation used for Madoc Inc. or allocation according to labour hours, which is also common). Only activity-based costing can capture the relation between activities and costs.

Exhibit 11.5: Product Cost Report Using Activity-Based Costing

Madoc Inc.
Revised Product Cost Report

	Hole Punches	Staplers	Total
Sales units	500,000	200,000	700,000
Selling price	$1.64	$2.5	
Sales revenue	$820,000	$500,000	$1,320,000
Direct costs:			
Raw materials	$180,000	$ 80,000	$ 260,000
Labour	90,000	40,000	130,000
	$270,000	$120,000	$ 390,000
Overhead:			
Unit-related costs	$ 50,000	$ 20,000	$ 70,000
Batch-sustaining costs	100,000	250,000	350,000
Product-sustaining costs	10,000	50,000	60,000
	$160,000	$320,000	$ 480,000
Total product cost	$430,000	$440,000	$ 870,000
Product profitability	$390,000	$ 60,000	$ 450,000
Net profit as % of sales	47.6%	12.0%	
Business-sustaining costs (not allocated to products)			160,000
Net profit			$ 290,000

11.4.6 *Activity-Based Costing and Customer Profitability*

In the same way that products are not all equal causes or users of cost, not all customers are equal. Activity-based costing can be used to analyze customer profitability.

Tryfan Inc. sells building materials to five major hardware retailers. Activated Hardware is the biggest customer, taking half of all output. In 2011, Tryfan's total sales were $10 million at full selling price. Contribution margin was 25% of this, or $2.5 million. Selling expenses total $1 million. Activated Hardware is seen as the most important customer because of the high proportion of sales made on its account.

Because Activated Hardware's volume is so high, it is allowed a 5% volume discount of $250,000. Sixty percent of all sales-personnel time is spent dealing with the Activated account ($150,000), while the other 40% is spent dealing with the other customers ($100,000). Deliveries have to be made to each of Activated's retail outlets (at a cost of $375,000), whereas the other customers have their purchases delivered to their central warehouses (at a total cost of $125,000). An activity-based costing analysis of customer profitability shows that Activated is not Tryfan's best customer by any means, as shown in Exhibit 11.6.

Exhibit 11.6: Activity-based Costing Analysis

Tryfan Inc.
Customer Profitability Analysis

	Activated Hardware	Four Smaller Customers	Total
Sales	$5,000,000	$5,000,000	$10,000,000
Contribution margin	$1,250,000	$1,250,000	$ 2,500,000
Customer specific costs			
5% discount	250,000		
Sales staff	150,000	100,000	
Delivery costs	375,000	125,000	
	$ 775,000	$ 225,000	$ 1,000,000
Profit	$ 475,000	$1,025,000	$ 1,500,000
Profit as % of sales	9.5%	20.5%	15%

Although Activated Hardware is a good customer, the high costs of servicing it makes it less profitable than the other four, smaller customers.

Once again, like the production situation, it is the differential demands placed on the system by different customers (or products) that make simplistic cost allocations problematic and make activity-based costing the only sensible way to allocate costs.

11.5 Over- and Under-Allocation of Overhead

An overhead recovery rate is used to allocate overhead to products. This is true whether the company is using a traditional recovery rate based on labour hours or a recovery rate that is established by a more precise system, such as activity-based costing. It is important to remember that overhead recovery rates are based on estimates, and the estimates may not tie in exactly with the actual data.

The overhead recovery rate is calculated by dividing the budgeted overhead (an estimate) by the budgeted recovery base, such as labour hours (another estimate). If either of these is materially different from the actual value, then the recovery rate will have been set at either too high or too low a level.

Over-recovery

If the recovery rate is too high, the overhead allocated to products will be too much. This could be a problem because it might have made the company charge too high a price for the product. The logical effect of too high a price is that sales will be lost. Lost sales result in lost profitability.

Over-recovery of overhead would be the result of either underspending on overhead or more than expected overhead recovery base (e.g., labour hours).

Under-recovery

If the overhead recovery rate is set too low, then the overhead allocated to products will be too little. This could be a problem because at the end of the year there will be overhead incurred that has not been carried by any of the products. Product prices may have been set too low for the products to be truly profitable.

Under-recovery of overhead would be the result of overspending on overhead compared to the budget, or the overhead recovery base is set too high (e.g., working fewer labour hours than were planned).

In Exhibit 11.7, the Sebastian Co. has budgeted its production overhead to be $500,000 for the year. The company anticipated working 20,000 labour hours, so the overhead recovery rate throughout the year was $25 per labour hour. Every time a product used a labour hour it would be charged with $25 of overhead. The expectation was that by the end of the year the total overhead charged to all products would be exactly $500,000.

In Exhibit 11.7, (1), a combination of $20,000 of underspending on overhead plus an additional 2,000 labour hours charged to production at $25 per hour has resulted in a $70,000 over-recovery.

In Exhibit 11.7, (2), $25,000 of overspending on overhead combined with not working 5,000 of the planned labour hours charged to production at $25 per hour has resulted in a $150,000 under-recovery.

Exhibit 11.7: Over- and Under-Recovery of Overhead

Details of Sebastian Co.'s budgeted production overhead:

Budgeted production overhead	$500,000	
Budgeted labour hours	20,000	
Overhead recovery rate ($500,000 ÷ 20,000 hours)	$25	

(1) Over-Recovery

Number of labour hours worked	22,000	
Total overhead charged to products (22,000 hrs. × $25)		$550,000
Actual overhead incurred		480,000
Over-recovered overhead		$ 70,000

(2) Under-Recovery

Number of labour hours worked	15,000	
Total overhead charged to products (15,000 hrs. × $25)		$375,000
Actual overhead incurred		525,000
Under-recovered overhead		($150,000)

Under-recovery of a significant amount is a major problem, as it results in losses. It is also important, though less so, if overhead is over-recovered by a significant amount, as it erodes competitiveness.

A significant amount of under- or over-recovery may also signal a problem of the company or department's budgeting process.

11.6 Using Costs to Set Prices for Products or Services

We calculate the cost of products because we want that information for some specific purpose (all management accounting should be purpose driven). Cost information can be used in a variety of management activities, including the following:

1. Planning: Cost information is essential to the preparation of budgets and other financial plans.
2. Control: By comparing planned costs with actual costs, we can see whether or not the organization is exercising good cost control.
3. Decision-making: When we have to make a choice between two courses of action, a reliable estimate of the cost of products is sometimes the deciding factor.
4. Pricing.

11.6.1 Price Makers

Where the organization is producing a unique product and there is no competition, the cost can be used to decide what price to charge. The organization is acting as a "price maker".

Madoc Inc. currently makes hole punches and staplers, and (as per Exhibit 11.2 and Exhibit 11.4) the company's profit as % of sales is 22% at present. The company has been approached to manufacture a new product, which is a laser document shredder. Madoc Inc. believes that it has the expertise and spare capacity to take on this job, but it does not yet have a price in mind. In Exhibit 11.8, we show the estimated costs and the estimated selling price.

11.6.2 Price Takers

Where the organization is producing a more or less generic product and there are many competitors, there will be an established market price. Costs can be used to see if we, too, can charge that market price and still be profitable.

Madoc Inc. currently sells its staplers for $2.50, and that is in line with what its competitors charge for similar staplers. A new competitor has entered the market with a stapler that will sell for $2.00. It is expected that other suppliers will bring their prices down to about $2.00 to match the new competition. Madoc's stapler manager wants to know if he can

Exhibit 11.8: Using Costs to Develop Prices

The cost details for Madoc's new laser shredder are as follows:

Budgeted costs:	
Raw materials	$ 8.50
Direct labour (1/2 hour @ $25)	12.50
Overhead:	
Machine hours (1/3 @ $30)	10.00
Assembly hours (1/2 @ $16)	8.00
Total budgeted cost	$39.00

Assuming Madoc Inc. would like to have the same profit margin (22%) for its laser shredder, the total cost would be 78% of the price.

Target selling price ($39 ÷ 78%)	$50.00
Operating profit (22% of price)	$11.00

Exhibit 11.9: Matching Competitors' Prices

Madoc Inc.
Price Profitability Analysis for Staplers

Proposed selling price	$2.00	100%
Current estimated costs:		
Raw materials ($80,000 ÷ 200,000 units sold)	$0.40	20%
Direct labour ($40,000 ÷ 200,000 units sold)	0.20	10%
Overhead ($240,000 ÷ 200,000 units sold)	1.20	60%
Total cost	1.80	90%
Operating profit	$0.20	10%

match that price and still be profitable. The analysis of that decision is shown in Exhibit 11.9.

It seems that if Madoc were to sell its staplers for $2.00 each, the operating profit as % of sales would fall to 10%. This is far below the company's existing operating profit as % of sales, which is 22%. This may be unacceptable.

If Madoc Inc. wants to (i) stay in the staplers market and (ii) maintain its current operating profit of 22% of sales, it will have to look very carefully at its costs to see where cost savings can be made.

In this example, raw materials and labour are already a very low percentage of product costs (respectively, 20% and 10% of sales revenue). It is not likely that enough cost could be saved by economizing on raw

335

materials or labour. It is likely that any cost savings would come from a serious look at the overhead costs. Overhead costs should be considered carefully to make sure that they are all necessary. If they are not necessary, they should be eliminated. The essential overhead costs that remain should be subjected to a process of cost reduction wherever possible. By doing this, it may be possible to reduce overheads. If overheads per unit can be brought down from $1.20 to $0.96, then the operating profit per unit would rise by $0.24, from $0.20 to $0.44 per unit. The operating profit would then become 22% of sales revenue. This would maintain the existing rate of overall company profitability.

Note that Exhibit 11.9 applies costs information from Exhibit 11.2, where the single cost-recovery rate method was used for overhead allocation. If Macdoc were to use costs information from Exhibits 11.4 and 11.5, where multiple cost-recovery rates and activity-based costing were used for overhead allocation, respectively, Macdoc would be selling the stapler at a loss at $2.00 a piece. See for yourself by substituting the overhead cost in Exhibit 11.9 with those in Exhibit 11.4 ($308,000 ÷ 200,000 = $1.54) and Exhibit 11.5 ($320,000 ÷ 200,000 = $1.60).

11.7 Summary

Cost allocation is a necessary part of planning, controlling, and setting selling prices. Direct costs (such as raw materials and labour) can be traced directly to the products that used them. That tracing is not possible in respect of overheads. Overheads have to be allocated to products through an overhead cost recovery process. In the most straightforward situations, a single overhead recovery rate will accomplish this effectively. In an organization with multiple departments, it may be better to have a different overhead recovery rate for each department. In the most complex situations, activity-based costing must be used to allocate overhead accurately to the activities that caused them and the products that used those activities. Cost information is a key input into setting the prices at which products should be sold and in managing costs to maintain profitability.

Self-Study Problems

1. Michael Manufacturing has budgeted overhead of $5 million. The company has chosen to allocate overhead to products on the basis of direct labour hours. Budgeted labour hours in 2010 were 100,000.

    Actual results for 2011 showed that the company spent $5.4 million on overhead, and incurred 110,000 direct labour hours. Product X93 incurred $700,000 of direct material cost, and $400,000 of direct labour cost (10,000 direct labour hours).

    Required
    (a) What is Michael Manufacturing's overhead recovery rate for the year 2011?
    (b) How much overhead would be charged to product X93?
    (c) How much is the overhead over- or under-recovered for the company as a whole?

2. The human resources department at Treblanc Inc. has estimated its costs for 2011 as $500,000. This is based on a careful activity-based costing exercise that establishes the following cost drivers and expected levels of activity:

Hiring for new positions	20 @ $5,000	$100,000
Replacing existing positions	50 @ $2,000	100,000
Maintaining existing positions	1,000 @ $ 100	100,000
Fixed costs		200,000
Total budgeted costs		$500,000

    There are five departments (including HR), and each should be charged with one-fifth of the fixed costs.

    Required
    (a) Using the traditional cost allocation method, calculate an overhead recovery rate for the human resources department, based on charging overhead to user departments on the basis of the existing workforce of 1,000 employees.
    (b) Using the overhead allocation rate calculated in (a), how much would be the budgeted expense charged to the production department, which has 200 employees?
    (c) How much expense would be charged to the production department using the activity-based costing information if you are told that the shop has 200 employees and that it is proposing to hire no new positions but replace two existing positions?
    (d) Which is fairer, (b) or (c)?

Solutions

1. (a) Overhead recovery rate:

= budgeted overhead ÷ budgeted direct labour hour
= $5,000,000 ÷ 100,000
= $50 per direct labour hour

(b) Overhead for product X93 would be:

= 10,000 × $50
= $500,000

(c) Overhead charged to production

($50 × 110,000 direct labour hours)	$5,500,000
Actual overhead incurred	5,400,000
Over-recovered overhead	$ 100,000

2. (a) Traditional cost allocation: single overhead cost pool and charge-out rate:

= $500,000 ÷ 1,000 employees
= $500 per employee

(b) Overhead expense charged to the production department:

= 200 employees × $500
= $100,000

(c) Activity-based costing overhead allocation for the production department:

Hire new employees	0 × $5,000	$ 0
Replace existing employees	2 × $2,000	4,000
Maintain existing employees	200 × $100	20,000
Share of fixed costs	$200,000 × 1/5	40,000
Total overhead allocated		$64,000

(d) The activity-based costing allocation is fairer: it charges the human resource department costs to users based on the causes of those costs. Because the production department is very stable (low turnover of staff), it causes less cost. This is reflected in the lower cost allocation ($64,000 compared to $100,000).

Discussion Questions and Problems

Discussion Questions

1. What is the objective of allocating overheads to products?
2. Why is it more problematic to allocate overhead than it is to trace raw materials and labour to products?
3. What are the advantages of using labour hours to allocate overhead?
4. What are the disadvantages of using labour hours to allocate overhead?
5. What are the advantages of using machine hours to allocate overhead?
6. What are the disadvantages of using machine hours to allocate overhead?
7. What is a cost pool for purposes of activity-based costing?
8. What is a cost driver?
9. How is overhead recovered in prices?
10. Which determines price: costs or competition?

Problems

1. Tilbury Co. has budgeted overhead of $9 million for the year. The company has decided to allocate overhead to products on the basis of labour hours. Budgeted labour hours for the year are 600,000. Job # X95 is budgeted to use 540 labour hours.

   Required
   (a) Calculate the overhead recovery rate.
   (b) Calculate the overhead that will be charged to job # X95.

2. Muskoka Inc. has budgeted production overhead of $600,000 per year. The company allocates overhead costs to products on the basis of machine hours. Last year, Muskoka Inc. budgeted to use 5,000 machine hours. Products are priced by calculating the estimated raw materials, direct labour, and production overhead, and then adding 70% to cover selling and administration and a profit margin.
      Job # 05.2011 X32 has had the following estimate prepared:

Raw materials	$10,000
Direct labour	200 hours @ $20 each
Machine time	40 hours

   Required
   (a) Calculate the total cost for job # 05.2011 X32.
   (b) Calculate the selling price for job # 05.2011 X32.
   (c) Is this price estimation method fair?

3. Muskoka Inc. has budgeted production overhead of $600,000 per year. The company allocates overhead costs to products on the basis of machine hours. Last year, Muskoka Inc. budgeted to use 5,000 machine hours. Products are priced by calculating the estimated raw materials, direct labour, and production overhead, and then adding 70% to cover selling and administration and a profit margin.

Last year, the actual cost of production overhead was $670,000. Actual machine hours used totalled 6,000.

Required
Calculate the over-recovery or under-recovery of production overhead.

4. Arnold's Extrusions designs and manufactures plastic components for metalworking manufacturers. Its three main departments where variable manufacturing overhead is incurred are as follows:

   • Computer Aided Design
   • Prototype Production
   • Manufacturing

   There are two principal customers: Aluminium Inc. and Steel Co. In 2012, machine hours were budgeted to be 4,000.
   Variable manufacturing overhead was budgeted to be $600,000 in 2012, and it was allocated to contracts on the basis of machine hours. The actual variable manufacturing overhead for 2012 was $617,200.
   During 2012, contracts from Aluminium Inc. used 3,000 hours and contracts from Steel Co. used 1,200 hours.

   Required
   (a) Calculate a plant-wide overhead recovery rate for Arnold's Extrusions.
   (b) Calculate how much variable manufacturing overhead would be allocated to jobs for (i) Aluminium Inc., and (ii) Steel Co.
   (c) Calculate how much variable manufacturing overhead was over-recovered or under-recovered.
   (d) Are machine hours the correct way to allocate variable manufacturing overhead at Arnold's Extrusions?

5. You have been given the budgeted variable manufacturing overhead costs for each of the three departments: Computer Aided Design (CAD), Prototype Production (PP), and Manufacturing (M). Also, your team of consultants has carried out interviews with the key workers and managers in the three departments. The managers inform you that the most appropriate cost drivers for their departments are as followings:

	CAD	PP	M
Budgeted overhead	$100,000	$100,000	$400,000
Cost driver (hours)	CAD	Engineering	Machine
Budgeted cost driver (units)	800	200	4,000

During 2012 the use of cost drivers was as follows:

	CAD	PP	M
Aluminium Inc.	500	200	3,000
Steel Co.	250	50	1,200
Total	750	250	4,200

Required

(a) Calculate the cost-driver rates for the three departments.

(b) Calculate how much variable manufacturing overhead would be allocated to (i) Aluminium Inc., and (ii) Steel Co.

(c) Which of the three overhead allocation methods — plant-wide overhead allocation rates, departmental overhead allocation rates, and activity-based costing — is more precise?

6. Halifax Co. has calculated the following cost pools for production overhead:

Pool	Budgeted Cost per Month	Cost Driver	Budgeted Level
Set-ups	$200,000	# of set-ups	100 set-ups
Material handling	$75,000	# of material moves	50 moves
Material storage	$100,000	# tonnes stored	50 tonnes
Maintenance	$200,000	# of machine hrs	200 hrs
Inspection	$200,000	# of inspection hrs	100 hrs
Labour hours			5,000 hrs

The following data refers to two jobs that were completed in June:

Details	Job A	Job B
Direct material cost	$5,000	$7,500
Direct labour cost	$7,500	$5,000
Direct labour hours	300	100
Set-ups	5	1
Materials moves	10	3
Tonnes of material stored	2	5
Machine hours	10	5
Inspection hours	1	1

Required

(a) Using labour hours as the overhead allocation base, calculate a plant-wide overhead recovery cost rate, and calculate the cost of each job.

(b) Using activity-based costing, calculate the cost of each job.

(c) Between the plant-wide overhead allocation and the activity-based costing allocation, which provides a more precise cost?

7. Killarney Wholesale distributes car parts to independently owned repair shops in Northern Ontario. The company has gathered the following data about three types of customer:

	Dealers	Chains	Independents
Monthly sales revenue	$500,000	$300,000	$20,000
Gross profit %	10%	12%	15%
Monthly costs:			
Sales visits (@ $500 each)	1	1	1
Order processing (@ $200 each)	10	5	1
Deliveries (@ $100 each)	5	5	1
Rush deliveries (@ $200 each)	10	2	0
Sales promotions	$2,000	$1,000	0

Required

(a) Calculate the profitability of each type of customer as % of sales revenue.

(b) If you wanted to improve the profitability of the "Dealers" sector, where would you look for cost reductions?

3

Financial Decision Making

Finance:

"...the acquisition, management and financing of resources needed by firms."

A.H.R Davis & G.E Pinches
Canadian Financial Management, *4th Canadian Edition*
Toronto, Addison Wesley Longman, 2002

12

Analysis of Short-Term Decisions

Learning
Objectives

After studying this chapter you should be able to do the following:
→ Identify differential costs and revenues
→ Describe the role of capacity
→ Explain how to decide whether to make or buy
→ Identify sunk costs and committed costs
→ Explain the difference between a short-term and a long-term decision

12.1 Introduction

In Section 1 of this book, we examined financial accounting, which is the use of accounting for scorekeeping; in Section 2, we discussed the use of accounting for attention directing, through budgets and budgetary control. In this section (Section 3), we deal with the ways accounting can support decision making. The topic is addressed, first, with respect to short-term decisions (Chapter 12) and second, with respect to long-term decisions (Chapters 13 and 14). In Chapter 15 we tie together all the strands in an analysis of a company's financial statements.

12.2 Differential Costs and Revenues: New Orders

In Chapter 10, we looked at cost behaviour: understanding cost behaviour is essential for competent planning and control. Those same ideas of cost behaviour will now be used as the basis for making short-term decisions. The simple approach to cost behaviour splits costs into variable (those that change as production or sales activity changes) or fixed (those that do not change when production or sales go up or down). That idea is close to (but not identical to) the idea of differential costs and revenues.

Differential costs and revenues are those that change as a result of a decision. Variable costs are normally differential costs, and fixed costs are normally not differential costs. In making a decision, the only elements that are relevant are those that are differential to the decision.

Revenues are generally differential, in the sense that they behave in a variable way: as sales rise or fall, revenue from sales rises or falls in proportion. There is seldom a problem incorporating sales revenues into a decision. More revenue is virtually always better than less revenue.

Costs, on the other hand, frequently give rise to confusion, and the way they are reported may lead to incorrect decision making. The principle problem is that, typically, organizations use full cost as their way

Exhibit 12.1: Standard Cost at Gery's Gelati

Gery's Gelati makes ice cream. The budget for each 100-litre batch is as follows:

		100 litres	per litre
Raw material:			
Dairy products	100 litres @ $0.50/litre	$ 50	$0.50
Flavouring	2 kg @ $20/kg	40	0.40
Additives	1 kg @ $10/kg	10	0.10
		$100	$1.00
Labour	1 hour @ $25	25	0.25
Overhead (2 machine hours @$25/hour)		50	0.50
Standard manufacturing cost		$175	$1.75
Selling and administrative overhead ($50/batch)		50	0.50
Standard cost of goods sold		$225	$2.25
Profit margin		75	0.75
Standard selling price		$300	$3.00

of reporting accounting information. The financial accounts tend not to split costs on the basis of behaviour (fixed vs. variable); instead, costs are reported functionally (materials, wages, utilities, rent, etc.). Inventories are normally valued at full cost, rather than variable cost.

If full cost accounting data is used in short-term decision making, the effect of the decision will be inaccurately perceived.

For example, in the normal course of events, Gery's Gelati's product is sold to customers for $3 per litre, as shown in Exhibit 12.1. Suppose a new customer offers $2 per litre for a special order of 10,000 litres — would it be worthwhile?

The initial response may be negative. We should look at the reasoning behind the "no" decision.

First, the company may not be prepared to consider any sales at less than its "normal" selling price of $3 per litre. There are frequently good behavioural reasons for such an attitude. This is not, however, an answer that can be supported by short-term economic analysis.

Second, suppose the decision was based on the fact that the standard cost of goods sold is $2.25/litre, and the $2 offer does not cover the full cost. Is "no" still a reasonable answer? To analyze this, we have to know more about the costs included in the $2.25.

It is clear that the ingredients ($1/litre) will be incurred to make the order for the new customer. Likewise, it is probable that the order will require additional labour ($0.25/litre). As a selling price, $1.25 would cover the materials and labour.

Suppose that all the production overhead is fixed cost. As long as there is production capacity to make the additional order, there is no differential cost. The production overhead allocation is, therefore, irrelevant to the decision and should not influence the decision. It can be ignored.

Suppose the selling and administrative overhead ($0.50/litre) is half fixed and half variable. Half ($0.25) is relevant to the decision, and the other half, which is fixed cost, is irrelevant to the decision.

So a minimum selling price of $1.50 (materials $1.00, labour $0.25, and variable selling overhead $0.25) is required to cover the differential (or marginal) cost. Any selling price in excess of $1.50 will create additional contribution margin for the firm.

At a selling price of $2, the contribution margin is $0.50/litre. An order for 10,000 litres will add $5,000 to total contribution and to operating income.

The "full cost" reporting system (which is prevalent in organizations) does not reveal the effect of the decision; it merely confuses matters.

With the differential cost information, the decision maker is now in a position to make an informed decision. The answer may still be negative because of other qualitative factors. For example, Gery's may perceive that lowering the cost to this customer would have knock-on effects with other customers, who would also negotiate for lower prices. Or Gery's may consider that additional contribution of $5,000 not to be worth the effort of the additional production. At least Gery's now has all the relevant information to make a rational decision.

12.3 Capacity Issues

One of the keys to Gery's Gelati's decision is the existence of idle capacity. If the additional 10,000 litres cannot be made within the existing capacity, then a decision to sell the 10,000 litres at $2 each would be incorrect. If there is insufficient spare capacity, then either more capacity would have to be added (at an additional cost) or sales to "regular" customers would have to be sacrificed, with an associated loss of contribution margin.

Using unused capacity is, effectively, free. Where there is no unused capacity, then capacity has to be created and this always has a cost.

Consider Gery's Gelati again, but this time assume the company has spare capacity to make only 7,000 litres. Gery's has several choices:

(a) Accept the order for 7,000 of the 10,000 litres requested.
(b) Accept the order for the full 10,000 litres, and reduce sales to regular customers by 3,000 litres.
(c) Accept the order for 10,000 litres, and incur an additional fixed cost of $2,800 to temporarily increase capacity.

Choice (a) will result in additional contribution margin, but not as much as before. Gery's will get $0.50 contribution margin on 7,000 litres, for a total of net $3,500 benefit.

Choice (b) will result in losing the contribution margin on regular sales of 3,000 litres. The regular contribution margin is $1.50 (selling price, variable cost, $3 – $1.50 = $1.50).

$$3,000 \times \$1.50 = \$4,500$$

This must be set against the $5,000 of additional contribution margin from the special order. The net effect is an increased contribution margin of $500.

We should also recognize the potential drawback associated with failing to supply the regular customers with the products they normally buy from Gery's. There are few things more expensive in the business world than a dissatisfied customer. Unfortunately, it is very difficult to put an accurate dollar value on dissatisfaction and, for that reason, it is frequently omitted from the calculation.

Choice (c) will result in increased contribution margin of $5,000 from the new order, less the additional capacity cost of $2,800. The net effect is a $2,200 profit increase.

All three alternatives increase profit, so there is a good economic argument for accepting the order, whichever way it is to be satisfied. Of the three, choice (a) is the best since it adds the greatest amount of profit: $3,500.

12.4 Make or Buy

The same type of analysis can be applied to situations calling for a decision to produce something internally, or to sub-contract it to a third party. Once again, the issue is to discover what costs and revenues are differential to the decision. Costs that can be eliminated by sourcing outside are differential costs, and costs that continue are not differential. Once again, the use of full costing in the accounting system is likely to provide misleading information.

Consider Cumberland Sausage Co., which produces food products. All production and service activities are subject to rigorous cost control. Among other things, use of office space in the corporate headquarters is charged out at cost, based on square metres occupied, and corporate overhead is charged to all departments at a rate of $1,000 per full-time employee.

The human resource department has the following budget for 2012:

Salaries and wages (25 employees)	$1,000,000
Fringe benefits (10% × salaries and wages)	100,000
Computer system costs	500,000
Office expense	500,000
Corporate overhead (25 × $1,000)	25,000
Total	$2,125,000

HR Solutions, a specialist human resources agency, has offered to take over the entire HR function for Cumberland Sausage at a cost of $1,800,000 per year.

The initial response might be that this is a good deal. The reported cost will decrease from $2,125,000 to $1,800,000, and savings of $325,000 will result. However, the "full cost" approach has introduced some irrelevant data. The salaries and wages will be eliminated (we assume, otherwise it's never going to be a good idea) as will the fringe benefits and the computer system costs. The office expense, however, which is an allocation of head office occupancy, will probably not change, and the corporate overhead will not change.

Outsourcing will not affect the office expense, and corporate overhead will also stay the same in total, but will now have to be allocated to other parts of the business, increasing the reported costs.

The effect of the outsourcing will be to add $1,800,000 of additional cost, and eliminate $1,600,000 of avoidable costs. The net effect is that Cumberland Sausage Co. will be $200,000 worse off.

12.5 Sunk Costs

One of the costs that is always irrelevant is a sunk cost. A sunk cost is one that has already happened or has been committed, so that it is unavoidable.

Take the computer system costs of $500,000 in the previous Cumberland example. If those are currently incurred costs, such as hardware rental, software licensing, and supplies, then they may be avoidable costs. By sub-contracting the HR department, they could be cancelled.

Alternatively, suppose the computer system was set up two years ago, at which time there was a major acquisition of hardware, and special software was custom-written for the Cumberland Sausage applications. The costs are now predominantly amortization of computer hardware and software. Discontinuing the use of the computer will not make these costs go away. They are sunk costs.

Sunk costs are typical when the financial accounting model uses matching to spread a cost incurred in one period to future periods where the use is to continue. Amortization is the most frequently found sunk cost.

12.6 Committed Costs

A committed cost is one that the organization is obliged to incur, even though it has not yet been spent. An example of a committed cost is the rent payable on a lease, or the salary of an employee on a five-year employment contract.

Even though the money has not yet been spent, the obligation to spend it is unavoidable. Such costs may be treated exactly the same way as sunk costs.

Suppose that the manager of the HR department of Cumberland Sausage Co. is on a two-year employment contract. His salary for the next two years should be added to the unavoidable costs in making the decision of whether or not to outsource the HR function.

12.7 Short-Term vs. Long-Term

The shorter the timespan of the decision, the more likely that the differential cost and revenue will be the appropriate way to make the decision. As timespans get longer, the choices available to the organization become wider, and marginal approach cost will give way to something nearer a full-cost model.

Capacity, for example, may be unused in the short term. If there is spare production capacity today, or this week, there is little or nothing that can be done about it. As time goes by, the company can reduce its spare capacity by replacing machines with smaller ones, or moving to smaller premises when the lease comes up for renewal. In the long term, very few costs are totally unchangeable, and the idea of a truly fixed cost disappears. Perhaps the company will be able to introduce new products that absorb the spare capacity. In the longer term, unused capacity should not exist.

Full costs are the current costs of providing the existing capacity. As the time horizon of the decision gets longer, these costs become more and more relevant as they become a closer approximation of the long-term differential costs.

The short-term analysis presented earlier implies that every new decision may be made with a price that just covers the variable cost. If that approach is used for all decisions, it will rapidly lead to a disastrous situation where none of the products or services provides enough contribution to pay the fixed costs, let alone any profit.

In the longer term, fixed costs must be covered by contribution from the various activities of the company, and full costs have a role to play in establishing the fair share each product or service must generate.

12.8 Short-term Decisions and the Functional Manager

Functional managers, such as the human resources manager, need to bear in mind the process of short-term decision making when forming recommendations about the resources they control.

Many of the costs in a human resources department are either fixed costs or committed costs. As such, when a decision is made to change management practice, those costs are unlikely to go away. The costs merely remain unchanged, making some potential cost savings illusory.

An example would be the costs associated with a computer system dedicated to the IT department. Its sunk costs (the cost of buying the computer hardware and the associated software) will seldom be avoidable, even if it is no longer in use. In a similar way, the costs of the human resources department will mostly be the salaries of personnel. These are fixed costs and can only be eliminated by discharging people from their jobs. Even then, there are severance costs involved in de-hiring them, reducing the benefit that could be achieved by outsourcing the human resources function.

12.9 Summary

Decisions in general should be based on differential factors: the costs and revenues that change as a result of the decision. Short-term decisions should reflect short-term differential factors, which are very close to being contribution margin analysis (i.e., revenues less variable costs), although other differential factors should also be considered. These would include costs such as special packaging and additional design costs, a or reduction in costs resulting from deleting features that are normally part of the product. In the short term, capacity constraints and unused capacity are unalterable; but as the decision horizon becomes longer, it will be possible to raise or lower capacity to deal with capacity constraints and unused capacity. Full costs tend to give inappropriate short-term signals for decisions; but as the decision horizon gets longer, full costs become more appropriate measures of the relevant costs. In the longest term, all costs, fixed and variable, must be covered by revenues, or the organization will fail.

Self-Study Problem

1. Marcia's Millinery makes women's hats. The company has a workshop in the Toronto garment district. The capacity of the workshop is 1,500 hats per week. Each hat uses $6 of materials and takes 40 minutes to make. The cutters and machinists earn $12 per hour. The fixed expenses total $6,000 per week. The hats are sold to retailers for $30 each, and the retailers sell them to customers for $50 each. In recent months, Marcia's has sold 1,000 hats per week.

   Canadian Tire has decided that it wants to sell women's hats as well as its existing line of hardware products. They have asked Marcia's Millinery to supply 400 hats per week every week for the next year at a price of $18.

   Required
   (a) What are the variable costs per hat, the fixed costs per week, the full cost per hat, the profit per hat, and the contribution margin per hat for Marcia's Millinery's existing trade?
   (b) Should Marcia's accept the offer from Canadian Tire?
   (c) If Canadian Tire wanted Marcia's Millinery to sell the company 1,500 hats per week, what price per hat would be necessary so that Marcia would make the same profit as before?
   (d) If the capacity of Marcia's workshop was 1,000 hats instead of 1,500 hats, how would this affect the decision to accept Canadian Tire's offer of 400 hats at $18?
   (e) What are the qualitative factors in this decision?

Solution

1. (a) Variable cost per hat

Materials	$ 6
Labour ($12 × 40 minutes)	8
Total variable cost per hat	$14
Fixed cost ($6,000 ÷ 1,000 hats)	6
Full cost per hat	$20
Profit per hat	10
Price per hat to retailers	$30
Contribution margin per hat ($30 – $14)	$16

   (b) The price offered by Canadian Tire is $18.

   If Marcia's compares this to the normal selling price of $30, the company would reject the Canadian Tire offer.

   However, the additional cost of making a hat is $14 (i.e., the variable cost), and Marcia's has enough spare capacity to make the additional hats. At a price of $18, Marcia's will make a $4 contribution margin per hat.

   Increased contribution margin:

   Per week = $4 × 400 = $1,600

   Per year = $1,600 × 52 weeks
   = $83,200

As there is no increase in the fixed cost, this $83,200 will all be profit.

(c) Existing situation

1,000 hats × $16 contribution margin	$16,000 per week
$16,000 contribution margin ÷ 1,500 hats	$10.67
Variable cost	14.00
Required price	$24.67

Note: It is not necessary to use the fixed cost in this comparison as it is the same whether the hats are sold to regular customers or to Canadian Tire; it is not a cost that is marginal to the decision.

(d) If the capacity of the workshop is only 1,000 hats, then Marcia's is currently operating at capacity. To sell 400 hats to Canadian Tire at a contribution margin of $4 each means not selling 400 hats to regular customers at a contribution margin of $16 ($30 – $14). Marcia's will be worse off by:

$$= (\$16 - \$4) \times 400 \text{ hats} \times 52 \text{ weeks}$$
$$= \$12 \times 400 \text{ hats} \times 52 \text{ weeks}$$
$$= \$249,600 \text{ per year}$$

(e) Qualitative factors in this decision:
- Can sales of 1,000 per week to regular customers be maintained for the foreseeable future?
- Is there any growth in sales likely?
- What will happen to the reputation of Marcia's Millinery?

Discussion Questions and Problems

Discussion Questions

1. What are the characteristics of a cost that is relevant to a short-term decision?
2. Describe a sunk cost and give two examples.
3. Why is it important to know whether a plant is operating at or below full capacity?
4. What are the qualitative factors that affect the make-or-buy decision?
5. Are direct materials and direct labour always relevant costs for short-term decisions?
6. Why do managers rely on full costs for pricing decisions?
7. Is the cost of raw materials a fixed cost or a variable cost?
8. Is the cost of raw materials a relevant cost or an irrelevant cost?
9. Is amortization of production equipment a fixed cost or a variable cost?
10. Is amortization of production equipment a relevant cost or an irrelevant cost?

Problems

1. Brazil Co. is planning on adding an additional shift of workers in its production facility. Production would be increased from 500 units per week to 1,000 units per week.

   Required
   Identify each of the following costs as (i) fixed (F), variable (V), or mixed (M); and (ii) whether it is relevant (R) or not relevant (NR) to the additional shift decision.

   (a) Direct materials
   (b) Direct labour
   (c) Production overhead
   (d) Plant amortization (calculated on the straight-line basis)
   (e) A production-based royalty of $0.25 per unit
   (f) Energy costs of $200 per machine hour to operate production machines
   (g) Insurance
   (h) Sales commissions, based on units sold

2. For the Brazil Co., identify each of the following as a sunk cost (S), a committed cost (C), or neither (N):

   (a) Direct materials (not yet ordered)
   (b) Direct materials (ordered, but not yet delivered)
   (c) Direct materials (in inventory)
   (d) Next year's payments on a lease for a truck
   (e) Plant amortization
   (f) Sales commissions (sales staff get a commission of 5% of year's net sales)
   (g) An annual bonus payable at the discretion of management

355

(h)   Plant maintenance payable monthly under a contract
(i)   Plant maintenance payable at the discretion of management
(j)   Warranty costs on products sold

3.   Church Co. makes chairs and tables. The income statement for last year was as follows:

Sales revenues (100,000 units)		$800,000
Direct materials	$150,000	
Direct labour	75,000	
Production overhead	125,000	350,000
Gross margin		$450,000
Selling and distribution	$150,000	
Administration	100,000	250,000
Operating income		$200,000

Production overhead is estimated to be 40% variable and 60% fixed. Selling and distribution expense includes $50,000 variable expense, and the remainder is fixed. All the administrative expense is fixed.

Required
(a)   Calculate the variable cost per unit manufactured.
(b)   Calculate the variable cost per unit sold.
(c)   Calculate the full cost per unit manufactured.
(d)   Calculate the full cost per unit sold.
(e)   Calculate the minimum price at which a unit could be sold while covering its marginal cost.
(f)   Calculate the minimum price at which a unit could be sold while covering its full cost.
(g)   Calculate the minimum price at which the products could be sold so that operating income is $200,000.

4.   Church Co. makes chairs and tables. The income statement for last year was as follows:

Sales revenues (100,000 units)		$800,000
Direct materials	$150,000	
Direct labour	75,000	
Production overhead	125,000	350,000
Gross margin		$450,000
Selling and distribution	$150,000	
Administration	100,000	250,000
Operating income		$200,000

Production overhead is estimated to be 40% variable and 60% fixed. Selling and distribution expense includes $50,000 variable expense, and the remainder is fixed. All the administrative expense is fixed.

Kabul Supply Inc. has asked Church Co. to supply 1,000 tables at a price of $5 each, for export to Afghanistan. There would be no variable selling and distribution cost incurred.

Required

(a) Should Church Co. accept the order if there is adequate capacity to make the additional units?

(b) Should Church Co. accept the order if there is no spare capacity to make any of the additional units?

(c) Should Church Co. accept the order if there is adequate capacity to make 500 of the additional units but the remaining 500 units would have to come from reductions in sales to regular customers?

5. Church Co. makes chairs and tables. The income statement for last year was as follows, with an analysis of the profitability of the two product lines:

	Chairs	Tables	Total
Sales units	80,000	20,000	100,000
Sales revenues	$400,000	$400,000	$800,000
Direct materials	$100,000	$ 50,000	$150,000
Direct labour	50,000	25,000	75,000
Production overhead	83,333	41,667	125,000
Direct cost	$233,333	$116,667	$350,000
Gross margin	$166,667	$283,333	$450,000
Selling and distribution	$100,000	$50,000	$150,000
Administration	66,667	33,333	100,000
	$166,667	$ 83,333	$250,000
Operating income	$ nil	$200,000	$200,000

Production overhead is a fixed expense. Selling and distribution expense is a variable expense. All the administrative expense is fixed. All overheads are allocated to products on the basis of direct labour cost.

The production manager wants to stop making chairs as the company makes no profit on chairs. If the company does that, it could make and sell an additional 10,000 tables.

Required

Calculate the change in operating profit that would result from switching from chairs to tables.

6. The Famous Fish Farm breeds salmon and trout for sale to supermarkets across Canada. The company has prepared a product cost analysis for 2011. The analysis suggested that the trout product should be discontinued as it is making a loss.

All costs have been allocated to the two product lines on the basis of kilograms of fish shipped. Fish feed, labour, and distribution costs are variable costs; all the remaining costs are fixed, and none of them would be eliminated if trout were discontinued.

Required

Famous Fish Farm's 2011 product cost analysis for Salmon and Trout is as follows:

	Salmon	Trout	Total
Kg shipped	50,000	200,000	250,000
Sales revenue	$200,000	$250,000	$450,000
Costs			
Fish feed	$ 24,000	$ 96,000	$120,000
Labour	15,000	60,000	75,000
Distribution costs	15,000	60,000	75,000
Maintenance	3,000	12,000	15,000
Amortization	5,000	20,000	25,000
Administration	15,000	60,000	75,000
Total costs	$ 77,000	$308,000	$385,000
Operating income	$123,000	$(58,000)	$ 65,000

Do you agree with the suggestion to discontinue the trout product? (Calculate how much the net income would be after making that decision.)

7. The Famous Fish Farm breeds salmon and trout for sale to supermarkets across Canada. The company has prepared the following product cost analysis for 2011:

	Salmon	Trout	Total
Kg shipped	50,000	200,000	250,000
Sales revenue	$ 200,000	$ 250,000	$ 450,000
Costs			
Fish feed	$ 24,000	$ 96,000	$ 120,000
Labour	15,000	60,000	75,000
Distribution costs	15,000	60,000	75,000
Maintenance	3,000	12,000	15,000
Amortization	5,000	20,000	25,000
Administration	15,000	60,000	75,000
Total costs	$ 77,000	$ 308,000	$ 385,000
Operating income	$ 123,000	$ (58,000)	$ 65,000

In order to improve performance, it has been suggested that the maintenance should be outsourced to a local engineering company. The engineering company has quoted $12,000 as an annual maintenance fee. If it were to be outsourced, the existing part-time maintenance employee (salary cost: $8,000 per year) would be de-hired, and maintenance supplies of $2,000 would be avoided. Famous Fish Farms would still have to pay $5,000 per year on a maintenance contract for its computer system.

Required
(a) Should the maintenance be outsourced?
(b) What qualitative factors should be considered?

8. The Famous Fish Farm breeds salmon and trout for sale to supermarkets across Canada. The company has prepared the following product cost analysis for 2011:

	Salmon	Trout	Total
Kg shipped	50,000	200,000	250,000
Sales revenue	$ 200,000	$ 250,000	$ 450,000
Costs			
Fish feed	$ 24,000	$ 96,000	$ 120,000
Labour	15,000	60,000	75,000
Distribution costs	15,000	60,000	75,000
Maintenance	3,000	12,000	15,000
Amortization	5,000	20,000	25,000
Administration	15,000	60,000	75,000
Total costs	$ 77,000	$ 308,000	$ 385,000
Operating income	$ 123,000	$ (58,000)	$ 65,000

All costs have been allocated to the two product lines on the basis of kilograms of fish shipped. Fish feed, labour, and distribution costs are variable costs; all the remaining costs are fixed, and none of them would be eliminated if trout were discontinued.

The current set-up has the capacity to grow 400,000 kg of fish per year.

It has been suggested that the company should add a third fish — koi — to its product lines. The estimates show that 100,000 kg of koi can be shipped each year, at a selling price of $1.5 per kg. Variable costs would be the same rate as for salmon or trout.

Required
(a) Should koi be added to its product lines?
(b) Show how the income statement would appear if the koi product line were to be added.

9. Constable Co. sells three products: meat, fish, and cheese. The company has prepared the following departmental income statement for year 2011 ($ '000s):

	Meat	Fish	Cheese	Total
Sales revenue	$800	$ 200	$1,500	$2,500
Cost of goods sold	400	150	1,000	1,550
Gross margin	$400	$ 50	$ 500	$ 950
Direct fixed expenses	100	90	210	400
Departmental operating income	$300	$ (40)	$ 290	$ 550
Common fixed expenses				300
Operating income				$ 250

The cost of goods sold is all variable expense. The direct fixed expenses consist of the amortization of specialized refrigeration equipment used in each department. None of this equipment could be sold by itself. The common fixed expenses represent expense that cannot be traced to any one department.

It has been suggested that the fish department be closed as it is losing money.

Required
(a) Do you agree with the proposal to drop the fish department? (Hint: calculate the profit that would remain after dropping the fish department.)

(b) Assume that 25% of sales in the meat department would be lost if the fish department were closed. Calculate the effect of dropping the fish department.

(c) Assume that all fish sales would be transferred to meat sales if the fish department were dropped. Calculate the effect of dropping the fish department.

10. Elora Inc. makes hydraulic equipment for industrial applications. The company has always manufactured the flow control valves itself. The standard cost of a typical flow control valve is $40.50, made up of the following:

Direct material:

Aluminium casing	$ 2.00
Neoprene bushings	1.00
	$ 3.00

Direct labour	10.00	(15 minutes @ $40 per labour hour)
Variable overhead	12.50	(15 minutes @ $50 per machine hour)
Fixed overhead	15.00	(15 minutes @ $60 per machine hour)
Total	$40.50	

Elora Inc. used 2,000 hydraulic control levers in 2010. The Mainland Machine Co. imports hydraulic control levers from the Far East and is anxious to get a contract to supply Elora Inc. Mainland Machine Co. has quoted a price of $40.00 per unit.

Required
Should Elora Inc. accept the offer from Mainland Machine Co.?

11. Personal Planners provides financial advice to its clients on investment, retirement planning, and tax management. The cost of providing retirement planning is $594 per client, details as follows:

Textbook, "Personal Finance"	$ 37.00
Photocopying	10.00
Advisor's time (2 hours @ $100)	200.00
Computer simulation fee	50.00
Direct costs	$297.00
Overhead (100% of direct costs)	297.00
Total	$594.00

The overhead is typical for this type of business and consists of 40% variable costs and 60% fixed costs. Last year, Personal Planners advised 100 clients on retirement planning.

Robert Bruce Inc., a specialist retirement planning company, has offered to service all of Personal Planners' retirement planning clients.

Required
Assume all "direct" costs are variable for the following questions.

(a) If the offer from Robert Bruce Inc. is $500 per client, should the offer be accepted?

(b) If the offer from Robert Bruce Inc. is a $50,000 lump sum, for which Robert Bruce Inc. would advise up to 120 clients, should the offer be accepted?

Sources of Capital

13

Learning
Objectives

After studying this chapter, you should be able to describe the role of the following in raising capital:

→ Common shares
→ Dividends and retained earnings
→ Preferred shares
→ Equity capital
→ Debt and interest
→ Assessing risk through the interest cover ratio
→ The effect of financial leverage

13.1 Introduction

A business may be thought of as two separate, but related, decision activities: raising capital and investing capital.

Investing capital in short-term assets is dealt with earlier (in Chapters 4 and 5) under working capital management (how much inventory to carry, how much credit to allow our customers, how much credit to get from our suppliers, how much cash liquidity to keep on hand, etc.). Investing capital in long-term assets is dealt with in Chapter 14 by capital budgeting techniques (net present value, accounting rate of return, payback, etc.).

In this chapter, we shall discuss the other part of the equation: the sources of capital, deciding how much capital to raise, and from where. The sources of capital will be discussed under the following headings: common shares, retained earnings, preferred shares, equity capital, and debt. We shall also include a discussion of the cost of capital and the effect of leverage.

13.2 Common Shares

A business that is just starting up has no capital until the owners put some in. The double entry principle tells us that for every investment in an asset, there must have been a source of capital of the same value. All organizations will have some capital provided by the owners to get the company going.

In a sole proprietorship, this is *owner's equity*.

In a partnership, this is *owners' equity* (note the apostrophe has moved, indicating there are multiple owners in a partnership).

In a corporation (a limited liability company), this is *common stock* (otherwise known as common shares or ordinary shares). We shall concentrate on corporations, as they are the most important type of business structure.

In the simplest situations, this initial investment is all the share-related activity that happens, and it remains unchanged from one balance sheet to the next over the life of the company. All companies have at least one common share class in issue. Most situations, however, are more complex.

The initial investment is an exchange process: the investor gives something of value to the business (typically cash, though it could equally well be business assets); in return, the company gives the investor a share certificate.

The bookkeeping entry shows the cash received being added to the cash balance in the company, and the common shares account credited with an equal dollar amount. This preserves the balance sheet equation. Where the shares are issued in exchange for non-cash assets, the fair market value of the assets is recorded, and that same dollar amount is credited to the common shares account. Share certificates are then issued to the contributors.

The share certificate is an acknowledgement that the investor owns, literally, a share in the business. If there is only one share issued, then the owner of that share owns 100% of the company. If there are two shares, each owns 50%. With 100 shares, each owns 1%; with one million shares, each share represents a one-millionth part of the ownership in the company. The more shares there are, the less the proportion of the company each share owns.

Common shareholders are said to have a residual interest in the company. That means they own everything left over after all the other claims have been met. In the normal course of events, where a company is a continuing entity, that really does not mean a lot. However, when a company is wound up (officially terminated), that residual status may make a very big difference. If the company is wound up because it has failed, it generally means that the common shareholders will get nothing. In other situations, where assets are in excess of liabilities, closing the company may mean a large surplus that would be paid out to common shareholders.

The nature of the residual interest makes common shares a relatively high-risk investment for shareholders and, by counter argument, a relatively low-risk source of capital for the company.

13.2.1 Net Income and Dividends

The residual interest concept applies to winding up situations; it also applies to the ongoing activities during the normal operation of the company. When a company generates sales revenue, its first obligation is to pay the costs and expenses that were incurred. What is left over is net income, which is beneficially owned by the shareholders. They do not always get their hands on it, however, due to the existence of dividend policies, which are under the control of the board of directors.

Companies are owned by their shareholders, but they are frequently run by others. In smaller (typically family-owned) businesses, the shareholders may be the directors. In larger companies, particularly ones where the shares are publicly traded on a stock exchange, the directors are elected by the shareholders to manage the company on their behalf, but the shareholders themselves play no part in the day-to-day management of the company. This is only practical. Imagine what would happen if shareholders in Bell Canada Enterprises Inc. felt that they could dabble directly in the active management of the company: it would be chaos.

When a company makes a net income, the directors of the company must make a decision about what to do with it. Their choices are to pay the net income to the shareholders as a dividend; to retain the net income in the company for reinvestment; or to pay some as dividend, and retain the rest for reinvestment.

Many shareholders (though not all) will want to maximize the amount of their dividend from the company whose shares they hold. The quicker they get their money, the sooner they are able to spend it or reinvest it in another company. Most company directors (and some shareholders), by contrast, will want to minimize the amount of the dividend. The smaller the dividend, the more there is to reinvest in the company and the larger the company will grow. There is, thus, a conflict of interest between the two. The result is often the payment of a compromise dividend that is part of the net income, but not all of it.

The process is that the directors are in charge of the decision that a dividend should be paid. The shareholders cannot initiate a dividend payment; the proposal can come only from the directors. Thus, if the directors feel that there is not enough liquidity to pay a dividend (or for any other reason), merely by not acting they can ensure that there will be no dividend. If, and only if, the directors propose a dividend will it be paid.

How much dividend is being paid out can be measured through the dividend cover ratio:

$$\text{Dividend cover ratio} = \text{net income} \div \text{dividend}$$

A company that makes $5 million in net income, for example, and pays a total dividend of $1 million has a dividend cover ratio of 5 (which could also be described as a dividend payout % of 20%).

In theory, the amount of the dividend should not matter. One dollar earned as net income makes the common shareholders $1 richer. If it is paid out as dividend, they have the $1 in their hands and they can use their increase in wealth in whatever way they wish. One dollar earned as net income that is then plowed back into the company means that their share certificates now represent a share of a company that has $1 more assets than it had before. In a just and proper world, the market price of the shares should rise by exactly $1 to reflect this. Sadly, we live in a naughty world, and it does not always work out exactly as the theory tells us it should. In general, though, the theory is fairly robust, and reduced dividends are largely reflected in increased share prices. Share price increases are frequently referred to as "capital growth".

13.2.2 *Stock Splits and Stock Dividends*

A company that does well, making substantial profits, will find its share price increase over time. The lower the dividend payout, the greater this growth is likely to be. While this is a benefit to the shareholder, it

---

Exhibit 13.1: Stock Splits and Stock Dividends

P. Bunyan Inc.
Balance Sheet as at December 31, 2011

Assets		Equity	
Various assets	$100,000	100 common shares of $500 each	$ 50,000
		Retained earnings	50,000
	$100,000		$100,000

(a) After a 5-for-1 stock split, the balance sheet would be:

Assets		Equity	
Various assets	$100,000	500 common shares of $100 each	$ 50,000
		Retained earnings	50,000
	$100,000		$100,000

(b) After a 20% stock dividend, the balance sheet would be:

Assets		Equity	
Various Assets	$100,000	120 common shares of $500 each	$ 60,000
		Retained earnings	40,000
	$100,000		$100,000

---

may result in an unmanageably high share price. If the price of an individual share gets to be too high, buying the shares may be beyond the resources of some small investors. Stock splits alleviate this problem. (See Exhibit 13.1.)

In a stock split, the total value of the company remains unchanged, as does the balance sheet value of the common shares. The number of common shares, however, is increased. The value of each individual share should fall in proportion to the rate of the split.

A company that wishes to pay a dividend, but has insufficient liquidity to pay the dividend in cash, may pay a stock dividend. In a stock dividend, additional shares are allocated to existing shareholders. If the shareholders so wish, they can sell these in the stock market, turning their stock dividend into a cash dividend.

From the company perspective, this is very similar to a stock split. The one difference is that in a stock dividend, the market value of the new shares issued is deducted from retained earnings and added to common stock. Because both accounts are part of equity, there is no effect on the rest of the balance sheet, but now some of the retained earnings (which is a distributable reserve) has been reclassified as (non-distributable) common shares. Neither stock splits nor stock dividends change the amount or types of asset.

13.2.3 *Rights of Common Shareholders*

Common shareholders have the following rights:

- To be informed about the company's financial performance by being given copies of the annual financial statements.
- To attend annual general meetings and to vote on important issues, including the appointment of the auditor and the directors.
- To receive dividends, when approved, on an equal footing with all other common shareholders.
- To receive the net proceeds of winding up the company, on an equal footing with other common shareholders.
- Limited liability: if the company goes into bankruptcy, the shareholders are not required to contribute to the shortfall, except to the extent of their investment in the company's shares.

13.3 Retained Earnings

The payment, or non-payment, of dividends needs to be reflected in the financial records and reports.

The company that always pays out 100% of its net income as dividend will maintain its common equity at the same level (as long as there are no increases or decreases in the number of shares themselves). All other things being equal, the company will stay the same size.

The company that pays out less than 100% of its net income as dividend will grow. The amount plowed back will be invested in new assets, and total company assets will increase. This is reflected in the financial statements by the creation of a new heading called retained earnings in the equity section of the balance sheet. Retained earnings are profits made by the company but not distributed as dividends to shareholders.

Over time, the retained earnings can become a very large amount; they often exceed the recorded amounts of the common equity. Canadian Tire, for example, had, at the end of 2010, $711 million in share capital and $3,394 million in retained earnings.

Where retained earnings are significant, the market value of the common shares is likely to be much higher than the amount originally contributed to the company for the shares.

13.4 Preferred Shares

A preferred share is a share that has some preferential right attached to it. Typically, this is a right to receive a dividend before the common shareholders. A $1, 8% preferred share, for example, is entitled to receive 8% of its nominal value ($1) in dividend (i.e., eight cents). Only when this preferred dividend has been paid can common shareholders receive any dividend.

Preferred shares are a way of reducing the risk for investors. If, however, the risk is a finite amount, by reducing the risk for preferred shareholders the risk level of the common shares is increased.

From a legal perspective, preferred shareholders are still part owners of the company. In the same way that common shareholders cannot force the directors to pay them a dividend, preferred shareholders cannot force their dividend to be paid to them. Like common shares, then, preferred shares represent a low-risk way of financing the company.

There are many variations on the theme of preferred shares. The more important ones are listed below:

- *Redeemable:* A redeemable preferred share is required or allowed to be repaid at some future time. To be redeemable, a preferred share has to have a nominal value: a stated cash amount at which it will be redeemed. Common shares, by contrast, are not normally redeemable.
- *Convertible:* A convertible preferred share is one that is allowed or required to be exchanged for common shares at some future time, and at a stated rate of conversion.
- *Cumulative:* A cumulative preferred share is one that allows unpaid preferred dividends to accumulate, and only after all arrears of preferred dividends are paid can common shareholders get any dividend.
- *Participating:* A participating preferred share is one that enjoys the regular dividend preference at a set rate, and is also entitled to a further dividend on a par with the dividend paid out to common shareholders.
- *Capital preference:* In the event of the winding up of the company, a preferred share may carry the right to repayment of its nominal amount before the common shareholders get anything.
- *Voting preference:* Some preferred shares carry a right to outvote common shares in company meetings, though this feature is rare and is frowned on by most stock exchanges.

Preferred share capital has its own heading within the equity section of the balance sheet.

13.5 Equity Capital

The three categories discussed so far (common shares, retained earnings, and preferred shares) are the main items found in the equity section of the balance sheet. In order, preferred shares will generally be listed first, followed by common shares, followed by retained earnings.

Other categories that may be encountered, but that are less important, include the following:

- *Contributed surplus:* This is the excess amount received for shares over their nominal value. Current practice is to issue common shares without a nominal value (no par value shares), so this heading is not very important, except to accountants.
- *Foreign exchange adjustments:* Some of the wilder results of translating numbers originally expressed in foreign currencies are recorded in this heading.

In general, equity represents a pool of capital with two important features:

- First, it does not have to be repaid (with the exception of redeemable preferred shares). This means that it is low risk for the company. There is never a threat to the liquidity situation from having to repay the capital.
- Second, it is rewarded through the payment of dividends, and dividends do not have to be paid if the directors are against them. Again, this is a low risk for the company.

Both features are in stark contrast with the nature of debt, which is discussed later.

13.5.1 **Cost of Equity**

Equity has a cost to the company, though it is sometimes difficult to see.

Investors have expectations about investing in the company. If they do not receive a reward of some type, then they will not want to continue as investors and they will sell their shares.

The company's profits are the source of investors' rewards: they can be paid to the investor as they are earned in the form of a dividend, or the earnings can be plowed back into the company as retained earnings. If some or all of the profits are retained by the company, we expect the share price to increase, as it has more assets than it had previously.

The return to the shareholders is, therefore, a combination of dividends received and growth in share price. (See example in Exhibit 13.2.)

The shareholders' expected return and the cost of equity to the company are mirror images of each other.

Exhibit 13.2: Dividends and the Cost of Equity

Market value of shares at start of 2011	$100,000
Net income for 2011	$ 20,000
Shareholders expected return on equity	20%

1. If a dividend of $20,000 is paid, the shareholders will get a return of 20% ($20,000 ÷ $100,000 = 20%).

2. If the profit is plowed back into the company, then assets are greater by $20,000, so market value should increase from $100,000 to $120,000.

   The shareholder has gained $20,000, but this is because the market value of the shares has increased. ($20,000 ÷ $100,000 = 20% return on equity)

3. The company could also pay a dividend that is less than $20,000. The result would be a smaller rise in the market value of the shares, but the shareholders' return would still total 20%.

13.6 Debt

A company that wants to invest in assets can choose to raise money through selling shares and/or by plowing back retained earnings. It can also choose to borrow (i.e., debt). Shares represent an ownership relationship between the shareholder and the company. Debt is a creditor relationship, which is very different. Debt has an interest obligation and a repayment obligation, and so it is much riskier for the company.

There are several features of debt that need to be described: level, interest, repayment, and security.

13.6.1 Level

The level of debt is commonly expressed as a ratio. (See Exhibit 13.3.) This may be the ratio of debt to equity, or the ratio of debt to total assets:

Debt-to-equity ratio: $\dfrac{\text{total debt}}{\text{total equity}} \times 100\%$

Debt-to-assets ratio: $\dfrac{\text{total debt}}{\text{total assets}} \times 100\%$

From the accounting equation we know that the total debt and the total equity add up to the total assets, so these two are not really different ratios, just a different way of expressing the same idea. The debt-to-equity ratio is potentially infinitely large; the debt-to-assets ratio cannot exceed 100% (apart from very unusual circumstances where the equity is negative).

Exhibit 13.3: Debt Ratios

Creative Consultants Inc. has total assets of $900,000. Current liabilities are $100,000; long-term liabilities are $200,000; equity consists of common shares of $50,000 and retained earnings of $550,000.

Debt-to-equity ratio: $\dfrac{(\$100,000 + \$200,000)}{(\$50,000 + \$550,000)} \times 100\% = 50\%$

Debt-to-assets ratio: $\dfrac{(\$100,000 + \$200,000)}{(\$900,000)} \times 100\% = 33.33\%$

These could also be expressed this way: there is $0.50 of debt for every $1 of equity (debt-to-equity ratio of 50%), or there is $0.33 of debt for every $1 of assets (debt-to-assets ratio of 33.33%).

The higher the level of debt, the greater the risk of default. Generally speaking, debt-to-equity ratios of more than 100% are regarded as excessive. Likewise, debt-to-asset ratios of more than 50% are regarded as excessive.

13.6.2 *Interest*

When a company borrows, there is a contractual relationship that provides for, among other things, interest payments. The interest is normally expressed as an annual percentage rate on the amount outstanding. Thus, a 10% bank loan carries interest at 10% of whatever the loan balance is.

The company is required to pay this interest whether or not it has sufficient profit and whether or not it has sufficient liquidity. The company is, therefore, exposed. This makes debt a high-risk source of capital for the company, but a low-risk investment for the lender.

The company's ability to service its debt interest is measured by the interest cover ratio (also known as times interest earned ratio):

$$\frac{\text{operating income (income before taxes and interest)}}{\text{interest expense}}$$

A company with an operating income of $11 million, interest of $2 million, and taxes of $5 million will have net income after tax and interest of $4 million. The interest cover ratio will be 5.5:

$$\frac{\$11,000,000}{\$2,000,000} = 5.5$$

The smaller this ratio, the higher the risk that interest cannot be paid.

An additional feature of debt interest is that it is a tax-allowable expense, unlike a dividend. When $1 of interest is paid, the taxable net income falls by $1 too. The effect is that the after-tax interest rate is less than the nominal rate, by the amount of the tax rate.

After-tax interest rate $=$ nominal interest rate $\times (1 - \text{tax rate})$

If the nominal interest rate is 10%, and the marginal tax rate is 40%, then the after-tax interest rate is 6% and this is called the after-tax cost of debt.

13.6.3 *Repayment*

All debt has to be repaid eventually. The terms of the contract will show whether it has to be repaid sooner or repaid later. Debt that is to be repaid within one year is recorded in the current liabilities section of the balance sheet. Debt that is to be repaid after one year is classified as long-term debt and is shown as a long-term liability.

Repayment may be at a fixed future date (e.g., debt borrowed in 2010, repayable in 2015). Repayment may be over an extended period (e.g., debt borrowed in 2010, repayable in equal annual instalments from 2015 to 2020).

Whatever the date of repayment, it may come at an inconvenient time, when corporate liquidity is low. Repayment obligations are a risk to the company.

13.6.4 Security

The good name of the borrowing company is always important in lending situations. Having a good reputation for paying interest on time and repaying debt when due improves access to further borrowing. A poor reputation for meeting loan obligations can make borrowing virtually impossible. In some situations the lender will reduce risk exposure by taking a legal charge against some assets of the company.

This is common in the case of families or individuals buying a house. The house itself is the security for the loan. In fact, mortgagors limit their risk further by lending (typically) 75% or less of the house's value. If the mortgagee defaults, the house may be seized and sold to pay off the debt.

Companies may be subject to similar terms. A loan may be advanced, secured on specific assets (e.g., the inventory). If there is default, the pledged assets may be seized and sold to pay the debt. This reduces the risk for the lender.

13.6.5 Reporting

When the debt is recorded in the balance sheet, it is required that the interest rate, the repayment terms, and any security be disclosed, too. Frequently there are so many different debt issues with different terms that the disclosure has to take place in the "notes to the accounts", rather than in the balance sheet itself.

13.7 Debt, Risk, and Financial Leverage

The following are from the perspective of the providers of capital:

1. Equity capital earns a return, which is in the form of dividends or growth in the market value of shares.
2. Debt has a return, which is in the form of interest received.

From the perspective of the company, we see the mirror image of these costs:

1. Equity capital has a cost to the company represented by shareholder's expectations of a return.
2. Debt has a cost to the company represented by interest paid. Because interest is a "tax allowable" expense, its net cost is the gross amount of interest less the tax savings it causes.

Taken together, the cost of equity and the cost of debt are the cost of capital of the company.

If the company is financed wholly by equity, the cost of equity is the company's cost of capital. If the company is financed wholly by debt, the cost of interest (net of tax) is the company's cost of capital. And if the company is financed partly by equity and partly by debt, then its cost of capital will be a weighted average of the cost of equity and the cost of debt, weighted according to their relative proportions on the balance sheet. This is called the *weighted average cost of capital*.

Because of the terms relating to interest, repayment, and security, debt is low risk for the lender. However, it is for the same reasons that debt is a relatively high-risk source of capital for the company.

Because it is low risk, lenders will have modest expectations about return. They will charge a relatively low interest rate. Thus, it should be cheaper for companies to borrow money than to get additional investors to buy shares. Additionally, as interest expense is tax allowable, the net cost of debt is again lower.

If a company uses a judicious amount of debt to finance its investments, it can engage in financial leverage. Financial leverage is a way of reducing a company's overall cost of capital and making it more profitable.

A company that is financed entirely by common stock has the cost of common stock as its cost of capital, which is normally a relatively high cost. However, when a company borrows money, as long as the cost of debt is lower than the cost of equity, its cost of capital overall will fall.

> **Example:** Assume that the return required by investors for ABC Co.'s shares is 15%, and interest has a nominal rate of 10%. The marginal tax rate is 40%.

For ABC Co. to be financed entirely by equity, its cost of capital will be 15%. If ABC Co. finances half its assets by borrowing and half from equity, it will have a cost of capital of 10.5%. (See Exhibit 13.4.)

Also, a company that can reduce its cost of capital will increase its earnings per share and thereby increase the share price.

Exhibit 13.4: Weighted Average Cost of Capital (WACC)

Weighted average cost of capital is an average expected return on all of a company's capital. It is calculated by weighting each source of capital proportionately. The WACC for ABC Co. is as follows:

Source	Rate with tax effect	After-tax rate	Proportion	Weighted average
Debt	$10\% \times (1 - 0.4) =$	6% ×	50% =	3.0%
Equity	15%	15% ×	50% =	7.5%
Total			100%	10.5%

Suppose ABC Co.'s operating income is $50, and the company is financed entirely from equity. Its shares, therefore, will be worth $200:

Operating income	$ 50
Interest	0
Taxes (40%)	(20)
Net income	$ 30
Required return on equity	15%
Value of equity ($30 ÷ 15%)	$200

If ABC Co. were to borrow $100 at an interest cost of 10% and use it to repay $100 of its equity, its return on equity would increase:

Operating income	$ 50
Interest ($100 × 10%)	10
Taxable income	$ 40
Taxes (40%)	(16)
Net income	$ 24
Value of equity: less repaid ($200 – $100)	$100
Return on equity [($24 ÷ $100) × 100%]	24%

By moving from 100% equity to 50% debt and 50% equity, ABC Co.'s weighted average cost of capital reduces from 15% to 10.5%. Its common shareholders are also better off because their returns increase (from 15% to 24%).

It appears that it would be beneficial for ABC Co. to move even further along the same path. The company would perhaps like to finance itself entirely by debt, at a net cost of 6%.

Unfortunately, that reasoning is flawed. By the time 100% of the company is financed by debt, all of the company's risk would have been transferred from the shareholders to the debt holders. Beyond a certain point of "reasonable" levels of debt, the 10% rate of interest will no longer apply. Realizing how risky their situation has become, lenders will demand higher interest rates, which erodes the benefit of extreme leverage.

What is considered a reasonable level of debt is a judgment call, and it varies from one industry to another. Measurement of the situation is done through the debt ratio, or the debt-to-equity ratio. Typically, debt ratios greater than 50% (which is equivalent to a debt-to-equity ratio of 100%) are regarded as the limit for prudent investors.

Borrowing, instead of using all equity to finance a company, increases the earnings for the common shareholders but also increases their volatility. Exhibit 13.5 shows what happens to return on equity when operating earnings fluctuate.

Take operating earnings of $50 as a base case, and increase them by 10% or decrease them by 10%, for a company entirely financed by equity. The results would be what appear in Exhibit 13.5, (1).

A 10% change, up or down, in operating income results in the same 10% change in the return on equity. If the required return on equity

Exhibit 13.5: Impact on Return on Equity Using Borrowing to Finance

(1) Through Equity Alone

Results	Base	Change in Operating Earnings	
		Good (+10%)	Bad (−10%)
Operation earnings	$ 50	$ 55	$ 45
Interest	nil	nil	nil
Taxes (40%)	(20)	(22)	(18)
Net income	$ 30	$ 33	$ 27
Shareholders' equity	$200	$200	$200
Return on equity (ROE)	15.0%	16.5%	13.5%
Increase/decrease of ROE from base		+10%	−10%

(2) Using Borrowing and Equity

	Base	Change in Operating Earnings	
		Good (+10%)	Bad (−10%)
Operation earnings	$ 50	$ 55	$ 45
Interest	(10)	(10)	(10)
Taxable income	$ 40	$ 45	$ 35
Taxes (40%)	(16)	(18)	(14)
Net income	$ 24	$ 27	$ 21
Shareholders' equity	$100	$100	$100
Return on equity (ROE)	24%	27%	21%
Increase/decrease of ROE from base		+12.5%	−12.5%

is 15%, then the $200 value of the shares would increase or decrease to reflect this. The market price of the shares increases from $200 to $220 ($33 ÷ 0.15), or decreases from $200 to $180 ($27 ÷ 0.15), thus restoring the 15% return for shareholders.

Now look at what happens if the company is financed half from equity and half from debt. Interest of $10 (10% of $100) has to be paid in each case as is shown in Exhibit 13.5, (2).

The same 10% change in operating income has been translated into a much larger gain or loss in return on equity. A 10% increase results in a 12.5% increase in the return on equity (from 24% to 27%), while a 10% decrease brings a 12.5% loss to the return on equity (from 24% to 21%). The debt has levered the return, making not only net income higher, but also the ROE more variable.

13.8 Summary

In capital structure, there is a fundamental choice between debt and equity financing. Equity is lower risk, but higher cost; debt is higher risk, but lower cost. A reasonable level of debt will minimize the cost of capital, as this will make the company more profitable for the equity shareholders. At extremely high levels of debt, there is a risk of bankruptcy, so high levels of debt are to be avoided. Minimizing the cost of capital is important, as we shall see in the next chapter: it is a constraint on which projects the company can invest in.

Appendix 13.1
Risk and Return

Students coming to this subject for the first time often find that the question of where the rates of return on shares and debt come from is problematic. Earlier in this chapter, in order to make the topic relatively straightforward, the source of these rates is deliberately glossed over. Statements are made such as "the debt pays 10% interest" or "the required return on equity (shares) is 15%". In this appendix, we discuss the market model. The market model tells us that risk and return have a positively correlated straight-line relationship. Basically, the market sets interest rates.

The market model starts with the idea that return (the benefit an investor gets from holding an investment) is a good thing: all other things being equal, an investor will prefer more return to less return.

Return comes partly in the form of dividends from profit and partly in the form of change in the share price. Where the directors pay only a fraction of the profit as dividends and plow the rest back into the business, it is logical to expect the share price to increase because the reinvestment of profits would make the company bigger. Most investors would also expect share prices to rise because of other factors, such as the company's ability to make good investment decisions and the general upward trend of the economy.

When the return is expressed as a percentage of the share price, we get a measure of return on equity. (Note that this is similar to, though not identical with, the return on equity calculated in Chapters 2 and 15, where it is done entirely on the basis of the company's financial statements and does not include any reference to the share price.)

Shareholders' return:

= (dividend received + change in share price)
÷ beginning share price

Example: Common shares of the Energen Co. had a market price of $10 each on January 1, 2011. During 2011, the shares paid a dividend of $1. At the end of the year the share price had risen to $10.50.

Shareholders' return:

= ([$1 + ($10.50 – $10.00)] ÷ $10.00) × 100%
= 15%

As the calculation above indicates, the return is independent of the dividend decision. The company profit is either paid now, as dividend, or is reflected in share price increases (which can be rationalized as the expectation of future dividends).

The holder of a common share in Energen Co. has achieved a return of 15% per annum. This would be compared with other available returns to see how well the share had performed relative to the alternative investments available. It would also be used to estimate future returns, on the basis that shares that have performed well in the past are likely to continue to perform well in the future.

If shareholders find or expect this return to be lower than other available returns they will sell their shares in Energen Co. and buy those other investments. The effect of selling pressure will be that the share price of Energen Co. starts to fall. As the share price falls, the expected future return increases. Eventually the expected future return will become the same as that of any comparable alternative investment, and there will no longer be any need to sell the shares. At that point selling pressure will cease and the share price will stabilize at the new, lower level.

On the other hand, if investors see that Energen's share is expected to yield a higher return than other investments, they will try to buy its shares. This will put upward pressure on the share price, and it will rise. As the share price rises, Energen's expected future return will fall. Eventually the price will stabilize where the expected future return is the same as that of any comparable investment.

Thus, the market rules in both situations. It is theoretically impossible for two shares that are alike in every respect to have different share prices. The effect of buying and selling causes share prices to stabilize at a point where equivalent investments produce equivalent returns, all other things being equal.

However elegant this theory is, there are a number of ways in which its practical application makes it somewhat less tidy. In the first place, we are talking about expected future returns. Predicting the future is an uncertain process. The greater the uncertainty, the more divergent individual investors' expectations will be. Different expectations lead to different buying and selling decisions.

Second, it is not easy to find shares that are exact equivalents of each other. Two different companies will always have some features that are unique. To make the market model work effectively, we would, at the very least, need a way of reflecting the most basic of these differences: the level of risk of each company.

Third, not all investors are created equal. Some are tax-exempt on their earnings (charities, for example). Most individual investors pay different rates of tax on the return that is received as dividend and the return that is received due to an increase in the share price. Investors are, therefore, not indifferent to whether they receive their return as dividends, or as capital growth. Also, different investors have different attitudes toward risk. While most investors are risk averse, some are "risk prone": they actually like to gamble.

Because of these (and other) differences, there is a lot of uncertainty about the whole investing process, particularly in investing in the shares of companies. As we shall see, there are some investments that are less uncertain, but they tend to give a lower return.

One of the underlying ideas of finance is that the market is efficient. Efficiency in respect of shares implies that the share price at any given point in time accurately represents the available information about that share. If this is true, then it is impossible to beat the market. However, investors constantly strive to beat the market, so they buy and sell shares in pursuit of improved returns. Logically, investors can only be doing so because they believe the market is inefficient. Ironically, it is this investor buying and selling pressure that makes the market efficient. The market is, therefore, efficient because investors do not believe that selfsame efficiency.

An important feature of company shares is that they are risky. The common usage of the term *risk* is entirely negative. We would talk about the risk of losing our job, or the risk of becoming ill. We would not, normally, talk about the risk of winning Lotto 6/49.

In finance, risk generally includes upside risk as well as downside risk, and all volatility is equated with risk. Risk is perceived as something to be avoided. All other things being equal, investors would prefer less risk to more risk. Once again, the actions of investors in the marketplace, buying and selling shares, reflect this preference.

If, as is suggested, investors are risk averse (and most are), then faced with two investment opportunities with equal returns but different levels of risk, investors will sell the one with the higher risk and use the proceeds to buy the investment with the lower risk. In doing so, they will drive the price of the high-risk share down (increasing its expected future return) and the price of the low-risk share up (decreasing its expected future return). Eventually the prices will stabilize at a point where the difference in risk levels is adequately compensated for by the difference in prices and, hence, the differences in expected future returns.

At the lowest end of the risk scale, there are some investments that carry virtually no risk. The Government of Canada, for example, is a regular borrower from the financial system. It does so by selling treasury bills (T-bills) to banks and other financial institutions. These are sold by an auction process, with the potential buyers putting in bids for the T-bills; the highest bidders get them. Because they paid the highest prices, the return they get is the lowest return. Once again, the market has determined the return to the investor and the rate of interest that the government has to pay. As of early 2011, the return on Government of Canada 91-day T-bills is about 1%. An average of bonds maturing within the next two years is about 2%, so we could say that the risk-free return is somewhere between 1% and 2%, say 1.5%.

At the normal level of risk, there is the market. In the case of Canada, this could be taken as a well-diversified portfolio of the shares listed on the Toronto Stock Exchange. Suppose, for illustration, that this market return is 15%. We can plot the risk and return of both the risk-free investment and the normal risk investment on a graph with the horizontal axis representing risk and the vertical axis representing return. (See Exhibit 13A.1.) Having plotted these two points (the risk-free rate and the return on a normal-risk portfolio), we can join them up with a straight line that represents any combination of risk and return. As long as we assume that the relationship is linear (and that is no more than an assumption), we now have a market line that enables us to rationally price any investment, as long as we know its expected risk level. This market line is where we get the returns that are used so blithely in ideas such as the weighted average cost of capital.

Exhibit 13A.1: The Market Model

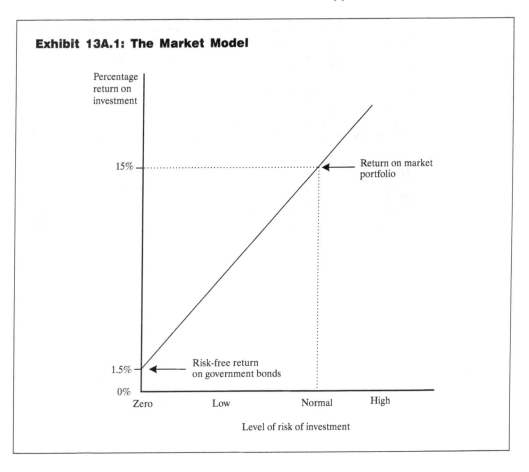

The return on a common share that is equally as risky as the rest of the market will be the same as the market earns, on average. If that return is out of line, investor buying and selling pressure will push it back into line.

The return on a common share that is riskier than the market should earn a higher return, through the same process. The amount of the additional return should depend on the amount of the additional risk.

The return on a common share that is less risky than the market should earn a lower return, through the same process. The amount of the reduction in return should depend on the extent of the reduced risk.

The return on a preferred share, being inherently lower risk to the investor than a common share, should be lower than the return on a similar common share.

The return on borrowed money, being inherently lower risk (for the lender) than that of an equity investment, should always be lower than a return on an equity investment.

The return on a secured investment, such as a mortgage loan, should be lower than the return on an unsecured loan, because it is lower risk.

The government should be able to borrow at the lowest rates as it offers a no-risk investment.

Some rates of return as at early 2011:

What you can earn:

Government of Canada: 91-day T-bill	1.00%
TD Guaranteed Investment Certificates (depending on the term)	0.5% to 2.2%

What you must pay:

TD Bank prime rate	6.25%
Mortgage interest rates (best bank rate for a 5-year fixed mortgage)	5.84%
TD Visa interest rate	19.75%
TD Bank interest on unsecured loan	8.75%
Store-specific credit card	25% to 28%

Self-Study Problems

1. As at January 31, 2002, Bombardier Inc. had assets of $27,753 million. These were represented by the following sources of finance:

	$ million	
Short-term and other borrowings	$15,684	
Long-term debt	7,979	
Total liabilities		$23,663
Shareholders' equity		
Preferred shares (12 million × $25)	$ 300	
Ordinary shares (1,371 million)	896	
Retained earnings	2,894	4,090
Total liabilities and equity		$27,753

    Required
    (a) What were the ratios of debt to equity and debt to assets?
    (b) What is your opinion of the leverage (debt) situation at Bombardier?
    (c) The preferred dividend is stated as being a quarterly amount of $0.34375 per share. Calculate the total amount of the preferred dividend for the year.
    (d) The total dividend on the common shares was $248 million. How much was the dividend per share?
    (e) What was the (total) dividend cover ratio if earnings were $390.9 million?
    (f) Total earnings for the year were $390.9 million. What was the earnings per share figure for the common shares? (First deduct the preferred dividend from the earnings, then divide it by the number of common shares.)
    (g) Total interest expense was $477 million for the year. Calculate the rate of interest per the dollar amount of the debt and the interest cover ratio. (Operating income was $1,700 million.)

2. The Gearing Co. is financed 30% by debt, carrying an interest rate of 8%, and 70% by equity, which has a cost of 12%. The marginal tax rate is 50%.

    Required
    What is the weighted average cost of capital?

3. The Bonzer Corporation and the Dinkum Company are the same size: each has $100,000 of assets. They both make $25,000 operating profit and pay income taxes at a rate of 30%. Bonzer is financed entirely by $100,000 of equity. Dinkum is financed 40% by debt, which requires 10% interest, and 60% by equity (i.e., equity = $60,000).

    Required
    (a) Calculate the return on equity for the two companies.
    (b) Suppose earnings in Year 2 fall from $25,000 per year, by 40%, to $15,000 per year. Calculate the return on equity for the two companies in Year 2.

Solutions

1. (a) Debt-to-equity ratio:

   $$= (\$23,663 \div \$4,090) \times 100\%$$
   $$= 579\%$$

   Debt-to-assets ratio:

   $$= (\$23,663 \div \$27,753) \times 100\%$$
   $$= 85\%$$

   (b) There is too much debt here. (Debt to equity exceeds 100%; debt to assets exceeds 50%.)

   (c) Total preferred dividend for the year:

   $$= \text{preferred dividend per share} \times \# \text{ of preferred shares}$$
   $$= (\$0.34375 \times 4) \times 12 \text{ million shares}$$
   $$= \$1.375 \text{ per share} \times 12 \text{ million shares}$$
   $$= \$16.5 \text{ million}$$

   (d) Dividend per share:

   $$= \$248 \text{ million} \div 1,371 \text{ million shares}$$
   $$= \$0.18 \text{ per share}$$

   (e) Dividend cover ratio:

   $$= \text{earnings} \div \text{dividend}$$
   $$= \$390.9 \text{ million} \div (\$16.5 \text{ million} + \$248 \text{ million})$$
   $$= 1.48$$

   (That is a low but reasonable cover ratio.)

   (f) Earnings available for common shares:

   $$= (\$390.9 \text{ million} - \$16.5 \text{ million preferred dividend})$$
   $$\div 1,371 \text{ million common shares}$$
   $$= \$374.4 \text{ million} \div 1,371 \text{ million common shares}$$
   $$= \$0.27$$

   (g) Interest rate:

   $$= (\text{interest paid} \div \text{amount of debt}) \times 100\%$$
   $$= (\$477 \text{ million} \div \$23,663 \text{ million}) \times 100\%$$
   $$= 2.02\%$$

   Interest cover ratio:

   $$= \text{operating income} \div \text{interest}$$
   $$= \$1,700 \text{ million} \div \$477 \text{ million}$$
   $$= 3.56$$

2. After-tax cost of debt [8% × (1 − 0.50)]   4.0%
   Cost of equity   12.0%
   Weighted average cost of capital
   [(4% × 0.3) + (12% × 0.7)]   9.6%

3. (a)

Year 1	Bonzer	Dinkum	
Operating income	$ 25,000	$25,000	
Interest on debt	0	4,000	($40,000 × 10%)
Taxable income	$ 25,000	$21,000	
Taxes @ 30%	7,500	6,300	
Net income	$ 17,500	$14,700	
Equity capital	$100,000	$60,000	
Return on equity	17.5%	24.5%	

(b)

Year 2	Bonzer	Dinkum	
Operating income	$ 15,000	$15,000	
Interest on debt	0	4,000	($40,000 × 10%)
Taxable income	$ 15,000	$11,000	
Taxes: @ 30%	(4,500)	(3,300)	
Net income	$ 10,500	$ 7,700	
Equity capital	$100,000	$60,000	
Return on equity	10.5%	12.8%	

A 40% decline in operating income causes a 40% decline in the return on equity in Bonzer Corporation.

A 40% decline in operating income causes a 47.76% decline in the return on equity in Dinkum Company because of leverage.

Dinkum shareholders get a higher return, but it is also a riskier investment.

Discussion Questions and Problems

Discussion Questions

1. What are the rights and benefits of owning common shares?
2. What are the features that distinguish preferred shares from common shares?
3. How is debt different from equity? (Answer the question from the perspective of both the borrower and the lender.)
4. Who has control over dividend policy?
5. Explain why retained earnings appear on the balance sheet of most companies.
6. What is the meaning of the interest cover ratio?
7. What is the meaning of the debt-to-equity ratio?
8. What is the leverage effect?
9. How can a lender reduce the risk of default on debt?
10. What are the features of a good leverage policy for a company?

Problems

1. Below is a list of transactions of Govan Co.:

   (a) M. Brough invests $200,000 in cash to get the company going. He is issued 100 common shares.
   (b) M. Brough deeds a shopping mall to Govan Co. The shopping mall has an appraised value of $800,000. M. Brough is issued 400 common shares.
   (c) Mrs. Brough pays $50,000 to the company. In return, she is issued 50,000 cumulative, redeemable, convertible 5% preference shares with a nominal value of $1 each.
   (d) The common shares are split: 10 for 1.
   (e) There is a public offering of shares, and 100,000 common shares are sold for $5 each.
   (f) Govan Co. buys a commercial property in the Lowlands region for $5,000,000: $500,000 is paid in cash and the balance is financed by a mortgage loan from the Merlin Bank. The loan carries an interest rate of 10% and is for a five-year fixed term.
   (g) The company made a net profit for the year of $750,000.
   (h) The company paid the preference share dividend.
   (i) The company paid a dividend of $0.50 per share on the common shares.
   (j) The 50,000 preference shares were converted into 50,000 common shares.

   Required
   Show the balance sheet of Govan Co. after each of the transactions.

2. Prince Inc. was started up in 2007. It has 20,000 common shares of no par value and 5,000 cumulative 5% preference shares of $10 each. The company made a net profit of $300,000 per year each year from 2007 through 2011, but it did not pay any dividend so far.

As a result, prior to paying the 2011 dividend, the company had retained earnings of $1,500,000.

In 2011, the company wants to pay a dividend of $10 per common share.

Required
Show the statements of retained earnings for 2011, including all dividend payments.

3. There are 25,600,000 common shares of Height Ltd. in issue. Height Ltd. had net income (after tax and interest) of $640,000 in 2011. Interest expense for 2011 was $260,000, and tax expense was $400,000. A common share dividend of $512,000 was paid.

Required
(a) Calculate the interest cover ratio.
(b) Calculate the dividend cover ratio.
(c) Calculate the earnings per share.
(d) Calculate the dividend per share.

4. Height Ltd. had total assets of $9,360,000. These were financed by the following: current liabilities, $2,680,000; long-term debt, $2,000,000; common shares, $512,000; retained earnings, $4,168,000.

Required
(a) Calculate the debt-to-assets ratio.
(b) Calculate the debt-to-equity ratio
(c) Comment on the risk level of the company.

5. Pike Co. has $10 million of secured debt, which carries interest at 6%, and $20 million in common shares, which have a required rate of return of 12%. The company tax rate is 40%. There are no retained earnings.

Required
(a) Calculate the net of tax cost of debt.
(b) Calculate the debt-to-assets ratio.
(c) Calculate the weighted average cost of capital.

6. Pike Co. has $20 million of secured debt, which carries interest at 6%, and $20 million in common shares, which have a required rate of return of 10%. The company tax rate is 40%. There are no retained earnings.

Required
What would be the effect on the weighted average cost of capital if the company takes out additional borrowings of the following amounts, each at 10% interest?

(a) $2 million
(b) $10 million
(c) $20 million
(d) $50 million

7. Milton Inc. has made a net income of $1,000,000. How much dividend should the company pay to the common shareholders?

8. Dave Inc. and Buster Ltd. are both wholesalers of machine parts. Each has an operating income of $500,000 in year 2011. Dave Inc., which is financed entirely by common shares, has a total market value of $500,000. Buster Ltd. is also worth $500,000, but it is financed 40% by common shares and 60% by long-term debt, which carries an interest rate of 5%. The tax rate for both companies is 40%.

    Required
    (a) Calculate the return on equity for each company.
    (b) If, in 2012, the operating income increases by 15% for both companies, by what percentage will the return on equity change for each company?
    (c) If, in 2012, the operating income falls to $200,000 for both companies, by what percentage will the return on equity change for each company?

9. Lemmy's Inc. has the following financial statements:

Lemmy's Inc.
Balance Sheet as at December 31, 2011
($ millions)

Current assets			Current liabilities		
Cash	$ 120		Trade creditors		$ 800
Receivables	600		Bank loans		100
Inventory	400				$ 900
Prepaid	80		Long-term debt		300
	$1,200				$1,200
			Equity		
Long-term assets (net)	600		Common shares	$100	
			Retained earnings	500	600
Total assets	$1,800		Total liabilities & equity		$1,800

Lemmy's Inc.
Statement of Retained Earnings
Year to December 31, 2011
($ millions)

Retained earnings as at January 1, 2011	$300
Net income for 2011	600
	$900
Dividend paid	400
Retained earnings as at December 31, 2011	$500

Required
(a) If there were one million common shares in issue, what was the dividend per share?
(b) What were the dividend payout ratio and the dividend cover ratio for 2011?

(c) What is the maximum dividend that Lemmy's Inc. could have legally paid out in 2011?

(d) What is the maximum dividend that Lemmy's Inc. could have paid out in 2011 without recourse to additional borrowing?

(e) If Lemmy's Inc. wants to invest $100 million in a new plot of agricultural land, how could the company finance it?

(f) Would you, as a bank lending officer, lend Lemmy's Inc. $5 million to buy a new office building? If so, under what terms?

(g) Would you, as a bank lending officer, lend Lemmy's Inc. $5 million to launch a new weed-killer product the company has developed? If so, under what terms?

10. Lemmy's Inc. has the following financial statements:

Lemmy's Inc.
Balance Sheet as at December 31, 2011
($ millions)

Current assets		Current liabilities		
Cash	$ 120	Trade creditors		$ 800
Receivables	600	Bank loans		100
Inventory	400			$ 900
Prepaid	80	Long-term debt		300
	$1,200			$1,200
Long-term assets (net)	600	**Equity**		
		Common shares	$100	
		Retained earnings	500	600
Total assets	$1,800	Total liabilities & equity		$1,800

Lemmy's Inc.
Statement of Retained Earnings
Year to December 31, 2011
($ millions)

Retained earnings as at January 1, 2011	$300
Net income for 2011	600
	$900
Dividend paid	400
Retained earnings as at December 31, 2011	$500

Required

(a) If the common shares of Lemmy's Inc. were split six for one, how would the balance sheet change?

(b) If Lemmy's Inc. declared a stock dividend of $250 million, how would the balance sheet change?

(c) Which is better: a stock split or a stock dividend?

11. Punters Co. made a net profit of $50,000 in 2011. Its equity consists of $200,000 in common shares and $100,000 in 10% preference shares. The directors recognize that the company has to pay the preference dividend first, but they want to pay a dividend totalling $10,000 to the directors who own half the common shares and a div-

idend totalling $5,000 to the outside shareholders who own the other half of the common shares. Can they legally do so? If not, how can they legally achieve their planned distribution?

12. Hoopla Co. has a capital structure that consists of $500,000 of common shares, $100,000 of retained earnings, and $400,000 of long-term debt. The debt carries an interest rate of 10%. The corporate tax rate is 40%. The required rate of return on the equity is 20%.

Required
(a) Calculate the net-of-tax cost of debt.
(b) Calculate the weighted average cost of capital.

14

Long-Term Decision Making

Learning
Objectives

After studying this chapter you should be able to explain the following:
→ Why capital budgeting is important to corporate strategy
→ The payback technique
→ The return on investment technique
→ The net present value technique
→ The weighted average cost of capital
→ The role of uncertainty

14.1 Introduction

Long-term decisions are those such as buying new equipment, moving to new premises, and launching new products. These decisions are critically important as they commit the organization to a particular way of doing things over a number of years. Additionally, the long-term decisions tend to involve large amounts of money. Because of these two factors (size of investment and time period), there is a special class of decision-analysis techniques that deal with the assessment of long-term decisions. By making such decisions in a more structured and thoughtful way, we try to avoid committing significant amounts of money to a direction that will not help the organization achieve its long-term objectives.

We can contrast long-term decisions with short-term operating decisions, such as hiring a worker or buying raw materials. If a short-term decision is made in error, there is a way of escaping from it. We could sell the unwanted raw materials, or we could terminate the unwanted employee. There would be a cost, but not an unbearably high cost. Those "get out" options are not so easily available for long-term decisions, or are only available at a very high cost. Suppose that, after buying a new plant, the chosen location proved to be grossly inefficient. There may be no alternative use for a specially constructed building and its specialized equipment. If no buyer can be found, its value is worthless.

Long-term decision making is sometimes referred to as the "capital budgeting" decision as it monitors the process through which the capital of the company is budgeted to be spent. There are three main decision-analysis techniques: payback, the return on investment, and present value. Each technique has a role to play, but the third (present value) is theoretically rigorous. Ideally, no long-term decision should go ahead without having successfully passed the screen of present value analysis.

The capital investment proposals that a company examines may come from various sources: proposals to replace machinery may come from the production manager; proposals to increase efficiency may come from engineering; new product ideas may come from the marketing department; a proposal to invest in a training facility may come from the human resources department; strategic analysis may result in a proposal to relocate operations to a more favourable site.

It is important that, no matter where the proposal originates, the same standard of care is exercised over the decision, and the same criteria are used to judge whether the proposal is acceptable or not. If not, that same proposal might get a "yes" from one source and a "no" from another. This would be illogical. So we shall try to develop decision rules that we can apply across the whole organization in an even-handed way.

All proposals must provide the same quality and quantity of information, including, at a minimum, the following:

• A strategic analysis
• The amount of the investment
• The effect on revenues, costs, and, hence, profits
• The effect on cash flows
• A consideration of the risk

14.2 Strategic Analysis

Organizations are purposive: they have objectives, and they act in pursuit of those objectives. Once objectives have been identified, it is necessary to have a strategy to achieve them. Subsequent to setting the strategy, operational activities are initiated to give effect to it. Long-term decisions should be ways of moving that strategy forward. A proposal that does so is worthy of further consideration, and a proposal that militates against the strategy should be rejected.

Consider Exxon Mobil Corporation. Suppose it identified "functional and geographic diversity" as a core strength upon which its strategy is based. ExxonMobil is considering a proposal to increase the range of chemical manufacturing in its Australian subsidiary. By doing so it would increase its functional and geographic diversity. The proposal is therefore appropriate to the strategy. It would pass this strategic screening.

Strategy could include ideas such as being a "least cost" manufacturer. For that, strategy proposals that increase production efficiency are appropriate. Strategy could equally well be based on consumer satisfaction through product differentiation. In that case, a proposal that increases the range of products or increases the products' suitability in meeting the needs of customers would be ideal.

As an aspect of strategic analysis, most companies will assess the ethical dimension of a proposal. Having an ethical position is inevitable, and with increased publicity and scrutiny of their ethics, companies are likely to wish to appear more responsible. Capital projects frequently have strong ethical implications. Assessing whether or not a proposal contravenes ethical standards is part of deciding whether or not to proceed with the analysis.

Let's return to the ExxonMobil example. Thirty-five of the shareholders of Exxon Mobil Corporation proposed a motion at the 2001 AGM to shift away from fossil fuels and into ecologically friendly fuels. For a variety of reasons, the directors of ExxonMobil urged shareholders to vote against this motion. They can only have made that recommendation after considering the ethics of capitalism, the ethics of the ecological lobby, and the ethical position of the company. In the view of the dissenting shareholders, ExxonMobil may be perceived as having allowed the economic aspects to take precedence over the ethical dimension.

(Of course, an organization that has not clearly identified its strategy and/or its ethics is at a disadvantage when doing any form of strategic analysis. If you don't know where you are going, it really does not matter which bus you catch: they all go there.)

Having passed the strategic analysis, a project should then be judged on its economic consequences for the company. Most proposals (or projects, as they are often called) will call for an investment of a substantial amount of cash at the beginning, and they will generate cash and earnings over a period of years. The key to any decision-analysis technique is that it should measure whether the future returns justify the investment.

In comparing the three main capital budgeting decision-analysis techniques — payback, the return on investment, and present value — we shall see how the three techniques would treat a proposal to acquire a patent:

> The investment consists of the cost to the company: $300,000. The patent has six years to run, and the best estimate of the outcome is an increase in revenues of $500,000 per year. Costs will increase by $475,000 per year. These estimated costs consist of materials, wages, and other cash costs totalling $425,000 per year, and amortization of $50,000 per year. At the end of six years, the patent will expire, and it will have no residual value.

For ease of analysis, we shall ignore the fact that there will be some increases in the receivables, the payables, and the inventory, although such changes are likely in reality.

14.3 Payback

The first technique we shall look at is called payback. Payback considers the cash invested in a project and the cash generated by that project. When the cash generated is sufficient to repay the investment, then payback is said to have occurred.

Consider our initial investment of $300,000. Each year, the project's sales revenues are $500,000, and each year the cash expenses total $425,000. Each year the project generates $75,000 in cash. Note that the amortization expense is not relevant to a payback calculation, as it is not represented by a cash flow.

At the end of the first year, $75,000 is generated to pay off the $300,000 investment, so the cumulative cash flow becomes –$225,000. At the end of year two, another $75,000 is paid back, so the cumulative cash flow becomes –$150,000. At the end of year three, another $75,000 is paid back, so the cumulative cash flow becomes –$75,000. At the end of year four, another $75,000 is paid back, so the cumulative cash flow becomes

Exhibit 14.1: Payback

				Year			
	0	**1**	**2**	**3**	**4**	**5**	**6**
Cash flow ($ '000s)	$(300)	$ 75	$ 75	$ 75	$75	$75	$75
Cumulative cash flow	$(300)	$(225)	$(150)	$(75)	nil		

↑
Payback point
(end of Year 4)

nil. At the end of year four the initial investment has been completely recovered and payback is said to have occurred. (See Exhibit 14.1.)

It is a quick and easy calculation, and it has some merit. A project that never achieves payback, for example, is never going to be acceptable. Also, if you are comparing two very similar projects it is probable that the one with the shorter payback is less risky than the one with the longer payback. However, this technique has at least two serious drawbacks.

The first deficiency is that it considers only part of the project's life. Everything that happens after the payback date is ignored. That cannot be right. Suppose you were offered an investment opportunity that cost $300,000 now, and with the following choices of future cash inflows:

- $75,000 per year for years one to four
- $75,000 per year for years one through six
- $75,000 per year forever

Comparison of these alternatives is made easier by deducting years one through four, which are common to all three. After eliminating the first four years, the following cash flows remain:

- Nothing
- $75,000 in year five and $75,000 in year six
- $75,000 per year from year five onward, forever

It does not take much imagination to recognize that the third option is preferable to the other two. Yet each of these three situations would be described as having a four-year payback period. Only if we have no preference among them is it logical to have our screening technique regard them all equally, but we do have a preference. (See Exhibit 14.2.)

The second deficiency is that payback ignores the pattern of cash flows. Suppose there are two projects, each with a payback period of two years. The initial investment is $100,000, and the two projects have the following cash inflows:

- Project A: year one, $99,000; year two, $1,000
- Project B: year one, $1,000; year two, $99,000

Exhibit 14.2: Cash Flow
— Which One Would You Rather Have?

Year

Choice	0	1	2	3	4	5	6	7 to Infinity
1	($300,00)	$75,000	$75,000	$75,000	$75,000			
2	($300,00)	$75,000	$75,000	$75,000	$75,000	$75,000	$75,000	
3	($300,00)	$75,000	$75,000	$75,000	$75,000	$75,000	$75,000	$75,000

↑
Payback point
(end of Year 4)

Payback fails to consider what happens after the investment is repaid!

Most investors would prefer to get their money sooner, rather than later. Project A would be preferred according to that criterion. However, the payback period regards both projects as equally good as each has a two-year payback.

Despite its shortcomings, payback has some popularity among managers, and it is used in a number of organizations. We stress again, though, that it is an imperfect appraisal technique, and it is insufficient, by itself, to judge whether a project is acceptable or not.

14.4 Return on Investment

The second technique we shall examine is return on investment. This is a ratio that should already be familiar to you. It was introduced earlier in this book to show how ratios can be used to assess the overall performance of a company. In that context, the ratio was defined as:

ROI = (operating income ÷ total assets) × 100%

If that is how we are going to judge the company as a whole, then it makes some good sense to apply the same criterion to assessing an individual investment project. After all, what is a company but a portfolio of interconnected investment projects? If each of them is justified according to return on investment, then the company as a whole will achieve an acceptable return on investment.

In assessing the project we will want to compare the income that the project creates with the investment for the project.

ROI = (operating income from the investment ÷ investment) × 100%

Exhibit 14.3: Return on Investment

($ '000s)	0	1	2	Year 3	4	5	6
Cash flow	(300)	75	75	75	75	75	75
Amortization		50	50	50	50	50	50
Operating income		25	25	25	25	25	25

$$ROI = \frac{\$25,000}{\$300,000} \times 100\% = 8.33\%$$

The return on investment for this project is 8.33%.

The operating income from the investment in the patent we looked at earlier is $25,000 per year for six years. (See Exhibit 14.3.) We had previously calculated cash flow as $75,000 per year. To get from cash flow to net income, the major difference is that we have to deduct amortization. Using a straight-line amortization approach, the entire $300,000 investment will be written off in six annual amounts of $50,000 each. Cash flow of $75,000, less $50,000 of amortization expense, leaves operating income of $25,000 per year.

The return on investment for this project is 8.33%. This is actually the return on the initial investment of $300,000. Another version of ROI expresses the operating income as a percentage of the average investment. Because the average investment is assumed to be half of the initial investment, the return on average investment is always exactly two times the return on initial investment. The return on average investment for this project would be 16.67%:

Return on average investment (ROAvI)

$$= \frac{\$25,000}{(\$300,000 \div 2)} \times 100\%$$

$$= 16.67\%$$

In general, either ROI or ROAvI ratio will be compared with some sort of standard or expectation. So, an investment might be considered acceptable if it had an ROI of 12%. When using the ROAvI, the expectation would be twice as much: the investment would need to show an ROAvI of 24% to be regarded as acceptable.

ROI, whether based on initial investment or on average investment, is superior to payback as it uses the estimated income from all six years of the project's life. However, it is still a deficient technique because it does not consider the pattern of cash flows over the life of the project any more than the payback does.

Exhibit 14.4: Cash Flow
— Which One Would You Rather Have?

		Year		
	0	1	2	3
Project X	($600,000)	$340,000	$220,000	$220,000
Project Y	($600,000)	$220,000	$220,000	$340,000

Both X and Y produce the same total cash flow and the same total profit; they have the same return on investment: ($180,000 ÷ 3) ÷ $600,000 = 10%.

X produces its cash flow sooner and is, therefore, preferable to Y.

This is not captured by the return on investment calculation, which averages profits out over the project's life.

Suppose there are two projects, each with a cost of $600,000, and with the following cash inflows (see Exhibit 14.4):

- Project X: year one, $340,000; year two, $220,000; year three, $220,000
- Project Y: year one, $220,000; year two, $220,000; year three, $340,000

Straight-line amortization will reduce each year's profit by $200,000, leaving the following operating income:

- Project X: year one, $140,000; year two, $20,000; year three, $20,000
- Project Y: year one, $20,000; year two, $20,000; year three, $140,000

The total profit for each project is $180,000 over the three years, which is $60,000 per year on average. With an initial investment of $600,000, both projects have a 10% return:

$$\frac{(\$180,000 \div 3)}{\$600,000} \times 100\% = 10\%$$

Although the total income and ROI are the same, the pattern of earning income over time is different, and that causes the pattern of receiving cash inflows to be different also. If we compare the two projects, we can see what that different pattern of cash flows is. Once again, the deduction of one series of cash flows from the other highlights the effect. In each year the $200,000 amortization charge has been added to the income to show the cash flow:

- Project X: year one, $340,000; year two, $220,000; year three, $220,000
- Project Y: year one, $220,000; year two, $220,000; year three, $340,000

Difference $(X - Y)$:

- Year one: $120,000
- Year two: nil
- Year three: ($120,000)

With the similar deficiency as the payback period, it is only logical to regard these two projects as equally worthwhile if investors are indifferent about getting their money back sooner rather than later. But we know they want it sooner, because only with the cash in their hand are they able to spend it or reinvest it. The ROI method is faulty because it fails to discern the cash flows between the two projects. Note that return on investment ratios can be used to assess both new investments (as discussed here) and also ongoing situations (as shown in Chapter 2, page 26).

14.5 Present Value

The third technique is called present value. What we are faced with is a theoretical approach along the following lines:

- The assessment of a project should be based on its cash flows.
- Cash flows arising at different times are not directly comparable to one another.
- It is possible to discount a future cash flow back to the present time by allowing for the interest effect: this calculates its present value.
- Present values can be meaningfully added to one another.
- When the present values of all the cash flows from a project are added, a project with a positive net present value will increase the value of the firm, while a project with a negative net present value will decrease the value of the firm.

The present-value approach is the underpinning of techniques with the following names:

- Present value
- Net present value
- Discounted cash flow
- Discounting
- Internal rate of return

To understand present value, we will have to begin with a small discussion of interest.

14.5.1 Simple and Compound Interest

A dollar today is not worth the same as a dollar tomorrow. There are at least two good reasons for this phenomenon: interest and risk. We shall look at risk later in this chapter. For now, let us consider only the interest effect.

The reason $1 today is not worth the same as $1 tomorrow is that between today and tomorrow there is the opportunity of earning interest. One day's interest is, of course, trivial (unless you are a bank or a financial institution, in which case the amounts are so enormous that even one day's interest is significant). To make the issue sensible, we shall consider not one day, but one year: a period when the interest effect becomes meaningfully large.

The accounting equation treats assets as if they were equivalent and interchangeable. For example, the asset Cash on the balance sheet is treated in almost the same way as the asset Accounts Receivable. From a present value perspective, however, they are not equivalent.

If you have $100 cash on hand, you can invest it to earn interest. If, however, instead of cash, you have $100 in the form of an account receivable, you do not have that investment opportunity. You cannot invest expectations, and an account receivable is an expectation. How much that opportunity is worth depends on two factors: how long you have to wait before the cash is received and how high the rate of interest is. The longer you have to wait, the more interest opportunities are passed up. The higher the rate of interest, the greater the interest opportunity that is passed up.

Assume you are trying to compare $100 cash in hand against $100 that might be received in one year. Assume that the rate of interest is 5%, 10%, 15%, 20% per year. The $100 invested at these rates would grow in one year to the following:

		Interest Rate			
		5%	**10%**	**15%**	**20%**
Present value	$100				
Future value in 1 year		$105	$110	$115	$120

Clearly, the higher the rate of interest, the greater the interest opportunity. In 2011, interest rates in Canada were at a very low level. You could get a medium-term mortgage to buy a house for about 6%, for example. Because of this, the interest effect was substantially less than it would have been in times of higher interest rates. However, it is still important.

The calculation above is called simple interest. The interest rate per year is multiplied by the principal ($100) and added to the principal to get its future amount at the end of the year. If more than one year elapses, then the interest-earning process is repeated.

In compound interest it is assumed that the principal and the first year's interest are available to earn interest in the second year. The future amount at the end of the second year is available to earn interest in the third year, and so on.

A $100 investment with an interest rate of 10% per annum will grow to $161.05 in five years:

$110.00 in 1 year:	$100.00 + ($100.00 × 0.10) = $110.00
$121.00 in 2 years:	$110.00 + ($110.00 × 0.10) = $121.00
$133.10 in 3 years:	$121.00 + ($121.00 × 0.10) = $133.10
$146.41 in 4 years:	$133.10 + ($133.10 × 0.10) = $146.41
$161.05 in 5 years:	$146.41 + ($146.41 × 0.10) = $161.05

If the interest rate were higher, the growth would be greater. For example, $100 invested at 20% per annum would grow to $248.83 in five years:

$120.00 in 1 year:	$100.00 + ($100.00 × 0.20) = $120.00
$144.00 in 2 years:	$120.00 + ($120.00 × 0.20) = $144.00
$172.80 in 3 years:	$144.00 + ($144.00 × 0.20) = $172.80
$207.36 in 4 years:	$172.80 + ($172.80 × 0.20) = $207.36
$248.83 in 5 years:	$207.36 + ($207.36 × 0.20) = $248.83

The effect of compound interest can be seen by looking at the way $100 will grow if invested at different interest rates and for different periods of time:

Interest rate:		5%	10%	15%
Present value	$100			
Future value in:				
1 year		$105.00	$110.00	$ 115.00
2 years		110.25	121.00	132.25
3 years		115.76	133.10	152.09
4 years		121.55	146.41	174.90
5 years		127.63	161.05	201.14
10 years		162.89	259.37	404.56
20 years		265.33	672.75	1,636.65

The formula to calculate future value is as follows:

$$FV = PV (1 + i)^n$$

where:

FV   is the future value (the amount to which the investment will grow).
PV   is the present value (the amount originally invested).
i   is the interest rate.
n   is the number of years the amount is invested for.

This formula makes it possible to calculate the future value for any combination of amount, interest rates, or number of years. To make life easier, the formula is built into the functions of all business calculators. Check your calculator's instruction book to see how to enter the data and get the result. That will not be possible with really simple calculators or those designed mainly for other applications. The formula is also built into many computer programs and applications (Excel spreadsheets, for example).

Future values are very useful for some calculations: for example, they will be handy in finding out how much your RRSPs are expected to increase over your working life so that you will be able to estimate your wealth at retirement. They are not so useful for project appraisal, however, and the main reason they are being described is so that we can turn the interest concept (which people largely understand) into its corollary: discounting. By inverting the interest process, we get discounting.

14.5.2 *Discounting*

If a present amount can grow to a larger future amount through the process of compound interest, then a future amount can be expressed as its present equivalent by eliminating the interest opportunity.

If $100 would grow to $110 in a year when invested at 10%, then a future amount of $110 receivable in one year's time is equivalent to $100 now. In other words, discounting $110 at 10% for one year gives it a present value of $100.

The compound interest factor in the FV formula is

$$(1 + i)^n$$

Discounting uses the inverse of the compound interest factor, and its formula is as follows:

$$PV = FV \times \frac{1}{(1+i)^n}$$

Or, if you prefer:

$$PV = \frac{FV}{(1+i)^n}$$

The effect of the discounting process varies with the interest rate and the number of years. High interest rates and long time periods make future values far higher than the initial investment. In the same way, high interest rates and long time delays before receiving a cash flow mean that its present value may be far less than the dollar amount eventually received.

So, if the interest rate is 10% and you have to wait two years for $100, it is the same as having $82.64 now. The 10% interest would grow the $82.64 into $100 over two years. (See Exhibit 14.5.)

$82.64 × 1.1 = $90.91 at the end of year one
$90.91 × 1.1 = $100.00 at the end of year two

If the interest rate is 15% and you have to wait 20 years for your $100, it is worth only $6.11 in present value. That is because $6.11 invested now at 15% interest would grow into $100 in 20 years:

$$FV = PV \times (1 + i)^n$$
$$FV = \$6.11 \times (1 + 0.15)^{20}$$
$$= \$100$$

With very high interest rates and/or with long time periods, the present values of future cash flows approach (but never quite reach) zero.

As with future value, the discounting formula is readily available as a function of calculators, computers, and software. As a leftover from the days when calculators and computers were less readily available, there are also tables that show the value of $1 \div (1 + i)^n$ for a range of values of i and n. These are called discount tables or present value tables,

Exhibit 14.5: The Effect of Discounting

	Interest Rate		
	5%	10%	15%
Future value $100			
Present value if time period is:			
1 year	95.24	90.91	86.96
2 years	90.70	82.64	75.61
3 years	86.38	75.13	65.75
4 years	82.27	68.30	57.18
5 years	78.35	62.09	49.72
10 years	61.39	38.55	24.72
20 years	37.69	14.86	6.11

as they enable calculating the amount by which a future value must be discounted to get its present value. (A present value table is included in Exhibit 14.6.)

To use the table for a particular combination of i and n, look up the number at the intersection of the i (interest rate) column and n (number of years) row. Multiply the future cash flow by that discount factor to get its present value.

Suppose a contract entitles you to receive $1,000 in two years, and 10% is the relevant interest rate. The discount factor (Exhibit 14.6) for a 10% interest rate and a two-year time period is 0.8264 (all discount factors are less than 1); the contract's present value, therefore, is $826.40. You should see no difference between receiving $826.40 now and receiving $1,000 in two years.

The discounting process enables all future cash flows to be restated at their present equivalents. These present values can be added or subtracted as they are at a common point in time, unlike the future values, which could not be meaningfully added as they were stated at different times. When present values of all future cash flows are added, we get "net present value".

14.5.3 Net Present Value

The cash flows that were estimated to arise from an investment in the patent proposal are as follows:

Initial investment now	$300,000
Years one through six	
Revenues	$500,000
Cash expenses	425,000
Annual cash inflow	$ 75,000

Exhibit 14.6: Present Value of $1

Interest rate	3%	5%	8%	10%	12%	14%	16%	18%	20%	25%
Number of years										
1	0.9709	0.9524	0.9259	0.9091	0.8929	0.8772	0.8621	0.8475	0.8333	0.8000
2	0.9426	0.9070	0.8573	0.8264	0.7972	0.7695	0.7432	0.7182	0.6944	0.6400
3	0.9151	0.8638	0.7938	0.7513	0.7118	0.6750	0.6407	0.6086	0.5787	0.5120
4	0.8885	0.8227	0.7629	0.6830	0.6355	0.5921	0.5523	0.5158	0.4823	0.4096
5	0.8626	0.7835	0.6806	0.6209	0.5674	0.5194	0.4761	0.4371	0.4019	0.3277
6	0.8375	0.7462	0.6302	0.5645	0.5066	0.4556	0.4104	0.3714	0.3349	0.2621
7	0.8131	0.7107	0.5835	0.5132	0.4524	0.3996	0.3538	0.3139	0.2791	0.2097
8	0.7894	0.6768	0.5403	0.4665	0.4039	0.3506	0.3050	0.2660	0.2326	0.1678
9	0.7664	0.6446	0.5002	0.4241	0.3606	0.3075	0.2630	0.2255	0.1938	0.1342
10	0.7441	0.6139	0.4632	0.3855	0.3220	0.2697	0.2267	0.1911	0.1615	0.1074
15	0.6419	0.4810	0.3152	0.2394	0.1827	0.1401	0.1079	0.0835	0.0649	0.0352
20	0.5537	0.3769	0.2146	0.1486	0.1037	0.0728	0.0514	0.0365	0.0261	0.0115

Exhibit 14.7: Calculating Net Present Value

Year	Cash Flow	12% Discount Factor*	Present Value
0 (now)	($300,000)	1.0000	($300,000.0)
1	$75,000	0.8929	66,967.5
2	75,000	0.7972	59,790.0
3	75,000	0.7118	53,385.0
4	75,000	0.6355	47,662.5
5	75,000	0.5674	42,555.0
6	75,000	0.5066	37,995.0
Present value of cash inflows			$308,355.0
Net present value of the project			$ 8,355.0

* Taken from Exhibit 14.6.

To restate these cash flows at their present values we would multiply each one by an appropriate discount factor. If 12% is the relevant interest rate, we can read the discount factors from the 12% column of Exhibit 14.6.

Note that the initial investment is not discounted. It occurs now and, therefore, its present value is equal to its cash value.

Each of the $75,000 annual cash flows is multiplied by the applicable discount factor to reduce it from a cash amount of $75,000 to some lower present value. As the time period increases, so the effect of discounting becomes more. Thus the $75,000 we are to receive in year six is only worth $37,995 today ($75,000 × 0.5066).

The discounted cash inflows can be added. They total $308,355. (See Exhibit 14.7.) That is the total present value of the inflows from this patent project, and it is a good measure of how worthwhile the project is. If these cash flows had cost more than $308,355 to "buy", it would not be worthwhile.

By deducting the investment from the total of the inflows, we get the "net present value". If the net present value of a project is positive, it is acceptable. If the net present value is negative, the project is not acceptable. And if the net present value is zero, we should be indifferent between investing and not investing. (See Exhibit 14.8 for steps in a net present value calculation.)

Here, the patent project costs $300,000 to invest; the present value of its cash inflows ($308,355) is greater than the present value of its cash outflows ($300,000). With a positive net present value of $8,355, the project is worthwhile.

Exhibit 14.8: Steps in a Net Present Value Calculation

1. Estimate the amount of the cash investment.
2. Estimate the amount and timing of the cash flows that the investment will cause.
3. Decide on an appropriate discount rate (i.e., interest rate).
4. Discount each future cash flow to its preset value.
5. Add the present values of all the inflows.
6. Deduct the investment, leaving the net present value.
7. If the net present value is a positive number, the investment is acceptable; if the net present value is a negative number, the investment is unacceptable.

14.5.4 *Annuities*

A series of cash flows that is the same each year for a period of time is called an annuity. As such, the cash flow of the patent proposal is an annuity since its cash inflows are the same each year — it will give cash flows of $75,000 per year for six years. There are some shortcuts to doing the calculations for annuities. First, your business calculator or computer will have annuity routines, much like the present value routines. Second, there are the tables.

Exhibit 14.6 shows the discount factors for any combination of i and n so that a cash flow arising at a known future date can be discounted. Exhibit 14.9 shows discount factors for annuities. As with Exhibit 14.6, it is an array, with columns for i and rows for n. The big difference is that n in Exhibit 14.9 means every year for that number of years, rather than arising at year n, as it would in Exhibit 14.6.

Technically, Exhibit 14.9 is a cumulative version of the numbers in Exhibit 14.6. Compare the two tables. The first row in each table is identical. That is because an annuity for one year is the same as receiving a single payment one year from now. The second row in Exhibit 14.9 is the total of the first and second rows in Exhibit 14.6. The third row in Exhibit 14.9 is the total of the first three rows in Exhibit 14.6, and so on.

Exhibit 14.9 is used in much the same way as Exhibit 14.6. A known or estimated annual cash flow is multiplied by the annuity factor from Exhibit 14.9 to get its present value:

For i of 12% and n of six years, the annuity factor is 4.1114.
A six-year annuity of $75,000 is worth $75,000 \times 4.1114 = \$308,355$

If the initial investment was $300,000, the net present value would be $8,355. This is the same answer that we get from the calculation in Exhibit 14.7. There should be no surprise to that, as they are just different presen-

Exhibit 14.9: Present Value of an Annuity of $1 per Year

Interest rate	3%	5%	8%	10%	12%	14%	16%	18%	20%	25%
Number of years										
1	0.9709	0.9524	0.9259	0.9091	0.8929	0.8772	0.8621	0.8475	0.8333	0.8000
2	1.9135	1.8594	1.7832	1.7356	1.6901	1.6467	1.6053	1.5657	1.5277	1.4400
3	2.8286	2.7232	2.5770	2.4869	2.4019	2.3217	2.2460	2.1743	2.1064	1.9520
4	3.7171	3.5459	3.3399	3.1699	3.0374	2.9138	2.7983	2.6901	2.5887	2.3616
5	4.5797	4.3294	4.0205	3.7908	3.6048	3.4332	3.2744	3.1272	2.9906	2.6893
6	5.4172	5.0756	4.6507	4.3553	4.1114	3.8888	3.6848	3.4986	3.3255	2.9514
7	6.2303	5.7863	5.2342	4.8685	4.5638	4.2884	4.0386	3.8125	3.6046	3.1611
8	7.0197	6.4631	5.7745	5.3350	4.9677	4.6390	4.3436	4.0785	3.8372	3.3289
9	7.7861	7.1077	6.2747	5.7591	5.3283	4.9465	4.6066	4.3040	4.0310	3.4631
10	8.5302	7.7216	6.7379	6.1446	5.6503	5.2162	4.8333	4.4951	4.1925	3.5705
15	11.9379	10.3797	8.5595	7.6061	6.8109	6.1422	5.5755	5.0916	4.6755	3.8593
20	14.8775	12.4622	9.8181	8.5136	7.4694	6.6231	5.9288	5.3257	4.8696	3.9539

tations of the same mathematical process. However, using annuity tables makes for a much shorter calculation.

PV of an annuity = annual amount × annuity discount factor

14.5.5 *Weighted Average Cost of Capital*

One of the deliberate omissions in all the previous calculations is any indication of where the discount rate, or relevant interest rate, comes from. There are a number of possibilities, but we are going to restrict ourselves to one of them — the weighted average cost of capital (WACC), which was introduced in the previous chapter. WACC is the appropriate discount rate because it represents the cost of all financing (debt and/ or equity) that a company can use to invest in projects. And by using WACC, the proposal will only be accepted if its return is sufficient to maintain the company's share price and if it keeps its shareholders and creditors happy.

14.6 **Uncertainty**

It cannot be stressed too strongly that assessment of long-term projects is an inaccurate science. The assessment is based on future cash flows, and the future is always uncertain. At best, we have estimates of what the cash flows will be; at worst, we have wild guesses. Clearly, we will be better at estimating some things than at estimating others.

A proposal that consists of a relatively minor change in existing operations would tend to be low risk. To sell a 10-tonne truck and replace it with a 15-tonne truck, for example, would be subject to very little uncertainty.

A proposal that involves a more radical change would likely be less well understood and more uncertain. For example, the introduction of a performance-related bonus scheme may represent a completely new way of rewarding employees, and its outcomes may be highly uncertain.

Proposals that involve brave new ventures (introduction of new products, excursions into new markets) offer the least reliability and the greatest levels of uncertainty. Such proposals are often the most lucrative, as well as being the riskiest.

It is not good management practice to ignore risk, though that is clearly the behaviour we see exhibited on occasion. We should, as a first step, try to understand where risk comes from (changing prices, changing technology, developments in markets, etc.), and we must try to measure the risk associated with major long-term decisions. Once the risk has been measured, however crudely, we must incorporate it into the decision process.

One way of doing this is through the discount rate. If the WACC is the appropriate rate at which to discount a cash flow of "normal" risk, then it can be argued that a higher discount rate should be used for a riskier cash flow. Several companies adopt this approach. They will use different rates to discount different projects, perhaps adding two percentage points to the rate where the project is perceived as risky.

Another method is to use what is called "sensitivity analysis". If all the data in respect of a project are entered into a spreadsheet, then it is a relatively simple process to vary the input factors one by one to see what effect a change would have on the outcome. This is called sensitivity analysis.

In the first edition of this book, which was written in 2003, the following example of risk was given:

> A project might critically depend on there being crude oil available as an input at a price of $25 or less per barrel. If the price is $25 or less, the net present value would be positive. If the price rises to $27, then the net present value would become negative.

As of this writing (March 2011), the price of crude oil is hovering at around $115 a barrel, a price that was unimaginable in 2003. The decision to go ahead with the project would then become an exercise in estimating the future price of crude oil, as that is what the project is sensitive to.

Risk analysis is a complex art, and sophisticated modelling techniques may be necessary to incorporate it into the long-term decision process. Just because it is difficult, however, is no reason to ignore it.

14.7 Summary

Long-term decisions have to be carefully vetted to make sure they move the company forward toward its objectives. Such decisions may be assessed using payback, return on investment, and present value. Of these, present value is far more rigorous than the others. Because these projects are about the future, there is risk involved, and that is another dimension to be considered in making the decision.

Self-Study Problems

1. A project has a required investment of $100,000. It will result in cash inflows as follows:

Year	$
1	10,000
2	20,000
3	35,000
4	35,000
5	55,000

Required
(a) Calculate the payback period.
(b) Calculate the return on initial investment and the return on average investment.
(c) Calculate the net present value using a cost of capital of 16%.
(d) Is this investment acceptable?

2. A project has an initial investment of $1.2 million. It will result in cash flows of $600,000 per year for each of the next six years.

Required
(a) Calculate the payback period.
(b) Calculate the return on initial investment.
(c) Calculate the net present value, using a cost of capital of 12%.
(d) Would you recommend this investment?

Solutions

1. (a)

Year	$ Cash Inflow	$ Cumulative Cash Inflow
0	($100,000)	($100,000)
1	10,000	(90,000)
2	20,000	(70,000)
3	35,000	(35,000)
4	35,000	nil

Payback is at the end of year 4.

(b) Amortization: $100,000 ÷ 5 years = $20,000 per year

Year	$ Cash Inflow	Amortization	Operating Income
1	$ 10,000	$ 20,000	($10,000)
2	20,000	20,000	nil
3	35,000	20,000	15,000
4	35,000	20,000	15,000
5	55,000	20,000	35,000
Total	$155,000	$100,000	$55,000

Average annual operating income:

= $55,000 ÷ 5 years
= $11,000

Return on initial investment:

= (average annual operating income ÷ initial investment)
× 100%
= ($11,000 ÷ $100,000) × 100%
= 11%

Return on average investment:

= (average annual operating profit ÷ average investment)
× 100%
= [$11,000 ÷ ($100,000 ÷ 2)] × 100%
= 22%

(c)

Year	Cash flow	16% Discount Factor	Present Value
1	$10,000	0.8621	$ 8,621
2	20,000	0.7432	14,864
3	35,000	0.6407	22,425
4	35,000	0.5523	19,331
5	55,000	0.4761	26,186
Present value of cash inflows			$ 91,427
Initial investment			100,000
Net present value			($ 8,573)

(d) No, this investment does not pass the financial hurdle, as it has a negative net present value. It is not acceptable.

409

2. (a) Payback:

$$= \text{investment} \div \text{annual cash flow}$$
$$= \$1,200,000 \div \$600,000$$
$$= 2 \text{ years}$$

(b) Annual amortization expense, using the straight-line method:

$$= \$1,200,000 \div 6 \text{ years}$$
$$= \$200,000 \text{ per year}$$

Annual operating income:

$$= \text{cash flow} - \text{amortization}$$
$$= \$600,000 - \$200,000$$
$$= \$400,000$$

Return on initial investment:

$$= (\text{annual operating income} \div \text{initial investment}) \times 100\%$$
$$= (\$400,000 \div 1,200,000) \times 100\%$$
$$= 33.33\%$$

Return on average investment would be twice that: 66.67%

(c) Net present value of project:

Net present value of cash flows:
Annual cash flow × (12%, 6-year annuity discount factor)
= $600,000 × 4.1114* $2,466,840

Investment: 1,200,000
Net present value $1,266,840

* From Exhibit 14.9

(d) Yes, the project has a positive net present value, so it is acceptable on financial grounds.

Discussion Questions and Problems

Discussion Questions

1. Why is long-term decision making so much more important than short-term decision making?
2. What are the likely sources of proposals for long-term investments?
3. Name the three appraisal techniques used for long-term investment analysis, and describe how each one is applied.
4. What are the main weaknesses of the payback method?
5. What are the main weaknesses of the return on investment method?
6. Should return on investment be calculated on the basis of the original investment or the average investment?
7. In the net present value method, what interest rate should be used to discount future cash flows?
8. Why is amortization "added back" to net income to get cash flow?
9. What is risk, and how can it be accommodated in project appraisal?
10. Describe the relationship between strategic planning and capital project appraisal.

Problems

1. The Software Solutions Corporation is a software development company based in Southern Ontario. The company has decided that its strategy is to be based on offering state-of-the-art, differentiated, high-end software solutions to organizations that are prepared to pay for the best products available. The company is considering a number of long-term investment decisions:

    (a) Acquisition of a new software management program that would integrate existing software development activities and enable products to be more functional when they were introduced to the market: cost, $2 million
    (b) Acquisition of an existing software development company that had unique expertise in an area Software Solutions wanted to develop: cost, $55 million
    (c) Relocation of company offices from downtown Toronto to Richmond Hill, which would save substantial operating costs: cost, $1 million
    (d) Hiring Jennifer Wong, who is currently the software manager of a rival company: proposed salary, $250,000 per year
    (e) Spending $750,000 on an advertising campaign in trade magazines to attract new customers
    (f) Outsourcing programming activities to a specialist organization in Southeast Asia: expected savings of $500,000 per year

    Required
    For each investment, describe how well it fits with the company's strategy, and decide whether or not the company should proceed to evaluate the proposal's economic merits.

2. Handiman Hardware Inc. manufactures and sells computer peripherals for industrial applications. Its philosophy is to make high-demand products in large quantities and to sell them at prices lower than the competitors' products. The company is considering a number of investment decisions:

   (a) Purchase of a new production machine that will reduce variable costs by 3%: cost, $200,000
   (b) Purchase of new product design software that will enable more innovative products possible: cost, $50,000
   (c) Relocation of the company's manufacturing plant from downtown Oshawa to Richmond Hill so as to be nearer some main customers: cost, $500,000
   (d) Relocation of the administrative offices from downtown Oshawa to Geraldton, which will reduce administrative expense by $50,000 per year: cost, $100,000
   (e) Spending $200,000 on television advertising to improve customer awareness among the general public
   (f) Spending $200,000 on advertising in *Production Manager Monthly* to improve product awareness among professional production managers
   (g) Outsourcing production to the Far East: expected cost is $400,000, but production costs would fall dramatically

   Required
   For each decision, describe how well it fits with the company's strategy, and decide whether or not the company should proceed to evaluate the proposal's economic merits.

3. A project has an initial investment of $60,000, and estimated future cash inflows of $12,400 per year for six years.

   Required
   (a) Calculate the payback period.
   (b) Calculate the return on initial investment.
   (c) Calculate the return on average investment.
   (d) Is the investment worthwhile?

4. For each of the following alternatives, state which is preferable:

   (a) $1,000 per month at the end of every month for a year, or $12,000 now
   (b) $1,000 per month at the end of every month for a year, or $12,000 at the end of the year
   (c) $12,000 now or $12,500 at the end of one year

5. Calculate the present value, using the relevant interest rate of 10%, for each of the following amounts:

   (a) $10,000 now
   (b) $10,000 at the end of one year
   (c) $10,000 at the end of five years
   (d) $10,000 at the end of each of the next five years
   (e) $10,000 at the end of each year forever

6. Purdy Co. has a cost of capital of 25%. The company is considering a project that has the following cash inflows:

Investment	Now	($500,000)
Cash inflow	Year 1	300,000
Cash inflow	Year 2	250,000
Cash inflow	Year 3	200,000
Cash inflow	Year 4	150,000

Required
(a) Calculate the payback period.
(b) Calculate the return on the initial investment.
(c) Calculate the return on the average investment.
(d) Calculate the present value of the cash inflows.
(e) Calculate the net present value of the project.

7. Purdy Co. is considering a new project that will yield an operating profit of $1,250,000 per year for each of the next four years. The operating profit is calculated after amortizing the initial investment of $5,000,000 on the straight-line basis. The company has a cost of capital of 25%.

Required
For this project, calculate the following:
(a) The payback period
(b) The return on original investment
(c) The return on average investment
(d) The annual cash inflow
(e) The net present value of the project

8. Erie Electrical has a number of wholesale outlets in Ontario. The company is considering opening at a new location in Oshawa. The investment required is $10 million, which will buy and equip a new "state-of-the-art" store. The entire $10 million would be amortized over a 10-year period. Sales are expected to be $25 million per year each year for the next 10 years. The gross margin percentage is 20%. Other cash operating expenses are budgeted to be $500,000 per year. The company's cost of capital is 10%.

Required
(a) Calculate the annual operating income.
(b) Calculate the annual cash inflow.
(c) Calculate the payback period.
(d) Calculate the return on initial investment.
(e) Calculate the return on average investment.
(f) Calculate the net present value of the project.
(g) Would you advise the company to go ahead or not?

9. Erie Electrical has a number of wholesale outlets in Southern Ontario. The company has identified a number of projects that are in line with company strategy, all of which have positive net present values and acceptable payback periods:

413

(a) Purchasing a new packing machine for the Oshawa warehouse
(b) Refitting all service vehicles to run on environmentally friendly natural gas
(c) Outsourcing all service operations
(d) Redesigning one of the warehouses so that fewer inventory movements are required
(e) Opening a new electrical supplies outlet in Mississauga
(f) Opening a new electrical supplies outlet in California
(g) Introducing a new line of plumbing supplies
(h) Diversifying into building a new subdivision
(i) Diversifying into computer software development in Argentina

Required
For each one, consider how reliable the underlying estimates are likely to be, and state whether you think the project is "normal risk", "low risk", or "high risk".

10. Erie Electrical is considering investing in a new warehouse management system. This is budgeted to cost $654,900, which will be amortized on the straight-line basis over the project's expected five-year life. The project is expected to increase cash inflows by $200,000 per year. The company's cost of capital is 20%. Because this investment is perceived as being "low risk", it has been suggested that the project be evaluated using a "risk adjusted" cost of capital of 14%.

Required
(a) What is the net present value of the project when the cash inflows are discounted at 20%?
(b) What is the net present value of the project when the cash inflows are discounted at 14%?
(c) Is the investment justified?
(d) What would happen if the cash inflows were to be discounted at 16%?

11. Erie Electrical has a capital structure that consists of 20% long-term debt, earning 8% before tax. The effective corporate tax rate is 20%. The other 80% of the capital is common shares, and these expect a return of 20%.

Required
Calculate the weighted average cost of capital.

Financial
Statement
Analysis

15

Learning
Objectives

After studying this chapter you should be able to calculate and interpret financial accounting ratios that deal with the following:

→ Liquidity
→ Profitability
→ Debt
→ Efficiency
→ Market-related measures

15.1 Introduction

Accounting ratios are used to better understand the numbers in financial statements. When an accounting number is compared to another accounting number, the ratio is sometimes very informative: more informative than the numbers would be by themselves. Thus, the dollar value of inventory from the balance sheet, by itself, tells us little. The value of inventory compared to the sales revenue gives us a valuable clue to assess the efficiency of the company's inventory control; it expresses the information as the number of times per year the inventory is turned over. The value of the inventory turnover ratio for one year when compared with the same ratio for a subsequent year tells us whether inventory management is improving or getting worse.

Within the various chapters of this text we have introduced a number of financial accounting ratios. In order to understand these ratios better and understand their interrelationships, in this chapter we carry out a financial ratio analysis on the results of Leon's Furniture Ltd.

We start off with the financial statements themselves. To make the task more straightforward, the financial statements have been summarized to some extent. (See Exhibit 15.1.) Their principal characteristics, however, remain intact.

The analysis will concentrate on the following:

• *Liquidity:* Whether or not the company is likely to run out of cash.
• *Profitability:* How well the company has performed.
• *Debt:* The extent to which debt increases company risk.
• *Efficiency:* How well the company used its assets.
• *Market-related measures:* Information about share values.

This is not an exhaustive list of financial ratios, but it is sufficient to give a reasonable assessment of the company's performance and prospects.

Exhibit 15.1: Summarized Financial Statements

Note that the following financial statements of Leon's Furniture Ltd. have been some-what simplified for the purposes of illustrating the concepts covered in this textbook.

Leon's Furniture Ltd.
Balance Sheet
($ '000s)

	As at December 31		
	2007	2008	2009
ASSETS			
Current assets			
Cash and marketable securities	$142,279	$139,275	$170,726
Accounts receivable, etc.	34,966	34,507	32,634
Inventory	75,640	92,904	83,957
Total current assets	$252,885	$266,686	$287,317
Long-term assets (net)	222,341	246,722	241,839
Total assets	$475,226	$513,408	$529,156
LIABILITIES & EQUITY			
Current liabilities	$126,837	$129,585	$122,558
Long-term liabilities	26,384	30,465	31,460
Total liabilities	$153,221	$160,050	$154,018
Common shares	$ 14,020	$ 16,493	$ 17,704
Retained earnings	307,985	336,865	357,434
Shareholders' equity	$322,005	$353,358	$375,138
Total liabilities and equity	$475,226	$513,408	$529,156

Leon's Furniture Ltd.
Income Statement
($ '000s)

	For the Years Ended December 31		
	2007	2008	2009
Sales revenue	$637,456	$740,376	$703,180
Cost of sales	363,261	440,360	419,819
Gross profit	$274,195	$300,016	$283,361
Operating expenses:			
Salaries, etc.	$103,661	$116,591	$103,977
Advertising	32,008	33,752	34,732
Rent & property taxes	10,486	11,268	12,165
Other expense (net of other income)	22,983	28,016	33,391
Total cash expenses	$169,138	$189,627	$184,265
Amortization	14,034	16,253	16,562
Total operating expenses	$183,172	$205,880	$200,827
Operating income	$ 91,023	$ 94,136	$ 82,534
Income tax	32,529	30,746	25,670
Net income	$ 58,494	$ 63,390	$ 56,864

Exhibit 15.1 (continued)

Leon's Furniture Ltd.
Statement of Retained Earnings
($ '000s)

	For the Years Ended December 31		
	2007	2008	2009
Retained earnings brought forward	$ 276,037	$ 307,068	$ 338,960
Add: Net income for the year	58,494	63,390	56,864
Deduct: Cost of share purchases	(7,635)	(4,625)	(4,297)
Deduct: Dividend paid	(19,828)	(26,873)	(33,951)
Retained earnings carried forward	$ 307,068	$ 338,960	$ 357,576

Leon's Furniture Ltd.
Statement of Cash Flows
($ '000s)

	For the Years Ended December 31		
	2007	2008	2009
Operating Activities:			
Net income	$ 58,494	$ 63,390	$ 56,864
Add: Non-cash expenses (including amortization)	17,151	18,820	16,616
Deduct: Net increase in non-cash working capital	(7,112)	(12,482)	4,035
Cash from operations	$ 68,533	$ 69,728	$ 77,515
Investing Activities:			
Net cash used as investment in long-term asset	$ (43,629)	$ (24,402)	$ (20,215)
Financing Activities:			
Dividends paid	$ (19,671)	$ (26,870)	$ (33,965)
Repurchase of shares	(7,706)	(4,672)	(4,517)
Cash used in financing	$ (27,377)	$ (31,542)	$ (38,482)
Net increase (decrease) in cash	$ (2,473)	$ 13,784	$ 18,818
Cash brought forward	28,172	25,699	39,483
Cash carried forward	$ 25,699	$ 39,483	$ 58,301

Additional Information

1. Number of common shares in issue: 2007, 70,777,000; 2008, 70,729,000; 2009, 70,714,000.
2. Average share prices for 2007 to 2009 were $14.90, $8.30, and $11.80, respectively.

15.2 Liquidity

A major concern to any organization is its ability to survive. Short-term survival is critically dependent on the relationship between immediate obligations and the liquid assets that are available to pay them. Cash will be needed to pay these short-term debts, but cash is not the only available resource: other short-term assets may also be turned into cash and used to pay liabilities. Thus, liquidity analysis is concerned primarily with the current assets and the current liabilities. The greater the ratio of current assets to current liabilities, the more liquid the company is, and the lower the threat of running out of cash. Two ratios are used for liquidity analysis: the current ratio and the quick ratio.

15.2.1 Current Ratio

Definition: current assets ÷ current liabilities

2007	2008	2009
$252,885	$266,686	$287,317
$126,837	$129,585	$122,558
= 1.99 : 1	= 2.06 : 1	= 2.34 : 1

Analysis: Leon's is adequately liquid. Its current ratio is almost exactly the same as the 2 : 1 norm in years 2007 and 2008, and over 2 : 1 in 2009.

15.2.2 Quick Ratio

Definition: (current assets – inventory) ÷ current liabilities

The quick ratio recognizes that inventory, though a current asset, is less liquid than other current assets, and its availability to pay off obligations is questionable. Hence, inventory is removed, and the more liquid current assets are compared to current liabilities.

2007	2008	2009
($252,885 – $75,640)	($266,686 – $92,904)	($287,317 – $83,957)
$126,837	$129,585	$122,558
= 1.40 : 1	= 1.34 : 1	= 1.66 : 1

Analysis: Leon's is adequately liquid. Its quick ratio is well above the 1 : 1 norm in all three years.

15.3 Profitability

Once it has survived extinction in the short term, a company has an objective of profitability to meet. Profitability ratios express some measure of profits against the resources used to create them. In this way the results are scaled. This means that the results of different-sized companies can be compared. You would not expect the same dollar amount of profit from IBM and a corner grocery store, but you might expect the same percentage return on their respective assets. The profitability ratios we shall calculate are return on sales (%), return on assets (%), and return on shareholders' equity (%).

15.3.1 Gross Profit on Sales (%)

Definition: (gross profit ÷ sales) × 100%

This ratio measures what is left over out of sales after the direct cost of sales is deducted. In a retail organization such as Leon's the direct cost is the replacement of the inventory that has been sold. It is a very useful control measure that monitors whether the company is controlling its merchandising activities effectively. If sales revenue or inventory are being misappropriated, this ratio will be lower than what would be expected from the official profit markups.

Canadian company law does not require disclosure of the direct costs as a separate category, but Leon's has chosen to report it anyway. It is always calculated internally, for control purposes.

2007	2008	2009
$\dfrac{\$274{,}195}{\$637{,}456} \times 100\%$	$\dfrac{\$300{,}016}{\$740{,}376} \times 100\%$	$\dfrac{\$283{,}361}{\$703{,}180} \times 100\%$
= 43.0%	= 40.5%	= 40.3%

Analysis: Leon's has suffered a small reduction in its gross profit as % of sales between 2007 and 2009, falling from 43.0% to 40.3%.

In 2008 and 2009, it is just over 40%. A 40% gross profit ratio is consistent with a 66-2/3% markup on costs. For example, if an item has a cost of $600, a markup of 66-2/3% would add $400 to make the selling price $1,000. The $400 gross margin is 40% of the selling price.

15.3.2 Return on Sales (%)

Definition: (operating income ÷ sales) × 100%

This ratio measures what is left over out of each dollar of sales after all the operating expenses have been paid. It measures many things that are under the control of the management (such as the total number of employees and their remuneration) and also a number of things that are outside management's control (such as the purchase price of raw material inputs). The more carefully management controls the costs under their influence, the higher this ratio will be.

2007	2008	2009
$\dfrac{\$91{,}023}{\$637{,}456} \times 100\%$	$\dfrac{\$94{,}136}{\$740{,}376} \times 100\%$	$\dfrac{\$82{,}534}{\$703{,}180} \times 100\%$
= 14.3%	= 12.7%	= 11.7%

Analysis: The operating income as % of sales fell from 14.3% in 2007 to 12.7% in 2008, and 11.7% in 2009.

In the case of Leon's, the company has given us comprehensive information about its expenses, so we can do a complete vertical analysis of the component parts of the income statement, expressing each item as a percentage of the sales revenue:

	2007		2008		2009	
Sales revenue	$637,456	100.0%	$740,736	100.0%	$703,180	100.0%
Cost of sales	363,261	57.0%	440,360	59.5%	419,819	59.7%
Gross profit	$274,195	43.0%	$300,016	40.5%	$283,361	40.3%
Operating expenses:						
Salaries, etc.	$103,661	16.3%	$116,591	15.8%	$103,977	14.8%
Advertising	32,008	5.0%	33,752	4.6%	34,732	4.9%
Rent & taxes	10,486	1.6%	11,268	1.5%	12,165	1.7%
Other expenses	22,983	3.6%	28,016	3.8%	33,391	4.7%
Amortization	14,034	2.2%	16,253	2.1%	16,562	2.4%
Total operating expenses	$183,172	28.7%	$205,880	27.8%	$200,827	28.5%
Operating income	$ 91,023	14.3%	$ 94,136	12.7%	$ 82,534	11.8%
Income tax	32,529	5.1%	30,746	4.1%	25,670	3.7%
Net income	$ 58,494	9.2%	$ 63,390	8.6%	$ 56,864	8.1%

Analysis: Leon's had an increase in sales revenue. In 2007, sales revenue was $637,456; by 2008, it had risen to $740,376, which is a 16% increase. Despite having made this increase in the sales revenue, the gross profit did not rise proportionately, and gross profit as % of sales fell from 43.0% to 40.5%. Operating expenses increased in dollar value but did not increase by the same 16% as sales revenue had, falling in total from 28.7% of sales revenue to 27.8%. As a result of all the above, the operating profit as % of sales fell from 14.3% to 12.7%. Taxes were a smaller percentage of the sales revenue (4.1% in 2008 instead of 5.1% in 2007). This resulted in net income as % of sales falling from 9.2% in 2007 to 8.6% in 2008.

In 2009, sales fell slightly to $703,180. The gross profit percentage stayed constant (just over 40%). Expenses rose slightly (from 27.8% to 28.5%) and taxes fell slightly (from 4.1% to 3.7%). Net income as % of sales fell to 8.1%.

Put in other words, for every $1 of sales in 2007, there was 9.2 cents left over after all outgoings. By 2008 this had fallen to 8.6 cents, and by 2009 it was 8.1 cents

15.3.3 *Return on Assets (%)*

Definition: (operating income ÷ total assets) × 100%

The return on assets measures how well the company has used its assets in carrying out its business mission. (Here, it is retailing.)

2007	2008	2009
$\dfrac{\$91,023}{\$475,226} \times 100\%$	$\dfrac{\$94,136}{\$513,408} \times 100\%$	$\dfrac{\$82,534}{\$529,136} \times 100\%$
= 19.2%	= 18.3%	= 15.6%

Analysis: Between 2007 and 2009, operating income rose from $91,023 to $94,136 (an increase of 3.4%), and total assets rose from $475,226 to $513,408 (an increase of 8%). The net effect is that the return on assets fell from 19.2% to 18.3%. In 2009, operating income fell to $82,534, while total assets increased to $529,156. Return and assets fell to 15.6%.

 This steady decline (19.2%, 18.3%, 15.6%) is a worrying trend.

Comment: There is a connection between the return-on-sales ratio, the return-on-assets ratio (both are shown above), and the total asset turnover ratio (which is shown later in this chapter).

Return on sales	×	Total asset turnover	=	Return on assets
2007				
14.3%	×	1.34 times	=	19.2%
2008				
12.7%	×	1.44 times	=	18.3%
2009				
11.7%	×	1.33 times	=	15.6%

Analysis: Between 2007 and 2008, the drop in return on sales (from 14.3% to 12.7%) was partially offset by the increase in the asset turnover ratio (from 1.34X to 1.44X). In 2009, both return on sales and total asset turnover declined, so return on assets fell to 15.6%.

15.3.4 *Return on Equity (%)*

Definition: (net income ÷ shareholders' equity) × 100%

This is similar to the return on assets, in that it attempts to measure overall economic performance; however, it does so from the perspective of the shareholder, rather than the business unit. There are two differences between these two ratios.

 First, the return on equity is measured on the basis of income after interest, which is then compared to the assets, net of liabilities (in other words, the owners' equity). This means, effectively, that the finance provided by borrowings and the interest cost of borrowings have both been excluded. Thus, a smaller definition of income is being compared with a smaller definition of investment. Return on equity compares the income to which the shareholders are entitled to the finances they have supplied. All other things being equal, this should result in the return on equity being the same as or higher than the return on assets. This is because interest costs on debt (low-risk) should be lower than the required return on equity.

 Second, the return on equity is measured on an after-tax basis. This is because investors are really interested in what is left over for them after taxes have been paid. All other things being equal, this should cause the return on equity to be lower than the return on assets.

 Because these two effects (leverage, taxes) work in opposite directions (leverage increases the return on equity; taxes decrease the return on equity), it is not always clear what the net effect will be.

2007	2008	2009
$\dfrac{\$58{,}494}{\$322{,}005} \times 100\%$	$\dfrac{\$63{,}390}{\$353{,}358} \times 100\%$	$\dfrac{\$56{,}864}{\$375{,}138} \times 100\%$
$= 18.2\%$	$= 17.9\%$	$= 15.2\%$

Analysis: Both the net income and the shareholders' equity rose in dollar value between 2007 and 2008. However, the percentage increases were different. Net income rose from $58,494 to $63,390, which is an increase of 8.4%, and shareholders' equity rose from $322,005 to $353,358, which is an increase of 9.7%. The net effect is a slight fall (from 18.2% to 17.9%) in the return each shareholder got per dollar of assets invested in the company.

When this return (around 18%) is compared with alternative investment opportunities, it is clear that Leon's is doing a good job for its investors in both years.

By 2009, the return on equity had fallen to 15.2%, which is lower than 2008 or 2007, but still a good return in a recessionary economy.

15.4 Debt

When a company uses debt to finance its activities, two things happen. First, because debt is less risky to the investor (i.e., the cost of debt is lower) and because debt interest is a tax-allowable expense for the borrower, the greater the debt, the greater the return on equity should be. Second, the greater the debt, the riskier the equity return becomes: both the variability of returns and the probability of default increase as a result of borrowing capital. Investors and creditors will want to measure the debt in relation to the equity (debt-to-equity ratio or debt-to-total-assets ratio), and will also want to measure the debt interest in relation to the income (interest cover ratio).

The two ratios, debt to equity and debt to total assets, are just different ways of measuring the same concept. It is redundant to consider both.

15.4.1 Debt to Assets (%)

Definition: (total debt ÷ total assets) × 100%

2007	2008	2009
$\dfrac{\$153{,}221}{\$475{,}226} \times 100\%$	$\dfrac{\$160{,}050}{\$513{,}408} \times 100\%$	$\dfrac{\$154{,}018}{\$529{,}156} \times 100\%$
$= 32.2\%$	$= 31.2\%$	$= 29.1\%$

15.4.2 Debt to Equity (%)

Definition: (total debt ÷ shareholders' equity) × 100%

2007	2008	2007
$\dfrac{\$153{,}221}{\$322{,}005} \times 100\%$	$\dfrac{\$160{,}050}{\$353{,}358} \times 100\%$	$\dfrac{\$154{,}018}{\$373{,}138} \times 100\%$
$= 47.6\%$	$= 45.3\%$	$= 41.1\%$

Analysis: Where debt is greater than 50% of total assets or is greater than 100% of shareholders' equity, the conclusion would be that the company has too much debt. An unhealthy reliance on borrowed funds is symptomatic of a risky company. Leon's debt ratios are well below these cut-off levels in all three years, so debt does not present a high level of financial risk.

15.4.3 *Interest Cover Ratio*

Definition: operating income (income before taxes and interest)
÷ interest paid

This ratio measures the ability of the company to pay interest expense out of current earnings. The earnings before interest and taxes are divided by the interest expense.

In the case of Leon's, the company has no debt that carries interest (its liabilities consist of mainly accounts payable and other non-interest–bearing amounts). Its long-term liabilities consist of deferred income taxes. Therefore, it is not possible to calculate the interest cover ratio.

A high interest cover ratio is associated with low risk and a low interest cover ratio is associated with high financial risk. With no interest payable, Leon's has no risk arising from borrowings and interest payments.

15.5 Efficiency

To be efficient can be thought of as getting a high level of sales out of a given set of assets, or, to put it the other way around, using a small quantity of assets to support a given level of sales. Efficiency ratios examine this feature by relating the assets on the balance sheet to the sales revenue.

This can be done for all assets (total assets turnover) or individual asset classes (e.g., receivables turnover, inventory turnover). In each case a judgment may be made on whether the asset is well managed or not.

15.5.1 *Total Asset Turnover*

Definition: sales ÷ total assets

2007	2008	2007
$\dfrac{\$637{,}456}{\$475{,}226} = 1.34\text{X}$	$\dfrac{\$740{,}376}{\$513{,}408} = 1.44\text{X}$	$\dfrac{\$703{,}180}{\$529{,}156} = 1.33\text{X}$

Analysis: The greater the sales revenue per dollar of assets, the more efficiently the company is operating. In 2007, Leon's generated $1.34 for every $1 of assets. By 2008, this had increased to $1.44. The company had therefore become more efficient in its use of assets. In 2009, it fell to 1.33X, so the company was less efficient in 2009.

The total asset turnover ratio can be broken down into its component elements by looking at similar ratios for each of the assets. The two assets that are most commonly examined are the accounts receivable and the inventory.

15.5.2 Receivables Turnover Ratio and Number of Days' Receivables

Companies that let their customers buy goods on credit terms probably expect to increase their sales by doing so. There is a cost, however, in that the accounts receivable have to be financed. An efficient company is one that allows customers credit terms, but is then rigorous about collecting the amounts owing. Comparing receivables to sales revenue shows the turnover ratio. The more frequently these are turned over, the more efficiently the company is operating.

An alternative way of presenting the same information is the number of days' worth of sales that the receivables represent. It is unnecessary to calculate both ratios.

Receivables Turnover Ratio

Definition: sales ÷ receivables

2007

$$\frac{\$637,456}{\$34,966} = 18.2X$$

2008

$$\frac{\$740,376}{\$34,507} = 21.5X$$

2009

$$\frac{\$703,180}{\$32,634} = 21.5X$$

Receivables Collection Period

Definition: receivables ÷ (sales ÷ 365)

2007

$$\frac{\$34,966}{(\$637,456 \div 365)}$$

= 20 days

2008

$$\frac{\$34,507}{(\$740,376 \div 365)}$$

= 17 days

2009

$$\frac{\$32,634}{(\$703,150 \div 365)}$$

= 16.9 days

Analysis: Between 2007 and 2008, although sales revenue increased by 16%, accounts receivable actually fell slightly (from $34,966 to $34,507). The receivables turnover ratio increased from 18.2 times per year to 21.5 times per year, indicating higher efficiency. The same story is told by the receivables collection period. In 2007, it took 20 days on average to collect accounts receivable; in 2008, that had fallen to 17 days; and in 2009, the collection period went down further, to 16.9 days.

15.5.3 Inventory Turnover and Inventory Holding Period

A retail company such as Leon's needs inventory so that its customers can see what they are buying. Holding inventory is, however, expensive. It has to be warehoused and moved around. It may suffer deterioration. It has to be financed. All other things being equal, the less the inventory for a given level of sales revenue, the more efficiently the company is operating.

Inventory Turnover

Definition: sales ÷ inventory

2007	2008	2009
$\frac{\$637,456}{\$75,640} = 8.4X$	$\frac{\$740,376}{\$92,904} = 8.0X$	$\frac{\$703,180}{\$83,957} = 8.4X$

Inventory Holding Period

Definition: inventory ÷ (sales ÷ 365)

2007	2008	2009
$\frac{\$75,640}{(\$637,456 \div 365)}$	$\frac{\$92,904}{(\$740,376 \div 365)}$	$\frac{\$83,957}{(\$703,180 \div 365)}$
= 43 days	= 46 days	= 44 days

Analysis: Sales revenue increased by 16% from 2007 to 2008, but inventory increased even faster. In 2007, inventory was $75,640; in 2008, it increased by almost 23% to $92,904. As a result, the inventory turnover ratio fell from 8.4 times per year to 8.0 times per year, and the inventory holding period increased from 43 days to 46 days. The company's use of inventory has become less efficient.

In 2009, turnover was back to 8.4X and inventory holding period was back to 44 days.

15.6 Market-Related Ratios

Ratios that shareholders will use in assessing the value of their shares include the earnings per share, the price-to-earnings ratio, and the dividend cover ratio.

15.6.1 Earnings Per Share

Definition: net income ÷ number of common shares

The higher the earnings, the better it is for the shareholders. Earnings will either be paid to shareholders now as a dividend, or they will get the benefit of capital growth through increased share prices if the earnings are plowed back into the company to finance growth. Whatever the total earnings, they have to be shared among the shareholders, so the greater the number of shares, the lower each share's proportion of earnings.

2007	2008	2009
$\frac{\$58,494}{70,777} = \$0.83$	$\frac{\$63,390}{70,729} = \$0.90$	$\frac{\$56,864}{70,714} = \$0.80$

Analysis: Leon's had a higher net income in 2008 ($63,390, compared to $58,494 in 2007), but the number of shares in issue had shrunk slightly (from 70,777 to 70,729). As a result, the earning per share increased from 83 cents to 90 cents. In 2009, EPS fell to 80 cents.

Leon's also has some share options in existence, which would enable some managers to purchase additional shares. If that were done, the number of shares would increase, but the net income would remain the same. This would dilute the earnings per share to a slightly lower level in all three years: EPS would be 80 cents in 2007, 87 cents in 2008, and 78 cents in 2009.

15.6.2 Price-to-Earnings Ratio

Definition: share price ÷ earnings per share

The relationship between the earnings of the company and the price of the shares is a judgment by the investing public on how well the company is regarded. A company with a high price-to-earnings ratio is looked on favourably, while a company with a low price-to-earnings ratio is viewed unfavourably.

2007	2008	2009
$\dfrac{\$14.19}{\$0.83} = 17.1X$	$\dfrac{\$8.30}{\$0.90} = 9.2X$	$\dfrac{\$11.80}{\$0.80} = 14.75X$

Analysis: In March 2009, the market price of an ordinary share of Leon's Furniture Ltd. was $8.30. The 2008 earnings per share were $0.90. This gives a price-to-earnings ratio of 9.2 times. This is about average for the retail sector in early 2009.

During 2007 the market price varied from a low of $12.18 to a high of $16.20. The average of these two gives a share price of $14.19. Based on $14.19, the price-to-earnings ratio for 2007 would be 17.1 times.

In May 2010, the share price was $11.80, EPS was $0.80, and P/E ratio was 14.75 times.

15.6.3 Dividend Cover Ratio and Dividend Payout (%)

Definition: net income ÷ dividend

The dividend cover ratio shows the extent to which the earnings are being paid back to shareholders as current dividend and, by implication, the level of profits being plowed back into capital growth. You can't have both!

2007	2008	2009
$\dfrac{\$58,494}{\$19,828} = 2.9X$	$\dfrac{\$63,390}{\$26,873} = 2.4X$	$\dfrac{\$56,864}{\$33,951} = 1.7X$

The same information can be presented in a different form as the dividend payout percentage:

Definition: (dividend ÷ net income) × 100%

2007	2008	2009
$\dfrac{\$19,828}{\$58,494} \times 100\%$	$\dfrac{\$26,873}{\$63,390} \times 100\%$	$\dfrac{\$33,951}{\$56,864} \times 100\%$
$= 33.9\%$	$= 42.4\%$	$= 59.7\%$

Analysis: Between 2007 and 2008, net income rose by 8.4%, but the dividend paid rose even more. Dividend payments went up from 27-1/4 cents per share to 38 cents per share (an increase of 39%). The dividend cover (at 2.4) is quite healthy and there is little risk of the dividend not being affordable, but it has fallen from 2.9X coverage to 2.4X cover. Also, the dividend payout increased from 33.9% of net income to 42.4%.

In 2009, the dividend cover ratio fell to 1.7X and the payout rose to 59.7%. This was because a higher dividend was paid out of lower net income.

15.7 Summary

Leon's Furniture Ltd. is profitable. It earns a good return on its assets and a good return for its shareholders; expenses seem to be well under control. The company is also very low risk. It has adequate liquidity and has negligible amounts of interest-bearing debt. A relatively high proportion of earnings is paid to shareholders as dividend. Its market price and price-to-earnings ratio imply that investors perceive it as a "normal" retail investment.

Appendix 15.1
The Dupont Pyramid
of Operating Ratios

Return on Assets

Way back in the 1920s, the Dupont Company developed a "pyramid" of operating ratios to help it analyze its business operations and to guide the company toward appropriate remedial actions if things went off-track.

The apex of the pyramid is the profitability ratio, return on assets (ROA). ROA is defined as operating income divided by total assets. At the operating unit level, this is seen as the main business objective. However, if the ROA has fallen below the expected level, it is not easy to pinpoint exactly what actions to take to raise it back to where it should be.

General Trading in recent years had ROA of between 12% and 14%, and the business was seen as doing just fine. In 2011, the ROA fell to 9%, and the owners became concerned that it was not profitable enough. Because the ROA was only 9%, the return on equity was lower than the company had expected. (Return on equity is net income, after tax and interest, divided by owners' equity, and is the main ratio for judging investors' returns.)

If the ROA is down to 9%, the owners should be telling the operating managers to increase it. The question is, how? Either increasing the operating income or decreasing the assets would improve the ratio, but what actions can the managers take? The answer is that the ROA ratio does not, by itself, identify any practical steps that managers can take to fix this situation. There is nothing obvious that can be done to magically increase operating profit, nor to decrease total assets.

Dupont broke the ROA down into two parts by relating each of the two terms in the formula to the sales revenue:

$$\text{ROA} = \text{operating profit} \div \text{total assets}$$

That is the same as:

$$= \text{return on sales} \times \text{total asset turnover}$$
$$= \left(\frac{\text{operating profit}}{\text{sales revenue}}\right) \times \left(\frac{\text{sales revenue}}{\text{total assets}}\right)$$

Thus, there are now two ratios to explain the ROA. The return on sales shows how much of every sales dollar is left over as profit after all the costs and expenses have been met. The higher the return on sales, the higher the ROA becomes. The total asset turnover tells us how many

429

Exhibit 15A.1: Understanding General Trading's ROA

Income Statements ($ '000s)	2010	% to Sales	2011	% to Sales
Sales revenue	$500	100	$600	100
Cost of goods sold	250	50	330	55
Gross margin	$250	50	$270	45
Less: Expenses				
Rent, utilities, and taxes	50	10	54	9
Wages	100	20	132	22
Other expenses	40	8	48	8
Total expenses	$190	38	$234	39
Operating profit	$ 60	12	$ 36	6

Asset Turnover Ratios

For General Trading the assets on the balance sheet for 2010 and 2011 have been expressed as turnover rates in relation to the sales of those years as follows:

($ '000s)	2010	Turnover Ratio	2011	Turnover Ratio
Sales revenue	$500		$600	
Cash	$ 50	10.0	$ 50	12.0
Accounts receivable	100	5.0	120	5.0
Inventory	250	2.0	130	4.6
Long-term assets	100	5.0	100	6.0
Total assets	$500	1.0	$400	1.5

The dramatic improvement in the total asset turnover ratio (from 1.0 to 1.5) can be attributed to a number of causes:

- The cash balance stayed the same ($50,000) but, because the sales were higher, the turnover ratio increased from 10 to 12.
- The accounts receivable increased from $100,000 to $120,000, but this exactly matched the rate of increase in sales revenue, so the turnover ratio stayed the same.
- A substantial drop in inventory level (from $250,000 to $130,000) means that the inventory turnover ratio has risen (from 2.0 to 4.6).
- The long-term assets having stayed the same ($100,000) and sales revenue having increased, the long-term asset turnover ratio has increased from 5.0 to 6.0.

times each dollar of assets creates its own value in sales revenue each year. The higher the asset turnover ratio is, the more times per year the return on sales is earned, and so the higher the ROA becomes.

For General Trading, the ROA of 12% in 2010 can be broken down into a return on sales of 12% and a total asset turnover of 1.0. (See Exhibit 15A.1.) The 12% was earned 1.0 times, so the ROA is also 12% (12% × 1.0 = 12%).

In 2011, the return on sales fell to 6%, but the total asset turnover increased to 1.5. The 6% was earned 1.5 times, and that resulted in a ROA of 9% (6% × 1.5 = 9%).

Vertical Analysis of the Income Statement

The Dupont system does not stop at breaking the ROA into return on sales and total asset turnover. It takes each of these and breaks it down into its component parts.

Managing the elements of the income statement (the gross margin percentage, the percentage of sales spent on wages, etc.) is a route to increasing the ROA. By breaking down every element of the income statement and expressing it as a percentage of sales, we get a picture of where the sales revenue is disappearing to. By tracking changes in these percentages, we can see why the ROA has declined and, perhaps more important, we can identify management improvements that would put the organization back on track. This percentage analysis of the income statement is sometimes referred to as a "vertical analysis of the income statement". (To calculate the expenses as a percentage of sales, the dollar value of the expense is divided by the dollar value of sales revenue, and then multiplied by 100.)

The 2010 and 2011 income statements for General Trading are summarized in Exhibit 15A.1, and the expenses shown as percentages of each year's sales revenue. From the vertical analysis of the income statement, some of the reasons for the decline in the return on sales (and, hence, ROA) can be determined:

- The cost of goods sold as a percentage of sales has increased, as a result of which the gross margin has declined by five points, from a 50% gross margin to a 45% gross margin.
- The rent, utilities, and taxes have gone down by one percentage point.
- The wages have increased by two points.
- Other expenses have stayed at the same percentage level.

The management question at this point is: why did these changes occur? Then the next question is: were they deliberate? For example, the reduction in gross margin may be a deliberate decision to reduce selling prices in order to boost sales volume. If this was the case, it worked, as sales volume increased from $500,000 to $600,000. The additional wage expense may have been because of a deliberate decision to hire more staff or pay a sales-related bonus in order to boost sales. Again, if that was the case, it worked. On the other hand, it may be that the decline in gross margin was due to poor stock control or poor purchasing decisions, and it may be that the increase in wage expense was due to hiring unnecessary staff. Neither the accountant nor the accounting system can answer these questions; the managers responsible for the operation of the stores must address them. Once their input has been received, there may be a clear way to redress the situation, such as increasing selling prices, or reducing stock losses through theft, or reducing staffing levels.

Efficiency Analysis of the Balance Sheet Assets

Measuring the elements of the asset side of the balance sheet (inventory, receivables, long-term assets, etc.) in relation to sales also enables us to understand the dynamics of the change in ROA, and engage in practical ways to improve it.

The lower the dollar value of the asset base on which the organization operates, the more efficiently it is operating, all other things being equal. By reducing the value of receivables, inventory, or long-term assets, we can improve the asset turnover ratio, and so improve the ROA. Conversely, if we relax control over an asset such as inventory and let it build up to an unnecessarily high level, it makes the asset turnover ratio fall, and eventually reduces ROA.

As with the vertical analysis of the income statement, we must differentiate between what the accounting reports tell us (that the turnover ratios have changed) and what the causes of those changes were; only the managers concerned can explain why the changes happened.

It could be, for example, that the increase in sales revenue or the decrease in gross margin percentage was directly linked to the reduction in inventory levels because they had a sale to get rid of old, slow-moving stock. The reduction in inventory could also be an independent initiative in pursuit of greater efficiency and totally unconnected to sales volume or sales margins.

Whatever the reasons, the total asset turnover ratio has shown a substantial increase between 2010 and 2011 (see Exhibit 15A.1), so there is probably little that can be done to increase it further. However, if management did plan to make further increases in the total asset turnover ratio, this breakdown would show them where their actions would be felt most strongly. Informed by these individual asset turnover ratios, they would make decisions about whether to try to reduce receivables (by chasing poor-paying customers) or reduce inventories (by moving to a just-in-time inventory management system), or concentrate on long-term asset efficiency.

Summary

The Dupont Pyramid of Operating Ratios is a powerful way of using the financial accounting ratios. (See Exhibit 15A.2.) It takes the descriptive benefits of the ratios and moves them toward management applications by suggesting areas where managers can change business practices in ways that improve the return on assets.

Exhibit 15A.2: The Dupont Pyramid of Operating Expenses

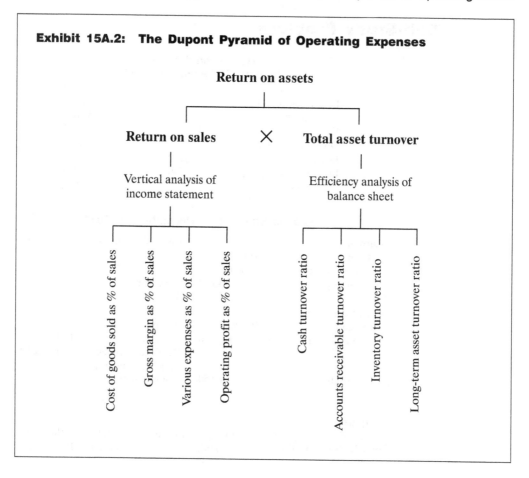

Self-Study Problem

1.

Randy the Retailer
Income Statement for 2011

Sales revenue		$5,000
Direct cost of sales		2,000
Gross profit		$3,000
Expenses		1,250
Operating income		$1,750
Interest	$250	
Income taxes	500	750
Net income		$1,000

Balance Sheet as at December 31, 2011

Current assets			Current liabilities		$2,000
Cash	$1,000				
Accounts receivable	1,400				
Inventory	2,600	$5,000	Long-term debt		500
			Total liabilities		$2,500
Long-term assets					
At cost	$6,000		Equity		
Amortization to date	3,500	2,500	Share capital	$1,000	
			Retained earnings	4,000	5,000
			Total liabilities		
Total assets		$7,500	and equity		$7,500

Required

Calculate appropriate accounting ratios and comment on the company's (a) liquidity, (b) profitability, (c) risk, and (d) efficiency.

Solution

(a)   Liquidity

Current ratio:

= current assets ÷ current liabilities
= \$5,000 ÷ \$2,000
= 2.5 : 1

Quick ratio:

= (current assets – inventory) ÷ current liabilities
= (\$5,000 – \$2,600) ÷ \$2,000
= 1.2 : 1

Comment: This company is adequately liquid according to both these ratios.

(b)   Profitability

Gross profit on sales %:

= (gross profit ÷ sales revenue) × 100%
= (\$3,000 ÷ \$5,000) × 100%
= 60%

Return on sales %:

= (operating income ÷ sales revenue) × 100%
= (\$1,750 ÷ \$5,000) × 100%
= 35%

Return on assets %:

= (operating income ÷ total assets) × 100%
= (\$1,750 ÷ \$7,500) × 100%
= 23.33%

Return on equity %:

= (net income ÷ total equity) × 100%
= (\$1,000 ÷ \$5,000) × 100%
= 20%

Comment: The gross profit ratio is 60% (it is not known whether or not this is what would be expected). Return on sales is 35%, return on assets is 23.33%, and return on equity is 20%. None of these figures seems problematic.

(c)   Risk

Debt-to-assets %:

= (total debt ÷ total assets) × 100%
= (\$2,500 ÷ \$7,500) × 100%
= 33.33%

OR

Debt-to-equity %:

$$= \text{(total debt} \div \text{total equity)} \times 100\%$$
$$= (\$2,500 \div \$5,000) \times 100\%$$
$$= 50\%$$

Interest cover ratio:

$$= \text{operating income} \div \text{interest paid}$$
$$= \$1,750 \div \$250$$
$$= 7 \text{ times}$$

Comment: The amount of debt is reasonable (less than 50% of assets, less than 100% of equity) and interest is well covered. The company is low risk.

(d) Efficiency

Total asset turnover:

$$= \text{sales revenue} \div \text{total assets}$$
$$= \$5,000 \div \$7,500$$
$$= .6667 \text{ times}$$

Receivables turnover ratio:

$$= \text{sales revenue} \div \text{receivables}$$
$$= \$5,000 \div \$1,400$$
$$= 3.6 \text{ times}$$

OR

Receivables collection period / Number of days' receivables:

$$= \text{receivables} \div \text{(sales revenues} \div 365)$$
$$= \$1,400 \div (\$5,000 \div 365)$$
$$= 102 \text{ days}$$

Inventory turnover:

$$= \text{sales revenue} \div \text{inventory}$$
$$= \$5,000 \div \$2,600$$
$$= 1.92 \text{ times}$$

OR

Inventory holding period:

$$= \text{inventory} \div \text{(sales revenue} \div 365)$$
$$= \$2,600 \div (\$5,000 \div 365)$$
$$= 190 \text{ days}$$

Comment: Receivables and inventory are turned over very slowly. As a result, total asset turnover is very low ($1 of assets does not even generate $1 of sales per year). The company's efficiency is poor.

Note the relationship between efficiency and profitability:

Return on sales	×	Total asset turnover	=	Return on assets
35%	×	0.6667	=	23.33%

An increase in either the return on sales or the total asset turnover would increase the return on assets. This, in turn, would increase the return on equity.

Discussion Questions and Problems

Discussion Questions

1. Why are accounting ratios more useful than raw accounting data?
2. What is the objective of liquidity analysis?
3. What is the objective of profitability analysis?
4. What is the objective of debt analysis?
5. What is the objective of efficiency analysis?
6. How do market-related ratios increase our understanding of corporate performance?
7. Between the current ratio or the quick ratio, which is more important, and why?
8. Between the return on sales % or the return on assets %, which is more important, and why?
9. Between the return on assets % or the return on equity %, which is more important, and why?
10. How can efficiency ratios be used to increase profitability?

Problems

1. You are given the (summarized) financial statements of Nortel Networks Corporation.

Nortel Networks Corporation
Income Statement
($ millions)

	For the Year ended December 31		
	2008	2007	2006
Sales revenue	$ 10,421	$ 10,948	$ 11,418
Cost of sales	6,136	6,334	6,979
Gross margin	$ 4,285	$ 4,614	$ 4,439
Operating expenses			
Selling, general & administrative	$ 2,153	$ 2,490	$ 2,503
Research & development	1,573	1,723	1,961
Amortization	2,425	50	26
Other	316	125	(333)
Total	$ 6,467	$ 4,388	$ 4,157
Operating income (loss)	$ (2,182)	$ 226	$ 282
Non-operating income (expense)	$ (212)	$ 91	$ 6
Interest & dividend income	110	221	140
Interest expense	(322)	(381)	(340)
Income tax	(3,193)	(1,114)	(60)
	$ (3,617)	$ (1,183)	$ (254)
Net income (loss)	$ (5,799)	$ (957)	$ 28

Notes
• During 2008, the company was required to write off the amount of $2,379 as impairment of its goodwill. This has been included in amortization expense.
• No dividend was paid in 2006, 2007, or 2008.

Nortel Networks Corporation
Balance Sheet
($ millions)

| | As at December 31 | |
	2008	2007
Current assets		
Cash	$ 2,498	$ 3,608
Accounts receivable	2,154	2,583
Inventory	1,477	2,002
Other	499	954
Total current assets	$ 6,628	$ 9,147
Long-term assets	2,209	7,921
Total assets	$ 8,837	$ 17,068
Current liabilities	$ 4,506	$ 6,772
Long-term liabilities	7,460	6,708
Total liabilities	$ 11,966	$ 13,480
Equity		
Common shares	$ 39,962	$ 39,883
Accumulated deficit	(43,091)	(36,295)
Shareholders' equity (negative)	$ (3,129)	$ 3,588
Total liabilities & equity	$ 8,837	$ 17,068

Note
• Approximately 5 million common shares were in existence at the end of 2006, 2007, and 2008.

Required
(a)   (i) Calculate the current ratio and the quick ratio for 2007 and 2008.
  (ii) Was the company liquid?

(b)   (i) Calculate the ratio of debt as % of total assets for 2007 and 2008.
  (ii) Calculate the interest coverage ratio for 2007 and 2008.
  (iii) Calculate the dividend coverage ratio for 2007 and 2008.
  (iv) Was the company exposed to high levels of financial risk?

(c)   (i) Calculate the gross profit as % of sales for 2006, 2007, and 2008.
  (ii) Calculate the operating income as % of sales for 2006, 2007, and 2008.
  (iii) Calculate the operating income as % of total assets for 2007 and 2008.
  (iv) Calculate the net income as % of shareholders' equity for 2007 and 2008.
  (v) Was the company adequately profitable?

(d)   (i) Calculate the total asset turnover for 2007 and 2008.
  (ii) Calculate the receivables turnover ratio for 2007 and 2008.

439

(iii) Calculate the inventory turnover ratio for 2007 and 2008.
(iv) Was the company efficient?
(v) Show how the return on sales, the total asset turnover ratio, and the return on assets ratio are connected.

(e) Calculate the earnings per share for 2006, 2007, and 2008.

2. You are given the summarized financial statements of Exact Metal for 2011:

Exact Metal
Statement of Earnings and Retained Income for 2011
($ '000s)

Gross operating revenue		$9,000
Less: Cost of goods sold and operating expenses		
Various	$6,500	
Amortization	1,000	(7,500)
Operating income		$1,500
Less: Interest	$ 150	
Taxes	500	(650)
Net income		$ 850
Add: Retained earnings at start of year		500
		$1,350
Less: Dividends paid		300
Retained earnings at end of year		$1,050

Exact Metal
Balance Sheet As At the End of 2011
($ '000s)

Current assets		
Cash	$ 300	
Accounts receivable	900	
Inventory	1,800	
Total current assets		$3,000
Long-term assets (net)		2,000
Total assets		$5,000
Current liabilities		$1,800
Long-term liabilities		1,200
Total liabilities		$3,000
Shareholders' equity		
Share capital	$1,950	
Retained earnings	1,050	
Total shareholders' equity		2,000
Total liabilities and shareholders' equity		$5,000

Required
Using financial ratio analysis, prepare a report on how well the company is doing.

3. You are given the financial statements of Google Inc. Note that these financial statements have been simplified in order to demonstrate the material covered in this book.

Google Inc.
Balance Sheet
($ millions)

	As at December 31	
	2009	2010
ASSETS		
Current assets		
Cash	$ 10,189	$ 13,630
Marketable securities	14,296	21,345
Total cash and marketable securities	$ 24,485	$ 34,975
Accounts receivable	3,178	4,252
Inventory	nil	nil
Other current assets	1,504	2,335
	$ 29,167	$ 41,562
Long-term assets	11,330	16,289
Total assets	$ 40,497	$ 57,851
LIABILITIES AND EQUITY		
Current liabilities	$ 2,747	$ 9,996
Long-term liabilities	1,746	1,614
Total liabilities	$ 4,493	$ 11,610
Equity		
Common shares	$15,817	$18,235
Retained earnings	20,187 36,004	28,006 46,241
Total liabilities & equity	$ 40,497	$ 57,851

Google Inc.
Income Statement
($ millions)

	For the Year Ended December 31	
	2009	2010
Sales revenue	$ 23,651	$ 29,321
Costs of revenues	8,844	10,417
Gross profit	$ 14,807	$ 18,904
Research & development	$ 2,843	$3,762
Sales & marketing	1,984	2,799
General & administrative	1,668	1,962
Total expenses	6,495	8,523
Operating income	$ 8,312	$ 10,381
Non-operating items		
Interest income	69	415
Income before taxes	$ 8,381	$ 10,796
Income taxes	1,861	2,291
Net income	$ 6,520	$ 8,505

Google Inc.
Statement of Retained Earnings
($ millions)

	For the year ended December 31	
	2009	**2010**
Balance at January 1	$ 13,789	$ 20,187
Net income for the year	6,520	8,505
Miscellaneous adjustments	(122)	(686)
Balance at December 31	$ 20,187	$ 28,006

Required

(a) (i) Calculate the current ratio and the quick ratio for 2009 and 2010.

(ii) Was the company liquid?

(b) (i) Calculate the ratio of debt as % of total assets for 2009 and 2010.

(ii) Calculate the interest cover ratio for 2009 and 2010.

(iii) Calculate the dividend cover ratio for 2009 and 2010.

(iv) Was the company exposed to high levels of financial risk?

(c) (i) Calculate the gross profit as % of sales for 2009 and 2010.

(ii) Calculate the operating income as % of sales for 2009 and 2010.

(iii) Calculate the operating income as % of total assets for 2009 and 2010.

(iv) Calculate the net income as % of shareholders' equity for 2009 and 2010.

(v) Was the company adequately profitable?

(d) (i) Calculate the total asset turnover for 2009 and 2010.

(ii) Calculate the receivables turnover ratio for 2009 and 2010.

(iii) Calculate the inventory turnover ratio for 2009 and 2010.

(iv) Was the company efficient?

(v) Show how the return on sales, the total asset turnover ratio, and the return on assets ratio are connected.

(e) Assuming the average number of shares was 318 million in 2009 and 321 million in 2010, calculate the earnings per share for 2009 and 2010.

4

Accounting for the Not-for-Profit Sector

Not-for-Profit and Government Organizations:

"A *nonprofit* activity is an integrated set of activities and assets that is capable of being conducted and managed for the purpose of providing benefits ... as a fulfillment of an organization's purpose or mission."

Financial Accounting Standards Board (U.S.), 2006

16

Accounting for Not-for-Profit and Government Organizations

Learning
Objectives

After studying this chapter, you should be able to do the following:
→ Understand the nature of not-for-profit organizations
→ Understand the three basic characteristics of not-for-profit organizations
→ Explain the differences between not-for-profit organizations and government organizations
→ Understand how financial accounting for not-for-profit and government organizations differs from financial accounting for for-profit companies
→ Explain how financial statement analysis can be used by not-for-profit organizations
→ Explain the concepts of effectiveness and efficiency in the evaluation of not-for-profit organizations
→ Understand the role of budgeting and budgeting control in the management of not-for-profit organizations

16.1 Introduction

Up to this point this book has focused on accounting for business organizations, or what we will call in this chapter, for-profit companies. Despite the predominance of for-profit companies in the economy of Canada, not-for-profit organizations and governments represent a sizable share of economic activity. The objectives of these organizations differ from for-profit companies, but accounting still plays an important role. This chapter surveys accounting principles and techniques for not-for-profit and government organizations.

16.2 Not-for-Profit and Government Organizations

16.2.1 For-Profit and Not-for-Profit Organizations

The principal objective of a business is to maximize profit — hence the term *for-profit company*, which we use to refer to business organizations in this chapter. There are, however, many activities for which self-interest and the profit-oriented form of organization is not appropriate. Organizations that are operated expressly to provide needed goods or services rather than to make a profit are called *not-for-profit organizations* (*NFPOs*).[1]

---

[1] Not-for-profit organizations are also called *non-profit* organizations (NPOs).

It is important to understand the distinction between for-profit companies and not-for-profit organizations. It is not the nature of the goods or services that they provide that distinguishes NFPOs from for-profit companies. NFPOs and for-profit companies can be found in all areas of economic activity. The essential difference between for-profit businesses and not-for-profit organizations is the motivation for their activities and the measure of their success. The assumption is that the objective of a for-profit company — to be more precise, the objective of the managers of a for-profit company — is to maximize profit on behalf of the owners. Whatever other personal motivations they may have, the common, basic interest of business owners, be they shareholders in incorporated companies, partners in partnerships or even sole proprietors, is financial self-interest. Profit — the growth of net worth from operations — is the measure of this objective, which explains the emphasis that accounting puts on the measurement of net income.

But not all economic activity is based on self-interest. Not-for-profit organizations exist to provide goods or services for some particular purpose rather than to maximize the profits of the business owners. There are various kinds of NFPOs. Charities, for example, are organizations that raise money based on appeals to people's humanitarian feelings and then use the resources raised to carry out their mission of relieving poverty, encouraging the arts, finding cures for disease, etc. The pursuit of profit plays no role in their activities. Financial issues are important, primarily because what such organizations can do is limited by the amount of money and other resources they can raise. Put another way, financial considerations represents a *constraint* rather than any sort of objective. Since their expenditure is limited by their revenue, we can say that charities aim to *break even*. Operating to break even in the long run is in fact characteristic of not-for-profit organizations. Other activities that are operated on the same premises are hospitals, social service organizations, schools, and universities.[2] For some NFPOs, the charitable aspect may not be present at all. Examples include clubs, unions, and other organizations, such as trade and professional associations, which offer services to their members, and co-operatives, which carry on business on behalf of their members. Not-for-profit organizations can be as small as personal charitable foundations or as large as national unions. What all of them have in common is the objective of providing services their revenue will support with no expectation of profit.

In a somewhat different category but still operating for the purposes of providing a service rather than making a profit are *governments* — in Canada, local, provincial, and federal governments. Governments are like NFPOs in that profit is not an objective. But governments are unlike NFPOs in that they have the *power to tax*. On the basis of various tax laws and, ultimately, the coercive power of the state, governments can compel individuals and companies to provide the money that is needed to

---

[2] These examples are given for illustrative purposes; such activities are not necessarily carried out on a not-for-profit basis. For instance, although not very common in Canada, there are schools and hospitals that operate on a for-profit basis. These would be called *proprietary* schools or hospitals to distinguish them from not-for-profit organizations.

carry out their activities.[3] The discussion that follows refers primarily to not-for-profit organizations but, in large part, applies to governments and government accounting as well. Significant differences between the characteristics or accounting of NFPOs and governments will be highlighted.

16.2.2 Characteristics of NFPOs

Not-for-profit organizations are defined by the presence of the following characteristics:

- **Service mission**. The objective of an NFPO is the provision of goods or services for a particular purpose rather than making a profit from its activities.

- **Break-even constraint**. The long-run financial objective of the organization is to ensure that total expenses are equal to total revenues.

- **No beneficial ownership**. Not-for-profit organizations have stakeholders and a governance structure, but do not have, as does a for-profit company, identifiable owners with an equity claim and the expectation of enjoying a financial return from the operation of the organization.

16.2.2.1 Service Mission

Every NFPO has its own particular mission. For example, charities exist to help the poor or afflicted or to support the arts or research; schools and universities, to educate students; hospitals, to heal the sick; clubs and co-operatives, to provide personal or business services to their members. Although the motivations differ, in all these cases the scope of the organization's activity is well-defined and resources are raised for that purpose. In some cases, such as charities, those that benefit and those that provide the resources are different; in others, such as clubs, associations, and co-operatives, they are the same. In many cases, such as schools and hospitals, there are elements of both: those that use the services (parents, students, patients) pay part of the costs, but funds are also provided by government or raised as charitable donations from alumni, friends, and others. In all cases, the objective of the NFPO is to raise resources and spend them in a way that most effectively and efficiently serves the NFPO's mission. This is its principal characteristic. (To illustrate, see "Purpose of the Organization" in the Canadian Red Cross Society's 2009 Financial Statement.)

16.2.2.2 Break-even Constraint

A second characteristic of an NFPO is a financial one: the scale of its activities is limited by its revenue. In other words, over the long term, an NFPO is constrained to break even. Of course, in a particular period it

---

[3] Many hospitals, schools, and universities in Canada, while organized as NFPOs, are effectively financed with public money and thus bear some of the characteristics of government organizations. Such organizations are sometimes referred to as *parapublic organizations*.

Objective of the Canadian Red Cross Society

1. Purpose of the Organization

The Canadian Red Cross Society (the "Society") is a not-for-profit volunteer-based humanitarian organization dedicated to helping people in Canada and around the world with situations that threaten their survival and safety, their security and well-being, or their human dignity. The Society relies on continuing support from various levels of governments and fundraising from other donors.

The Society, which is incorporated without share capital under the laws of Canada, is a registered Canadian charity and, as such, is exempt from income taxes.

Source: Excerpt from Notes to the Financial Statements, year ended March 31, 2009.

---

may happen that an organization raises more or less money than it spends. This "excess/(deficiency) of revenues over expenses" is called just that, rather than *profit*, and it is not normally sought for its own sake. It typically results from small, random variations of revenue and expense from budget; and, in the normal course of events, it will balance each other out over the longer term. Occasionally an NFPO may budget for a series of excess revenues over expenses to accumulate capital for a future expansion of its activities; but again, this is not a case of maximizing profits for the benefit of the owners. (The law sometimes puts restrictions on the ability of an NFPO to accumulate revenue in excess of expenses. For example, a charitable organization may lose its charitable status and the right to issue tax receipts if it does not distribute a substantial percentage of the donations it receives from the public.) Because not-for-profit organizations do not seek to make profits, they do not pay income tax.

16.2.2.3 *No Beneficial Ownership*

The absence of a profit motive brings out the third characteristic of NFPOs: the absence of beneficial owners. NFPOs are normally incorporated without share capital. The equity section of an NFPO is usually quite simple — just one or more lines titled net assets or "fund balance".[4] As corporations, they are legal persons or entities; they can own property and incur debt. As well, they have a governance structure that includes a board of directors and rules for determining who may elect the board and receive the financial reports. But although an NFPO is a legal person that

---

[4] An NFPO with more than one fund would have net assets of a fund balance for each fund — see section 16.4.2.1, pp. 454–455.

Co-operatives and Mutual Societies

Co-operatives and mutual societies are organizations of a somewhat hybrid nature. They are an exception to the no-beneficial-ownership rule in that they carry on business on behalf of the members in addition to providing services to them. Co-operatives issue shares to members when they join and can pay dividends (usually based on the volume of business between the member and the organization). They pay taxes on undistributed income. Mutual societies, using different terminology, do much the same.

Historically, these organizations have not sought to maximize profits, although this is changing. Successful commercial activity carries with it pressure to conform fully to the business organizational model and has led some co-operatives and mutual insurance companies to operate effectively on a for-profit basis, and even in some cases to convert to the for-profit organizational form.

We can see an example of this pressure in the report of the chief executive officer in the 2004 annual report of the Mountain Equipment Cooperative (MEC). MEC was founded 33 years earlier to serve hikers and mountain climbers in the Vancouver area. In 2004, it had grown to be an organization with two million members across Canada and over $150 million in annual sales (and to 3 million members and over $250 million in sales in 2009). In 2004, the CEO made the point that growth "has stretched and strained the business in ways the founders could not have envisioned". This has led to a "major restructuring of the organization" with the key priorities that include "... *planning for a modest annual surplus of 3–4%. This last goal sometimes seems incongruous, given that the Co-op is not about profit, but the size of the business dictates that we plan on achieving a surplus ... otherwise MEC has little flexibility to react to what is happening in the broader context* [emphasis added]." The CEO felt it necessary to remind the members that the organization was still being run as a co-operative: "Any surplus at the end of the year, of course, goes back to members in the form of dividends to their share accounts."

It is difficult to avoid the conclusion that the more an NFPO operates like a for-profit business, the more likely it is that it will become one. The main pressure has been the difficulty of access to capital when opportunities or threats arise. This is of course what many companies have faced in the last two years. MEC's response was little different from that of most for-profit companies. In the words of the Board chair, recalling plans how they dealt with the unfolding challenge of doing business in 2009: "The Board of Directors and the Senior Management Team worked together to chart a conservative course. Early in the year the Board decided against share redemptions, and Senior Management implemented a short-term freeze on hiring and wage increases. Staff worked hard to keep expenses down." MEC is not a for-profit company, but its directors and executives talk in for-profit terms. Will it stop there? Other large Canadian co-operatives have found it necessary to convert to the standard for-profit corporations. It will be interesting to see if the MEC can maintain its status as a co-operative.

can own property, an NFPO itself has no owners in the sense of persons who have a claim on the net assets of the organization or who have an expectation of enjoying a financial return from its operation. Rather, an

IFRS and Not-for-Profit Organizations

Although the Canadian Institute of Chartered Accountants (CICA) replaced Canadian GAAP with International Financial Reporting Standards (IFRS) for public, for-profit companies beginning January 1, 2011, this change will not be required for not-for-profit organizations. NFPOs may continue to use current standards, but, if they wish, they may adopt IFRS.

NFPO has a membership or a community that contributes resources to the organization for the purpose of furthering its objectives.[5]

Clubs, co-operatives, and mutual societies are an exception to the no-beneficial-ownership principle. Though they have no profit objective, some clubs do issue shares to members who might then benefit from enhanced property values if the club is liquidated. Co-operatives and mutual societies have evolved in the not-for-profit tradition, but in many ways they have come to take on many for-profit characteristics, including shares, retained earnings, and profit maximization.

16.2.3 Differences Between NFPOs and Government Organizations

These three characteristics — service mission, break-even constraint, and no beneficial ownership — define the not-for-profit organization. Government organizations share these characteristics, but there are other important differences. Governments, like NFPOs, have no beneficial ownership and pay no dividends. Governments pay no taxes (though they do collect them).

The biggest differences between governments and NFPOs are in governance, mission, and financing. The differences in governance are generally understood and will not be pursued here. It is sufficient to note that governance in government organizations is essentially political and is based on constitutional law, whereas governance in NFPOs is based on corporate law.

The mission of governments, even small municipal governments, is much broader in scope than most NFPOs. Unlike an NFPO, the service mission of government is multi-faceted, politically determined, and constrained only by constitution and convention. The break-even constraint is not so restrictive for governments. NFPOs are primarily revenue-financed

---

[5] We can also speak of the potentially broader category of NFPO *stakeholders*, which would include, in addition to the membership or community that contributes to the organization, those who are served by the organization. For not-for-profit organizations, the category of stakeholders can be very broad. *Creditors*, of course, have legal claims on the organization for interest and repayment of the loans they have extended, and they therefore have a stake. But governments, the press, and even members of the public at large can also have a say in how some not-for-profit organizations operate. The widespread public nature of the controversies that arose over the role of the Red Cross in blood collection is a case in point.

through a combination of voluntary contributions, sale of services, and grants and subsidies from other organizations, all of which can easily dry up. Governments' power to tax makes a big difference in their financial management. Even if taxes are not actually levied in the short run, sovereign governments normally have no problem financing deficits with debt. Even though long-term deficit financing by government raises economic questions beyond the scope of this book, deficits are more of an option for governments than they are for NFPOs. Still, at some point, even sovereign governments are subject to a break-even constraint; it is just that they have a much longer time horizon over which they must balance revenue and expense than any private sector NFPOs do.[6]

16.3 Accounting Techniques for Not-for-Profit Organizations

The focus in this book up to this point has been on the accounting principles and procedures of for-profit organizations. Many of the principles and most of the procedures of for-profit accounting are applicable to NFPO accounting (and to a somewhat lesser extent to governmental accounting), so we will focus on the differences between them.

Accounting for NFPOs grew out of the accounting practices of governments. Historically, government accounting has been heavily influenced by legal and political considerations. This is reflected in the use of fund accounting and, at least in the past, the use of cash-basis accounting in government accounting reports. Accounting for NFPOs has evolved in the same tradition with its use of the cash basis recording of transactions, its emphasis on fund accounting and stewardship reporting, and the importance given to control through budgets. This is changing, however. In the past few years, accounting standard setters have acted to bring accounting standards for not-for-profit organizations more in line with those of for-profit companies. Measurement of assets and liabilities, revenues and expenses using the principles of accrual accounting is the main focus of these changes. The fundamental differences in organizational objectives between for-profit and not-for-profit, of course, remain. Though in many ways they have moved toward business accounting, the use of fund accounting by NFPOs (and governments) is a reflection of basic differences (see Exhibit 16.1). In addition there are differences in the areas of revenue recognition and the treatment of capital assets and, more generally, in accounting form and terminology. It is important to note, too, that because profit is neither sought nor measured, the use of accounting reports for scorekeeping in NFPOs is much more limited.

---

[6] Parapublic NFPOs, such as hospitals, school boards, and port and airport authorities, enjoy significant or full government support and, under certain conditions, can borrow money with a government financial guarantee that can allow them to operate with expenses in excess of revenues for relatively long periods of time.

Exhibit 16.1: Reporting Objectives and Accounting

It is helpful to consider differences in accounting for for-profit businesses, not-for-profit organizations, and governments in terms of the underlying reporting objectives. Communication of information to shareholders (both current and potential) is an underlying principle of accounting for business enterprises. Government accounting, on the other hand, has been influenced by the demands of political accountability and the constraints of the law with a focus on such questions as these: How were revenues raised? Was expenditure within budget? Was spending in accordance with the law? Since accounting for not-for-profit organizations evolved in this tradition, it took on the basic form of government accounting, including the use of fund accounting and an emphasis on reporting cash transactions. In recent years, however, more of a measurement and information focus has been adopted, and NFPO accounting has taken on many of the characteristics of business accounting. We can represent this as follows:

Informational Focus   **Political–Legal Focus**

●───●

Accounting for:

For-profits   **NFPOs** ◄─────────── *NFPOs*   **Governments**
                         (today)   (historically)

16.4 Financial Accounting for Not-for-Profit Organizations

Broadly speaking, many of the principles of accounting used by for-profit companies apply to not-for-profit organizations as well. For this reason there is considerable similarity in accounting practice and terminology. There are at the same time important differences, and we will highlight the principal ones in the following areas:

- Financial statements
- Organizational entity
- Revenue and expense
- Amortization

16.4.1 Financial Statements

The general form of financial reports for both for-profit companies and not-for-profit organizations are the same, but there are differences in terminology reflecting their different objectives and legal structure. Both the balance sheet and the cash flow statement have the same names and same general form for for-profit companies and not-for-profit organizations. Both for-profit and not-for-profit organizations prepare operating

---

Exhibit 16.2: Financial Statement Terminology

Not-for-Profit Organization	For-Profit Company
Balance sheet	Balance sheet
Statement of operations (or revenue and expense)	Income statement (or statement of earnings)
Statement of net assets (or fund balances)	Statement of retained earnings
Statement of cash flows	Statement of cash flows

---

statements, but what would normally be called an *income statement* or *earnings statement* by for-profit companies is a *statement of operations* or *statement of revenue and expense* by NFPOs. Since NFPOs are organized without share capital and do not earn profits, the equity change statement is much simpler and the terminology more appropriate to not-for-profit organizations: *statement of net assets* or *statement of fund balances* instead of the for-profit companies' *statement of retained earnings*. (The term *fund balance* will often be used even if there are no other features of fund accounting.) It is common for NFPOs to combine the Statement of Operations with the Statement of Net Assets (or Fund Balances) as a Statement of Operations and Net Assets (or Fund Balances).

Exhibit 16.2 compares the names of the financial statements of NFPOs and for-profit companies. An example of combined statements of operations and fund balances and a multi-column balance sheet can be found in Appendix 16.1. It is worth pointing out that this organization, Centraide of Montreal, a large charitable fundraising organization (similar to United Way in other Canadian cities), does not prepare a cash flow statement. Lack of a cash flow statement is common among NFPOs. Even though it is clear from this organization's balance sheet that the statements are prepared on at least a modified accrual basis, in a note to the financial statements the directors state that a statement of cash flows has not been presented as it would not provide any additional meaningful information. The auditors have accepted this assessment.

16.4.2 *Organizational Entity*

The basic notion of a business or organizational entity is the same for both for-profit companies and not-for-profit organizations. A difference arises, however, in the way in which the entity can be sub-divided. In a for-profit organization, these sub-entities are themselves legally independent incorporated companies and produce their own financial statements. For reporting purposes of the controlling parent, however, they are subsidiaries and their financial results are combined with those of the parent in consolidated statements (see Chapter 4, Appendix 4.3). Such parent–subsidiary relationships are not typically found in not-for-profit organizations. It is common, however, for the board of an NFPO, especially a large NFPO, to divide the entity internally by objective or by operating restriction. Thus, an NFPO may contain two or more accounting entities, and they are called *funds*. This system of accounting is called *fund accounting*.

16.4.2.1 *Fund Accounting*

A fund is a self-balancing *accounting entity* within the legal entity that is the organization itself. *Fund accounting* refers to the accounting procedures underlying sets of self-balancing accounts in an organization, one for each fund established by law, contract, or policy. A fund will typically include a balance sheet (assets, liabilities, fund balance, or net assets), operating statement (revenues, expenses), and statement of fund balance (or net assets). The separation of resources in fund accounting is normally of an accounting nature only, although there may be physical segregation of some assets.

Fund accounting is characteristic of NFPOs and governments, though not all such organizations use it. Fund accounting is found in organizations that have independent service objectives or that administer segregated resources for which there are specific restrictions on how they are used. Fund accounting is never found in the for-profit sector. In a for-profit organization, the entity as a whole has the one overriding objective: to maximize the profits of the whole organization. Since a for-profit company's various activities are designed and operated with this goal in mind, any breakdown of these activities for reporting purposes is for information only — it is not a structural principle of the organization.

Every not-for-profit organization must have an *unrestricted* or *general fund*, although it may not be so named if it is a small organization with only one fund (and even in these cases, the term *fund balance* is frequently used in place of the term *net assets* now preferred by the standard-setters as the name of the equity section of the balance sheet). Other funds that are typically found in NFPOs are the *restricted fund* (or funds), the *endowment fund*, and the *capital* or *plant fund*. In a very large NFPO, the funds reported in the financial statements may in fact be groupings of smaller funds, since each legal or operating restriction will give rise to a separate fund. For example, each scholarship endowment in a university is accounted for in a separate fund, though for simplicity the numerous endowment funds would be grouped and reported together on the financial statements in one "endowment fund".

There are different ways of presenting the funds on the financial statements, but the multi-column format, which shows the funds in parallel columns, is the clearest accounting representation. When funds have transactions with one another (as is often the case) and there are balances owing/receivable at year-end, these balances will be shown on the financial statements. See Appendix 16.1 for an example of the financial statements of a charity that uses fund accounting.

16.4.3 *Revenue and Expense*

Traditionally, like governments, not-for-profit organizations operated on a cash basis rather than on an accrual basis. It was felt that accounting for cash was by far the most important responsibility of NFPOs. Conversely, income measurement, which uses the accrual basis of accounting and is used to assess how much "better off" the entity is after each period of operations, was seen as inappropriate for a not-for-profit organization. This view has changed. Today, there is a consensus that, so far as possible, NFPOs should follow the rules of accrual accounting, namely, that revenue and expenses be recognized when the event takes place rather than when cash changes hands. What this means is that there is an increasing use of accrual accounting procedures in NFPOs, and we now see revenues and expenses measured in a manner similar to that used in business accounting with corresponding accruals of receivables and payables. In addition, amortization accounting is often practised. (Because it is not always appropriate or even possible to apply all the principles of accrual accounting to NFPOs, the method used is often described as "modified accrual-basis accounting".)

The purpose of using accrual accounting in NFPOs is to measure real resource flows, not to determine income as such. Since an NFPO does not have owners and there is no profit to account for, there must be a change in terminology. Instead of *net income*, the difference between revenues and expenses is normally labelled *excess/(deficiency) of revenue over expense* or just *net result*. The statement that corresponds to the income statement in for-profit financial statements becomes, in not-for-profit terminology, the *statement of operations* or *statement of revenue and expense*.

It should be noted that many NFPOs, especially smaller organizations, feel that the advantages of using even modified accrual-basis accounting do not justify the additional bookkeeping cost. Such organizations would then do their reporting on a cash basis. In a pure cash-basis system, revenues are cash receipts and expenses are cash expenditures. Receivables and payables will not be recognized, nor will capital assets, which will be expensed fully and immediately when purchased. The balance sheet will have only two items: the asset (cash) and net assets (or fund balance). There will be no statement of cash flows because it would be identical to the statement of operations.[7]

16.4.3.1 *Revenue Recognition*

By definition, revenue is the gross increase in net assets corresponding to the inflow of assets (or reduction of liabilities) from operations. The major issue in revenue recognition is timing: when do we recognize revenue in a particular series of transactions? Or to use the technical terms, *when is revenue realized*? Accountants have traditionally insisted that there should be a completed exchange before revenue can be considered earned. In other words, goods or services must be transferred to the buyer in exchange for cash or an enforceable claim to cash.

In the case of a typical for-profit company, realization is almost always directly linked to delivery, in other words to the provision of goods or services. The organization itself must fulfill its part of the contract, or at least

---

[7] As we can see from the sample financial statements in Appendix 16.1, even an NFPO that uses modified accrual accounting with limited recognition of receivables and payables may not prepare a cash flow statement because it would add so little additional information to what is presented in the statement of operations.

Examples of Revenue Recognition Policies

Inter Pares, 2009

Excerpt from Notes, 1. Significant Accounting Policies

(b) Revenue recognition: ... Donations are recorded as revenue when received.

Centraide, 2010

Excerpt from Notes, 3. Accounting Policies

Revenue recognition
Unrestricted contributions are recognized as revenue of the Operating Fund in the year they are received or receivable if the amount to be received can be reasonably estimated and collection is reasonably assured....

---

a significant part of it, before revenue can be recognized. For not-for-profit organizations, however, this criterion must be interpreted differently because revenue is not based on an exchange. In fact, there is often no link between the supply of resources and the organization's provision of goods or services. This is most clearly the case for a charity with revenue coming from one group (e.g., the donors) and goods and services provided to a second group (i.e., the beneficiaries of the charity). Since there is no direct relationship between revenues and expenditures, the service-provision test is not really applicable. Thus, a not-for-profit organization normally chooses to recognize contributions as they are received. This is an exception to the general recognition rule, and the use of a fund accounting framework minimizes the possibility that it will be misinterpreted.

For NFPOs, expenditure is the measure of service provided (even though it is not matched to revenue), but there remains the separate question of an enforceable claim. For a for-profit company, there must be a reasonable expectation that any money owed on a transaction will be collected. Because of the difficulty in enforcing charitable pledges, many NFPOs wait until the money is received before recognizing the revenue rather than treating it as an account receivable. Others follow normal commercial principles and recognize pledged contributions as revenue if "collection is reasonably assure". Inter Pares and Centraide are examples of the two different revenue recognition policies (see focus box, above).

16.4.3.2 *Fixed Assets and Amortization*

Amortization is the measure of the use of long-term capital assets over time. It requires making a distinction between the capital expenditure at the time the capital asset was purchased and the subsequent series of amortization expenses. Traditionally, under the influence of governmental accounting where stewardship of cash was the principal concern, the financial statements of not-for-profit organizations measured the *expenditure* (payment) of funds. Amortization did not involve the expenditure of funds and consequently it was not recognized in the financial statements. According to this view, purchases of fixed assets must be accounted for in the period they take place. The transaction may be treated like all other current expenditures, and the asset is effectively "expensed" on purchase. An alternative treatment is to have the asset capitalized and then left on the balance sheet without any subsequent amortization. In either case there are no further transactions with respect to the asset. As far as NFPOs are concerned, this did not represent a particular problem. An income measure was not needed to provide information to financial markets, nor for tax purposes or dividend purposes. Financial statements with a conventional measure of income including amortization might have been useful for presentation to a bank or other financial institution in support of a loan application, but in fact revenue guarantees from a government or a granting agency, or the security of mortgaged fixed assets would be worth much more. Moreover, some would argue that recording amortization would mislead statement users by recording a cost in the operating statement that was not properly a cost to operations since operating transactions and capital transactions should be kept separate.[8] To sum up, many preparers and users of NFPO financial statements were of the opinion that amortization was unnecessary and even misleading.

The current view on amortization (by no means universally held) is more in line with the business income model with its focus on information for decision making. Preparing statements to show appropriable resources realized and disposed of (essentially a cash flow statement) does not preclude recognizing amortization. To ignore amortization throws away information. For all its faults, accounting amortization is the best estimate we have of asset consumption. Without it, expenses are an incomplete measure of the true economic cost of the organization's operations. The advantages of an amortization measure for costing should be self-evident, particularly where the operation is meant to be self-sustaining. It can be added that charges of "unfair competition"[9] from businesses operating in the same line will be more easily avoided if the NFPO's fees are set on a full-cost basis including a fair measure of amortization.

Finally, there is a legitimate concern over the criticism that amortization would involve double charging if the assets were purchased with the proceeds of a capital campaign. If full-cost fees include amortization (assuming (i) that the amortization policy is appropriate, (ii) that prices

---

[8] A clear distinction between operating transactions and capital transactions has a long tradition in government and NFPO accounting. Finding the money to purchase the capital asset is one decision (and one basis of accounting), and getting the resources on a year-by-year basis to operate the service is another. For example, a hospital or university might finance the purchase of a new building by approaching a wealthy donor or organizing a capital campaign for that purpose. The building could be expected to last for a very long time, and in any case would presumably be replaced by mounting another capital campaign. In such circumstances, the cost of using the asset (i.e., amortization) was not an operating cost and should not be an expense in the statement of revenue and expense. In the same way, organizations that charge users fees should not include amortization as part of the cost of the service since to do so would be overcharging: both the donor and the user would be paying for the capital asset.

[9] Complaints are sometimes made by for-profit health clubs and studios that feel the fees charged by neighbourhood YMCA/YWCAs and other NFPOs unfairly undercut the commercial prices because they don't cover amortization of facilities (or pay a fair rent, which would include an allowance for amortization). Such arguments have validity if the NFPO facility costing does not charge amortization.

are stable, and (iii) that all other costs are covered), break-even operations will imply that cash is accumulating for the replacement of the fixed asset at the original cost. Under these circumstances, it is true that a capital campaign to replace the organization's assets at the end of their expected useful lives would in fact be redundant. Thus, if amortization is charged in the accounts, capital campaigns should only be undertaken to expand or significantly upgrade an NFPO's facilities.

In the past decade, full amortization accounting along the same lines as that used in for-profit accounting is required by NFPOs in Canada. According to the CICA Handbook, *capital assets* should be carried at cost on the balance sheet and be *amortized*. If the amortization transactions are carried out in the operating fund, the effect will be essentially the same as conventional business amortization accounting. However, if the NFPO uses fund accounting and segregates capital asset and related long-term debt in a capital asset fund, the result will be much different. Rather, it will appear in the statement of revenue and expense of the capital asset fund. See, for example, the revenue and expense statement (called *statement of operations...*) of the capital asset fund in Appendix 16.1 on p. 467.

16.5 Financial Statement Analysis

Compared to its use with for-profit companies, conventional financial statement analysis as summarized in Chapter 15 has limited usefulness in assessing not-for-profit organizations. Any ratio that uses a measure of profitability has no meaning for an organization that does not seek to make a profit, cannot pay dividends, and has no shares to trade on the market. This means that all the profit-based ratios (return on sales, assets, equity, and the interest cover ratio) and all market-related measures (earnings per share, price-to-earnings ratio, dividend cover ratio, and dividend payout) have no application for NFPOs. Even debt ratios have limited usefulness. A debt-to-asset ratio might be helpful in assessing an organization's capacity to finance new capital assets with long-term debt, but financial management for the purpose of taking advantage of leverage (the debt-to-equity ratio) is meaningless for an NFPO. All the same, interest on long-term debt is an ongoing commitment to make interest payments, and some measure of the relative burden of interest can be useful to readers. For an NFPO, this could be measured by a variant of the interest cover ratio using revenue available for general operations instead of net income as the numerator. The higher the ratio, the lower the burden of interest.

Liquidity ratios — current ratio and quick ratio — can be useful, but only if the organization uses a full accrual basis that measures current assets and current liabilities in the same way that for-profit companies do. Since not all NFPOs do so, one must ensure that a full accrual basis is used for the ratios to be meaningful. Similarly, some of the efficiency ratios may be useful with the right circumstances. If receivables arise out of revenue and are managed on a commercial basis, receivable turnover and collection period measures are applicable, but these conditions do not always exist. Readers of the financial statements of private schools and universities might find these measures useful, but there are not many other situations where they would apply. Even rarer in an NFPO context are situations where inventory turnover and holding period measures could convey useful information. These measures could only be used for the rare NFPO that carries and sells goods on a commercial basis and manages its inventory accordingly.

Financial statements of NFPOs are used primarily to reveal the scale of the organization's operations and to check that it is satisfying the break-even constraint over the long run. To assess the success of the organization in carrying out its mandate in an effective and efficient manner, other tools are needed. These are discussed in the next section.

16.6 Evaluating Effectiveness and Efficiency in Not-for-Profit Organizations

How can we measure the success of a company or an organization? Consider the for-profit company first. In principle, the success of a for-profit organization is directly measured by net income. Net income is the difference between revenue (the value the market has paid for the goods and services produced and sold by the company, or the social value of its output) and expense (the cost of all the inputs used to produce the output). Net income thus is a measure of the value added by the company, above and beyond all the measured inputs, and represents the pure profit for the company owners. This profit can be compared to a previous period's profit to give us a sense of how the company is doing over time. If the profit (net income) is compared to the owners' investment in the company (i.e., in accounting terms, the book value of shareholders' equity), we have a scale-free measure of rate of return, which can be compared to that of other companies of any size in the same line or, more generally, to any company. In general, the higher the net income, the higher the rate of return, and the more successful the company has been.

A similar assessment cannot be done for a not-for-profit organization. Making a profit is not an objective, and, in the long run, it is expected to be zero in any case. Even looking at revenue or expense alone as a measure of total output or total input is problematic. Revenue for most not-for-profit organizations is simply contributions, not a measure of what the organization produces as for a for-profit company. Some NFPOs, such as theatre groups, symphonies, and opera companies, do earn revenue from sales of tickets. But if prices are subsidized by other revenue from government and private donations, it would be inappropriate to take total revenue as a market measure of how much the public values what these organizations produce. Expenses are also not necessarily reliable measures of resources used. While some inputs of not-for-profit organizations are purchased at market price, other inputs, especially those of intrinsic value such as volunteer labour, are supplied at nominal or zero cost. In short, to the extent that there are outputs or inputs for which a market price has not been paid, there is no independent measure of the value of these resource flows. Consequently, conventional accounting measures and financial reports are of little help in evaluating the success of not-for-profit organizations.

As we have seen, conventional financial statement analysis has a very limited role in the assessment of not-for-profit organizations. Other tools and techniques do exist for this purpose. What follows is a brief overview of effectiveness and efficiency as principles for evaluating not-for-profit organizations. It must be emphasized that, unlike the concepts of financial accounting, there is not as yet a body of "generally accepted" evaluation criteria for NFPOs. In certain industries, some indicators and measures might be widely used, but this does not mean that they are generally accepted. When a general standard of evaluation is accepted, it is most likely to come through the influence of governments, which have the power to mandate regulatory reports in fields such as health care (hospitals) and education (schools and universities).

16.6.1 Effectiveness

Effectiveness is solely concerned with *output* — how well does the organization do in what it has set itself to do. This involves a comparison between some desired, expected, or standard output on the one hand, and what is actually achieved on the other. There is no reference to inputs in the concept of effectiveness.

If the objective of a not-for-profit organization is to provide a single, well-defined service, then measuring the organization's effectiveness in providing that service is the most direct assessment of how well the organization has succeeded in its mission. Because effectiveness is an important measure, however, does not mean that it can be easily or unambiguously determined. This is especially true for not-for-profit organizations that provide a range of services, or for NFPOs whose services are not easily identified or measured. Since for many large NFPOs — hospital, universities, social service agencies, for example — there is no agreement on what they should be doing except in the broadest terms, it is easy to see that even identifying effectiveness measures will be fraught with difficulty. Listed below are some examples of effectiveness measures for common NFPOs:

Hospitals: Number of patients served/cured/stabilized
Number of emergency cases treated
Measure of hospital-generated disease....

Schools: Percentage of eligible population served
Percentage of students entering who complete the year
Percentage of students placed in prestigious colleges....

Universities Percentage of eligible population served
Percentage of students entering who graduate
Size of library
Number of library places
Number of Nobel prize winners on faculty....

16.6.2 Efficiency

Efficiency is concerned with the *relationship of inputs to outputs*. This can be measured as a ratio of output to input, or as a difference between output and input. The ratio has more general application as there is no need for the numerator and the denominator to be in the same terms (for example, average annual graduates per full-time teacher). Still, if we want to compare two situations in terms of an efficiency ratio (for example, two different organizations or the same organizations at different times), we must be sure that in both situations the measure used as the numerator and the measure used as the denominator are the same. If, for example, the efficiency measure of a hospital is the number of patients per full-time nurse, we must be sure that the mix of patients is the same for the other hospital that is being compared. Otherwise, the measure must take that into account.

Consider another example. If we compare the efficiency of various universities by looking only at the number of full-time equivalent students per full-time faculty member, it will give very misleading results because some universities have medical schools and large graduate programs and others do not. For a meaningful comparison, one either weights the number of students in the different schools and programs in some unbiased fashion — which may be difficult to do — or avoids the problem by comparing only similar schools and programs rather than the university as a whole. In other words, it would be appropriate to compare undergraduate programs in two universities in terms of teaching efficiency (measured by number of students per faculty member); however, any *overall* comparison of the two universities would be invalid unless they had very similar structures.

Finally, efficiency and effectiveness are not unrelated. For example, the efficiency of public service in different jurisdictions is often compared. Take the case of garbage collection. If one city collects twice a week and the other only once, it would be quite surprising if the latter were not cheaper since the cost of garbage storage is largely borne by the households. From the municipality's point of view, cheaper generally means more efficient. But is it? Garbage collection costs per household are lower with once a week collection as compared to twice a week collection, but in fact they are different services even if there is no explicit measure of the storage costs to the householders of additional containers, loss of amenity, etc., of the less frequent service. This is not to say that less frequent garbage collection might not, on balance, be a wiser policy, but in making a proper judgment about efficiency, effectiveness must either be explicitly measured or held constant. It is for this reason that effectiveness and efficiency have to be dealt with together.

16.7 Budgeting and Budgetary Control

16.7.1 *The Importance of Budgets for NFPOs and Governments*

Because, as a rule, not-for-profit organizations do not have measured output and do not sell their output in a market, management accounting techniques that focus on production (activity-based costing) or units sales (break-even analysis) have limited applicability to not-for-profit organizations or government. Budgeting and budgetary control are, however, widely used in the management of not-for-profit organizations. In fact, because the discipline of the market is largely absent from not-for-profit organizations — and even more so for governments — budgeting and budgeting control are key management techniques for these organizations.

16.7.2 *Techniques of Budgeting in NFPOs*

The mechanics of budgeting — operating budgets, cash (financial) budgets, and control — are much the same for NFPOs as they are for for-profit organizations as described in Chapters 7 and 9. The differences lie in the objective. Unlike for-profit organizations that also use budgets for planning and motivating (target) purposes, the primary purpose of budgeting in NFPOs is for organizational control. Selling, even when the organization does produce and sell some output, is very rarely a central activity of an NFPO. The operating constraint for most NFPOs is the revenue budget. The scale of activity of the organization and any financial planning and cash budgeting all flow from the organization's expectations of revenue. The objective of the budget is therefore to ensure — so far as possible — that expenditures are kept in line with expected revenues.

16.8 Summary

Not-for-profit and government organizations differ fundamentally in purpose from for-profit companies. The difference in purpose has historically affected the manner of accounting and the form of financial statements of both NFPOs and governments. These differences have been narrowed in recent years, but the absence of profit as an objective requires that we use NFPO and government financial statements as accountability reports rather than as the basis for analysis and prediction. Without the summary measure of efficiency that profit provides, concern for effectiveness and efficiency requires that accounting information from NFPOs and governments be supplemented by non-financial measures, such as measures of frequency of service (e.g., case load for a social service agency, emergencies handled by an ambulance service) and measures of quality (percentage of graduates of an NPO school going on to university, dollar value of research grants held by medical staff at a hospital). Management accounting techniques have to be similarly adapted for use with NPOs and government organizations.

Appendix 16.1

Example of Financial Statements of a Not-for-Profit Organization Prepared Using Fund Accounting

This appendix presents the 2009–2010 financial statements for Centraide of Greater Montreal, a large charitable fundraising organization.[1] The notes that follow the statements are an integral part of the financial report. Note 3, Accounting Policies, can be a particularly useful guide for reading unfamiliar financial statements such as these. Note 3 will provide a useful introduction to these financial statements.

The statements comprise the auditors' report, statements of operations and fund balance for the four funds, and a balance sheet for all four funds in multi-column format. As is common for not-for-profit organizations, the financial statements do not include a statement of cash flows.

---

[1] Financial Statements of Centraide of Greater Montreal, 2010, **http://centraide-mtl.org/static/media/4059/ Annualreport2010.pdf**, pp. 36–46. © Centraide of Greater Montreal. Reproduced with permission of Centraide du Grand Montréal.

AUDITORS' REPORT

To the Members of
Centraide of Greater Montreal

We have audited the balance sheet of Centraide of Greater Montreal as at March 31, 2010 and the statements of operations and fund balance of the Operating Fund, Stabilization Fund, Capital Asset Fund and Development Fund for the year then ended. These financial statements are the responsibility of Centraide of Greater Montreal's management. Our responsibility is to express an opinion on these financial statements based on our audit.

We conducted our audit in accordance with Canadian generally accepted auditing standards. Those standards require that we plan and perform an audit to obtain reasonable assurance whether the financial statements are free of material misstatement. An audit includes examining, on a test basis, evidence supporting the amounts and disclosures in the financial statements. An audit also includes assessing the accounting principles used and significant estimates made by management, as well as evaluating the overall financial statement presentation.

In our opinion, these financial statements present fairly, in all material respects, the financial position of Centraide of Greater Montreal as at March 31, 2010 and the results of its operations and its cash flows for the year then ended in accordance with Canadian generally accepted accounting principles.

Samson Bélair/Deloitte & Touche p.e.n.c.r.l.[1]

April 21, 2010 (May 12, 2010 for Note 10)

---

[1] Chartered accountant auditor permit No. 20238

OPERATING FUND
Statement of operations and fund balance
YEAR ENDED MARCH 31, 2010

	2010	2009
	$	$
		(Restated)
Revenue		
Subscriptions	53,252,623	53,691,865
Uncollectible subscriptions	(1,767,409)	(1,432,733)
	51,485,214	52,259,132
Interest and other revenue	120,850	573,828
	51,606,064	52,832,960
Expenses		
Fundraising, communication and administrative costs (Note 9)	6,499,521	6,546,240
Excess of revenue over expenses before allocations and assistance to agencies	45,106,543	46,286,720
Allocations and assistance to agencies		
Allocations to agencies (Note 5)	42,824,130	42,931,918
Assistance to agencies, social research and community services (Note 9)	3,136,092	3,287,390
	45,960,222	46,219,308
(Deficiency) excess of revenue over expenses	(853,679)	67,412
Fund balance, beginning of year		
Previously recorded balance	400,825	460,673
Changes in accounting policies (Note 2)	43,541,217	43,939,975
Restated balance	43,942,042	44,400,648
Interfund transfers (Note 7)	—	(526,018)
Fund balance at end	**43,088,363**	43,942,042

STABILIZATION FUND
Statement of operations and fund balance
YEAR ENDED MARCH 31, 2010

	2010	2009
	$	$
Revenue		
Investments	814,053	(733,372)
Net result (deficit)	**814,053**	(733,372)
Fund balance at beginning	4,522,838	4,988,992
Interfund transfers (Note 7)	(600,000)	267,218
Fund balance at end	**4,736,891**	4,522,838

CAPITAL ASSET FUND
Statement of operations and fund balance
YEAR ENDED MARCH 31, 2010

	2010	2009
	$	$
Revenue		
Donations		
Fondation Centraide du Grand Montréal	600,000	—
Investments	2,690	17,133
	602,690	17,133
Expenses		
Amortization of fixed assets	271,159	302,065
Other	51,043	47,500
	322,202	349,565
Excess (deficiency) of revenue over expenses	280,488	(332,432)
Fund balance at beginning	4,784,159	4,857,791
Interfund transfers (Note 7)	600,000	258,800
Fund balance at end	5,664,647	4,784,159

DEVELOPMENT FUND
Statement of operations and fund balance
YEAR ENDED MARCH 31, 2010

	2010	2009
	$	$
Revenue		
Investments	4,920	25,011
	4,920	25,011
Expenses		
Training, research and development expenses	304,471	52,370
Deficiency of revenue over expenses	(299,551)	(27,359)
Fund balance at beginning	822,816	850,175
Fund balance at end	523,265	822,816

BALANCE SHEET
AS AT MARCH 31, 2010

	Operating Fund	Stabilization Fund	Capital Asset Fund	Development Fund	Total 2010	Total 2009
	$	$	$	$	$	$
Assets						
Current assets						
Cash	631,687	—	—	—	631,687	928,887
Investments (0.26% to 0.34%, maturing until June 2010)	25,392,692	—	—	—	25,392,692	26,946,033
Subscriptions receivable	20,243,356	—	—	—	20,243,356	20,302,909
Interfund receivable	—	—	1,531,981*	523,265*	—	—
Other assets (Note 6)	978,444	—	—	—	978,444	235,981
	47,246,179	—	1,531,981	523,265	47,246,179	48,413,810
Investments	—	5,336,891	—	—	5,336,891	4,255,620
Fixed assets (Note 4)	—	—	4,132,666	—	4,132,666	4,361,767
	47,246,179	5,336,891	5,664,647	523,265	56,715,736	57,031,197
Liabilities						
Current liabilities						
Accounts payable and accrued liabilities	1,977,241	—	—	—	1,977,241	2,694,515
Balance payable to agencies	118,430	—	—	—	118,430	98,381
Interfund payable	1,455,246*	600,000*	—	—	—	—
Deferred revenue	606,899	—	—	—	606,899	166,446
	4,157,816	600,000	—	—	2,702,570	2,959,342
Fund balances						
Invested in fixed assets	—	—	5,664,647	—	5,664,647	4,784,159
Externally restricted	—	—	—	523,265	523,265	822,816
Internally restricted	43,088,363	4,736,891	—	—	47,825,254	48,464,880
	43,088,363	4,736,891	5,664,647	523,265	54,013,166	54,071,855
	47,246,179	5,336,891	5,664,647	523,265	56,715,736	57,031,197

* These items are not reported in the Total column on the balance sheet because they offset each other.

Approved by the Board

_____ , Chairman

Louis L. Roquet

_____ , Vice-president and Treasurer

James C. Cherry

NOTES TO THE FINANCIAL STATEMENTS YEAR ENDED MARCH 31, 2010

1. Status and nature of activities

Centraide of Greater Montreal, a not-for-profit organization incorporated under Part III of the *Companies Act* (Quebec), is recognized as a registered charity within the meaning of the *Income Tax Act*. Centraide of Greater Montreal collects public donations to promote involvement in the society through sharing and volunteer and community activities.

In order to maintain its registered charity status, Centraide of Greater Montreal must meet certain spending requirements ("disbursement quota") according to the *Income Tax Act*. The disbursement quota is a minimum amount that the registered charity must spend on charitable programs or as gifts to qualified donees. Failure to comply with this requirement could lead to a revocation of Centraide of Greater Montreal registered charity status. As at March 31, 2010, Centraide of Greater Montreal complies with the requirement

2. Changes in accounting policies

On April 1, 2009, Centraide of Greater Montreal adopted the changes made to Sections 4400 and 4460 and the new recommendations of Section 4470 of the *Canadian Institute of Chartered Accountants ("CICA") Handbook*.

As per these modifications, revenues and expenses must be recognized and presented on a gross basis when Centraide of Greater Montreal is acting as a principal in transactions. The new recommendations establish disclosure standards for a not-for-profit organization that classifies its expenses by function and allocates its expenses to a number of functions to which the expenses relate.

The adoption of changes to section 4400 and 4460 had no impact on the financial statements of Centraide of Greater Montreal. The new disclosures required under Section 4470 are provided in Notes 3 and 9.

Financial statement concepts

Section 1000, entitled Financial statement concepts, of the *CICA Handbook* has been changed to reflect less emphasis on the matching principle. This amendment has been in effect since January 1, 2009 and has resulted in the restatement of the previous year's financial statements. The most significant impact was that revenue previously recognized as deferred revenue was included in the fund balances. Consequently, the following adjustments were recorded:

	Initial balance for the year ended March 31, 2009	Restatement	Restated balance for the year ended March 31, 2009
	$	$	$
Revenue			
Subscriptions	53,592,273	99,592	53,691,865
Uncollected subscriptions	(1,311,635)	(121,098)	(1,432,733)
Expenses			
Fundraising, communication and administrative costs	6,168,988	377,252	6,546,240
Balance sheet			
Liabilities			
Deferred revenue	43,707,663	(43,541,217)	166,446
Fund Balances			
Internally restricted			
Initial balance	460,673	43,939,975	44,400,648
Ending balance	400,825	43,541,217	43,942,042

NOTES TO THE FINANCIAL STATEMENTS YEAR ENDED MARCH 31, 2010 (Continued)

3. **Accounting policies**

Centraide of Greater Montreal has elected to use the exemption provided by the CICA permitting not-for-profit organizations not to apply the following Sections of the *CICA Handbook*: 3862 and 3863, which would otherwise have applied to the financial statements of Centraide of Greater Montreal for the year ended March 31, 2010. Centraide of Greater Montreal applies the requirements of Section 3861 of the *CICA Handbook* concerning the presentation and disclosures on financial instruments.

These financial statements are not prepared on a cumulative basis and do not include the accounts of the Fondation Centraide du Grand Montréal. The financial statements have been prepared in accordance with Canadian generally accepted accounting principles ("GAAP") and include the following significant accounting policies:

Fund accounting
Centraide of Greater Montreal uses the restricted fund method to account for its activities:

i) *Operating Fund*
    The Operating Fund comprises the current operating activities of Centraide of Greater Montreal. The annual net result, less interfund transfers, is applied against the Stabilization Fund, according to the rules established in the following paragraph. Internally restricted Fund balances represent resources available for future years.

ii) *Stabilization Fund*
    The Stabilization Fund was created to provide financial stability to agencies financed by Centraide of Greater Montreal, to satisfy new initiatives and urgent needs of the community, to answer needs considered urgent and approved by the Board of Directors, and to satisfy the normal expenses associated with Centraide of Greater Montreal's activities during substandard campaigns. The Fund varies according to investment revenue, the amount of unallocated funds, the net result for the year, and an annual contribution from the Operating Fund that is equal to 0.5% of the previous campaign. The decision to contribute is made annually based on the financial results of Centraide of Greater Montreal. The balance of the Stabilization Fund, excluding the fair value variation on long-term investments, must not exceed 10% of the amount of the previous campaign.

iii) *Capital Asset Fund*
    The Capital Asset Fund comprises the amortized cost of the building, furniture and equipment and computer equipment. The Fund varies according to interest earned, amounts received for the purpose of acquiring fixed assets, amortization of fixed assets, other expenses related to fixed assets and an annual contribution from the Operating Fund for updating and ongoing development of computer systems. The decision to contribute is reviewed annually based on the financial results of Centraide of Greater Montreal.

iv) *Development Fund*
    The Development Fund was created to fund research and development activities and pilot and other projects that are not considered part of Centraide of Greater Montreal's usual activities, with the ultimate goal to significantly increase the funds donated to Centraide of Greater Montreal over the coming years.

Revenue recognition
Unrestricted contributions are recognized as revenue of the Operating Fund in the year they are received or receivable if the amount to be received can be reasonably estimated and collection is reasonably assured. Restricted contributions are recognized as revenue of the Fund corresponding to their restriction in the year in which the related expenses are incurred.

NOTES TO THE FINANCIAL STATEMENTS YEAR ENDED MARCH 31, 2010 (Continued)

3.   Accounting policies (Continued)

Allocated expenses

Expenses are accounted for in the statement of operations of the Operating Fund and are allocated as follows:

	Fundraising, communication and administrative costs	Assistance to agencies, social research and community services
Annual campaign and major donors	100%	—
Allocation and Impact in the community	—	100%
Communications	85%	15%
General management	60%	40%
Administration	75%	25%

Expenses related to each function include all direct costs related to this function, including salaries and other direct charges, and a portion of indirect costs.

When shared or indirect costs are related to more than one function, such as the management and administration of these activities, Centraide allocates these costs among the functions. These costs include payroll and other expenses that cannot be directly charged to specific activities. These expenses are allocated among the functions according to the percentage of direct costs attributable to each function.

The financial statements do not include the cost of services rendered by individual volunteers and staff loaned to Centraide of Greater Montreal by businesses and public institutions.

Financial instruments

Financial instruments are initially stated at their fair value. Subsequent annual re-evaluation considers the following items:

Cash and short-term investments

Cash and short-term investments are classified as assets held for trading. They are, therefore, valued at their fair value; the fair value being based on the redemption value established by the issuing institution for the short-term investments.

Long-term investments

Long-term investments are represented by units of the Foundation of Greater Montreal Investment Fund and are classified as assets held for trading. They are, therefore, valued at their fair value; the fair value being based on the most recent market prices, normally the most recent bid price.

The transactions related to the investments are recorded at the transaction date.

Subscriptions receivable, other assets, accounts payable and accrued liabilities and balance payable to agencies

Subscriptions receivable and other assets, classified as loans and receivables, accounts payable and accrued liabilities and balance payable to agencies, classified as other liabilities, are valued at amortized cost.

Fixed assets

Fixed assets are recorded at cost. Amortization is based on their estimated useful lives using the straight-line method over the following periods:

Building	40 years
Furniture and equipment	8 years
Computer equipment	4 years

NOTES TO THE FINANCIAL STATEMENTS YEAR ENDED MARCH 31, 2010 (Continued)

3. **Accounting policies (Continued)**

Top-up pension plan
The costs of the top-up defined benefit plan are established by independent actuaries. The pension expense charged to results for the year includes the cost of benefits for services rendered during the year, which is determined using the projected benefit method prorated on years of service, as well as the amortization of the benefit cost for past service and the amortization of actuarial gains or losses for the portion that exceeds the 10% corridor. Amortization is calculated using the expected average remaining service life of the employees covered under the plan, i.e. six years.

Use of estimates
The preparation of financial statements in conformity with Canadian GAAP requires management to make estimates and assumptions that affect the reported amounts of assets and liabilities and disclosures of contingent assets and liabilities at the date of the financial statements and the reported amounts of revenue and expenses during the reporting period. Actual results could differ from these estimates.

4. **Fixed assets**

	2010			2009
	Cost	Accumulated amortization	Net book value	Net book value
	$	$	$	$
Building	5,131,412	1,324,475	3,806,937	3,919,689
Furniture and equipment	619,586	493,084	126,502	163,450
Computer equipment	2,113,565	1,914,338	199,227	278,628
	7,864,563	3,731,897	4,132,666	4,361,767

During the year, the purchase of fixed assets totalled $42,058 ($179,280 in 2009).

5. **Allocations to agencies**

	2010	2009
	$	$
Support for families and youth	10,021,058	10,197,984
Support for neighbourhood life	9,949,632	9,973,024
Support for the improvement of living conditions	7,632,711	7,703,888
Support for social inclusion	7,513,741	7,370,503
Support for community development (representatives)	3,120,438	3,070,794
Support for volunteering	2,196,590	2,242,185
Support for the development of community action potential	1,022,240	1,014,307
Special projects	453,121	531,827
Miscellaneous allocations	519,499	432,545
United Way of Canada	395,100	394,861
	42,824,130	42,931,918

NOTES TO THE FINANCIAL STATEMENTS YEAR ENDED MARCH 31, 2010 (Continued)

6. **Related party transactions**

Fondation Centraide du Grand Montréal, a related organization, is a registered charity incorporated under Part III of the *Companies Act* (Quebec) where the goal is to collect donations, legacies or other contributions, manage its assets and give all net proceeds generated by the capital without expending any portion thereof to Centraide of Greater Montreal. The net assets of Fondation Centraide du Grand Montréal total $25,826,439 as at March 31, 2010 ($21,724,566 in 2009), revenue amounted to $5,501,521 ($2,765,927 in negative in 2009) and expenses including donation to Centraide of Greater Montreal amounted to $1,399,648 ($250,696 in 2009).

During the year, the transactions between Centraide of Greater Montreal and Fondation Centraide du Grand Montréal were:

	2010	2009
	$	$
Revenue		
Donations — Capital Asset Fund	600,000	—
Donations — Operating Fund — Annual campaign	500,000	—
Administrative fees presented in deduction of fundraising communication and administrative costs	9,000	9,000

In the other assets balance, an amount of $607,498 (nil in 2009) is receivable from Fondation Centraide du Grand Montréal.

The balance of accounts payable and accrued liabilities include an amount of $77,729 ($1,264,588 in 2009) due to Fondation Centraide du Grand Montréal.

These transactions were made in the normal course of operations and have been recorded at the exchange amount, which is the amount of consideration established and agreed to by the parties.

7. **Interfund transfers**

The Board of Directors approved the following interfund transfers:

	2010	2009
	$	$
From the Stabilization Fund to Capital Asset Fund	600,000	—
From the Operating Fund		
to Stabilization Fund	—	267,218
to Capital Asset Fund	—	258,800
	—	526,018

8. **Pension plan**

Multi-employer contributory defined benefit pension plan
Centraide of Greater Montreal participates in a multi-employer contributory defined benefit pension plan. The benefits are capitalized in the pension fund for all participants of the pension plan. The employer's contribution paid is $572,813 ($562,275 in 2009). Based on the last actuarial valuation of the multi-employer pension plan performed on September 30, 2007, there is an unfunded liability of $917,200.

NOTES TO THE FINANCIAL STATEMENTS YEAR ENDED MARCH 31, 2010

8. **Pension plan (Continued)**

Top-up defined benefit plan

Centraide of Greater Montreal also established an unfunded, top-up defined benefit plan in 2006. The benefits of this plan are based on years of service and final salaries. The pension expense for the year totalled $118,300 ($133,100 in 2009).

Information about the top-up defined benefit plan is as follows:

	2010	2009
	$	$
Accrued benefit obligations	550,300	460,200
Balance of unamortized amounts	(86,200)	(114,400)
Benefit paid during the year	(1,081)	—
Accrued benefit liabilities, included with accounts payable and accrued liabilities	463,019	345,800

As at December 31, 2006, Centraide of Greater Montreal valuated its accrued benefit obligations for accounting purposes. The next valuation will be performed no later than December 31, 2010.

The significant actuarial assumptions made by Centraide of Greater Montreal are as follows:

	2010	2009
	%	%
Recognized costs		
Discount rate	4.75	4.75
Rate of compensation increase	2.75	2.75
Accrued benefit obligations		
Discount rate	4.75	4.75
Rate of compensation increase	2.75	2.75

9. **Allocated expenses**

As provided in Note 3, on accounting policies, the expenses related to a number of functions are allocated as follows:

	Fundraising, communication and administrative costs	Assistance to agencies, social research and community services	Total
	$	$	$
Annual campaign and major donors	2,605,642	—	2,605,642
Allocation and Impact in the community	—	1,566,336	1,566,336
Communications	970,345	171,237	1,141,582
General management	1,272,023	848,015	2,120,038
Administration	1,651,511	550,504	2,202,015
	6,499,521	3,136,092	9,635,613

NOTES TO THE FINANCIAL STATEMENTS YEAR ENDED MARCH 31, 2010 (Continued)

10. Commitments

Centraide of Greater Montreal has committed to pay an amount of $1,226,000 in the following fiscal year related to renovations to be performed on the building.

In April 2010, Centraide of Greater Montreal has committed to pay allocations to agencies for an amount of $40,172,250.

11. Financial instruments

Because of its financial assets and liabilities, Centraide of Greater Montreal is exposed to the following risks:

Interest rate risk

A portion of the investments of the Foundation of Greater Montreal Investment Fund, in which Centraide of Greater Montreal holds units, is invested in bonds and debentures. Consequently, a change in market interest rate will have an impact on the fair value of the units held by Centraide of Greater Montreal.

Foreign currency risk

A portion of the investments of the Foundation of Greater Montreal Investment Fund, in which Centraide of Greater Montreal holds units, comprises shares and interests in foreign equity funds. The units held by Centraide of Greater Montreal are consequently exposed to changes in foreign currencies. The same applies to the earned income associated with these units.

Fair value

The fair value of all financial instruments, other than long-term investments, approximates their carrying value due to their short-term maturity.

12. Statement of cash flows

A cash flow statement has not been prepared since the cash flow information is readily apparent from other financial statements and related notes.

Self-Study Problems

1. Refer to Appendix 16.1 for the financial statements of Centraide of Greater Montreal for the year ended March 31, 2010, and answer each of the following questions.

   (a) Since charities are based on appeals to humanitarian feelings and not-for-profit organizations are based on self-interest, why should a charitable organization such as Centraide find it necessary to have its financial statements audited or have financial statements at all?

   (b) Evaluate Centraide's (short-term) liquidity position. How does its liquidity position at the end of March 2010 compare to that of the previous year?

   (c) What does the account Deferred Revenues represent? What is the relationship between Deferred Revenues and Revenues?

   (d) What was the amortization expense for the year ended March 31, 2010? Why does amortization expense not show on the statement of operations and fund balance of the operating fund?

   (e) What is the point of having separate funds, such as operating fund, stabilization fund, etc.?

2. The Faculty of Management at Holywell University offers a special intensive summer program for senior managers in the not-for-profit sector. Because it is a non-credit program, the program is not eligible for government grants and thus must be self-financing. Unfortunately, on account of shrinking enrolments, the program has been experiencing financial difficulties. Last summer, for example, the program attracted only 30 participants and lost money.

   Fees and costs are as follows:

   Per participant

Revenue: Tuition fees	$ 6,000
Expense: Books, residence rooms, meals, and other costs	$ 2,000

   General program costs

Teaching honoraria (10 courses @ $5,000)	$50,000
Office (including office salaries)	$60,000
Advertising and promotion	$30,000

   Required

   (a)   i. Calculate the current break-even level of participants.

          ii. How much money was lost last year?

   (b) The dean of the faculty is convinced that the class size can be increased to more economic levels without compromising the quality of the program. To this end she is prepared to authorize an additional $10,000 per year in promotional and other support expenses.

          i. If this strategy is followed, what would the new break-even level be, as measured in numbers of participants?

          ii. How many participants would be needed to generate an annual surplus of $60,000?

(c) The program director agrees that promotion is important but feels that pricing is the critical factor. He argues that a $1,000 reduction in tuition fees combined with just $5,000 in promotion will attract 80 participants. Of course, to maintain program quality the class would have to be split, doubling the number of sections offered.

    i. If the program director is right about the number of participants, what would the annual program surplus be?

    ii. What would the new break-even point be for the program?

(d) The associate dean of the faculty argues that a program of this nature should be required to contribute 15% of its tuition revenue toward general faculty and university overhead.

    i. How does this affect the break-even point? Recalculate for the original situation in part (a).

    ii. In general, is the requirement that such programs make a contribution to the general overhead reasonable? Briefly discuss.

Solutions

1. (a) The short answer is that an audit is legally required. Still, we should understand why this is so. The readers of the financial statements want to know that the charity's financial statements present fairly the results of its operations and its financial position in accordance with generally accepted accounting principles. Giving such assurance is an auditor's job. This is not primarily a question of looking for fraud or other kinds of malfeasance. Even if everyone who works for Centraide behaves in the most disinterested and high-minded fashion, errors in accounting procedure or policy can occur. It is the auditor's job to uncover them. And for essentially this reason, we need financial reports, even if we didn't have auditors. Moreover, malfeasance can occur. Even if a charity's appeal is to higher motives, this does not mean that we can ignore self-interest on the part of those who work for charities or indeed any individual or organization that deals with a charity. For example, although charities rely to a great extent on volunteers, they do have permanent employees. These people may earn less than those who do similar jobs in the for-profit sector, but they do not work for nothing. This is a reflection of self-interest. Self-interest does not necessarily lead to malfeasance, but it can. It is naive to assume that no one who deals with a not-for-profit organization would ever take advantage of their position to advance their own interest. Financial scandals have occurred in every kind of NFPO, including charities, hospitals, and religious organizations. An audit does not ensure that every incidence of malfeasance will be uncovered, but it will usually reveal the material ones.

(b) Short-term liquidity is evaluated using the current ratio: current assets ÷ current liabilities. Centraide's current ratios for 2009 and 2010 are as follows:

March 31, 2010	March 31, 2009
(47,246,179 ÷ 2,702,570 =)	(48,413,810 ÷ 2,959,342 =)
17.5	16.4

The current ratio at March 2010 has not changed very much from that of March 2009. Both are well over the acceptable level of 2 — indeed both are over 15 — and can be considered exceptionally strong.

(c) Some contributions are "restricted", meaning that they can be spent only in a specified way or time. See page 470, note 3, Revenue recognition: "Restricted contributions are recognized as revenue of the Fund corresponding to their restrictions in the year in which the related expenses are incurred." Thus, the policy is saying, if the year in which the project expenses are to be incurred is in the future, the revenues are "deferred" until then. The cash will have been received (or if it was a pledge, a contribution receivable would have been recorded), but, unlike a typical revenue transaction, the other side of this transaction is a liability ("deferred revenue") and not revenue. Only in the period in which the money is spent according to the terms of the restriction is the revenue "realized" and the liability converted to revenues.

It is important to understand that whether the receipt of cash (or contribution receivable) gives rise to revenue or deferred revenue is not necessarily a question of facts (money changes hands); it can simply be the result of the adoption of a new accounting policy (or, as here, the CICA's decision to change an accounting principle). The change in accounting policy that occurred at Centraide between the 2009 and 2010 financial years illustrates this. The accounting policy described above represents a change in accounting policy that was followed in previous years, see note 2 on page 469: "the *CICA Handbook* has been changed to reflect less emphasis on the matching principle.... The most significant impact was that revenue previously recognized as deferred revenue was included in the fund balances." The old policy for revenue recognition can be found in note 2 of the 2009 financial statements (http://www.centraide-mtl.org/static/media/4059/Annualreport2009.pdf): "The annual fall campaign is conducted to raise funds for Centraide of Greater Montreal and its agencies for the subsequent fiscal year. Consequently, the available net proceeds from the current campaign, i.e., subscriptions less deferred fundraising, communication and administrative costs, are shown as deferred revenue on the balance sheet." Under the old policy essentially all contributions raised in financial year X would be considered deferred revenue until the year $X + 1$. The revenues of years X would be the contributions raised in year $X - 1$. There would be significant balance under current liabilities — deferred revenues — on the balance sheet each year. For example, deferred revenues on March 31, 2009, were $43,707,663. The 2009 figures, appear for comparative purposes in 2010 financial statements, have to be restated according to the new accounting policy. Under the new policy, deferred revenue is $166,446, essentially just the contribution made with restrictions described in the paragraph above. Under the old policy *all* fall contributions would have been deferred. Note that the application of the new policy changes calculated ratios such as the current ratio. The current ratio we calculated above for March 2009 (16.4) used the value of current liabilities reflecting the new policy. Under the old policy (see url to 2009 financial statements above), the current ratio is 1.0 ($48,413,810/$48,912,985).

(d) Amortization expense (depreciation) for the year ended March 31, 2010, was $271,159. This is shown on the statement of operations and fund balance of the capital asset fund rather than on the statement of operations and fund balance of the operating fund because, as in most NFPOs using fund accounting, capital assets are accounted for in a separate fund.

(e) The objective of using separate funds is to keep separate the accounting of operations or activities, which have their own objectives, restrictions or are in some other way (such as capital assets) independent of other operations. This allows the readers of the financial statements to evaluate each activity on its own criteria.

2. (a) i. Break-even is

unit fixed costs ÷ unit contribution margin
= ($50,000 + $60,000 + $30,000) ÷ ($6,000 – $2,000)
= $140,000 ÷ $4,000
= 35 participants

Check:				
Revenue	35 @ $6,000	=	$210,000
Variable expenses	35 @ $2,000	=	70,000
Contribution margin	35 @ $4,000	=	$140,000
Less fixed costs			140,000
Net contribution			$ 0

ii. Last year's results

Revenue	30 @ $6,000	=	$180,000
Variable expenses:	30 @ $2,000	=	60,000
Contribution margin	30 @ $4,000		$120,000
Less fixed costs			140,000
Net contribution			($ 20,000)

(b) i. New break-even with $10,000 additional fixed costs would be ($140,000 + $10,000) ÷ $4,000
= $150,000 ÷ $4,000
= 37.5 or 38 participants

ii. Target net contribution of $60,000:
($140,000 + $10,000 + $60,000) ÷ $4,000
= $210,000 ÷ $4,000
= 52.5 or 53 participants required

(c) New unit contribution margin is $5,000 – $2,000 = $3,000.
New fixed costs (note that the number of courses is doubled):

Teaching honoraria (20 courses @ $5,000)	$ 100,000
Office (including office salaries)	60,000
Advertising and promotion ($30,000 + $5,000)	35,000
Total	$ 195,000

i. Profit with 80 participants:

Fees	80 participants @ $5,000	$ 400,000
Books, etc.	80 participants @ $2,000	160,000
Contribution margin	80 participants @ $3,000	$ 240,000
Fixed costs		195,000
Net contribution		$ 45,000

    ii. New break-even

        $195,000 ÷ $3,000 = 65 participants

        (If the number of classes were not doubled, the new break-even would be $145,000 ÷ $3,000 = 48.33 or 49 participants.)

(d)   i. A 15% overhead charge comes off the top (since it is a percentage of the fee, it is incorrect to add it directly to variable unit expenses):

Fees	$6,000
Overhead charge @ 15%	900
Net fees	$5,100
Variable expenses	2,000
Unit contribution margin	$3,100

        Break-even is fixed costs divided by unit contribution margin: $140,000 ÷ $3,100 = 45.16 or 46 participants, i.e., an increase of 11 participants or 31%.

    ii. The discussion up to this point is in terms of break-even or target profit of the program. These two outcomes take into account the direct costs of the program, but they do not take into account the general fixed costs of the university. Every university program draws on the general resources of the university and should, in fairness, make a contribution toward general operations. Another way of looking at this is to consider that the general operations of the university cost typically from 25% to 40% of total costs, and these can only be supported to the extent that fee- and grant-attracting programs generate a surplus, on average, of 33% to 67% of direct costs. If this sort of cost structure is the case at Holywell, the proposed 15% contribution to university overhead is far too low.

Discussion Questions and Problems

Discussion Questions

1. State the differences between a non-profit organization and a for-profit company.
2. How do governments differ from NFPOs?
3. What are the three defining characteristics of NFPOs?
4. Since NFPOs are organized for the purpose of providing a service rather than for making a profit for their owners, why should there be any concern for financial considerations in their operations?
5. Why don't NFPOs present income statements?
6. What is a "fund" in NFPO accounting?
7. List the financial statement analysis ratios that have no application to NFPOs.
8. Why are effectiveness and efficiency ratios particularly useful in the assessment of NFPOs?
9. Why are budgets of such great importance for NFPOs and governments?

Problems

1. The bookkeeper of the Langford Municipal Arena has prepared the following statement for the month of November, which he calls the Statement of Financial Results:

Langford Municipal Arena
Statement of Financial Results
for the Month of November 2011

Receipts		
Revenue from ice rentals	$84,000	
Revenue from admissions	36,000	
Borrowings from bank	30,000	$150,000
Expenses		
Payment for supplies purchased	$13,400	
Payment for equipment purchased	31,000	
Payment for a one-year insurance policy	12,400	
Wages paid in cash	32,950	
Miscellaneous cash expenses	9,760	
Deposit on ice cleaning machine to be		
* delivered in January*	20,000	119,510
Net		$ 30,490

Required
The bookkeeper wants advice on how to prepare an accrual-based statement of revenue and expense (SRE). Review the wording of each italicized caption in the statement above and specify, with one of the following three explanations: (1) likely be included in an SRE, (2) included if appropriately modified, and (3) excluded.

Example
Payment for supplies purchased: (2), included with modification: Supplies used, with the caption "Supplies" or "Supplies expense",

is an appropriate expense item, but not cash paid to purchase supplies as indicated above.

2. Consider the following information drawn from the financial statements of Cavendish University and Dalrymple University:

	Cavendish	Dalrymple
	in thousands of dollars	
Balance Sheet		
ASSETS		
Operating fund		
Cash	$ 3,000	$ 2,500
Student fees receivable	3,000	3,000
Total	$ 6,000	$ 5,500
Capital fund		
Fixed assets	$ 25,000	$ 21,000
LIABILITIES AND FUND BALANCES		
Operating fund		
Current liabilities	$ 5,000	$ 3,000
Fund balance	1,000	2,500
Total	$ 6,000	$ 5,500
Capital fund		
Mortgage payable	$ 20,000	$ 10,000
Fund balance	5,000	11,000
Total	$ 25,000	$ 21,000
Operating Fund —		
Statement of Operations and Fund Balance		
REVENUE		
Student tuition fees	$ 24,000	$ 15,000
Government grant	76,000	53,000
Total	$100,000	$ 68,000
EXPENSES	99,500	70,000
Excess of revenue over expense (expense over revenue)	$ 500	($ 2,000)

Required

Compare Cavendish and Dalrymple under each of the following headings. Support your conclusion with quantitative evidence and make a judgment in each case as to which university is in a stronger position:

(a) Liquidity
(b) Risk
(c) Management of receivables

3. The board of governors of the Bullstrode Museum of Fine Arts, concerned about cutbacks to its operating grant from the provincial government, is considering a proposal from its executive director that would, if successful, make the museum a little less dependent on government financing.

The proposal involves devoting a section of the museum's art restoration workshop that is not currently being used to the production of miniature copies of the most renowned piece of sculpture in its collection, Koppelheim's *The Hug*. These reproductions would then be sold in the museum's retail shop to contribute toward the museum's revenues.

Expected unit costs have been estimated by an industrial engineer as follows:

Direct materials (plaster, wood, paint)	$20.00
Direct labour	$10.00
Other variable costs (including selling)	$ 5.00

In addition, there would be fixed costs related to this operation of $140,000 per annum. The engineer further estimates that such an operation could produce a maximum of 10,000 units a year.

The museum hopes that it could generate around $50,000 a year from this activity. The members of the board, however, are a little concerned at the risks involved, especially the $140,000 in fixed costs, most of which would have to be committed at the beginning of the year. Finally, nobody has yet given serious thought to the selling price of the model when it goes on sale in the museum shop.

Required

(a) If the price of the model were set at $70, what volume would have to be sold to break even? To make a contribution of $50,000 to museum revenues?

(b) If the price of the model were set at $50, what volume would have to be sold to break even? To make a contribution of $50,000 to museum revenues?

(c) Advise the board on this proposal. Should the museum go ahead with the project or not? Indicate what additional information you would need to be able to give better advice.

4. Consider the following statistics about non-profit ambulance services in four districts: Arbury, Bellevue, Cardborough, and Darbton in a recent year:

		Districts		
Characteristics	**A**	**B**	**C**	**D**
1. Population	124,000	487,000	542,000	1,700,000
2. Population density	0.8	3.9	5.6	8.7
3. Pickup time (min.)	23	13	9	15
4. Cost per patient ($)	27.30	23.6	19.5	26.15
5. Cost per mile ($)	2.60	2.75	2.35	3.85
6. Cost per 1,000 pop. ($)	11,500	9,430	8,650	10,750

Explanatory notes:

Row 2 Population density per acre
Row 3 Average time from call to pickup of patient
Row 4 Total cost of service divided by number of ambulance calls
Row 5 Total cost of service divided by number of vehicle-miles
Row 6 Total cost of service divided by population in thousands

Required

(a) Review, in turn, each of the six measures of the districts and their ambulance services. Indicate what each measure tells us about the district or its ambulance service. In particular, evaluate each one as a measure of effectiveness and/or a measure of efficiency.

(b) On the basis of your answer to part (a), give a summary ranking of the four districts as to
   (i) their effectiveness,
   (ii) their efficiency.

   Indicate in what ways this ranking may be inadequate. Identify the key pieces of additional information you would need to refine it.

(c) The ambulance services described above are not-for-profit organizations. Performance evaluation of profit-oriented companies would be handled differently. Identify the main difference between performance evaluation of not-for-profit organizations and profit-oriented companies. Do we get a clearer appraisal of organizational success in one case or the other? What are the implications for public policy?

5. Activity at the Dryden Point Hospital reaches a peak in the second quarter of the year (April–June). The hospital catchment area includes a range of mountains greatly favoured by climbers. Unfortunately, many novice climbers cannot resist the temptation of climbing in the spring, the prime avalanche season. The lucky ones end up in the hospital's emergency wards and operating rooms, often for extended periods of time (the unlucky ones are never found).

   The hospital prepares quarterly cash budgets over the calendar year. The forecasted grants from the provincial medicare office for the current year are as follows:

1st quarter	$390,000
2nd quarter	$750,000
3rd quarter	$390,000
4th quarter	$390,000

   In general, two-thirds of grants are collected in the quarter that they are made and one-third in the following quarter. The opening balance of accounts receivable are expected to be collected in the first quarter. These grants account for 100% of hospital revenue.

   Hospital supplies costing $360,000 will be purchased evenly over the first quarter, none in the rest of the year. Payment will be made 30 days after purchase.

   Nursing salaries are $150,000 in the first, third, and fourth quarters, $250,000 in the second. Payment is made in the quarter that the cost is incurred. General hospital overhead costs are $100,000 in the first, third, and fourth quarters, $300,000 in the second quarter, including $50,000 amortization each quarter. Payment lags behind the cost by approximately one month.

485

The hospital maintains an operating line of credit with its bank and pays interest on borrowings at an annual interest rate of 7%, payable quarterly. The hospital plans to maintain a minimum cash balance of $8,000 at all times. It will borrow in multiples of $5,000 when necessary to maintain this minimum. All borrowings are made at the beginning of the quarter where the deficiency is predicted, and any repayments will be made at the end of the quarter.

The hospital plans to purchase new medical equipment in the second and fourth quarters in the amounts of $150,000 and $50,000, respectively.

The closing balance sheet from the previous year shows a balance of cash on hand of $23,000 and accounts receivable of $128,000.

Required

Prepare a cash budget for the hospital for the first two quarters of the current year in a recognized format. Be sure to show operating cash flow, ending cash balance before financing, amounts borrowed/repaid, interest payments, and final cash balance.

6. The exhibit presented on the following pages contains the financial statements from Inter Pares, an international charity headquartered in Canada.[1] Answer the following questions using the information provided:

   (a) On both the statement of changes in fund balances and the balance sheet, there is a section entitled fund balances. What are fund balances? Why do they appear on both statements? Is there a corresponding account on the statements of a for-profit company, and how would that account differ from a fund balance? Why is there more than one fund balance?

   (b) Where would we find dividends on these statements? Briefly explain.

   (c) Refer to the statement of revenue and expense. How does this statement differ from the income statement of a for-profit company? Why is there no line for net income? Why does it have multiple columns?

   (d) Evaluate each of the following, comparing the organization's success in 2009 with that of the previous year (year end):
      (i) The organization's liquidity
      (ii) Its ability to pay interest on its debt
      (iii) The proportion of revenue used for (1) fundraising and (2) administration

---

AUDITORS' REPORT TO THE MEMBERS, INTER PARES

We have audited the statement of financial position of Inter Pares as at December 31, 2009 and the statement of revenue and expense and changes in fund balances for the year then ended. These financial statements are the responsibility of the organization's management. Our responsibility is to express an opinion on these financial statements based on our audit.

We conducted our audit in accordance with Canadian generally accepted auditing standards. Those standards require that we plan and perform an audit to obtain reasonable assurance whether the financial statements are free of material misstatement. An audit includes examining, on a test basis, evidence supporting the amounts and disclosures in the financial statements. An audit also includes assessing the accounting principles used and significant estimates made by management, as well as evaluating the overall financial statement presentation.

In our opinion, these financial statements present fairly, in all material respects, the financial position of the organization as at December 31, 2009 and the results of its operations and its cash flows for the year then ended in accordance with Canadian generally accepted accounting principles.

Ottawa, Ontario
March 01, 2010
Ouseley Hanvey Clipsham Deep LLP
Licensed Public Accountants

STATEMENT OF FINANCIAL POSITION
As At December 31, 2009

	2009	2008
ASSETS		
CURRENT		
Cash	$ 658,237	$ 301,310
Accounts receivable	97,787	82,891
Program advances (note 3)	760,031	734,605
	1,516,055	1,118,806
INVESTMENTS (note 4)	1,458,845	1,558,140
CAPITAL ASSETS (note 2)	691,782	712,859
	$3,666,682	$3,389,805
LIABILITIES		
CURRENT		
Accounts payable and accrued liabilities	$ 100,794	$ 92,176
Deferred revenue (note 3)	746,177	639,658
	846,971	731,834
YEARS OF SERVICE BENEFITS PAYABLE	102,913	104,765
	949,884	836,599
FUND BALANCES		
Unrestricted	56,076	20,766
Invested in capital assets	691,782	712,859
Bequest Fund (note 5)	901,868	797,416
Reserve Fund (note 6)	811,524	779,880
Endowment Fund (note 7)	255,548	242,285
	2,716,798	2,553,206
	$3,666,682	$3,389,805

STATEMENT OF CHANGES IN FUND BALANCES
For the Year Ended December 31, 2009

	Unrestricted Net Assets	Invested in Capital Assets	Bequest Fund	Reserve Fund	Endowment Fund	2009 Total	2008 Total
FUND BALANCE—BEGINNING OF YEAR	$20,766	$712,859	$797,416	$779,880	$242,285	$2,553,206	$2,434,265
Excess of revenue over expense	14,233	—	104,452	31,644	13,263	163,592	118,941
Purchase of capital assets	(5,276)	5,276	—	—	—	—	—
Amortization of capital assets	26,353	(26,353)	—	—	—	—	—
FUND BALANCES—END OF YEAR	$56,076	$691,782	$901,868	$811,524	$255,548	$2,716,798	$2,553,206

STATEMENT OF REVENUE AND EXPENSE
For the Year Ended December 31, 2009

	General Operations	Bequest Fund	Reserve Fund	Endowment Fund	2009 Total	2008 Total
REVENUE						
Donations	$1,395,806	$79,191	$ —	$ 600	$1,475,597	$1,471,737
CIDA-VSP	1,718,694	—	—	—	1,718,694	1,437,888
CIDA—other projects	3,621,818	—	—	—	3,621,818	4,696,598
Project generated grants	199,286	—	—	—	199,286	138,517
Interest and other	77,286	25,261	31,644	12,663	146,854	153,455
	7,012,890	104,452	31,644	13,263	7,162,249	7,898,195
EXPENSE						
Program						
Projects	5,558,642				5,558,642	6,045,437
Operations	782,233				782,233	966,558
	6,340,875				6,340,875	7,011,995
Administration	260,957				260,957	300,827
Fundraising	396,825				396,825	466,432
	6,998,657				6,998,657	7,779,254
EXCESS OF REVENUE OVER EXPENSE FOR THE YEAR	$ 14,233	$104,452	$ 31,644	$ 13,263	$ 163,592	$ 118,941

NOTES TO FINANCIAL STATEMENTS — DECEMBER 31, 2009

1. SIGNIFICANT ACCOUNTING POLICIES

(a) **Organization:** Inter Pares works overseas and in Canada in support of self-help development groups, and in the promotion of understanding about the causes, effects and solutions to under-development and poverty. Inter Pares was incorporated without share capital under Part II of the *Canada Business Corporations Act*. The Corporation is a registered charity under Section 149(1)(c) of the *Income Tax Act* and as a result is not subject to income taxes.

(b) **Revenue recognition:** Inter Pares follows the deferral method of accounting for contributions. Restricted contributions are recognized as revenue in the year in which the related expenses are incurred. Funds received from CIDA for overseas programs are recorded as program advances when sent overseas, and are subsequently recorded as expense when amounts are spent by overseas partners. Donations are recorded as revenue when received.

(c) **Financial instruments:** Investments are classified as held to maturity and are recorded at amortized cost. Other financial instruments are recorded at their initially recognized amounts less appropriate allowances.

(d) **Capital Assets:** Capital assets are recorded at cost. Amortization is provided on a straight line basis over 5 years for office equipment. Computer equipment is amortized 50% in the first year and 25% in the remaining 2 years. The building is amortized on a straight line basis over 40 years.

(e) **Use of estimates:** The preparation of these financial statements in conformity with Canadian generally accepted accounting principles requires management to make estimates and assumptions that affect the reported amounts of assets and liabilities and disclosure of contingent assets and liabilities at the date of the financial statements and the reported amounts of revenues and expenses during the reporting period. Actual results could differ from those estimates.

2. CAPITAL ASSETS

	Cost	Accumulated Amortization	2009 Net	2008 Net
Land	$ 200,000	$ —	$ 200,000	$ 200,000
Building	582,230	110,750	471,480	486,230
Computer & office equipment	117,258	96,956	20,302	26,629
	$ 899,488	$ 207,706	$ 691,782	$ 712,859

During the year, amortization of capital assets amounted to $26,353 (2008 — $28,563).

3. PROGRAM ADVANCES AND DEFERRED REVENUE Program advances can vary significantly from year to year depending on the timing of funds sent overseas and the reporting back by overseas counterparts. Deferred revenue consists mainly of revenue related to unspent overseas program advances.

4. INVESTMENTS Investments consist primarily of government bonds and GICs earning interest at rates between 2.8% and 6.2% per year, with varying maturities from March 2011 to October 2014. The fair value of investments is $1,538,669 (2008 — $1,639,307).

5. BEQUEST FUND During 2004 a bequest fund was established. Bequests received are recorded as revenue in this fund.

continued....

NOTES TO FINANCIAL STATEMENTS (Continued)

6. RESERVE FUND Inter Pares maintains an unrestricted operational reserve to assure that obligations are honoured in the event of unanticipated changes in external funding.

7. ENDOWMENT FUND The Margaret Fleming McKay Endowment Fund receives gifts whose principal is invested and held for a minimum of ten years. In addition to such externally restricted gifts, the Endowment Fund contains transfers from Inter Pares which are subject to the same restrictions. As at the year end, the Endowment Fund includes $82,700 (2008 — $82,100) in externally restricted gifts.

8. FINANCIAL INSTRUMENTS The organization's financial instruments consist of cash, accounts receivable, investments, accounts payable and years of service benefits payable. Unless otherwise noted, it is management's opinion that the organization is not exposed to significant interest, currency, or credit risks arising from these financial instruments and that carrying amounts approximate their fair value.

9. CAPITAL DISCLOSURE The organization defines its capital as its net assets, which are not subject to external requirements other than a portion of the Endowment Fund. Management's objective, when managing capital, is to safeguard the organization's ability to continue as a going concern, so that it can continue to provide services in accordance with its mission.

Glossary of Important Terms

Glossary

Absorption cost (full cost): the valuation of a product or service, including its flexible (unit-variable) cost and an allocation of fixed overhead.

Account: a financial record where transactions of a similar nature are recorded. All the accounts together constitute the *general ledger*.

Accounting: the process of recording, organizing, and communicating financial information.

Accounting cycle: the sequence of accounting procedures from identifying transactions, recording journal entries, posting to general ledger, adjusting and closing the books, and preparing the financial statements.

Accounting equation: recording transactions in terms of their effect on the assets, liabilities, and equity of the organization — i.e., assets = liabilities + equity.

Accounts payable: amounts owed by the company to suppliers of goods and services.

Accounts receivable: amounts owed to the company from customers.

Accrual concept: the recording of revenues and expenses in the time period when the economic flow occurs, rather than when the cash is received or paid.

Accrue: to record revenue or an expense that has occurred even though the related cash flow may not have happened.

Accumulated amortization: a contra-account. The total amortization taken over the lifetime of an asset or an asset group since its purchase. Presented as a deduction from the corresponding asset on the balance sheet.

Acid-test ratio (quick ratio): a measure of liquidity — i.e., (current assets less inventory) ÷ current liabilities.

Activity: a unit of work carried out to achieve an objective and that incurs a cost.

Activity-based costing: analysis of cost and cost behaviour using activities as the drivers of costs.

Activity-based management: use of activity-based costing information to make decisions.

Actual cost: the (historical) cost of an asset or expense.

Adjusting journal entry: an end-of-period journal entry made to bring the books up-to-date or to correct an error.

Allowance account: a *contra-account* that is used when the valuation is revised periodically, such as an *allowance for doubtful accounts (doubtful debts)*, or an *allowance for inventory decline*.

Allowance for bad and doubtful debts: an amount deducted from accounts receivable to provide for debts that will, eventually, be discovered to have been bad debts.

Amortization: the systematic allocation of cost of a long-term asset to the time periods during which the business should benefit from it (also called depreciation).

Annuity: an amount of money received each year for a specified period of time.

Appraisal cost: (in quality management) a cost incurred in inspecting products or services to assess their quality conformance.

Asset: an economic resource that is expected to benefit a future accounting period.

Asset turnover: an efficiency measure of assets and how they are employed to generate sales: sales ÷ total assets.

Attention directing: the role of accounting in bringing significant events to the notice of managers or shareholders.

Audit: the examination of a company's records and financial statements by an outside body.

Auditor: a professional accountant who carries out an audit.

Avoidable cost: a cost that, subject to a decision being taken, may be avoided.

B

Bad debt: an expense, the loss due to a customer's failure to pay for goods or services.

Bad debt allowance: an amount deducted from accounts receivable for potential bad debts, reducing them to their net realizable value.

Balance: in an account, taking the difference between total debits and credits, the net value of the account, debit, or credit as the case may be.

Balance sheet: a list of the company's assets, liabilities, and equity at a point in time.

Balanced scorecard: a systematic process for reporting on operations that bases its contents on the company strategy; it balances the past against the present and the future, and balances financial results against the perspectives of the customer, internal process improvements, and learning and growth objectives.

Batch-related costs: costs incurred by running a batch of production (rather than unit-driven variable costs).

Benchmarking: using the results of comparable organizations as the standard of performance.

Beneficial ownership: a characteristic of for-profit companies that have identifiable owners with an equity claim and the expectation of enjoying a financial return from the operation of the organization in the form of dividends. By definition, not-for-profit organizations do not have beneficial ownership, do not aim to make a profit, and do not pay dividends.

Book value: (of an asset) the historical cost, less accumulated amortization to date (also: written-down value); (of a company) the balance sheet totals of all assets, less all liabilities (i.e., the balance sheet value of the equity).

Books: an informal term for all the accounting records of the company — in particular, the journals, general ledger, and financial statements.

Break-even: a situation where revenues equal expenses.

Break-even (a.k.a. cost/volume/profit) analysis: use of the contribution margin to see how many units must be sold (the break-even point) to cover fixed costs.

Break-even constraint: the long-run financial requirement of an NFPO that total expenses are equal to total revenues.

Budget: a list of revenues and/or costs that are expected for a future control period.

Budgetary slack: a discrepancy between the budget and what the budget would be if set to "tight" standards of performance.

Business entity concept: each business enterprise is considered separate and distinct from its owners.

Business-sustaining activity (or cost): an activity or its related cost incurred for the benefit of the business as a whole and not traceable to units, batches, products, customers, etc. (formerly known as fixed costs).

C

Canadian Institute of Chartered Accountants (CICA): the main organization of professional accountants and auditors in Canada.

Capacity-related costs: costs incurred to give a company the capacity to carry out activities such as manufacturing, customer service, research, etc.; once committed, total capacity costs do not change in the short term — the capacity may be used or left idle, but the cost remains.

Capital asset: an asset that is held over a long period of time for its value in use, such as a *fixed asset* (property plant and equipment) or an *intangible asset*.

Capital budget: a budget for spending large amounts of money on long-term assets.

Capital budgeting: a decision process for assessing the viability of capital spending (*see also* payback, return on investment, and net present value).

Capitalize (verb): to recognize that an expenditure creates or increases a *capital asset* rather than an *expense*.

Cash budget: a forecast of cash inflows and outflows and, hence, cash balances for a specified future time period.

Cash flow statement: a financial statement that summarizes the sources and uses of cash under the following headings: Cash From/Used in Operations; Cash From/Used in Financing Activities; Cash From/Used in Investing Activities; Change in Cash (also called Statement of Changes in Financial Position).

Cash from/used in financing activities: cash flow resulting from borrowing or repaying loans, issue, or repayment of shares.

Cash from/used in investing activities: cash flow resulting from the purchase or sale of long-term assets.

Cash from/used in operations: cash flow resulting from the operating activities of the company: it is calculated as operating income plus amortization, plus the decrease (or minus the increase) in non-cash working capital.

Centralized (decision making; organization; responsibility): a system where all major decisions are made by senior management (*see also* decentralized....) on the basis that only senior management can see the big picture.

Certified General Accountants' Association (CGA): a body of professional accountants.

Change in cash: the difference between cash resources at the beginning and end of a time period.

CICA: *see* Canadian Institute of Chartered Accountants.

Closing the books: the process of transferring the balances of the revenue and expense and dividend accounts to retained earnings.

Committed cost: a cost that is legally committed even if the event has not taken place; a cost that will still be incurred even if the project is terminated.

Common cost: the cost of an activity or resource that is used by more than one responsibility unit.

Common share: the basic ownership units of a company: they have a residual interest in the assets of the company. (Also called common stock; ordinary shares.)

Competition; competitive market: a situation where there are many suppliers and many customers, and no supplier or customer can affect prices through their own actions.

Compound interest: interest earned being reinvested so that both principal and interest can then earn interest.

Conservatism concept: a systematic process for not overstating profits; expenses are recognized whenever they possibly may occur; revenues are not recognized unless they are highly likely.

Consolidation: aggregation of the financial results of companies that are linked through ownership or control.

Constant dollar: an accounting concept that assumes dollars are directly comparable whatever time they arose.

Continuity concept: the assumption that an organization will continue to exist and operate unless there is evidence to the contrary (also called going concern concept).

Continuous improvement: a philosophy of regular reductions in costs through increased efficiency.

Contra-account: an account that adjusts an asset account to the correct valuation at the balance sheet date, such as *accumulated amortization* or an *allowance account*.

Contribution margin (unit): the difference between the selling price and the unit-variable cost: the benefit of selling one additional unit (*see* break-even).

Control: the set of procedures used to assess how well the organization is achieving its objectives.

Controllability: a cost is controllable by a manager if its level is determined by the actions of that manager; the manager can be held responsible for costs he/she controls.

Controller: a senior accounting manager of a company (occasionally known as comptroller).

Conversion cost: the cost of transforming raw materials into finished goods; traditionally, conversion cost consisted of labour and overhead, but would now be defined with respect to whatever conversion activities have occurred.

Cost: a monetary value placed on a resource (*see* actual c., full c., historical c., standard c., variable c.); costs become expenses when they are used up.

Cost accounting: techniques and reports that deal with the cost and profitability of products and processes.

Cost accumulation: collecting and classifying costs according to their functional nature.

Cost allocation: tracing costs to cost pools or cost objects; allocation of cost pools to other cost objects through cost allocation rates.

Cost allocation base: a measure of use or activity (such as labour or machine hours) used to allocate cost (e.g., overhead), which cannot be traced to cost objects directly.

Cost behaviour: the analysis of the causes of costs (*see* flexible cost, fixed cost, activity-based cost) so that forecasting and control are made possible.

Cost centre: a control unit that is expected to carry out an activity, and incur costs to do so (*see also* revenue c., profit c., investment c.).

Cost concept (historical c.c.): that an asset should initially be valued at its original cost to the enterprise.

Cost driver: an activity that gives rise to a cost.

Cost driver rate: the rate of cost incurred per activity unit.

Cost function: a mathematical function relating a firm's or an industry's total cost to its output and factor costs.

Cost leadership: a business strategy based on minimizing costs through efficiency (*see also* differentiation).

Cost object: a product, service, process, etc., of which the cost is being calculated.

Cost of capital: (*see also* weighted average cost of capital) the minimum rate of return required to pay the providers of debt and equity capital; it is used in capital budgeting to assess the viability of investment proposals.

Cost of goods sold: in retailing, the direct (unit variable) costs of making a sale; in manufacturing, the direct costs will also include a proportion of (fixed) manufacturing overhead.

Cost of quality report: a systematic process for reporting on the costs incurred to achieve and monitor quality levels.

Cost of unused capacity: a capacity cost incurred, but not utilized.

Cost-plus pricing: an approach to pricing by reference to the cost of a product or service and the addition of a markup (a dollar amount or a percentage).

Cost pool: an account where the costs that are driven by a single cost driver are accumulated.

Cost/volume/profit analysis: *see* break-even.

Cr: *see* credit.

Credit (1): as a verb, to make credit entry.

Credit (2): entry on the right side of a double-entry bookkeeping system that represents the addition to a liability, equity, or revenue, or the reduction of an asset (*see* debit).

Credit (3): to buy or sell goods on delayed payment terms.

Creditor: a person or company that has lent money to the company.

Current asset: an asset that is likely to be recycled within one year (e.g., cash, accounts receivable, inventory).

Current liability: an amount owed that is due for payment within one year.

Current ratio: a measure of liquidity: current assets ÷ current liabilities.

Customer profitability analysis: use of activity-based costing information to assess the relative profitability of customers.

Customer-sustaining activity/cost: an activity carried out (with a cost incurred) to maintain a customer.

Cycle time: for repetitive activities, the time taken to go through one complete iteration of the process.

D

Debenture: a formal written notice of a long-term debt, specifying terms such as interest and repayment.

Debit: entry on the left side of a double-entry bookkeeping system that represents the addition of an asset or expense, such as an increase in dividends, or the reduction of a liability or revenue, or a reduction in shareholder's equity (*see* credit).

Debt ratio (debt-to-equity ratio; debt-to-assets ratio): a measure of relative indebtedness.

Decentralized (decision making; organization; responsibility): a system where major decisions are made by lower level management on the basis that the people near to the decision are best informed to decide.

Decision (making): choice between alternative courses of action for the future.

Depletion: the process similar to amortization that allocates the cost of using up a wasting asset, such as mineral or timber rights, to the appropriate accounting period.

Depreciation: *see* amortization.

Differentiation: a strategy based on the provision of goods or services that are very well suited to customers' needs and that may be sold at a premium price.

Direct cost: a cost that can be traced directly to a cost object (e.g., materials, labour).

Direct manufacturing cost: a cost that can be traced directly to the manufacture of a product.

Disclosure concept: an obligation to provide additional information wherever it is needed to allow a full appreciation of the financial reports.

Discounting: (in capital budgeting) the restatement of a future cash flow to its present value by eliminating (discounting) the interest opportunity.

Discretionary cost: a cost incurred as a result of management's (discretionary) decision about an activity (*see also* engineered cost).

Distribution cost: a cost incurred in distributing a product or service to a customer.

Dividend: a payment to shareholders (especially common shareholders) as a distribution of profit.

Dividend cover ratio/dividend payout ratio: a measure of the sustainability of dividends: dividend cover ratio = net income ÷ dividend paid; dividend payout ratio = (dividend ÷ net income) × 100%.

Double entry: a recording system that recognizes that every transaction must be recorded in accordance with the accounting equation (assets = liabilities + equity); the assumption that every asset has had a source, etc.

Doubtful debt: an amount that is set aside for the possibility that some customers may not pay the amounts they owe (also bad debt allowance).

Dr: *see* debit.

E

Earnings: (also net earnings) net income.

Earnings per share: net income divided by the number of shares in issue.

Earnings per share (diluted): net income divided by the number of shares in issue, plus any additional shares committed to be issued.

Economic flow: a change in a company's assets or liabilities. Also referred to as resource flow.

Economic value added: a measure of the difference between the return and the cost of an asset; it can be calculated as (operating income – interest charged for the use of the assets); formerly known as residual income.

Effectiveness: the extent to which an organization's objectives have been achieved.

Efficiency: the ability of an organization to carry out its activities (outputs) with a minimum of resources (inputs).

Efficient capital market: a market in which share prices fully and immediately reflect all relevant public information.

Engineered cost: a cost that is unavoidable in supplying a product or service.

Entity: *see* business entity concept.

Equity: the residual interest in a company (shares and retained earnings).

Expenditure: the payment of cash.

Expense (1): cost expired or liability incurred to earn income. A sub-account of retained earnings.

Expense (2): used as a verb — to recognize an expenditure as an expense, used often in contrast to *capitalize*.

External failure (cost): costs encountered after delivery or shipment to customers, resulting from products or services not conforming to requirements or customer needs. External failure costs result from errors detected after the output or product is delivered to a customer. These costs are incurred because the appraisal system failed to detect and remove all errors in the system.

F

Financial accounting: the process of preparing and disseminating general-purpose reports, such as the balance sheet and the income statement, for shareholders and external users.

Finished goods inventory: goods that have been manufactured but not yet sold.

First-in-first-out (FIFO): an inventory flow model that assumes items sold are those that have been in inventory longest (*see also* weighted average, last-in-first-out, and specific identification); in a time of rising prices, FIFO is relatively unconservative.

Fixed asset: a long-term asset with a physical presence (e.g., property, plant, equipment).

Fixed cost: a cost that does not change as a result of changes in units of activity (*see also* flexible cost); many fixed costs are period costs.

Flexible budget: a budget based on the same costs and efficiencies in the original (master) budget, but flexed (variable items are increased or decreased) to reflect changes between budgeted and actual activity levels.

Flexible budget variance: a measure of the difference between the actual costs incurred and the budgeted costs for the actual activity level projected by a flexible budget.

Flexible cost (unit-variable cost): a cost that increases or decreases in proportion to changes in numbers of units produced or sold (also called variable cost).

For-profit organization: an organization with a principal objective to maximize profit for the benefit of its owners (*see* not-for-profit organization).

Full cost: *see* absorption cost.

Fund: a self-balancing accounting entity within the legal entity that is the organization itself.

Fund accounting: refers to the accounting procedures underlying sets of self-balancing accounts in an organization, one for each fund established by law, contract, or policy.

Fund balances: *see* net assets.

G

General ledger: the collection of all the regular accounts in which assets, liabilities, equity, and transactions are recorded.

Generally accepted accounting principles (GAAP): a set of allowable methods for calculating and reporting financial reports for external users.

Goal congruence: a situation where the achievement of individual objectives is aligned with the achievement of corporate objectives.

Going concern: the assumption that the business will continue indefinitely.

Goodwill: the excess of the purchase price of an acquired entity over the fair market value of its assets and liabilities.

Government: an organization that is operated expressly to provide a wide range of goods or services rather than to make a profit, which is similar to an NFPO from an accounting point of view; unlike an NFPO, it has the power to tax and the ability to compel individuals and companies to provide the resources that are needed to carry out its activities.

Gross book value: the cost of an asset before deduction of amortization (*see also* net book value).

Gross margin (gross profit): the excess of sales revenue over the direct cost of sales (it may be a dollar figure or a percentage of sales).

H, I

Historical cost: the original cost of an asset to the company.

Imposed budget: a situation where a budget is imposed on an operating unit without consultation or agreement.

Incentive compensation: a system in which the monetary rewards are tied to achieving unit or corporate objectives.

Income statement: a financial accounting report of the revenues, expenses, and income for a period of time.

Incorporated company: a company that has received a charter as a legal person under the *Canada Business Corporations Act*, or the *Corporation Act* of a province. Shareholders in incorporated companies enjoy *limited liability*. Almost all companies incorporated in Canada (federally or provincially) have the words *limited* or *incorporated* (or an abbreviation) in their names.

Incremental budgeting: a budget based on a previous budget, possibly incorporating some changes (*see* zero-based budget).

Incremental cost/revenue: the additional cost or revenue of making or selling one additional unit (*see also* sunk cost); or the additional cost or revenue caused by taking a decision.

Indirect cost: a cost that cannot be uniquely traced to a cost object (*see also* direct cost).

Input: a resource used up in the course of a company's or NFPO's operations. For example, expenses are inputs to the earnings process for a company, and in the operations process for an NFPO.

Intangible asset: a long-term asset that has no physical form (e.g., goodwill, patents, trademarks).

Interest: a regular payment for the use of money.

Interest cover ratio: a measure of the sustainability of interest payments: operating income (income before taxes and interest expense) ÷ interest expense.

Internal failure (cost): costs encountered prior to delivery or shipment to customers resulting from products or services not conforming to requirements or customer needs. Internal failure costs result from errors detected within the enterprise before the output or product is delivered to a customer. These include all the costs associated with errors detected and removed by the appraisal system (e.g., re-inspecting and retesting all outgoing goods).

Internal rate of return: (in capital budgeting) the discount rate that results in a net present value of zero.

Inventory flow: an assumption about which units of inventory are represented by goods sold (*see* FIFO, weighted average, LIFO).

Inventory holding period: length of time inventory is held before it is sold; inventory × 365 ÷ sales revenue (equivalent to inventory turnover ratio).

Inventory turnover ratio: the number of times per year inventory is sold (turned over); sales revenue ÷ inventory (equivalent to inventory holding period).

Investment: (in capital budgeting) the initial amount of money spent on a capital project.

Investment centre: an organizational unit that has responsibility for costs, revenues, and investment decisions, and that can, therefore, be controlled through the return on investment ratio.

J

Job cost: a system that traces and assigns all costs incurred for a unique product, product line, job, or project. The costs must be directly attributable to the job.

Journal: the book in which all transactions are recorded in chronological order.

Journal entry: an entry recording a transaction in the journal. It includes at least one debit entry and one credit entry.

Just-in-time inventory management: an approach to organizing operations so that inventory of raw materials and finished goods is unnecessary, and inventory of work-in-process is substantially reduced.

K, L

Kaizen costing: *see* continuous improvement.

Last-in-first-out (LIFO): an inventory flow model that assumes items sold are those that have been most recently purchased (*see also* weighted average, first-in-first-out, and specific identification); in a time of rising prices, LIFO is relatively conservative.

Ledger (account): the collection of accounts in which assets, liabilities, equity, and transactions are recorded.

Liability: an amount owed by a company to an outside party.

Limited liability: the legal fact that a shareholder's liability for the debts of a company is limited to the amount the shareholder has invested in the shares.

Liquidity: whether or not a company has cash and other liquid resources available to pay its debts.

Liquidity ratio: *see* current ratio.

Long-run costs: the costs incurred to carry out an activity in the longer term.

Long-term debt: debt due to be repaid more than one year in the future.

Lower of cost or market price: an application of the conservatism concept in which inventory is valued either at cost or at market price if the market price is less than cost; market price may mean net sale proceeds or replacement cost.

M

Make or buy decision: analysis of choices between carrying out an activity internally and sub-contracting it to an outside agency.

Management accounting: the set of accounting activities that supports the internal processes and decisions of an organization.

Management by exception: the philosophy that things that have gone according to plan need not be investigated, but that exceptions should be investigated and give rise to corrective action as necessary.

Management by objectives: a process whereby reasonable objectives are agreed on between a manager and his/her superior, and progress toward achieving them is monitored through measurement and feedback.

Management control: use of accounting and other information systems to assess the performance of operating units and their managers.

Margin: the markup on costs to recover unallocated costs and profit.

Marginal (cost/revenue): *see* incremental cost/revenue.

Market share: the sales of a company expressed as a percentage of total sales for that market.

Markup: *see* margin.

Master budget: the budget set originally, based on forecasted sales/production levels (*see also* flexible budget).

Matching concept: the relating of sales revenues to the economic effort expended in achieving them: the relationship of expenses to time periods.

Materiality concept: the convention that trivial items need not be reported.

Minority interest: where financial reports are consolidated but where less than 100% of the shares are owned by the parent company, the share of ownership held by outside shareholders.

Mixed cost: a cost that is made up partly of variable cost and partly of fixed cost.

Motivation: the tendency of an individual to behave in a particular way.

N

Net assets: the residual claim or equity section of the balance sheet in a not-for-profit organization.

Net book value (NBV) the original cost of an asset or group of assets net of any associated allowance. It is usually seen in connection with long-term physical assets such as plant and equipment in which case the allowance deducted is accumulated amortization (NBV plant assets = cost less accumulated amortization). The term is sometimes used with reference to the whole company, in which case it is defined as total assets less total liabilities, in other words, total shareholders' equity.

Net income: revenues minus expenses, interest, and taxes; income available for the shareholders.

Net present value (NPV): (in capital budgeting) the cash flows arising from a project, discounted (*see* discounting), and added together; positive NPV implies an acceptable project.

Net worth: owners' equity.

Neutrality: to present information free from any bias (*see also* conservatism concept).

NFPO: *see* not-for-profit organization.

No par value: a share that has no stated monetary value.

Not-for-profit organization (NFPO): an organization that has a service mission, has no beneficial ownership, and is constrained to break even over the long term (in contrast to a *for-profit organization*, which seeks to maximize profit, *see* for-profit organization). Also called a *non-profit organization* (NPO).

NPO: *see* not-for-profit organization.

O

Objectivity concept: a philosophy that accounting values should not be systematically biased or distorted.

Operating budget: the part of the budget that forecasts revenues, expenses, and operating profit.

Operating income: revenues less operating expenses (but before deduction of interest expense or tax expense) (*see also* net income).

Opportunity cost: the cost of an asset as measured by its value in its next best alternative use.

Output: product or service, the provision of which is an object of an organization's or company's activities.

Outsource: to arrange to purchase a product or service from an external supplier rather than supply it internally.

Overapplied overhead: a situation where the overhead allocated to products is greater than the overhead incurred; it arises either because overhead spending is less than budgeted or because the overhead application base is greater than what was budgeted.

Overhead: expense other than direct materials and labour.

Overhead recovery: the use of a measure of activity, such as labour hours, to allocate budgeted overhead to products or processes through an overhead recovery rate.

Owners' equity: the amount of the shareholders' investment in the company; the assets less the liabilities; common shares plus retained earnings.

P

Par value: the legal or stated monetary face value of a share or a bond (*see also* no par value).

Parent company: a company that owns all the shares, or a majority of the shares, of another company (normally called the subsidiary company).

Participative budgeting: an approach to budget setting in which all levels contribute their inputs, and where the budget is not finalized until all parties agree to it (*see also* imposed budget).

Partnership: two or more individuals working together and sharing the profits of an enterprise, though not incorporated as a limited liability company.

Payback: (in capital budgeting) the point in time when future cash flows will have repaid the initial investment.

Perfect competition/perfectly competitive market: *see* competition.

Period cost: a cost that is incurred through the passage of time, rather than the level of output.

Periodicity concept: the assumption that the life of a business can be meaningfully divided into shorter (usually annual) periods for reporting to owners and managers.

Personal financial planning: application of accounting and finance concepts to individual situations (e.g., insurance, savings, investments, pensions).

Post: to copy a journal entry into the corresponding accounts.

Preferred dividend: the dividend paid to the owner of a preferred share.

Preferred share: a share that has some priority (e.g., being paid dividends) over the common shares.

Prepaid expense: an amount paid for an expense for which value has not yet been used (e.g., rent paid in advance).

Present value: a (future) cash flow after discounting to remove the opportunity cost of interest (*see also* net present value).

Prevention cost: (in quality control) a cost incurred to ensure conformance to quality standards.

Price setter: a company that can determine product price in a market.

Price taker: a company that must accept market prices for its products.

Process re-engineering: the radical rethinking and redesign of any business process to improve its performance.

Product cost: the cost associated with making/selling a product.

Production department: a functional unit that is responsible for transforming raw materials into finished products.

Product-sustaining activity: an activity and its related cost incurred in respect of a product or product line (as opposed to unit-variable cost, batch cost, or business-sustaining cost).

Profit centre: an organizational unit that is responsible for revenues and expenses and, hence, profits, and that can therefore be controlled by comparison of actual profit with budgeted profit.

Profitability ratios: measures of profit in relation to the resources used to sustain them: profit as % of sales; operating profit as % of assets (or return on assets); net income as % of equity (or return on equity).

Glossary

Q

Quality control: the activities and costs associated with quality conformance, including prevention, appraisal, and internal and external failures.

Quick ratio: *see* acid-test ratio.

R

Rate of return: *see* return on investment and internal rate of return.

Raw material inventory: materials on hand that have not yet been put into production.

Receipt: the collection of cash.

Recognition concept: the rules governing the point at which a transaction (especially a sale) will be recognized.

Re-engineering: *see* process re-engineering.

Relevance concept: (in relation to information) how useful information is for decisions, control processes, or beliefs.

Relevant cost/revenue: a cost or revenue that changes as a result of a decision.

Reliability concept: *see* objectivity concept.

Residual income: *see* economic value added.

Required rate of return: *see* cost of capital.

Responsibility centre: an organizational unit for which a manager is held responsible (*see* cost centre, revenue centre, profit centre, investment centre).

Retained earnings: profits made by a company since its date of incorporation (or reorganization) but not distributed to shareholders as dividends.

Return on assets: *see* profitability ratios.

Return on equity: *see* profitability ratios.

Return on investment (ROI): the profit from an operation expressed as a percentage of the investment in that operation.

Return on sales: *see* profitability ratios.

Revenue: the proceeds of sale of goods or services. Alternatively defined as the gross increase in owners' equity from operations.

Revenue centre: an organizational unit that has the responsibility to make sales; its performance can be judged by the variance between budgeted sales revenue and actual sales revenue.

Risk: the inherent uncertainty of the future.

S

Sales: revenue earned by providing goods in contrast to revenue from providing a service.

Sales forecast: a prediction of the sales level at a given price.

Scorekeeping: use of financial accounting information to assess how well assets have been utilized.

Security: an asset pledged to ensure repayment of a debt.

Sensitivity analysis: analysis of the effect of changes in input assumptions on the outcome of a decision.

Service mission: the principal objective of an NFPO — to provide goods or services for a particular purpose rather than to make a profit from its activities.

Share: *see* common shares and preferred shares.

Share capital: the accounting value of all the shares, common and preferred, issued and outstanding.

Shareholders' equity: share capital, retained earnings, and all other equity accounts.

Short-run: examination of the effect of decisions, costs, revenues, etc., in the very near future.

Society of Management Accountants: an organization of professional accountants whose members specialize in management accounting and strategy.

Sole proprietorship: an individual operating an unincorporated business.

Specific identification: an inventory flow model where uniquely identified units are recognized as being sold individually (*see also* weighted average, first-in-first-out, and last-in-first-out).

Stakeholder: any person or organization with a legal, moral, or organizational interest in the activities of a company or not-for-profit organization. Includes shareholders (if any), creditors, managers, employees, governments, members of the public, etc.

Standard cost: a pre-determined cost at which a product is expected to be made, a service rendered, etc.

Statement of changes in financial position: *see* cash flow statement.

Statement of fund balances: *see* statement of net assets.

Statement of net assets: the statement of an NFPO that reconciles the balance of net assets from the end of the previous reporting period to the end of the current period (also called the *statement of fund balances*). It corresponds to the statement of retained earnings in a for-profit financial statement.

Statement of operations: the statement of revenue and expense of a not-for-profit organization. It corresponds to the income statement in a for-profit financial statement.

Statement of retained income: a financial accounting report that shows the retained income at the start of the year, its increase due to the addition of net income, its decrease due to the payment of dividends, and the balance of retained income at the end of the year.

Statement of revenue and expense: *See* statement of operations.

Step fixed costs: a cost that is fixed within a given range, but then moves abruptly to a higher level when that range is exceeded.

Strategy: the process of choosing a basis for competing in the marketplace.

Subsidiary: a company of which all, or a majority, of the shares are owned by another (parent) company.

Sunk cost: a cost that was incurred in the past and that has, therefore, no relevance to decisions about the future.

T

T-account: a visual representation of a ledger *account*, with *debits* on the left-hand side and *credits* on the right-hand side.

Target cost: an appropriate cost that generates the target profit, given the target volume, target selling price, and target quality of the product.

Target costing: a market-driven strategy with a method of determining the appropriate cost of a product, and then designing and producing the product to meet this cost.

Time value of money: (in capital budgeting) the interest opportunity in respect of a future cash flow.

Total asset turnover: *see* asset turnover.

Transaction: an event that changes the assets, liabilities, or equity of a company and, according to generally accepted accounting principles, must be recorded in the books of a company.

Transfer pricing: the organizational rules that govern the setting of prices for the internal transfer of goods or services.

U

Underapplied overhead: a situation where the overhead allocated to products is less than the overhead incurred; it arises either because overhead spending is greater than budgeted or because the overhead application base is lower than budgeted.

Unearned revenue: collected sales revenue for which goods or services have not yet been supplied.

Unit-related activities: *see* flexible cost.

V

Value chain: the set of interrelated activities that delivers a product or service to the customer; each element of the value chain should add more value than it adds cost.

Variable cost: *see* flexible cost.

Variance (analysis): the difference between the budget and the actual cost, and its associated analysis and management.

W, Z

Weighted average: an inventory flow model that assumes commingling of assets for sale (*see also* first-in-first-out, last-in-first-out, and specific identification).

Weighted average cost of capital: the after-tax cost of debt capital multiplied by the proportion of debt in the capital structure plus the cost of equity capital multiplied by the proportion of equity in the capital structure: it is used in capital budgeting as the minimum required rate of return to assess the viability of investment proposals (*see also* cost of capital).

What-if analysis: *see* sensitivity analysis.

Work-in-process (work-in-progress) inventory: inventory of goods that have begun the manufacturing process but have not yet completed it.

Working capital: current assets less current liabilities.

Zero-based budget: a budget based on radical reassessment of the objectives of a functional unit and the most efficient and effective ways of achieving them.

Index

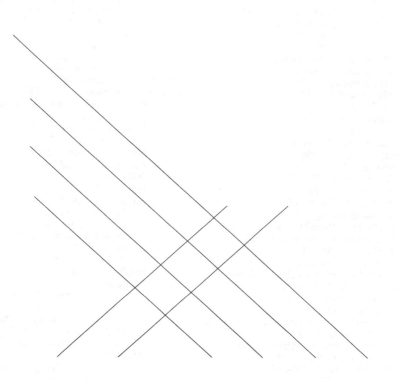

Index

Index

Index

tax expense *99–100*
total asset turnover *424*
trade credit *167*
    automated payments of *167*
trade payables *167–168*
trademarks *144*
    Coca-Cola *180*
traditional cost allocation *311–313*
transactions
    adjusting journal entries *59–62*
    amortization *115–117*
    bad debt expense *117–119*
    balance sheet accounts *179*
    bank loans *182–184*
    cost of goods sold *52–53, 56, 109–112*
    deferred delivery *108–109*
    effects on accounting equation *19–23*
    examples of *43–46, 49–59*
    expense *103–106, 109–119*
    identification of *32–33*
    intangible assets *180–181*
    long-term debt *184–185*
    measurement of *7*

    overhead expenses *112–115*
    recording of *7, 32–33, 42–43*
    revenue *51–53, 103–106*
    sales revenue *52, 55–56*
    shareholders equity *185–186*
treasury bills (T-Bills) *378*

U, V

uncertainty *406–407*
units of production amortization method *97–98*
variable costs *137–139, 301*

W, X, Z

weighted average cost of capital (WACC) *372, 406*
weighted average model *150*
"what-if" analysis *309–311*
work-in-process inventory *136*
working capital management *362*
Xerox Corporation *144*
zero-based budget *233*

Student Self-Study Resource

to accompany

Accounting for Non-financial Managers

The first purchaser of this book is provided access* to additional interactive multiple-choice tests for self-assessment and review. Available online, the tests can be accessed using the following information:

Access http://www.captus.com/anfm/student

Login: anfm-student115
Password: meuzep
Valid until 2014-12-31